THE
Bible
AS YOUR
GPS

To Melanie and Family,
Love thru Christ
Marilyn & Bruce
Kemb

THE *Bible* AS YOUR GPS

▸ KOBUS GENIS

WINEPRESS WP PUBLISHING

ISBN 13: 978-1-57921-920-8
ISBN 10: 1-57921-920-9
Library of Congress Catalog Card Number: 2007901438

TABLE OF CONTENTS

Preface xix
Acknowledgments xxiii

Our Point of Departure: Pre-History

Day 1: You Could Not Have Wished for a Better Start! 27
Day 2: Does Genesis 1 Have a Message for Us? 28
Day 3: The Crisis Confronting Us Every Day 30
Day 4: Can God Change His Plans? 32
Day 5: Ambition Can Be Dangerous! 33

Our First Stop: The Period of the Patriarchs and Slavery

Day 6: What Do We Do When Life Is a Dead End? 37
Day 7: People Who Are Arrogant Should Not Expect Support from Others! 38
Day 8: Sometimes It's Hard to Trust Others! 40
Day 9: Will We Escape from this Dark Hole? 41
Day 10: Where Should We Look for God? 42

Our Second Stop: From the Exodus to the Conquest of the Promised Land

Day 11: Can God Still Provide a Way Out? 47
Day 12: Why Do We Have to Suffer So Much? 49
Day 13: Can God Back Out? 51
Day 14: Religion Is Not Only About God! 53
Day 15: Where Is the Best Place to Hide from God? 54
Day 16: What Does God Look Like? 56

Day 17: Are There Limits to God's Forgiveness? 58

Day 18: Does God Expect Too Much of Us? 60

Day 19: Can God Really Use Us? 61

Day 20: The Lord Is Not Your Buddy! 62

Day 21: Ceremonies Can Be So Boring! 63

Day 22: Where Does Sex Belong? 64

Day 23: Does Everything in Life Involve God? 65

Day 24: What Should Our Lives Reflect? 66

Day 25: An Invitation Not to Be Refused! 67

Day 26: We All Admire this Characteristic! 68

Day 27: Has God's Light Been Dimmed? 69

Day 28: What Eats Away at Relationships? 70

Day 29: Love Is Not the Only Thing that Blinds! 71

Day 30: Will God Forgive the Sins We Commit Unknowingly? 72

Day 31: If Only We Could Start All Over Again 73

Day 32: God's Heart-Lung Machine 74

Day 33: Do We Fail if We Do Not Reach Our Goals? 75

Day 34: The Day When God Says No! 76

Day 35: How Can One Be Truly Happy? 77

Day 36: Good Theology Is Always Good Counseling! 78

Day 37: The Most Important Decision to Make Every Day 79

Day 38: Does God Have Friends? 80

Day 39: Imagine Two Spies and a Prostitute in One Room 81

Day 40: What Do I Do About My Sorry Past? 82

Day 41: God and War? 84

Day 42: A "Dog" that Took the Place of a Giant! 85

Day 43: The Big "J" that God Would Like to See on Earth! 86

Day 44: Don't Miss this Trip! 87

Day 45: The Last Chapters Reveal So Much 88

OUR THIRD STOP: JUDGES

Day 46: Does God Sometimes Forget About Us? 91

Day 47: Sometimes God Does Not Make Sense! 93

Day 48: When a Youngster Loses It 94

Day 49: Does God Work "Because of" or "in Spite of"? 95

Day 50: What Follows After Revenge Is Taken? 97

Day 51: Does God Easily Become Disheartened with Us? 98

Day 52: The Destructive Power of Sexual Desires 99

Day 53: God Moves Too Slowly at Times! 100
Day 54: How Does God Carry Out His Plans? 101
Day 55: Escape Never Brings Comfort 102
Day 56: What Should We Do in a Crisis? 103
Day 57: Dealing with Bitterness 105
Day 58: Merciful Coincidences! 106
Day 59: We Sometimes Have to Take Calculated Risks! 107
Day 60: The Defenseless Widow Becomes a Happy Grandmother 109

OUR FOURTH STOP: THE UNITED KINGDOM

Day 61: Why Are the Minister's Children So Naughty? 113
Day 62: How Should We See Things? 114
Day 63: From "Zero" to "Hero" 115
Day 64: An Impressive Beginning, But 116
Day 65: The Day When a Disabled Person's Life Changed 117
Day 66: The Three Words that Change Your Life! 118
Day 67: God Also Has a Mirror! 119
Day 68: Break the Silence! 120
Day 69: Parents Do Not Have Children, but Children Have Parents! 121
Day 70: In What Way Is God Involved in Our Lives and in History? 122
Day 71: Do We Really Need to Read These Genealogies? They Are So Boring! 123
Day 72: What Proof Is There that God Is Involved in Our Lives? 125
Day 73: Where God Often Surprises Us 127
Day 74: How Should We React to God's Care? 128
Day 75: Is Evil Taking Over? 129
Day 76: How Do We Make Sense of Life? 130
Day 77: Wisdom that Shows, Works! 131
Day 78: An Important Step Away from the Dumps of Despair! 132
Day 79: How Do We Deal with Heartache? 133
Day 80: How Do We Support Someone in Times of Heartache? 134
Day 81: Can We Protest Against God? 135
Day 82: So Many Questions About God 136
Day 83: How Great Is God? 137
Day 84: The Struggle to Find Answers to Our Questions 138
Day 85: We Cannot Aspire to Happiness! 139
Day 86: How to Cope with All the Violence! 140
Day 87: I Do Not Want To Tell Anybody 141
Day 88: Are We Being Honest with Ourselves? 142

Day 89: Do We See Too Little of This? 143
Day 90: The Ungodly Look So Happy! 144
Day 91: When Life Is Too Hard to Face 145
Day 92: Will God Really Forgive Us? 146
Day 93: The Many Questions of Life 147
Day 94: A Companion Who Will Never Let You Down! 148
Day 95: Is Wisdom Age-related? 149
Day 96: What Is Our Most Precious Possession? 150
Day 97: Every Dog Has His or Her Day! 151
Day 98: Small in Stature but Big at Heart! 152
Day 99: What Does a Dream Woman Look Like? 153
Day 100: Everything Seems So Meaningless! 154
Day 101: Are We Left to Our Own Fate? 155
Day 102: Is the Author of Ecclesiastes Too Pessimistic? 156
Day 103: Is Money the Key to Happiness? 157
Day 104: Don't Talk About Death! 158
Day 105: Life Doesn't Make Sense! 159
Day 106: Aging Is Not for Cowards! 160
Day 107: Is Death the End of Everything? 161
Day 108: How Can Our Happiness in Love Grow? 162
Day 109: Relationships on Autopilot 163
Day 110: Why Does Love Fade So Easily? 164
Day 111: Where Does Sex Fit In? 165
Day 112: Who Should Take the Initiative in Lovemaking? 166
Day 113: How Do We Ensure Intimacy? 167
Day 114: Does Sex Have to Wait for Marriage? 168

OUR FIFTH STOP: THE DIVIDED KINGDOM

Day 115: What Can We Expect to Follow After a High Point? 171
Day 116: The Day a Little Girl Made a Difference 172
Day 117: Is God Really Interested in Us? 173
Day 118: Does God Allow Us to Mess with Him? 174
Day 119: Is God Threatened by History? 175
Day 120: Ever Listen to a Sermon from Chronicles? 176
Day 121: God's Mercy Is Not Flat 177
Day 122: Was Jonah Really Swallowed by a Fish? 178
Day 123: Can God Change His Plans? 180
Day 124: We Must Not Keep This to Ourselves! 182

Day 125: To Read One's Own Obituary in the Newspaper 184

Day 126: When Should a Church Service End? 186

Day 127: What Makes Society Livable? 187

Day 128: God Has Messengers in Space! 188

Day 129: God Is No Cowboy! 189

Day 130: Where Is God's Training School? 190

Day 131: An Emotion We Need Never Feel Toward God 192

Day 132: The Day God Yielded! 194

Day 133: Low Points Become the Backdrop for High Points 196

Day 134: Religion Can Become Sin! 198

Day 135: What If We Had the Privilege of Asking God for a Sign? 200

Day 136: What Will Happen If We Can No Longer Dream? 201

Day 137: Sermons People Like to Hear 202

Day 138: Religion Can Be Dangerous! 204

Day 139: The One Thing God Does Not Bother About 205

Day 140: God Is Also Present Where the Cash Registers Ring! 206

Day 141: What Makes God So Unique and Unequalled? 207

Day 142: God Is More than Who We Think He Is! 208

Day 143: This Lion Is King No More 209

Day 144: How Do We Test Character? 210

Day 145: Theoretically Believers, But in Practice Atheists 211

Day 146: One Minute to Midnight 213

Day 147: Something of the Future in the Present! 214

Day 148: The Impossible Possibility! 215

Day 149: It Can Be Dangerous to Attend Church Services! 216

Day 150: What Makes Religion Dangerous? 217

Day 151: The Day When God Was Not Moved by Prayer 219

Day 152: A Point that Makes the Lord Intolerant! 220

Day 153: What Is the Difference Between a True and a False Prophet? 222

Day 154: God Is Full of Surprises! 224

Day 155: The Day When God Cried! 225

Day 156: How Do We Escape the Depths of Sorrow? 226

Day 157: The Day It Became Impossible to Serve the Lord 227

Day 158: Where Does Hope Begin? 228

Day 159: A Life Without Joy 229

Day 160: Lord, Why Do You Not Hear Us? 230

Day 161: God's Finger 231

Day 162: Faith Never Exists Without this Word! 233

Day 163: Two Evils We Should Guard Against! 234

Day 164: What Is God's Ultimate Aim? 236

Day 165: Should We Take a Chance with God? 238

Day 166: When We're Afraid 239

Day 167: A "Messiah" Who Did Not Know the Lord! 240

Day 168: How Can We Know that Our Faith Is Real? 241

Day 169: Seeing Is Not Always Believing! 242

OUR SIXTH STOP: EXILE

Day 170: "Lord, Can't You See My Suffering?" 245

Day 171: Can God Be Hurt? 246

Day 172: The Bible's Titanic Also Sank! 247

Day 173: The Mighty Pharaoh Was Nailed! 248

Day 174: If We Share Our Expectations, Our Problems Will Be Less! 249

Day 175: A Frightening Thought that Is Also Comforting 251

Day 176: What Do I Need in Dark Times? 252

Day 177: What Is God's Address? 253

Day 178: How Far Does Our Loyalty Reach? 255

Day 179: We Cannot Glorify and Praise God Without This! 257

Day 180: Is There A Lesson to Learn from History? 259

Day 181: What Gives the Weary and Depressed New Hope 261

Day 182: How Should We Understand Biblical Visions? 263

Day 183: What Can Biblical Visions Teach Us? 265

Day 184: How Do We Believe Despite Despair? 266

OUR SEVENTH STOP: RETURN FROM EXILE

Day 185: Excuses, Excuses, Excuses! 269

Day 186: How Do We Turn Priorities into Action? 270

Day 187: What Makes a Fresh Start Possible? 271

Day 188: Bigger and More Beautiful Is Not Always Better! 272

Day 189: Should We Cling to Tradition? 273

Day 190: The Bible's Limousine 274

Day 191: Something More Important than Territorial Advantage! 276

Day 192: A Bridge Links God's Wrath to His Mercy! 277

Day 193: How Lives Turn to Joy 278

Day 194: A Remarkable Story, Yet 279

Day 195: Beautiful, More Beautiful, Esther 281

Day 196: Bitterness, Conspiracy and Coincidence 283

Day 197: What Do We Do When Our Pride Gets Hurt? 284

Day 198: Even Power Cannot Resist This! 285

Day 199: A Word that Caused an Eclipse of God! 286

Day 200: A Quality that Can Cause a Drastic Change 288

Day 201: God Works Without Fanfare 289

Day 202: What This Congregation and a Rock Concert Have in Common? 290

Day 203: What Is Significant About March 12, 515 B.C.? 291

Day 204: How Important Is Timing? 292

Day 205: What to Do When People Disappoint Us 293

Day 206: Tears Link Our Pain to Something 294

Day 207: The Tearful Planner 295

Day 208: Sick and Tired of All the Discord? 296

Day 209: A Bittersweet Ending 298

Day 210: A Direct Question to God 299

Day 211: One of the Biggest Problems in the Church! 300

Day 212: Get a Glimpse of God's Heart! 301

Day 213: The Last Three Verses in the Old Testament! 302

OUR EIGHTH STOP: THE 400 SILENT YEARS

Day 214: How Do We Handle Embarrassing Relatives? 309

Day 215: The Only Way to Find True Happiness! 311

Day 216: How Can We Add Zest to Life? 313

Day 217: In What Way Is God the Light? 314

Day 218: I Also Like to Peep on the Sly! 315

Day 219: How Should We Treat Our Enemies? 316

Day 220: The Secret of a Successful Investment 317

Day 221: Do God's Miracles Depend on Our Faith? 318

Day 222: What Is the Secret to a Fulfilled Life? 319

Day 223: Step 1 for Walking on the Water: Recognize Your Calling! 321

Day 224: Step 2 for Walking on the Water: Overcome Your Fear! 323

Day 225: Step 3 for Walking on the Water: Be Bold in Your Faith! 324

Day 226: Step 4 for Walking on the Water: Get Out of the Boat! 326

Day 227: Step 5 for Walking on the Water: Remember that There Is Always Hope! 328

Day 228: Does Forgiveness Have Boundaries? 329

Day 229: To Be Doubtful Is Not as Bad as We Think! 331

Day 230: How Should We Understand Miracles? 332

Day 231: If We Lie Down with the Dogs We Will Get Up with Fleas! 333

Day 232: What Do We Mean When We Say that Jesus Is the "Son of God"? 334

Day 233: Blood Is Thicker than Water, But 336

Day 234: The Day When a Woman's Faith made Jesus' No Crumble! 337

Day 235: Does God Also Have Secrets? 338

Day 236: Is the Lotto Your Motto? 339

Day 237: Seven Days Without Sun: The Palms of Sunday! 340

Day 238: Seven Days Without Sun: The Whipping on Monday! 342

Day 239: Seven Days Without Sun: The Tricky Question on Tuesday! 344

Day 240: Seven Days Without Sun: The Sums on Wednesday! 346

Day 241: Seven Days Without Sun: The Betrayal on Thursday! 347

Day 242: Seven Days Without Sun: The Agonizing Cry on Friday! 348

Day 243: Seven Days Without Sun: The Irony of Saturday! 349

Day 244: The First Day of the Following Week! 350

Day 245: Nobody Really Cares! 351

Day 246: Evangelism? No Thanks! 352

Day 247: What If Things Become Too Much to Bear? 354

Day 248: The Worst Form of Disability 356

Day 249: The Game God Wants to Play with Us 358

Day 250: People Are Free to Raise Their Eyebrows! 359

Day 251: Strange and Reversed! 360

Day 252: How Does God Judge the Good Life? 362

Day 253: Every House Has Its Trials! 364

Day 254: The Big Question Concerning Our Problems 366

Day 255: This Is Too Good to Be True! 367

Day 256: Obstacles to Joy 369

Day 257: Why Is Pontius Pilate's Name in the Creed? 370

Day 258: If Jesus Is the Answer, What Is the Question? 371

Day 259: Does God Have a Handle? 372

Day 260: Life Can Sometimes Be So Unfair! 373

Day 261: What Constitutes a Threat? 374

Day 262: Why Was the Notice on Jesus' Cross in Three Languages? 375

Day 263: Why Does Life Sometimes Get So Lonely? 376

Day 264: The Most Famous Dying Words 377

Day 265: The First Witness to Jesus' Resurrection 379

Day 266: To Have Doubts Is Not As Bad As We Might Think! 380

Day 267: Afraid to Witness? 381

Day 268: What Do We Celebrate When We Celebrate the Ascension? 382

Day 269: The Revenge Of the Holy Spirit! 383

Day 270: A Congregation's Best Testimonial 385

Day 271: What "Good" People Also Need! 386

Day 272: Something God Never Does but We Do So Often! 387

Day 273: What Europe's First Convert Can Teach Us! 388
Day 274: Praise Does Not Always Require an Organ or a Guitar 389
Day 275: Meet the Spirit of God Anew . . . But Not as a Stepchild of Faith 391
Day 276: Meet the Spirit of God Anew . . . Through a Spirit-filled Life 393
Day 277: Meet the Spirit of God Anew . . . In the Shadows of Life............................ 395
Day 278: Meet the Spirit of God Anew . . . In Wrestling with Grief 397
Day 279: Meet the Spirit of God Anew . . . In Emotions... 399
Day 280: Meet the Spirit of God Anew . . . In Church 401
Day 281: Are We Good Enough for Heaven? 403
Day 282: What Makes Faith So Special? 404
Day 283: We Doubt So Easily 405
Day 284: Have We Been Accepted by God? 406
Day 285: Are You Super-Religious? 407
Day 286: Something a Government Cannot Conquer but We Can! 408
Day 287: The One Account We Will Never Be Able to Settle! 409
Day 288: What If Christians Differ Among Themselves? 410
Day 289: Godly Nonsense? 411
Day 290: There Is More on the Menu than Just Milkshakes! 412
Day 291: Effective People Live According to this Principle! 413
Day 292: Setting a Good Example.. 414
Day 293: Is There Life After Death? 415
Day 294: What Do We All Need from Time to Time? 416
Day 295: Is the Gospel Still Relevant? 417
Day 296: What Nobody Can Detect.. 418
Day 297: How Much Money Should We Give to the Church? 419
Day 298: Beware of the Plus Factor! 420
Day 299: Why Do You Believe? 421
Day 300: What Happens When God Forgives Us? 422
Day 301: Why Abraham Is Still a Hero! 423
Day 302: Jesus Had to Submit to the Law, but We Do Not! 424
Day 303: What Word Would Summarize the Gospel? 425
Day 304: What Does Faith Look Like? 426
Day 305: The Civil War Within Us! 427
Day 306: What Does Love Look Like? 428
Day 307: Is it "Because" or "In Spite of"? 429
Day 308: A Three-letter Word that Always Gives Things a New Turn! 430
Day 309: How Can We Make the Holy Trinity Part of Our Prayers? 431
Day 310: How Can We Convince the World that It Is Meaningful to Be a Christian? ... 432
Day 311: Shh! Nobody Should Hear About This!.. 433

Day 312: An E-mail to Father and Child 434

Day 313: How Do We Know If Someone Is a Leader? 435

Day 314: How Can We Solve Discord? 436

Day 315: The What Should Change to Who! 438

Day 316: What Does a Christian Look Like? 439

Day 317: What Do Faith, Hope and Love Have in Common? 440

Day 318: We Are Christians Because 441

Day 319: How Seriously Should One Approach Life? 442

Day 320: Should We Honestly Believe that People Can Change? 443

Day 321: What If We Are Not Chosen by God? 444

Day 322: One of the Greatest Mistakes in Our Prayer Life 445

Day 323: The Sermon that Will Reach People Outside the Congregation! ... 446

Day 324: How Can We Prepare Ourselves for the Second Coming? 447

Day 325: When Will Jesus Come? 448

Day 326: Where Does the Christian Life Begin? 449

Day 327: A Liberating Request of Only Three Words! 450

Day 328: It Is Good to Remember Our Sins! 451

Day 329: How Can We Silence Our Critics? 452

Day 330: What Do a Soldier, an Athlete and a Farmer Have in Common? 453

Day 331: Ever Doubt the Value of the Bible? 454

Day 332: We Do Not Like to Talk About Death! 455

Day 333: Where Do We Begin to Heal a Sick Society? 456

Day 334: Is the Bible Still Credible? 457

Day 335: Walls that Don't Belong in Churches! 458

Day 336: How Do We Put the Sparkle Back into Our Religious Life? 459

Day 337: Why Didn't an Angel Come to Die for Us Instead? 461

Day 338: Holding on to Faith Can Be a Battle! 463

Day 339: A Duel We Can Never Win 465

Day 340: Where Was God on September 11, 2001? 466

Day 341: The Only Way to Have Peace 467

Day 342: Why Is the Christian "Religion" So Unique? 469

Day 343: What Should We Do When We Are Spiritually Tired? 470

Day 344: Bitter or Better? 472

Day 345: What Is More Important than Appearance? 473

Day 346: Can Faith Without Good Deeds Save Us? 474

Day 347: What Do Our Tongues and a Tube of Toothpaste Have in Common? ... 475

Day 348: How Will We Be Able to Persevere in Troubled Times? 476

Day 349: Something a Christian Should Never Be Surprised About......... 477

Day 350: Grace in Suffering 478

Day 351: I Often Stumble! What Do I Do? 479

Day 352: Guard Against Them! 480

Day 353: Why Does God Wait So Long? 482

Day 354: The Essence of the Christian Faith 483

Day 355: We Easily Stumble over this Four-letter Word 484

Day 356: What Is Eternity? 485

Day 357: That Which We All Seek, but Which Is So Hard to Find 486

Day 358: This Causes No One Any Harm 487

Day 359: Something with Which We Should Never Gamble 488

Day 360: Evil Triumphs—Or So It Seems! 489

Day 361: What Does the Future Hold for Us? 491

Day 362: The Onslaught of the Evil Trio: The Dragon 493

Day 363: The Onslaught of the Evil Trio: The Antichrist! 495

Day 364: The Onslaught of the Evil Trio: The False Prophet! 497

Day 365: Another Strategy of the Evil Trio! 499

Day 366: From Paradise to Paradise 501

Index 503

PREFACE

My feelings are mixed as I drive through the vast snow-covered prairies of Alberta, Canada, on this March 16, 2004. Neil Diamond's music keeps me company. I'm excited that today marks the birth of this preface, but also sad because today is the birthday of my father who is no longer with us. Although I'm tearful, I realize that in fact this day is a joyous one. Joyous, because this devotional started with my dad—it was he who instilled a love for the Bible in me. In his unique handwriting, he wrote the following in each of his five children's Bibles:

> *The Bible is the most precious book.*
> *Reading it often*
> *will keep you safe.*
> *Read it again and again . . .*
> *Keep on praying . . .*
> *Live the life of the Bible*
> *and spread the word.*
>
> *—From Mom and Dad, with love*

These words speak to me because I witnessed it in my father's life, and I still do in my mother's. When I was young, I often asked my father questions about the Bible. Many of my questions brought a smile to his face, as if his smile was an attempt to tell me something about God's greatness. Today, I still have questions. God's greatness astounds me.

Despite six years of theology studies at the University of Stellenbosch, South Africa, reading the Bible had left me frustrated (probably because I was too young to appreciate theology). I had difficulty forming a complete picture of the Bible. I also did not always know how to apply the truths in the Bible to current issues, such as abortion and homosexuality.

I still had these frustrations when I joined the army for compulsory military training. Little did I know that while I was in the army, the way I understood and applied the Bible would change. This change took place as a fellow soldier and I polished our boots in the afternoons. Apart from the fact that he held a doctorate in theology, he also had the ability to channel my frustrations. So, while polishing our boots, he also polished my knowledge of theology. I'm grateful that to this day I can still depend on my friend for guidance.

I believe my frustrations were the impetus for my passion to help others understand the Bible and apply their understanding thereof. I am very grateful to my first congregation, the Port Natal congregation in Durban, South Africa, that gave me the freedom to equip members with this knowledge. For eight years, we engaged in the material of Veritas College on a weekly basis. I had the privilege to witness how the Holy Spirit (by means of the Word) addresses, frees and empowers people in their unique situations. It was there that I experienced how useful the Bible is on our journey through life. It is like a "GPS."

A GPS is a *Global Positioning System* that uses satellites, receivers and software to allow users to determine their exact geographical position. Although it was created and originally used by the U.S. military, GPS is now available to the general public all over the world. GPS navigation systems are currently installed in a number of luxury cars, complete with a map that shows drivers exactly where in the world they are. Advanced car GPS units can actually speak the directions to a certain destination and tell the driver when to turn. Isn't that amazing?

Our journey through life is guided by the Bible—our "GPS" or *God Positioning System*. According to Psalm 119:105, God's Word is a lamp to our feet and a light for our path. Our journey through life often leads us to unknown paths. We know that life can have rather sharp edges and that pain and sorrow are part of our existence. It is therefore not always easy to find our way in life. The Bible helps us to stay on course.

In reality, many people still believe in the gospel but do not *know* how to apply the message of the Bible on their life journey. So many people have told me that they started reading the Bible with great enthusiasm but that their enthusiasm did not last long because they found it difficult to understand. Some told me that they felt completely lost in the Bible. This is actually the last place you want to be lost—it is, after all, the Word of God!

This devotional is structured in a way to help you use the Bible as your daily guide. First, the daily readings indicate the form of writing used in a specific text. The Bible is written in *prose* form and in *poetic* form. It is important to determine the form of writing because you cannot read prose the same way you would read poetry. The following gives an outline of the different forms:

Prose

A. *Narrative:* the events that happen in time sequence without any explicit instructions to the reader. Narrative can be divided into:
1. Story: e.g., the story of Moses in the basket (Exod. 2)
2. Allegory: e.g., the parable of the sower (Matt. 13:3–23)
3. Dramatic history: e.g., the history of the birth and death of Jesus (Luke 1:26–45)
4. Parables: e.g., the parable of the Good Samaritan (Luke 10:25–37)
5. Conversation: e.g., Peter's confession of Christ (Luke 9:18–27)
6. Apocalypse: Apocalypse in the terminology of early Christian and Jewish literature, is a revelation of hidden things given by God to a chosen prophet. The word "apocalypse" is derived from the Greek word *apocalypses,* which means "to uncover" or a "revelation." Although it simply means "revealing" in everyday language, it is often used in regard to the end of the world. Apocalypse conveys a message in symbolism. The book of Revelation and Daniel 7–12 are examples of apocalyptic literature.

B. *Procedure*: explicit instructions to do things in a particular sequence; e.g., the instructions Aaron needed to follow before he could enter the Most Holy Place (Lev. 16).

C. *Explanation*: an explanation that serves as a basis for the instructions to follow; e.g., when Paul explains our life before Christ (Eph. 2:1–3).

D. *Instruction:* an explicit instruction based on an explanation; e.g., when Paul instructs fathers in how to deal with their children (Eph. 6:4).

Poetry

We see poetry primarily in:

A. *The Psalms:* the word "psalm" is derived from the Greek word *psalmos*—the meaning of which has been argued over for centuries. However, it is not wrong to say that *psalmos* means to "sing, making melody in your heart."

B. *Wisdom literature:* (Proverbs, Ecclesiastes, Job and some Psalms). A *proverb* is a short sentence with a lesson and advice concerning life that has been handed down from generation to generation:
   - *Proverbs* helps us master life.
   - *Ecclesiastes* helps us deal with death.
   - *Job* helps us deal with pain and suffering.

C. *The prophets:* The Hebrew word for "prophet" is *nabi,* which means "to call" or "to announce." The Greek word for "prophet" is *prophetes*. The prefix *pro* means "in the place of" or "in the name of." A prophet, therefore, was God's voice to His people.

Second, the way in which the journal is compiled will also help you to get a better picture of the Bible as a whole. The journal, with its 366 daily readings, starts at the beginning of Genesis and will accompany you through each book of the Bible right up to Revelation.

Note that the journal does not follow the sequence of books in the Old Testament. The books of the Old Testament are not divided according to a timeline but rather in main blocks such as the Law, Writings and Prophets. However, I have organized the books in such a way that they will follow a timeline. The journal is compiled according to the following schematic representation:

"Overview of the Bible" - Schematic representation.

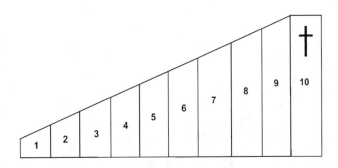

The Old Testament is represented by an ascending line because God's revelation to us becomes clearer as we encounter the cross-referencing of events. The Old Testament leads us to Christ.

1. Departure: Pre-History
2. First stop: The Patriarchs
3. Second stop: Exodus and Conquest
4. Third stop: Judges
5. Fourth stop: The United Kingdom
6. Fifth stop: The Divided Kingdom
7. Sixth stop: The Exile
8. Seventh stop: The Return from Exile
9. Eighth stop: The 400 Silent Years
10. New Testament

The New Testament is represented by a horizontal line because Jesus Christ, the culmination of God's revelation, has already come.

Third, every devotion starts with a relevant heading that serves as an invitation to you to use the Bible as your GPS. Finally, every day is accompanied by a closing prayer and a relevant quote.

Writing this journal seemed like running a marathon. It was exciting, but at times also tiring because it took longer than I had anticipated. I hope you will rediscover the almighty God as your companion while reading this journal. He wants to join you on your journey through life. In this way, your own journey will become a story about God.

May the words of Psalm 119:105 accompany you on your journey through life: "Your word is a lamp *to my feet* and a light *for my path*" (NIV).

ACKNOWLEDGMENTS

This work is the result of a lifetime of learning from my family, friends, colleagues, counselors and teachers who invested their time, energy, wisdom and interest in my life. For this, I am forever grateful!

Here are just a few who made this work possible:

To my wife, Anne-Marie, and my three children, Cara-Mari, Elsjé and James, for all the sacrifices they have endured to see this book to completion. I am as relieved as you are!

To my first congregation, the Dutch Reformed Church Port Natal, located in beautiful Durban, South Africa. I will always be grateful for the opportunity you gave me to grow spiritually and to take risks (together) for the kingdom of God.

To the Presbyterian Church in Wainwright and Chauvin in Alberta, Canada, for welcoming us to Canada with open hearts. You have helped me to add a Canadian touch to the book I started on African soil.

To Veritas College for igniting the passion of Bible teaching in me.

To the many proofreaders of the Presbyterian Church in Wainwright and Chauvin for your insight and sound advice.

To Dr. Berto Hendrikse for the many discussions and, above all, your friendship.

To my friend Dr. Danie Veldsman for his patience, integrity and wisdom. To his wife, Reneé, who patiently bore with all the time I spent with Danie on the phone.

OUR POINT OF DEPARTURE: PRE-HISTORY

(GENESIS 1–11)

The events in Genesis 1–11 bear no date and are therefore known as pre-history. Four important events occur during this time:

1. *Creation* (Gen. 1–2). Creation is God's announcement that He wants to accompany human beings on their life journey. The story of creation tells us who this God is who wants to join humankind on their journey through life. The rest of the Bible tells us how God wants to achieve this.
2. *The Fall* (Gen. 3–6:4). Human beings are the highlight of the creation. Created in the image of God, they have the position of power to reign over creation. The tragedy is that due to their disobedience, they disappoint God. In the Bible, the dark side of human nature is revealed at an early stage.
3. *The Flood* (Gen. 6:5–18). God regrets creating human beings (Gen. 6:6) and decides to use water to destroy them. God shows mercy by saving Noah and his family. After the flood, God makes a promise to never again repeat this event. The rainbow is proof of His promise. Yes, God is with us all the time.
4. *The Tower of Babel* (Gen. 11). Human beings once again disobey God. They decide to make a name for themselves by building the Tower of Babel. They do not proclaim the image of God throughout the world but prefer to congregate near the tower. God ruins their plans by creating confusion in their languages. It is nevertheless clear that the majority is unwilling to follow God.

The first 11 chapters of Genesis describe how human beings miss the mark. The rest of the Bible tells us how God accompanies human beings on their journey through life in order to create a community of believers—a family of faith!

YOU COULD NOT HAVE WISHED FOR A BETTER START!

The word "beginning" is a wonderful word because it contains elements of expectation, optimism and excitement. Think of a new day dawning, the first cry of a newborn baby, the opening chords of a music concert—or the beginning of a journey along the biblical paths. It is striking to note that the very first sentence in the Bible contains this word. It is here where our journey begins: the very first sentence in the Bible.

Genesis 1 (history)

[1] In the beginning God created the heavens and the earth.
[2] Now the earth was formless and empty, darkness was over the surface of the deep, and the Spirit of God was hovering over the waters. (NIV)

The first sentence in the Bible is an *announcement:* "In the beginning God created the heavens and the earth." This announcement reaches out to the heavens and the earth and proclaims that all and sundry are subservient to God. He has no equal. He is the creator of all. However, we must remember that the universe did not always have its present order. It was without life. The earth was still uninhabitable, desolate and empty. The mass of water that would give rise to everything was wrapped in darkness.

Uninhabitable and dark depths represent forces that frighten human beings and leave them feeling a sense of helplessness. Likewise, you might be starting this journey with the same feeling of helplessness—perhaps because of a child who has lost the way, a state of depression you are experiencing or even your deteriorating health. Helplessness about life can make you wonder if anyone is ever in control. You want to ask "where is God?" or even "is God truly God?" However, the feeling of helplessness and all the questions with which you may be wrestling should not prevent you from embarking on your journey. In fact, once you begin, you will discover that similar questions often crop up in the Bible.

Take comfort from the second part of Genesis 1:2: "The Spirit of God was hovering over the waters." Imagine a bird hovering graciously, but secretly, over the chaos (mass of water), ready to intervene. This symbolizes God's mysterious presence, which goes hand in hand with His creative power. It is this mysterious power that could equip a stutterer like Moses to lead his people, turn a defenseless widow like Naomi into a joyous grandmother, stop Saul in his tracks, or enable Jesus to rise from the dead.

On this journey, you will discover how God's Spirit is still alive. You should only learn to see this. In short, this journey begins with God. *You could not have wished for a better start!*

 Lord, I look forward to discovering how Your Spirit works in my life.

Start by doing what's necessary; then do what's possible; and suddenly you are doing the impossible.
—St. Francis of Assisi (1181–1226), *Roman Catholic saint who took the gospel literally*

DOES GENESIS 1 HAVE A MESSAGE FOR US?

The story of creation has given rise to much debate, but the question stands: Does Genesis 1 have a message for us? Let's take a look.

The schematic representation below shows that the story of the creation contains prose as well as poetic elements. It is a story containing repetition (a-e), which is characteristic of poetry. The schematic representation further shows that the first three days parallels the last three days:

Day	God's Actions	Day	God's Actions

1	**Light and Time**
	a And God said (v. 3)
	b "Let there be light," (v. 3)
	c and there was light (v. 3)
	d God saw . . . was good (v. 4)
	e evening . . . morning day (v. 5)
	    (NIV)
		4	**Sun, Moon and Stars**
			a And God said (v. 14)
			b Let there be lights (v. 14)
			c and it was so (v. 15)
			d and God saw . . . good (v. 18)
			e evening . . . morning (v. 19)
			    (NIV)

2	**Expanse (Space)** Water above (sky) Water under (sea)	5	**Living Objects to Occupy Expanse** Birds (sky) Creatures of the sea (sea)
3	**Land and Plants**	6	**Animals and Man**

Day 1: God uses an authoritative word to create *light*. The separation of day and night means that God also creates something else: *time*.

Day 2: God uses another authoritative word to separate the mass of water by creating a heavenly dome. Now there is water above (rain) and water beneath (sea), thereby creating *space*. On day 1 and 2, God creates the two basic preconditions for life, namely time and space.

Day 3: God uses yet another authoritative word to separate the uninhabited earth into soil and water. Then God lets plants flourish. The earth is ready to be inhabited. During the first three days, God thus tames the forces that struck fear into people in antiquity: darkness and barrenness.

During the last three days, God completes the cosmos in the same sequence as the first three days: the heavenly bodies (sun, moon and stars) to drive away the darkness; the birds to fill the air and the fishes to fill the seas; animals and human beings to live from its abundance. On the seventh day, God rests. This starts the cycle of work and rest.

The story of creation, which develops so wonderfully parallel, tells us *that* God created in an orderly fashion. The Bible does not tell us exactly *how* this came about—this is the concern of the natural sciences, which try to discover the secrets of creation. With the story of creation, God sets the table for *relationships* between God and human beings, between human beings themselves, and between human beings and creation. Shall we join God at the table?

Lord, I thank You for Your perfect creation. Thank You for letting me know You.

The most important single ingredient in the formula of success is knowing how to get along with people.
—Theodore Roosevelt (1858–1919), *Twenty-sixth American President (1901–1909)*

THE CRISIS CONFRONTING US EVERY DAY . . .

The well-known story told in Genesis 3 illustrates a crisis we experience each day.

Genesis 3 (story)

Tension: The serpent tempts Adam and Eve

> [1] Now the serpent was more crafty than any of the wild animals the LORD God had made. He said to the woman, 'Did God really say, 'You must not eat from any tree in the garden'?'

Relief of tension: Adam and Eve sin

> [6] When the woman saw that the fruit of the tree was good for food and pleasing to the eye, and also desirable for gaining wisdom, she took some and ate it. She also gave some to her husband, who was with her, and he ate it.

Result: Adam and Eve leave Eden

> [22]And the LORD God said, 'The man has now become like one of us knowing good and evil. He must not be allowed to reach out his hand and take also from the tree of life and eat, and live forever.' [23]So the LORD God banished him from the Garden of Eden to work the ground from which he had been taken. (NIV)

Human beings were created with free will. Two options confront them: (1) they can choose to lead their lives in a relationship with God, or (2) they can choose a way from God. The serpent very subtly states the alternatives. By emphasizing that he is a creature of God, the Bible stresses that the serpent represents any of the alternative choices. The text does not reveal anything further about the serpent, nor does it mention where the serpent obtained its knowledge. We therefore have to accept that the Bible draws a veil over the origin of evil and that it remains a mystery about which we can only speculate. (It is interesting to note that the serpent is often put on a par with Satan. The text does not state this, although later on in Revelation 12:9 and 20:2, the image of the serpent is equated to the devil or Satan.)

The serpent ensnares Adam and Eve by telling them that they can become equal with God. He makes them doubt God's word. The man and woman experience a crisis in which they have to decide. Perhaps their eyes will indeed be opened! They choose the alternative option. Adam and Eve's eyes do open as the serpent predicted, but with consequences they did not expect. Their choice leads to a rift between God and human beings and between human beings themselves. The gravity of Adam and Eve's transgression becomes clearer when the function of the trees are considered. The two trees, as a symbol of God's presence, indicate that the garden belongs to Him. The trees therefore set a boundary between God and the human beings. To transgress against the trees means to transgress against God.

This crisis in decision-making, with all its consequences, is not something from the distant past. Like Adam and Eve, we are also confronted (in subtle ways) with the alternatives on a daily basis.

The crises we face in our decision-making also involve *respect* for boundaries and a demonstration of our loyalties and respect.

 Lord, help me daily to choose a life that is grounded in a relationship with You.

He removes the greatest ornament of friendship, who takes away from it respect.
—Cicero (106–43 B.C.), *Ancient Roman lawyer, writer, scholar, orator and statesman*

CAN GOD CHANGE HIS PLANS?

We easily change our plans to suit ourselves. But can God also change His plans?

Genesis 6 (story)

Tension: God is grieved

> [5]The Lord saw how great man's wickedness on the earth had become, and that every inclination of the thoughts of his heart was only evil all the time.
> [6]The Lord was grieved that he had made man on the earth, and his heart was filled with pain.

Relief of tension: God makes a decision

> [7]So the LORD said, 'I will wipe mankind, whom I have created from the face of the earth—men and animals, and creatures that move along the ground, and birds in the air—for I am grieved that I have made them.'

Result: God's grace triumphs

> [8]But Noah found favor in the eyes of the Lord. (NIV)

God created human beings to be good, but because of their own doing they lost the way. Adam and Eve ate the forbidden fruit, Cain killed Abel, and the Titans thought they were immortal. Shortly after God created everything good, the Bible tells us of humankind's failure. This has an impact on God. He regrets ever having made them.

However, this does not mean that God erred. Humankind's sins cause Him tremendous pain because He loves them. The word "grieved" in this passage literally means that His heart was filled with pain. The same Hebrew word for "grief" is used in Genesis 3:16 to describe the pain women have to endure during childbirth and in Genesis 3:17 to describe men's toil to earn a living. By deliberately using the same word, the Bible says something remarkable: Our pain and toil have spilled over to God. God is therefore not detached from or indifferent to what happens to us.

Because God is disappointed, He decides to blot out humankind and even the animals. But then something impressive happens, as the word "but" in verse 8 indicates: God changes His mind. His love for humans is stronger than His wrath. This is what is wonderful about the God of the Bible. He is not a harsh, cold and clinical despot but a God who cares and understands. That is why He is prepared to give humankind another chance. This is the meaning of *grace*—God can change His plans!

 Lord, thank You for being a Father who cares and understands. Forgive me if I grieve You. Help me through the Holy Spirit not to continue in my sinful ways.

The will of God will never take you to where the grace of God will not protect you.
—Author unknown

AMBITION CAN BE DANGEROUS!

"Live your dream!" "If you can dream it, you can achieve it!" "Reach for the stars!" Ambitious people are inspired by utterances such as these. Ambition is a good thing, but it can be dangerous. The well-known story of the Tower of Babel illustrates the danger of ambition.

Genesis 11 (story)

Tension: Building the Tower of Babel

⁴Then they said, 'Come, let us build ourselves a city, with a tower that reaches to the heavens, so that we may make a name for ourselves and not be scattered over the face of the whole earth.'

Relief of tension: God causes confusion

⁵'But the Lord came down to see the city and the tower that the men were building.'
⁷'Come, let us go down and confuse their language so they will not understand each other.'

Result: The people are scattered

⁸So the Lord scattered them from there over all the earth, and they stopped building the city. (NIV)

In the past, people believed that the gods lived on the mountain tops. Because Mesopotamia did not have high mountains, people built ziggurats to perform this function. Ziggurats, which were common in Mesopotamia (modern-day Iraq), were built in the form of stairways that decreased in size from the bottom to the top of the structure. The base of a ziggurat could be about 300 square feet and have a height of about 300 feet. The room at the top was used for religious practices. It served as the meeting place between heaven and earth—between the gods and human beings.

The story of the Tower of Babel was most probably told with reference to the ziggurats. The purpose of the Tower of Babel was for the people to "make a name" for themselves by creating a tower "that reaches to the heavens" (v. 4). The phrase "reaches to the heavens" shows the human beings' ambition to compete with God, while "to make a name" reflects their pride. This reveals the sin committed by Adam and Eve, namely the desire to be like God (Gen. 3).

The story of the Tower of Babel goes on to relate that God came down to earth to see what was happening—which is rather ironic, as the people believed that their construction reached to the heavens. The words, "then nothing they plan to do will be impossible for them" (v. 6), reveal the human beings' revolt at its best. Human beings wanted to use their ambition to compete with God and to exclude Him.

Ambition without God leads to excessive pride and self-exaltation. Our ambition can lead us to trample on others and act just as we please—as if everything belongs to us. Ambition should always take God into account, for this will prevent us from becoming arrogant and crossing our boundaries.

The story of the Tower of Babel signals the end of pre-history in the Bible. Pre-historic times (in which people had only one language and one place name, namely Babel) will now make way for the historical era with its many languages and places—the historical time that starts with Abraham.

 Lord, I would like to always take You into account in my ambitions!

Ambition is the last refuge of failure.
—Oscar Wilde (1854–1900), *Irish poet and dramatist*

OUR FIRST STOP: THE PERIOD OF THE PATRIARCHS AND SLAVERY

(±2000–±1250 B.C.)
(GENESIS 12–50)

God is grieved because He created human beings (Gen 6:6). Nevertheless, He wants to accompany them on their journey. The means by which He chooses to do this is to single out one man and his family and turn them into a nation that will have a very special relationship with Him. God wants to reveal Himself to them and they, in turn (as the bearers of His image), have to reveal Him to others. God promises Abraham land and offspring. He forms the new community of believers in such a way that it does not happen naturally but through God's direct intervention.

God does this in two ways. First, He chooses an old sterile woman (Abraham's wife, Sarah) as the mother of the community of believers. Second, He calls someone from the heathens to be the father of the new community. By doing this, God wants us to realize that the community of believers is not the result of human thought and effort. It is the work of a God who wants to be reunited with us.

Abraham was the first father of the community. He and his descendants (such as Isaac and Jacob) are known as the patriarchs. "Patriarchs" is a Hebrew term that means "first father" or "ruling father." Joseph is another main figure. He was the favorite son of his father, Jacob. Genesis ends when Joseph and his family settle in Egypt, where they live for 430 years. During this time, they multiply in numbers and become slaves.

In these chapters in Genesis, we see the wondrous ways God goes about establishing a new community of faith.

WHAT DO WE DO
WHEN LIFE IS A DEAD END?

We often encounter situations in our lives when we feel trapped. These are times when it seems as if life has reached a dead end and there is no way forward. This episode might help us see the light!

Genesis 22 (story)

Tension: Abraham must offer up his son

²Then God said, 'Take your son, your only son, Isaac, whom you love, and go to the region of Moriah. Sacrifice him there as a burnt offering on one of the mountains I will tell you about.'

Relief of tension: The Lord provides a lamb

¹²'Do not lay a hand on the boy,' he said. 'Do not do anything to him. Now I know that you fear God, because you have not withheld from me your son, your only son.'
¹³Abraham looked up and there in a thicket he saw a ram caught by its horns. He went over and took the ram and sacrificed it as a burnt offering instead of his son. ¹⁴So Abraham called that place The LORD Will Provide. And to this day it is said, 'On the mountain of the LORD it will be provided.'

Result: The Lord promises blessing

¹⁶. . . 'I swear by myself, declares the LORD, that because you have done this and have not withheld your son, your only son, ¹⁷I will surely bless you and make your descendants as numerous as the stars in the sky and as the sand on the seashore . . .
¹⁸ and through your offspring all nations on earth will be blessed, because you have obeyed me.'
(NIV)

The episode in which Abraham was to sacrifice Isaac must have made Abraham doubt God's logic. How could God ask him to do such a thing? Had not God promised him land and numerous descendents? And now he was to sacrifice his only son. Yet despite his inability to understand, Abraham obeys God. In the end, Abraham sacrifices a ram, not Isaac. Was it a *coincidence that* the ram was there? No, Abraham sees this as a sign that God provides. He calls the place "the Lord will provide." What seemed like a dead end to Abraham was actually a new beginning.

We often explain things that happen to us as coincidence. Yet this may be God's way of providing in our lives. We do not have to understand everything, but we should realize that God wants to provide everything for us.

Right now, things may be happening in your life that just do not make sense. You may be asking questions such as, "Why is this happening to me?" or "How will I ever escape this?" Wrestling with God in situations in which there seems to be no way out will give you the opportunity to be like Abraham and say, "The Lord will provide."

 Lord, help me to trust You the way Abraham did, even though I do not always understand where You are leading me.

The pessimist sees difficulty in every opportunity. The optimist sees the opportunity in every difficulty.
—Winston Churchill (1874–1965), *British orator, author and Prime Minister during World War II*

PEOPLE WHO ARE ARROGANT SHOULD NOT EXPECT SUPPORT FROM OTHERS!

Dreams play a crucial role in the story of Joseph. They also bring about movement in the story. We will therefore focus on the following dreams during the next few days:

- Genesis 37: Joseph's dreams in his home—which lead to humiliation
- Genesis 40: The cupbearer's and the baker's dreams in prison—which draw attention to Joseph
- Genesis 41: Pharaoh's dreams in the palace—which lead to Joseph's promotion

Joseph's first dream reveals a characteristic of him that causes him to fall into disfavor with his family.

Genesis 37 (story)

Tension: Joseph gossips

[2]This is the account of Jacob. Joseph, a young man of seventeen, was tending the flocks with his brothers, the sons of Bilhah and the sons of Zilpah, his father's wives, and he brought their father a bad report about them.
[3]Now Israel loved Joseph more than any of his other sons, because he had been born to him in his old age; and he made a richly ornamented robe for him.

Relief of tension: Joseph's brothers take a dislike to him

[4]When his brothers saw that their father loved him more than any of them, they hated him and could not speak a kind word to him.
[5]Joseph had a dream, and when he told it to his brothers, they hated him all the more.
[10]When he told his father as well as his brothers, his father rebuked him and said, 'What is this dream you had? Will your mother and I and your brothers actually come and bow down to the ground before you?'

Result: Tension in the family

[11]His brothers were jealous of him, but his father kept the matter in mind. (NIV)

Joseph's two dreams have a detrimental effect on his relationship with his brothers. The meaning of the dreams is very clear: Joseph will become a ruler and his father and brothers will be subservient to him. Joseph's arrogance makes his brothers' blood boil. This is aggravated by the fact that he is their father's favorite child.

The way Joseph reports the dreams shows that he believes they will occur and that he is looking forward to their fulfillment. In those days, dreams were seen as revelations, and Joseph's dreams posed a threat to his brothers. This is why, in the next episode, they throw him into a cistern and sell him as a slave. This arrogant pet son learns the hard way that arrogance brings you into disrepute.

We have to listen earnestly to what is said in Proverbs 14:3: "A fool's talk brings a rod to his back, but the lips of the wise protect them" (NIV). The first dream leads to Joseph being thrown into a dry well and taken as a slave to Egypt.

 Lord, help me not to be conceited but to act wisely.

The truest characters of ignorance are vanity, and pride and arrogance.
—Samuel Butler (1835–1902), *English novelist, essayist and critic*

SOMETIMES IT'S HARD TO TRUST OTHERS!

Experience teaches us not to trust everybody. Some people even say that it is impossible to trust anyone. What should we do? This next episode in Joseph's life, which takes place between the first and second dreams, will help us to understand *trust* better.

Genesis 39 (story)

Tension: Potiphar's wife tries to seduce Joseph

> [6]So he left in Joseph's care everything he had; with Joseph in charge, he did not concern himself with anything except the food he ate.
> Now Joseph was well-built and handsome, [7] and after a while his master's wife took notice of Joseph and said, 'Come to bed with me!'

Relief of tension: Joseph flees and lands in prison

> [12]She caught him by his cloak and said, 'Come to bed with me!' But he left his cloak in her hand and ran out of the house. [19]When his master heard the story his wife told him, saying, 'This is how your slave treated me,' he burned with anger. [20]Joseph's master took him and put him in prison . . .

Result: Joseph achieves success while in prison

> [20]But while Joseph was there in the prison, [21]the LORD was with him; he showed him kindness and granted him favor in the eyes of the prison warden. [22]So the warden put Joseph in charge of all those held in the prison, and he was made responsible for all that was done there. [23]The warden paid no attention to anything under Joseph's care, because the LORD was with Joseph and gave him success in whatever he did. (NIV)

Potiphar sees that he can trust Joseph, so he leaves his whole household in Joseph's care—except for his food (v. 6). "His food" is a euphemism to describe sexual intercourse with his wife. Potiphar has barely left the scene when his wife starts flirting with Joseph. After all, Joseph is muscular and well built. Potiphar's wife wants to hand her husband's "food" to Joseph on a platter.

Joseph does not taste it, but because of a lie Potiphar's wife tells, he ends up in prison. In terms of the Law, Joseph should have been executed, but Potiphar has him locked up instead. Perhaps he did not find his wife's story convincing enough. Even in jail, Joseph radiates such self-confidence that the warden puts him in charge of everything. Not many people have Joseph's self-confidence.

Sometimes it's hard to trust others! However, without trust, relationships cannot be formed— and a life without relationships deprives us of one of our biggest needs: intimacy. This story does not ask us to consider whether we can trust people, but rather if we can be trusted. May the Lord help us all to be like Joseph!

Lord, I want to live in such a way that others will trust me.

> *I know God will not give me anything I can't handle. I just wish He didn't trust me so much.*
> —Mother Teresa of Calcutta (1910–1997), *Albanian born Indian missionary, founder of the Order of the Missionaries of Charity and winner of the Nobel Prize for Peace in 1979*

WILL WE ESCAPE FROM THIS DARK HOLE?

You might be down in the dumps because you could not cope with a difficult situation and now feel trapped in a dark hole of despair. If so, Joseph's second dream might set your life on track. This episode deals with the king's confidants (the cupbearer and the baker) who end up in prison with Joseph.

Genesis 40 (story)

Tension: Joseph must interpret dreams

[6]When Joseph came to them the next morning, he saw that they were dejected. [7] So he asked Pharaoh's officials who were in custody with him in his master's house, 'Why are your faces so sad today?' [8]'We both had dreams,' they answered, 'but there is no one to interpret them.' Then Joseph said to them, 'Do not interpretations belong to God? Tell me your dreams.' [9]So the chief cupbearer told Joseph his dream. He said to him, 'In my dream I saw a vine in front of me, [10]and on the vine were three branches. As soon as it budded, it blossomed, and its clusters ripened into grapes. [11]Pharaoh's cup was in my hand, and I took the grapes, squeezed them into Pharaoh's cup and put the cup in his hand.'

Relief of tension: Joseph interprets the dreams

[12]'This is what it means,' Joseph said to him. 'The three branches are three days. [13]Within three days Pharaoh will lift up your head and restore you to your position and you will put Pharaoh's cup in his hand, just as you used to do when you were his cupbearer.

Result: Joseph asks a favor

[14]But when all goes well with you, remember me and show me kindness; mention me to Pharaoh and get me out of this prison. [15]For I was forcibly carried off from the land of the Hebrews, and even here I have done nothing to deserve being put in a dungeon.' [23]The chief cupbearer, however, did not remember Joseph; he forgot him. (NIV)

When Joseph interprets the cupbearer's dream, we learn something about Joseph's own emotions (vv. 14–15). Although he did nothing to deserve it, he was made a slave and prisoner for 13 years. He asks the cupbearer to think of him and to ensure that he is released from prison.

The cupbearer is sympathetic towards Joseph when he hears how Joseph was abducted and thrown into the dungeon (prison) despite his innocence. The Hebrew word for "well" (cistern) also means dungeon (v. 15). This is a reference to his brothers who threw him into a dry well (cistern). Joseph's distress call of "remember me" expresses many people's call for help.

It is sad that the cupbearer forgets about Joseph (v. 23). Fortunately, the story does not end there. This dream paves the way for Joseph's release. In the same way, your own experience of distress in a dark hole may prove to be the way out of your difficulties.

 Lord, thank You that I can know that despite my circumstances, You are constantly working in my life.

Out of difficulties grow miracles.
—Jean de la Bruyere (1645–1696), *French satiric moralist*

WHERE SHOULD WE LOOK FOR GOD?

God sometimes seems absent in our lives. Where should we look for Him? The story of Joseph's third dream tells us where to look for God.

Genesis 41 (story)

Tension: Pharaoh is anxious

[8]In the morning his mind was troubled, so he sent for all the magicians and wise men of Egypt. Pharaoh told them his dreams, but no one could interpret them for him.

Relief of tension: Joseph is summoned from prison

[9]Then the chief cupbearer said to Pharaoh, 'Today I am reminded of my shortcomings. [10]Pharaoh was once angry with his servants, and he imprisoned me and the chief baker in the house of the captain of the guard. [11]Each of us had a dream the same night, and each dream had a meaning of its own. [12]Now a young Hebrew was there with us, a servant of the captain of the guard. We told him our dreams, and he interpreted them for us, giving each man the interpretation of his dream. [13]And things turned out exactly as he interpreted them to us: I was restored to my position, and the other man was hanged.' [14]So Pharaoh sent for Joseph, and he was quickly brought from the dungeon. When he had shaved and changed his clothes, he came before Pharaoh. [15]Pharaoh said to Joseph, 'I had a dream, and no one can interpret it. But I have heard it said of you that when you hear a dream you can interpret it.' [16]'I cannot do it,' Joseph replied to Pharaoh, 'but God will give Pharaoh the answer he desires.'

Result: Joseph is honored

[39]Then Pharaoh said to Joseph, 'Since God has made all this known to you, here is no one so discerning and wise as you. [40]You shall be in charge of my palace, and all my people are to submit to your orders. Only with respect to the throne will I be greater than you.' [41]So Pharaoh said to Joseph, 'I hereby put you in charge of the whole land of Egypt.' (NIV)

Joseph's first dream caused him to be thrown into a dry well. Here, following the last dream in the story about Joseph, he is brought to the mighty pharaoh's palace and becomes second in command in the whole land of Egypt. Joseph progresses from a prison to a palace—without pertinent mention of God (except in Genesis 45:5–8 and 50:19–20).

Was God absent? Certainly not! The Bible shows us that God often achieves His goal with the world inconspicuously by using ordinary people and ordinary events. We should not always look for God in the sensational. The story of Joseph also shows us that we should not look for God in pleasant things alone. Joseph's story proclaims that God is not hindered by people's shortcomings and wrongdoings. It is comforting to know that despite all society's ills and all our "dry well" experiences, God constantly works in our lives.

Thank You, Lord, for letting me know that You are constantly working in my life.

Small minds are concerned with the extraordinary, great minds with the ordinary.
—Blaise Pascal (1623–1662), *French mathematician, physicist and religious philosopher*

OUR SECOND STOP: FROM THE EXODUS TO THE CONQUEST OF THE PROMISED LAND

(±1250–1220 B.C.)
(EXODUS TO JOSHUA)

Genesis ends with Joseph and his family in Egypt. Exodus picks up the story 430 years later with Moses. As time went by, the Egyptians forgot how Joseph had saved them from starvation. During these 430 years, the Israelites multiplied in great numbers, even though the pharaoh forced them do slave labor in the hope of keeping their numbers in check. The following are highlights from this time:

Moses leads his people from Egypt—the 10 plagues
The Passover (Jewish Easter)—celebrating the exodus from Egypt
The people wander in the desert
- God makes a covenant with the people at Mount Sinai
- A constitution is formed for God's new people
  * Moral laws—the Ten Commandments (Exod. 20)
  * Ceremonial laws (e.g., Exod. 23:14–17)
  * Civil laws (e.g., Lev. 19:9–10)
- The sad episode of the golden calf
- God's presence with the people
  * The people are led by fire and cloud columns
  * The Tabernacle is built
  * God sends provision of manna and quails

Offerings—worshipers are unworthy to approach God on their own. Leviticus describes this in detail because the Levites are concerned with offerings.

Invasion of Canaan, the Promised Land

- Mission of the 12 spies
- Poisonous snakes afflict the people when they rebel
- The bronze snake on poles cures the people
- Moses bids farewell (Deuteronomy)
- Joshua leads the people across the Jordan
- The fall of Jericho
- The land is divided up
- The people still disobey (Deut. 7:2–4; Josh. 17:13)

We can now see that God is starting to fulfill His promises made to Abraham.

CAN GOD STILL PROVIDE A WAY OUT?

We live in a world with so much hurt and distress that one wonders if God can still provide a way out. This episode in the book of Exodus helps us to better understand the workings of God in our lives.

Exodus 2 (story)

Tension: Moses is hidden

[1]Now a man of the house of Levi married a Levite woman, [2]and she became pregnant and gave birth to a son. When she saw that he was a fine child, she hid him for three months. [3]But when she could hide him no longer, she got a papyrus basket for him and coated it with tar and pitch. Then she placed the child in it and put it among the reeds along the bank of the Nile.

Relief of tension: Moses' life is saved

[9]Pharaoh's daughter said to her, 'Take this baby and nurse him for me, and I will pay you.' So the woman took the baby and nursed him.

Result: Moses becomes the pharaoh's "grandchild"

[10]When the child grew older, she took him to Pharaoh's daughter and he became her son. She named him Moses, saying, 'I drew him out of the water.' (NIV)

The pharaohs were viewed as gods, and were therefore very mighty. After their 400-year stay in Egypt, the Israelites multiplied to such an extent that Pharaoh regards them as a threat. He orders that when Hebrew boys are born, they are thrown into the Nile. However, in this episode we see that women, who at that time had no real power, jeopardize the mighty Pharaoh's plans.

This starts with Moses' mother, who circumvents Pharaoh's decree by hiding her son in the reeds. Pharaoh's own daughter then comes to Moses' rescue and, by doing so, foils her father's plans. However, she does not want to take responsibility for his upbringing, so, without realizing it, she returns him to his own mother, who feeds him and takes care of him. The best part is that the princess pays Moses' mother to do this! God uses socially disempowered women to undermine the mighty Pharaoh's plans. Unbelievable!

Through this story, we learn that God can provide a way out in surprising and unpredictable ways. Yet human beings are not passive in all this. In this particular story, Moses' mother weaved a papyrus basket and hid Moses in it while his sister looked out for him. God works in our lives so that we can take responsibility. For instance, it does not help to pray for a safe neighborhood without taking the responsibility to form a neighborhood watch or work closely with the local police. God can and will use our involvement to provide a way out.

 Thank You, Lord, that You can provide a way out in surprising and unpredictable ways.

Tell me and I'll forget; show me and I may remember; involve me and I'll understand.
—Chinese Proverb

WHY DO WE HAVE TO SUFFER SO MUCH?

People do not see much sense in suffering and, therefore, do as much as possible to avoid it. In this next episode, we find a refreshing perspective on suffering.

Exodus 16 (story)

Tension: The Israelites in the desert complain to Moses

[2]In the desert the whole community grumbled against Moses and Aaron. [3]The Israelites said to them, 'If only we had died by the LORD's hand in Egypt! There we sat around pots of meat and ate all the food we wanted, but you have brought us out into this desert to starve this entire assembly to death.'

Relief of tension: Bread from heaven

[4]Then the LORD said to Moses, 'I will rain down bread from heaven for you. The people are to go out each day and gather enough for that day. In this way I will test them and see whether they will follow my instructions.

Result: Every family has enough

[15]When the Israelites saw it, they said to each other, 'What is it?' For they did not know what it was. Moses said to them, 'It is the bread the LORD has given you to eat. [16]This is what the LORD has commanded: 'Each one is to gather as much as he needs. Take an omer for each person you have in your tent." (NIV)

If you page through the Bible, you will find that deserts are always part of a life with God. John the Baptist and Jesus literally spent time in the desert. Many others experienced deserts in a figurative sense as part of their lives. This happened to such an extent that the "desert" came to symbolize suffering.

The Israelites suffered greatly in the desert. Their desert experience was aggravated by the shortage of water and food. The desert was also extremely hot and filled with uncertainties. However, in this story we see that the Bible paints a different picture of the desert. For the Israelites, the desert was not only a place of starvation but also a place of manna and quails. The desert was especially the place where human beings could become aware of their vulnerability and dependence on others, on nature, on their circumstances and on the mercy of God.

In the desert, God frees Israel a second time. At the Sea of Reeds, God had freed them *externally*—in other words, from the danger of Egypt that threatened them. Now, God frees them *internally* from selfishness and worry and enables them to trust Him because they had experienced His care. In our busy lives, suffering forces us to pause. It might be that the Lord uses our own suffering to free us internally to look at ourselves, our fellow human beings and at God anew.

 Thank You, Lord, for making me realize that at times it is necessary for me to suffer.

God whispers to us in our pleasures, speaks in our conscience, but shouts in our pains: it is His megaphone to rouse a deaf world.
—C.S. Lewis (1898–1963), *Oxford and Cambridge professor and perhaps the twentieth century's most famous convert to Christianity. Lewis was the creator of The Chronicles of Narnia.*

CAN GOD BACK OUT?

When entering into business contracts or work contracts—and yes, even marriage contracts—people normally ensure that they do not pin themselves down completely. They do this by including clauses to protect them and to keep their options open. The question is, Has God kept His options open where we are concerned? If He has, it means that He can still back out. Will He?

Exodus 19 (story)

Tension: Will Israel be obedient?

> ⁵Now if you obey me fully and keep my covenant, then out of all nations you will be my treasured possession. Although the whole earth is mine, ⁶you will be for me a kingdom of priests and a holy nation.' These are the words you are to speak to the Israelites.'

Relief of tension: Israel is willing to listen

> ⁷So Moses went back and summoned the elders of the people and set before them all the words the LORD had commanded him to speak. ⁸The people all responded together, 'We will do everything the LORD has said.' So Moses brought their answer back to the LORD.

Result: Guidelines for the covenant

Exodus 20

> ¹And God spoke all these words:
> ²'I am the LORD your God, who brought you out of Egypt, out of the land of slavery. (NIV)

These six chapters in Exodus (19–24) tell the story of how God enters into a covenant with the Israelites. A covenant is an agreement into which the parties concerned enter to ensure that a shaky relationship becomes more steadfast and permanent. In this episode, we find that God is prepared to commit Himself fully to Israel. His aim is to regain sinful human beings by means of Israel. The Lord expects a commitment by Israel to obey Him. As a guideline and policy for the commitment (the covenant), He gives Moses the Ten Commandments (Exod. 20).

Why would the Lord expect this kind of commitment from His people? According to Exodus 19:5–6, He does this because He wants to establish a group (a nation) for Himself. The words He uses in verses 5 and 6, namely "my treasured possession" and "a kingdom of priests," show that it has to be a special group of people. Indeed, they are special because they are the people whom God wants to use to regain the world for Himself.

Back then, this was the Lord's long-term plan with Israel. Today, the Church serves that same purpose. God did not keep His options open. When we realize that He wants to use us (as part of His Church) to regain the world for Himself, we have to take the covenant seriously. This is exactly where the problem in the Church often lies—a lack of commitment. It is time for us to show by the way we live that we believe in God and give priority to the Church!

Thank You, Lord, that Your covenant with us is so strong that You gave Your only Son
to die so that we can live.

*Think what a local church would look like if its people were radically devoted to Christ,
irrevocably committed to each other, and relentlessly dedicated to reaching
those outside God's family with the gospel of Christ.*
—Bill Hybels, *Senior Pastor of Willow Creek Community Church in Chicago, Illinois*

RELIGION IS NOT ONLY ABOUT GOD!

We tend to think of God when we hear the word "religion." This is quite understandable, as the connection between God and this word have become inseparable. The following section, however, shows us that religion has another side to it as well.

Exodus 20 (instruction)

[12]Honor your father and your mother, so that you may live long in the land the LORD your God is giving you.
[13]You shall not murder.
[14]You shall not commit adultery.
[15]You shall not steal.
[16]You shall not give false testimony against your neighbor.
[17]You shall not covet your neighbor's house. You shall not covet your neighbor's wife, or his manservant or maidservant, his ox or donkey, or anything that belongs to your neighbor. (NIV)

From this passage, we see that religion not only concerns God, but also people. This section is the well-known second tablet of the Ten Commandments, which deals with the relationship between human beings. If we read further than Exodus 20, we see that religion concerns even more than God and human beings—it involves the entire scope of life on earth. For example, Exodus 21 deals with good social order and with injuries and damages. Exodus 22 deals with theft, wildfires and goods left in the care of others. Religion, therefore, not only concerns elevated matters but also earthly matters.

John 3:16, perhaps the most famous verse in the Bible, proclaims, "For God so loved the world that he gave his one and only Son" (NIV). Our salvation in Christ is the result of the Lord's love and earnestness with this world. After all, He is the One who created it. The famous Dutch theologian, A.A. van Ruler, makes a striking observation by saying that the Lord did not create us in the Old Testament so that he could turn us into Christians in the New Testament. According to van Ruler, the Lord makes Christians of us in the New Testament so that we can become human beings again—human beings in the way God intended us to be.

Martin Luther, the famous reformer, also understood religion in this way. He said that the Lord called him twice: the first time from the world to a monastery and the second time from the monastery back to the world.

 Lord, I would like to be religious in all spheres of my life.

Preach the gospel at all times, and when necessary use words.
—Saint Francis of Assisi (1181–1226), *Roman Catholic saint who took the gospel literally*

WHERE IS THE BEST PLACE TO HIDE FROM GOD?

In the previous reading, we learned about God's covenant with the people. God commits Himself fully to the covenant, but He also makes demands on human beings. These demands are captured in the Ten Commandments. By nature, we tend not to obey demands. We like to hide from God and from the demands He sets for our lives. But where is the best place to hide from God?

Exodus 32 (story)

Tension: The people want another god

> [1]When the people saw that Moses was so long in coming down from the mountain, they gathered around Aaron and said, 'Come, make us gods who will go before us. As for this fellow Moses who brought us up out of Egypt, we don't know what has happened to him.'

Relief of tension: The people take action

> [3]So all the people took off their earrings and brought them to Aaron. [4]He took what they handed him and made it into an idol cast in the shape of a calf, fashioning it with a tool. Then they said, 'These are your gods, O Israel, who brought you up out of Egypt.'

Result: Festivities

> [5]When Aaron saw this, he built an altar in front of the calf and announced, 'Tomorrow there will be a festival to the LORD!' (NIV)

As Moses is experiencing a spiritual high on top of the mountain in the presence of God, the people are experiencing a spiritual low at the foot of the mountain. Because Moses stayed away for such a long time, they begin to believe that Moses has failed them. So they decide to make a golden calf to lead them into the desert.

There are many points of view on how we should interpret this action of Aaron and the people. Did they want to use the image of the golden calf to worship another god, or was the image merely intended as a substitute for God? Scholars are of the opinion that they wanted to create an image of God and not to worship another God, but we will never know for sure. Regardless, this request to Aaron meant that the Israelites were breaking the contract (covenant) that was still fresh in their memory. This is shocking!

In the second commandment (Exod. 20:4), God prohibited making images of Him. An image can never capture God's greatness, because an image can be manipulated in any way—it can be moved anywhere, and can even be discarded. The Israelites wanted to use the golden calf to manipulate God and worship Him on their own terms.

This is what makes religion so dangerous—it is often a subtle way to use the Lord to achieve our own objectives. It is not about the Lord's demands of the covenant but rather about what we demand from God. This is why Karl Barth, the famous Swiss theologian, said that the Church is the best place to hide from God's demands. The Church is exactly the place to be religious and to put our *demands* to the Lord. May God save us from this!

Lord, alert me to the fact that I should not use You to achieve my own aims.

How absurd men are! They never use the liberties they have; they demand those they do not have. They
have freedom of thought; they demand freedom of speech.
—Søren Kierkegaard (1813–1855), *Danish philosopher and theologian, generally recognized*
as the first existentialist philosopher

WHAT DOES GOD LOOK LIKE?

Moses is given the opportunity to ask the question we would probably all like to ask God: "What do You look like?" What did Moses see?

Exodus 33 (story)

Tension: *Moses wants to see God*

> [12]Moses said to the LORD, 'You have been telling me, 'Lead these people,' but you have not let me know whom you will send with me.'
> [18]Then Moses said, 'Now show me your glory.'

Relief of tension: *Moses sees God's back*

> [14]The LORD replied, 'My Presence will go with you, and I will give you rest.'
> [17]And the LORD said to Moses, 'I will do the very thing you have asked, because I am pleased with you and I know you by name. [22]When my glory passes by, I will put you in a cleft in the rock and cover you with my hand until I have passed by. [23]Then I will remove my hand and you will see my back; but my face must not be seen.'

Result: *Forgiveness*

> Forgiveness is implied because in Exodus 34 God once again makes a covenant with the people. (NIV)

In order to grasp Moses' question and God's answer, we need to understand the background to the conversation. This episode takes place in the desert immediately after the episode of the golden calf. The Lord is upset because the people forgot Him so soon, and so He decides to wipe them from the face of the earth (Exod. 32:10). However, when Moses pleads with God on behalf of the people, the Lord abandons His plan. God also grants Moses his wish to send an angel ahead of the people (32:34; 33:1–2), since He does not see His way clear to accompany them. Then, when it seems that Moses has been given everything he asked for, he says the following: "Now show me your glory" (v. 18).

Why would Moses ask this question? Scholars are of the opinion that by asking this question, Moses wanted to establish whether God had forgiven the people for creating the golden calf and whether He was still prepared to accompany them to the Promised Land. Moses knew that if God were to travel with them and was willing to reveal Himself, the people would be forgiven.

It is interesting to note that the Lord only gives Moses the opportunity to see His back. Why is this? Scholars believe that the Lord wanted to remind Moses of the fact that the Israelites were in His hands, not the other way round. By revealing His back, the Lord upheld His freedom and sovereignty. Without saying it explicitly, it is clear that the people are forgiven, because the covenant is restored in the following chapter. Moses has the opportunity to see God's back. Moses wants to know whether the Lord will go *along* with them, but God decides that He will *lead*.

It is wonderful to see God's back, because we can then know that we are following Him. It is more important to obediently follow the Lord than to know what He looks like.

 Thank You, Lord, not only for accompanying me today but also for leading the way. I want to follow You!

> *In the faces of men and women, I see God.*
> —Walt Whitman, *Nineteenth-century American poet*

ARE THERE LIMITS TO GOD'S FORGIVENESS?

Will God always forgive us everything? One would like to answer yes to this question. This episode in Exodus, in which God makes a second covenant with the people, gives us more insight into the question.

Exodus 34 (story)

Tension: What will God tell Moses?

¹The LORD said to Moses, 'Chisel out two stone tablets like the first ones, and I will write on them the words that were on the first tablets, which you broke. ²Be ready in the morning, and then come up on Mount Sinai. Present yourself to me there on top of the mountain. ³No one is to come with you or be seen anywhere on the mountain; not even the flocks and herds may graze in front of the mountain.'

Relief of tension: God speaks to Moses

⁴So Moses chiseled out two stone tablets like the first ones and went up Mount Sinai early in the morning, as the LORD had commanded him; and he carried the two stone tablets in his hands. ⁵Then the LORD came down . . .
⁶And he passed in front of Moses, proclaiming, 'The LORD, the LORD, the compassionate and gracious God, slow to anger, abounding in love and faithfulness, ⁷maintaining love to thousands, and forgiving wickedness, rebellion and sin. Yet he does not leave the guilty unpunished.

Result: The covenant is renewed

¹⁰Then the LORD said: 'I am making a covenant with you. Before all your people I will do wonders never before done in any nation in all the world.' (NIV)

Exodus 34:7 tells us that God forgives everything (injustice, trespassing and sin). However, the word "yet" in verse 7 gives us a serious warning: "Yet He does not leave the guilty unpunished." We should treat God's forgiveness respectfully and not take it for granted. His forgiveness is always a privilege that we should appreciate.

Forgiveness is always necessary in order to mend a broken relationship. This is why God forgave the people for making and worshipping the golden calf. Forgiveness is the bridge across the gulf that separates people. Therefore, forgiveness never operates in isolation but always leads to the mending of relationships.

Forgiveness and reconciliation are inseparable; the one cannot exist without the other. God will always forgive us for everything if our intentions are sincere in trying to restore our relationship with Him and our fellow human beings. One of the most liberating thoughts must be to know that God's forgiveness is boundless. Indeed, the Lord Himself told Moses, "The Lord, the Lord, the compassionate and gracious God, slow to anger, abounding in love and faithfulness" (v. 6).

 Lord, I would like to restore relationships through forgiveness.

Forgiveness is the fragrance that the violet sheds on the heel that has crushed it.
—Mark Twain (1835–1910), *American humorist, writer and lecturer*

DOES GOD EXPECT TOO MUCH OF US?

People will sometimes make unreasonable demands on us. In the Bible, God also makes demands on human beings. Are God's demands unreasonable? Let's take a look.

Leviticus 1 (procedure)—Offerings to the Lord

[1]The LORD called to Moses and spoke to him from the Tent of Meeting. He said,
[2]"Speak to the Israelites and say to them: 'When any of you brings an offering to the LORD, bring as your offering an animal from either the herd or the flock.
[3]If the offering is a burnt offering from the herd, he is to offer a male without defect. He must present it at the entrance to the Tent of Meeting so that it will be acceptable to the LORD.' (NIV)

The events in Leviticus take place in the desert near Mount Horeb. The book of Leviticus centers on the relationship between God and human beings. The truth is that the Israelites disturbed this relationship by being unfaithful. But God, by means of the system of offerings, made it possible for them to restore their relationship with Him.

The system of offerings and the way in which animals were sacrificed might seem repulsive to us, but this was not the case in those days. The people could worship God in a very concrete way by using what they had to eat as an offering. The Lord did not accept just any animal as sacrifice—a domestic animal, without defects and reared by the family, had to be used. A person had to give up this animal by offering it to God. This innocent animal would then act as the person's substitute in the eyes of God. The animal's blood replaced that of the human being—in other words, its life pays for the person's life. God suggests a wide range of offerings to enable both rich and poor to bring offerings.

This demonstrates that God is reasonable and enables everybody to be reconciled with Him. Fortunately, we no longer have to sacrifice animals to God, because the sacrificial death of Jesus restored the relationship between God and human beings. It is therefore no longer necessary to restore this relationship with actual offerings. However, God still expects us to give expression to this remedied relationship. How do we do this? Romans 12:1 explains it in terms of another offering, namely living sacrifices: "Therefore, I urge you, brothers, in view of God's mercy, to offer your bodies as living sacrifices, holy and pleasing to God" (NIV).

God's mercy toward us is characterized by love that involves sacrifice. He gave Himself as a sacrifice on the cross, which should be our motivation to show unselfish love toward God and our fellow human beings. If we want to love in this way, we will have to do things that we do not necessarily like (for example, washing the dishes) and be prepared to do things we would not normally be prepared to do. We simply perform the task out of love. Because we are motivated by love, God's expectations of us are not unreasonable. They are a joy and a privilege.

 Thank You, Lord, for being a reasonable and loving Father.

Only when we give joyfully, without hesitation or thought of gain, can we truly know what love means.
—Leo F. Buscaglia (1924–1998), *American guru and tireless advocate of the power of love*

CAN GOD REALLY USE US?

At times, we might feel that we are of no real use to God because we have so often failed Him and our fellow human beings. The following section in Leviticus will help us to see this differently.

Leviticus 8 (procedure)—Ordination of priests

[1]The LORD said to Moses, [2]'Bring Aaron and his sons, their garments, the anointing oil, the bull for the sin offering, the two rams and the basket containing bread made without yeast, [3]and gather the entire assembly at the entrance to the Tent of Meeting.'
[4]Moses did as the LORD commanded him and the assembly gathered at the entrance to the Tent of Meeting.
[5]Moses said to the assembly, 'This is what the LORD has commanded to be done.'
[30]Then Moses took some of the anointing oil and some of the blood from the altar and sprinkled them on Aaron and his garments and on his sons and their garments. So he consecrated Aaron and his garments and his sons and their garments. (NIV)

The ordination of Aaron as high priest and of his sons as priests marked a special day in Israel's history. A high priest had to perform very important duties. He was responsible for the daily offerings and functions in the Tabernacle. He was also responsible for conducting specific duties at the festivals at Passover and Pentecost and the Day of Atonement (Yom Kippur). During the Day of Atonement, only the high priest could enter the Holy Place to bring about reconciliation on behalf of the people. Someone in this position had to act extremely responsibly.

One would think that God would appoint an exceptional person to this position. Instead, God appointed someone with a less favorable record—Aaron. Aaron was the one who had made the golden calf while Moses met with God on Mount Horeb (Exod. 32–34). Aaron's sins drove God close to forsaking His people. Yet despite this incident, Aaron was ordained as high priest, and his sons were ordained as priests.

Aaron was not appointed because of his inherent qualities. Rather, he and his sons were empowered by means of the system of offerings when they were sanctified by the blood at the inauguration ceremony. The blood served as proof that their sins had been paid for. The appointment of Aaron and his sons therefore involved a ritual of offerings to sanctify them. From this, we see that God does not choose people because of their qualities and accomplishments. Our cleansing by the blood of Christ also makes us suitable candidates for God to use.

 Thank You, Father that You want to use me. Thank You that I no longer have to feel useless. Use me!

The purpose of life is not to be happy. It is to be useful, to be honorable, to be compassionate, to have it make some difference that you have lived and lived well.
—Ralph Waldo Emerson (1803–1882), *American poet, essayist and lecturer*

THE LORD IS NOT YOUR BUDDY!

The Lord wants us to have a relationship with Him, but any relationship has boundaries that should be respected. This next section in Leviticus shows us that the Lord also sets boundaries in our relationship with Him.

Leviticus 10 (story)

Tension: A wrong offering

[1]Aaron's sons Nadab and Abihu took their censers, put fire in them and added incense; and they offered unauthorized fire before the LORD, contrary to his command.

Relief of tension: A devouring fire

[2]So fire came out from the presence of the LORD and consumed them, and they died before the LORD.

Result: We must show respect for God

[3]Moses then said to Aaron, "This is what the LORD spoke of when he said: 'Among those who approach me I will show myself holy; in the sight of all the people I will be honored.'" (NIV)

What was intended as a joyous day ends in the tragic death of Aaron's two sons. They did not take the prescriptions of the system of offerings seriously and had to pay for it with their lives. This may seem cruel to us, but it serves as a reminder that God should always be taken seriously.

When I was a young student, one of my friends would often interrupt a respected professor during lectures by asking him questions, some of which were quite irritating. Once when this professor was about to conclude one of his lectures, my friend confronted him with the following question: "Professor, if the Lord is my friend, can I walk around on campus and talk to Him and tell Him that there is nothing like a pair of pretty legs?"

A dead silence fell over the lecture room, because this young man had once again dared to frustrate the distinguished professor. The professor answered with a loving, yet stern, expression: "Young man, the Lord is your friend but not your buddy." These words put an end to my friend's efforts to frustrate the professor. The professor instilled respect in all of us, and his life reminded us that we have to show great respect toward God.

 Lord, forgive me for not always showing You the necessary respect.

A true love of God must begin with a delight in his holiness.
—Jonathan Edwards (1703–1758), *American theologian, philosopher of British American Puritanism*
and stimulator of the "Great Awakening" revival

CEREMONIES CAN BE SO BORING!

Not everybody likes formal gatherings with rigid instructions. The whole book of Leviticus is about instructions and ceremonies. Leviticus 16, in which all the instructions are given, is the main focus of the book. It describes the day on which the high priest enters the Most Holy Place to make reconciliation for all the people. Why would God want reconciliation (the restoration of peace) to consist of so many ceremonies?

Leviticus 16 (procedure)—The annual reconciliation

³"This is how Aaron is to enter the sanctuary area: with a young bull for a sin offering and a ram for a burnt offering. ¹⁷No one is to be in the Tent of Meeting from the time Aaron goes in to make atonement in the Most Holy Place until he comes out, having made atonement for himself, his household and the whole community of Israel. ³⁴"This is to be a lasting ordinance for you: Atonement is to be made once a year for all the sins of the Israelites.' (NIV)

The ceremonies and rituals might seem senseless and even repulsive to us, but in those days they were considered part of daily life. The ceremonies were relevant to the culture and living conditions of the people. With these instructions, God connected Himself to the people's world. The Lord used these ceremonies to reveal something of Himself and of human beings. Let's look at a few aspects of this important day:

1. The high priest had to follow all the instructions for the ceremony carefully. This made the Israelites aware of the fact that they had to depend on God for reconciliation.
2. Only the high priest could enter the Most Holy Place once a year on behalf of the people. This restriction showed the people that God was holy and that access to Him was limited.
3. The annual sacrificial system showed that a substitute had to be sacrificed for reconciliation to take place.
4. The high priest had to sacrifice an animal before entering the Most Holy Place. This indicated that he, too, was sinful.

By introducing the Day of Atonement, the Lord created an opportunity to restore relationship with Him. This day, Yom Kippur, is still the most important day in the Jewish calendar. The Day of Atonement, with all its instructions, served to inform the people of God's *holiness* and their *dependence* on Him. This is the message that echoes throughout the Bible and that we must reflect by the way we live!

 Lord, help me to always remember that You are holy and that I am dependent on You.

Holiness is doing God's will with a smile.
—Mother Teresa of Calcutta (1910–1997), *Albanian born Indian missionary, founder of the Order of the Missionaries of Charity and winner of the Nobel Prize for Peace in 1979*

WHERE DOES SEX BELONG?

Sex is overemphasized and exploited in today's world. The question we should ask is: Where does sex belong?

Leviticus 18 (explanation and instruction)

[6] "No one is to approach any close relative to have sexual relations. (*instruction*) I am the LORD. (*explanation*)

[7] "Do not dishonor your father by having sexual relations with your mother. (*instruction*) She is your mother; (*explanation*) do not have relations with her.

[8] "Do not have sexual relations with your father's wife; (*instruction*) that would dishonor your father. (*explanation*)

[9] "Do not have sexual relations with your sister, either your father's daughter or your mother's daughter, whether she was born in the same home or elsewhere." (*instruction*) NIV

More and more teenagers and unmarried people today are sexually active than ever before, but this does not seem to satisfy the need for lasting relationships and intimacy. In fact, the contrary seems to be true: relationships are short-lived. Why? Because people buy into the lie that sex guarantees intimacy and true relationships. How many young people discover too late that sex is not the gateway to intimacy?

Fortunately, the Bible gives us guidelines to enable us to think about sex in the right way. There is much talk about whether or not premarital sex is wrong. This text in Leviticus 18 does not answer this issue, as it does pertain to premarital sex but rather with prohibited sexual activities. However, it is interesting to note that unmarried people are not mentioned. The warnings against illicit sex in Leviticus 18 seek to protect the close unity of the family.

Intimacy is only possible within a close relationship. A close-knit unit requires three elements: *mutual love, trust and commitment (longevity)*. Sex can flourish under these conditions! Can cohabitation guarantee these three elements? If so, why do some people prefer living together rather than getting married? Common sense tells us that sex without love, trust and commitment can be self-destructive. If a strong electric current passes through a thin electrical wire, the wire will be damaged beyond repair. This is the case with sex. It is worthwhile to wait for a safe and intimate environment that is based on love, trust and commitment.

Marriage seeks to ensure this kind of environment. However, the sad truth is that many marriages lack love, trust and commitment. Sex can cause frustration in marriages, especially if the partners are incompatible. So, how is your relationship doing?

 Lord, help me to create a safe environment for sex through love, trust and commitment.

The orgasm has replaced the cross as the focus of longing and the image of fulfillment.
—C.S. Lewis (1898–1963), *High-powered Oxford and Cambridge professor and perhaps the twentieth century's most famous convert to Christianity. Lewis was the creator of the Narnia series.*

DOES EVERYTHING IN LIFE INVOLVE GOD?

During service on Sunday, the sermon and hymns make us aware of God's presence and that worship involves God. However, during the course of the week, we tend to focus on other things and forget about God. The question is: Does everything in life involve God? The following section will help answer this question.

Leviticus 19 (explanation and instruction)

¹The LORD said to Moses, ² 'Speak to the entire assembly of Israel and say to them:
'Be holy (*instruction*) because I, the LORD your God, am holy.' ' (*explanation*)
³'Each of you must respect his mother and father, and you must observe my Sabbaths. (*instruction*) I am the LORD your God.' (*explanation*)
¹⁴'Do not curse the deaf or put a stumbling block in front of the blind, but fear your God. (*instruction*) I am the LORD.' (*explanation*)
¹⁶'Do not go about spreading slander among your people. Do not do anything that endangers your neighbor's life. (*instruction*) I am the LORD.' (*explanation*)
³²'Rise in the presence of the aged, show respect for the elderly and revere your God. (*instruction*) I am the LORD.' (*explanation*) NIV

Nearly all of the warnings in Leviticus 19 are written in the form of commands (Do not . . .). In this section, God admonishes His people to be holy. The reason (explanation) for this is because He is holy. This theme is of such importance in the book that the word "holy" is used 152 times. God wanted the Israelites to lead a holy life, because this would serve as a testimony to other nations that He was holy. Their lives were therefore a reflection of God's holiness. But how were they to live in order to reflect God's holiness?

Leviticus 17–26, known as the Law of Holiness, is the most important part of the book. These chapters contain instructions about how to dedicate oneself to God. For instance, Leviticus 18 refers to sexual relationships, while in Leviticus 19, God orders the Israelites to do things that will make them holy, such as show respect to their parents (v. 3), not curse the deaf (v. 14) and treat the elderly with respect (v. 32).

God asks us to act in good manner in all spheres of life. It is therefore clear that everything in our lives involves God. The Church is criticized for this very reason; namely that the people who attend on a Sunday often lack good behavior during the rest of the week. Many people no longer read the Bible, but they use the example each of us set to determine whether the Christian faith is worth following. As believers, we should be acutely aware of how we live. God's honor is at stake.

 Lord, help me to be aware of Your presence every day of the week and not only on Sundays.

Example is not the main thing in influencing others, it's the only thing.
—Albert Schweitzer (1875–1965), *German medical missionary, theologian, musician, philosopher and 1952 Nobel Peace Prize recipient*

WHAT SHOULD OUR LIVES REFLECT?

Every person's life reflects something. For example, a homeless person's life reflects poverty, despair and a bleak future. Young children playing in a park reflect innocence and pleasure. What should our lives reflect?

Leviticus 22 (explanation and instruction)

[27]'When a calf, a lamb or a goat is born, it is to remain with its mother for seven days. From the eighth day on, it will be acceptable as an offering made to the LORD by fire. *(explanation)*
[28]Do not slaughter a cow or a sheep and its young on the same day.
[29]'When you sacrifice a thank offering to the LORD, sacrifice it in such a way that it will be accepted on your behalf. [30]It must be eaten that same day; leave none of it till morning. I am the LORD.
[31]'Keep my commands and follow them. I am the LORD. [32]Do not profane my holy name. I must be acknowledged as holy by the Israelites. *(instruction)*
I am the LORD, who makes you holy [33]and who brought you out of Egypt to be your God. I am the LORD.' *(explanation)* NIV

In this section, with its many do's and don'ts, the Lord warns the people to present Him only with the best offerings. The Lord only accepts the best. The reason for this is explained clearly in verses 31 to 33: God is a holy God. He is holy because He differs from the other gods. Because He is God, only the best is good enough for Him, and His holiness should be reflected in the quality of the offerings.

The offerings mentioned in Leviticus 22 were the private offerings of the people that were either brought voluntarily or by making a promise. However, it is important to note that the mere fact that these offerings were voluntary was not to be used as an excuse to give second best. The offering could in no way dishonor the Lord's name—the offerings had to reflect God's holiness.

Today, parents will not hesitate to give their children bills for entertainment and small change for the church service. By doing this, children are subconsciously taught from an early age that small offerings are good enough to give to the Lord. I make a special effort to sometimes give my children bills for the collection plate on Sundays. But the Lord wants more than our money. Paul puts this very clearly in Romans 12:1 when he says, "Therefore, I urge you, brothers, in view of God's mercy, to offer your bodies as living sacrifices, holy and pleasing to God—this is your spiritual act of worship" (NIV).

God asks us to give our whole lives as offerings. We should live our whole lives in service to God. In everything we do, we should ask ourselves: *Do I reflect God's holiness?* Thinking about this makes me tremble. We have to live more responsibly!

 Lord, please give me the strength to ensure that my deeds reflect something of Your holiness.

Holiness, not happiness, is the chief end of man.
—Oswald Chambers (1874–1917), *Prominent early twentieth-century Scottish Protestant minister and teacher*

AN INVITATION NOT TO BE REFUSED!

The book of Numbers is a travel journal—a kind of diary—of the Israelites' travels from the time when they prepared for their journey at Mount Sinai to when they entered the promised land of Canaan. This journal in which the memories and experiences of the Israelites in the desert are recorded gives us a special invitation—one we cannot refuse.

Numbers 2 (procedure)

[1]The LORD said to Moses and Aaron: [2]'The Israelites are to camp around the Tent of Meeting some distance from it, each man under his standard with the banners of his family.' [3]On the *east*, toward the sunrise, the divisions of the camp of Judah are to encamp under their standard.
[5]The tribe of Issachar will camp next to them. [7]The tribe of Zebulun will be next.
[9]They will set out first.
[10]On the *south* will be the divisions of the camp of Reuben under their standard. [12]The tribe of Simeon will camp next to them. [14]The tribe of Gad will be next.
[16]They will set out second.
[17]Then the Tent of Meeting and the camp of the Levites will set out in the *middle* of the camps.
[18]On the *west* will be the divisions of the camp of Ephraim under their standard. [20]The tribe of Manasseh will be next to them. [22]The tribe of Benjamin will be next.
[24]They will set out third.
[25]On the *north* will be the divisions of the camp of Dan, under their standard. [27]The tribe of Asher will camp next to them. [29]The tribe of Naphtali will be next.
[31]They will set out last, under their standards.
[34]So the Israelites did everything the LORD commanded Moses; (NIV)

Before traveling to the Promised Land, the Lord gave the people a clear instruction that can be summed up by stating they had to set up camp in proper fashion. The camp was to be in the shape of a square, with three tribes on each side and the priests and Levites situated in the middle around the Tent of Meeting. The tribes were to be arranged in such a way that the Tent of Meeting was always visible.

The Tent of Meeting was symbolic of the Lord's presence. The camp's layout was symbolic of the central place of God in the people's lives. By using this specific placement, the Israelites acknowledged the Lord as the central point of their journey.

The camp's layout is, up to this day, an invitation to us to place the Lord in the center of our lives. What a privilege and honor to receive such an invitation! May our lives bear testimony to the fact that we have received the invitation to have the Lord as our companion on our journey through life.

 Lord, I would once more like to have You as the center of my life.

It is good to have an end to journey toward; but it is the journey that matters, in the end.
—Ursula K. LeGuin (b. 1929), *American writer, best known for tales of science fiction*

WE ALL ADMIRE THIS CHARACTERISTIC!

At one point, research was done to determine the one characteristic that people admire most in others. The following section describes that characteristic.

Numbers 6 (instruction)

¹The LORD said to Moses, ²"Speak to the Israelites and say to them: 'If a man or woman wants to make a special vow, a vow of separation to the LORD as a Nazirite,
³he must abstain from wine and other fermented drink and must not drink vinegar made from wine or from other fermented drink. He must not drink grape juice or eat grapes or raisins. ⁴As long as he is a Nazirite, he must not eat anything that comes from the grapevine, not even the seeds or skins.
⁵"During the entire period of his vow of separation no razor may be used on his head. He must be holy until the period of his separation to the LORD is over; he must let the hair of his head grow long. (NIV)

A Nazirite was someone who made a vow to commit himself or herself fully to the Lord. This passage in Numbers 6 contains the specific instructions for someone who made this vow. A Nazirite vow, which could be taken for a limited period or for the rest of the person's life, was not an easy one. It demanded that the person abstain from certain things, such as drinking wine and beer.

The items that the Nazirites had to give up were those that played an important role in the lives of the heathen and unbelievers. A person therefore had to be very committed to leading this kind of life. So, does this mean that only the Nazirites at the time were committed to the Lord? No, all the people had to be devoted to God, but the Nazirite was a visible symbol of devotion.

Devotion has a way of inspiring and motivating people. The Nazirites' devotion served as a source of inspiration and moral support to motivate others to follow a life of devotion. The reason why such people's devotion elicits so much admiration is because most people struggle to attain it. New Year resolutions are a good example of this. Soon after the start of a new year, we slip into our old ways of overindulging or not exercising. It is therefore important for us to associate with dedicated people. May their inspiration lead us to also become sources of inspiration and hope!

 Lord, I would like to be a symbol of devotion to those around me.

People often say that motivation doesn't last. Well, neither does bathing—
that's why we recommend it daily.
—Zig Ziglar, *American motivational speaker and author*

HAS GOD'S LIGHT BEEN DIMMED?

These days, I often hear people saying that we live in dark times. Thanks to Thomas Edison, we can use electricity to provide light during dark nights. But for dark times, God gives us His light. Yet so many people, even faithful ones, do not enjoy God's light and struggle to find direction in their lives. Does this mean that God's light has been dimmed?

Numbers 8 (procedure)

[1]The LORD said to Moses, [2]"Speak to Aaron and say to him, 'When you set up the seven lamps, they are to light the area in front of the lampstand."
[3]Aaron did so; he set up the lamps so that they faced forward on the lampstand, just as the LORD commanded Moses. [4]This is how the lampstand was made: It was made of hammered gold—from its base to its blossoms. The lampstand was made exactly like the pattern the LORD had shown Moses. (NIV)

The objects in the Tent of Meeting had symbolic meaning. The Ark, which was placed in the Most Holy Place of the Tent of Meeting, symbolized the Lord's presence. A priest could enter the Most Holy Place only once a year during the Day of Atonement to establish reconciliation for himself and the people of Israel. Before he could present himself to God, he first had to pass through the Holy Place of the tent. When he walked through the foyer to enter the Holy Place, he could see where he was going, because the lampstand with its small lamps lit up his way in the darkness. The priest saw this light as a symbol of God's light that lights up our lives.

The people experienced this in a physical sense as they traveled through the desert. God showed them the way by appearing as a column of cloud during the day and as a column of fire at night. Such columns of clouds and light are absent in our journey through life, but God has provided something else to guide us. The words of Psalm 119:105 say it all: "Your word is a lamp *to my feet* and a light *for my path*" (NIV).

God's light, the Word of God, has not been dimmed. His Word is written in the Bible. This devotional is my small attempt to help others to get a better understanding of the Bible. This task requires us to make regular stops on our journey through life and to check whether we are still on track.

 Lord, thank You that Your Word is the GPS for my life travels.

Reading the Bible without meditating on it is like trying to eat without swallowing.
—Author unknown

WHAT EATS AWAY AT RELATIONSHIPS?

We all long for healthy, long-term relationships. However, in our search to form relationships and maintain them, we often fail because of a certain "cancer" that we do not always take into account. What could this cancer be?

Numbers 12 (story)

Tension: Miriam and Aaron are jealous of Moses

[1]Miriam and Aaron began to talk against Moses because of his Cushite wife, for he had married a Cushite. [2]'Has the LORD spoken only through Moses?' they asked. 'Hasn't he also spoken through us?' And the LORD heard this.

Relief of tension: The Lord intervenes

[3]Now Moses was a very humble man, more humble than anyone else on the face of the earth. [4]At once the LORD said to Moses, Aaron and Miriam, 'Come out to the Tent of Meeting, all three of you.' So the three of them came out. [5]Then the LORD came down in a pillar of cloud; [9]The anger of the LORD burned against them, and he left them.

Result: Miriam contracts leprosy; Moses' reaction

[10]When the cloud lifted from above the Tent, there stood Miriam—leprous, like snow. [13]So Moses cried out to the LORD, 'O God, please heal her!' [14]The LORD replied to Moses, 'If her father had spit in her face, would she not have been in disgrace for seven days? Confine her outside the camp for seven days; after that she can be brought back.' (NIV)

Jealousy is the cancer in relationships. Aaron and his sister, Miriam, were very jealous of their brother, Moses. The reason for their jealousy was Moses' special position in Israel. Jealousy causes a person to be restless—to feel dissatisfied with their own lives and use criticism to trample on those around them. Many people like to hear that others have also failed, because this puts them all in the same boat. Jealousy wishes no one joy.

We do not know for certain why Aaron and Miriam wanted to speak to Moses about the Cushite woman. It could have been a smoke screen for their jealousy. Moses' answer to their jealousy was humility. He did not find their criticism threatening. When Miriam later contracted leprosy, Moses did not take delight in it. On the contrary, he prayed for his sister's recovery. Moses learned to use good to conquer evil. He left behind a good testimonial: "Now Moses was a very humble man, more humble than anyone else on the face of the earth" (Num. 12:3).

 Lord, help me not to be jealous but to be humble instead.

To cure jealousy is to see it for what it is, a dissatisfaction with self.
—Joan Didion (b. 1934), *American journalist and novelist*

LOVE IS NOT THE ONLY THING THAT BLINDS!

Love can blind us to the faults of others. However, love is not the only thing that can do this. Fear also has the ability to blind. This section demonstrates how fear can blind us.

Numbers 13 (story)

Tension: The spies get cold feet

²⁶They came back to Moses and Aaron and the whole Israelite community at Kadesh in the Desert of Paran. There they reported to them and to the whole assembly and showed them the fruit of the land. ²⁷They gave Moses this account: 'We went into the land to which you sent us, and it does flow with milk and honey! Here is its fruit. ²⁸But the people who live there are powerful and the cities are fortified and very large. We even saw descendants of Anak there.

Relief of tension: Two spies encourage

³⁰Then Caleb silenced the people before Moses and said, 'We should go up and take possession of the land, for we can certainly do it.' ³¹But the men who had gone up with him said, 'We can't attack those people; they are stronger than we are.'

Result: Bad rumors do the rounds

³²'And they spread among the Israelites a bad report about the land they had explored. They said, 'The land we explored devours those living in it. All the people we saw there are of great size. ³³. . . We seemed like grasshoppers in our own eyes, and we looked the same to them.' (NIV)

The 12 spies who explored the Promised Land to see what it had to offer drew different conclusions in their report to Moses and all the people of what they had seen. Ten of the 12 came to the following conclusion: "We can't attack those people" (v. 31), while only two (Joshua and Caleb) said, "We can certainly do it!" (v. 30). Why was the minority report so radically different from the majority report? The reason was because of fear.

The majority of the spies were scared of the big cities surrounded by thick walls and the gigantic Anakites. They were overwhelmed by fear, which made them forget God's promise that He would give them the land to live in. By doing this, they failed to appreciate God's plan for Israel. They did not so much fear that they would not survive as lack of trust in God—even though the camp's layout (see Day 25) was supposed to be a constant reminder of His presence! Joshua and Caleb, however, did not allow overwhelming circumstances to blind them to God and His promises. May we follow their example!

 Lord, please help me to guard against fear blinding me to You and Your promises.

I believe that every single event in life that happens is an opportunity to choose love over fear.
—Oprah Winfrey (b. 1954), *American television personality, actress and producer*

WILL GOD FORGIVE THE SINS WE COMMIT UNKNOWINGLY?

Does God treat unintentional offences differently from intentional ones? This next section in Numbers clarifies this issue.

Numbers 15 (procedure)

[22]"Now if you unintentionally fail to keep any of these commands the LORD gave Moses—[23] any of the LORD's commands to you through him, from the day the LORD gave them and continuing through the generations to come—[24]and if this is done unintentionally without the community being aware of it, then the whole community is to offer a young bull for a burnt offering as an aroma pleasing to the LORD, along with its prescribed grain offering and drink offering, and a male goat for a sin offering. [25]The priest is to make atonement for the whole Israelite community, and they will be forgiven, for it was not intentional and they have brought to the LORD for their wrong an offering made by fire and a sin offering. [26]The whole Israelite community and the aliens living among them will be forgiven, because all the people were involved in the unintentional wrong. [27]"But if just one person sins unintentionally, he must bring a year-old female goat for a sin offering. [28]The priest is to make atonement before the LORD for the one who erred by sinning unintentionally, and when atonement has been made for him, he will be forgiven. [29]One and the same law applies to everyone who sins unintentionally, whether he is a native-born Israelite or an alien. [30]"But anyone who sins defiantly, whether native-born or alien, blasphemes the LORD, and that person must be cut off from his people. [31]Because he has despised the LORD's word and broken his commands, that person must surely be cut off; his guilt remains on him." (NIV)

During their travels through the desert, the Israelites knew exactly what God expected of them (v. 22). The Lord severely punished those who were defiant, because they did not have the excuse of "not knowing" (v. 30). Intentional sin is a deliberate disregard for and a derision of the Lord's name. But what happens if one acts unintentionally? Fortunately, God understands that unintentional sin is not intended to dishonor His name. The fact that the people could say "we did not know" explains their behavior, although this is no excuse. In the desert, the Israelites had the opportunity to bring offerings in order to reconcile with God.

In the same way, God's Spirit wants to convince us and make us aware of unintentional sins. If we become aware of our sins and show remorse, the good news is that God forgives unintentional sins! He is also prepared to forgive us our intentional sins if we show remorse. This section serves as a serious warning that we need to stop doing those activities that we know are wrong. If we persist in being intentionally sinful, we create the impression that we do not take God seriously. God is serious about us! What is your position?

 Lord, thank You for always being willing to forgive.

You will know that forgiveness has begun when you recall those who hurt you and feel the power to wish them well.
—Lewis B. Smedes (1921–2002), *Best-selling author of more than 15 books and professor emeritus of theology and ethics at Fuller Theological Seminary in Pasadena, California*

IF ONLY WE COULD START ALL OVER AGAIN

If we are not satisfied with an e-mail we wrote, we can delete it and rewrite it. Unfortunately, the same does not apply to life. Fortunately, there is good news about this!

Numbers 29 (procedure)

¹'On the first day of the seventh month hold a sacred assembly and do no regular work. It is a day for you to sound the trumpets. ²As an aroma pleasing to the LORD, prepare a burnt offering of one young bull, one ram and seven male lambs a year old, all without defect.
³With the bull prepare a grain offering of three-tenths of an ephah of fine flour mixed with oil; with the ram, two-tenths; ⁴and with each of the seven lambs, one-tenth.
⁵Include one male goat as a sin offering to make atonement for you. ⁶These are in addition to the monthly and daily burnt offerings with their grain offerings and drink offerings as specified.
They are offerings made to the LORD by fire—a pleasing aroma.' (NIV)

The first day of the seventh month heralded the start of the New Year (Lev. 23:23–25). It was a festive day (Num. 29:1). The Israelites' New Year celebrations were religious. On that day, they brought different kinds of offerings. Why did they do this? To answer this question, we should look at the purpose of the different offerings:

Offering	Purpose
Burnt offering (Lev. 1)	To seek God's goodwill.
Grain offering (Lev. 2)	To show commitment to God and acknowledge that He provides food.
Sin offering (Lev. 4)	To be forgiven of unintentional sins (such as sins of negligence, irresponsibility and uncleanliness).
Drink offering (Num. 15)	To remind of the abundance of God's gifts and promises.
Fire offering (Lev. 1:9)	This is the name given to describe all the offerings that were burnt on an altar, completely or partially.

These offerings proclaimed that commitment, forgiveness and abundance were possible. This good news started the Israelites' New Year. Although we do not bring offerings in the same way, we still bring them with forgiveness, remorse and honesty. We cannot start all over again by turning back the clock, but through forgiveness, remorse and honesty, we can start afresh. Thank God!

 Thank You, Lord, for giving me the opportunity to start afresh.

To forgive is to set a prisoner free and discover that the prisoner was you.
—Lewis B. Smedes (1921–2002), *Best-selling author of more than 15 books and professor emeritus of theology and ethics at Fuller Theological Seminary in Pasadena, California*

GOD'S HEART-LUNG MACHINE

The main purpose of a heart-lung machine is to keep someone alive by performing the respiratory function. However, the intention is not that the machine should be connected to the person permanently. We are not created to be kept alive, but to live. This is exactly what Moses wanted to tell the Israelites.

Deuteronomy 1 (history)

¹These are the words Moses spoke to all Israel in the desert east of the Jordan—that is, in the Arabah—opposite Suph, between Paran and Tophel, Laban, Hazeroth and Dizahab.

²(It takes eleven days to go from Horeb to Kadesh Barnea by the Mount Seir road.)

³In the fortieth year, on the first day of the eleventh month, Moses proclaimed to the Israelites all that the LORD had commanded him concerning them.

⁴This was after he had defeated Sihon king of the Amorites, who reigned in Heshbon, and at Edrei had defeated Og king of Bashan, who reigned in Ashtaroth.

⁵East of the Jordan in the territory of Moab, Moses began to expound this law, saying:

⁶The LORD our God said to us at Horeb, 'You have stayed long enough at this mountain. (NIV)

Moses delivered this speech east of the Jordan River on the first day of the eleventh month of the fortieth year after the exodus. The twelfth and last month were a time of mourning following the death of Moses. The people entered the Promised Land during the next month (the first month of the forty-first year).

An 11-day journey eventually took 40 years. The distance was never the problem, but rather the Israelites' attitude. They were stubborn and rebellious, and their hearts were filled with doubt. God did not want them to enter the Promised Land with that kind of attitude, because such an attitude would not make a good impression about the God of Israel on other nations. So God decided to give them a "heart transplant," with the desert functioning as the operation table and the manna and quails as the heart-lung machine.

By having the Israelites wander in the desert for 40 years, God wanted the people to learn that He not only wanted to keep them alive but also that He wanted to prepare them for a life of service and devotion. Perhaps you, too, are on a spiritual journey through the desert. You experience life as difficult and painful. You do not always understand the workings of God in your life. This might be God's way of preparing you for something wonderful in your life. May you experience God's care (manna) on your journey through the desert.

 Thank You, God, for not merely keeping me alive but for letting me live!

What makes the desert beautiful is that somewhere it hides a well.
—Antoine de Saint-Exupery (1900–1944), *French pilot, writer and author of* The Little Prince

DO WE FAIL IF WE DO NOT REACH OUR GOALS?

It is always exciting to strive toward achieving an ideal. In reality, most people do not always achieve their goals, but this does not necessarily mean that they were at fault. The question is, should we be considered a failure if we do not achieve our ideals? This section might help to gain some insight into this question.

Deuteronomy 3 (history)

[12]Of the land that we took over at that time, I gave the Reubenites and the Gadites the territory north of Aroer by the Arnon Gorge, including half the hill country of Gilead, together with its towns.
[13]The rest of Gilead and also all of Bashan, the kingdom of Og, I gave to the half tribe of Manasseh. (The whole region of Argob in Bashan used to be known as a land of the Rephaites.
[14]Jair, a descendant of Manasseh, took the whole region of Argob as far as the border of the Geshurites and the Maacathites; it was named after him, so that to this day Bashan is called Havvoth Jair.)
[15]And I gave Gilead to Makir.
[16]But to the Reubenites and the Gadites I gave the territory extending from Gilead down to the Arnon Gorge (the middle of the gorge being the border) and out to the Jabbok River, which is the border of the Ammonites.
[17]Its western border was the Jordan in the Arabah, from Kinnereth to the Sea of the Arabah (the Salt Sea), below the slopes of Pisgah. (NIV)

Moses witnessed the beginning of the fulfillment of God's promise to the people when they conquered the area east of the Promised Land. Moses allocated the good grazing area of Sihon to Reuben and Gad because they had big herds of cattle (Num. 32:1–5). One half of the tribe of Manasseh received the area north of the Jabbok. However, Moses did not attain his goal to enter the Promised Land (west of the Jordan) because he had previously disobeyed God (Num. 2:12). Despite this, Moses was awarded the following titles:

- Man of God (Ezra 3:2)
- God's chosen one (Ps. 106:23)
- His friend (Exod. 33:11)

With titles such as these, nobody could call Moses a failure. Unfulfilled ideals easily blind us to what has already been achieved. Hebrews 11:13 provides the right perspective on unattained ideals: "All these people were still living by faith when they died. They did not receive the things promised; they only saw them and welcomed them from a distance. And they admitted that they were aliens and strangers on earth" (NIV).

 Thank You, God, that unattained ideals do not make me a failure.

Failure is a detour, not a dead-end street.
—Zig Ziglar, *American motivational speaker and author*

THE DAY WHEN GOD SAYS NO!

Parents sometimes say yes to their children after initially saying no. This often happens as a result of their children's pleas. But what do you do if God says no after you have pleaded with him? Let's read how Moses experienced God's no in his life.

Deuteronomy 3 (conversation)

²¹At that time I commanded Joshua: 'You have seen with your own eyes all that the LORD your God has done to these two kings. The LORD will do the same to all the kingdoms over there where you are going.
²²Do not be afraid of them; the LORD your God himself will fight for you.'
²³At that time I pleaded with the LORD:
²⁴"O Sovereign LORD, you have begun to show to your servant your greatness and your strong hand. For what god is there in heaven or on earth who can do the deeds and mighty works you do?
²⁵Let me go over and see the good land beyond the Jordan—that fine hill country and Lebanon.'
²⁶But because of you the LORD was angry with me and would not listen to me. 'That is enough,' the LORD said. 'Do not speak to me anymore about this matter.
²⁷Go up to the top of Pisgah and look west and north and south and east. Look at the land with your own eyes, since you are not going to cross this Jordan.
²⁸But commission Joshua, and encourage and strengthen him, for he will lead this people across and will cause them to inherit the land that you will see.'
²⁹So we stayed in the valley near Beth Peor. (NIV)

Moses' task to lead the stubborn Israelites through the desert was not an easy one. If there ever was a person who would have appreciated the Promised Land after 40 years of suffering, that person would have been Moses. In the desert, he had experienced the unparalleled greatness of God. He wanted to be part of the final destination: the Promised Land.

Moses dreaded the idea that after all the suffering he had endured as leader he would not be able to enter the Promised Land. For a long time, he pleaded with God to enter the land (v. 23), but God's answer was a clear no. Yet, as this prayer of Moses shows, he maintained his intimate relationship with God. His speech also confirms that he accepted God's answer.

We will not always understand God's ways. A well-known businessman once said that he was grateful that God did not always say yes to his prayers, because then he definitely would not have achieved what he did. By saying no, God had directed him to other wonderful paths. Let us learn from Moses to accept God's *no*.

 Lord, help me to accept Your no and to trust You with my tomorrow.

Pray, and let God worry.
—Martin Luther (1483–1546), *German priest and scholar whose questioning of certain Church practices led to the Protestant Reformation*

HOW CAN ONE BE TRULY HAPPY?

There are many answers to this question, but one thing is clear: Happiness is only possible within the confines of loving relationships. We all look for happiness, but we often stumble in our quest to obtain it. Let us read what Moses said about this to the people of Israel.

Deuteronomy 5 (explanation and instruction)

¹Moses summoned all Israel and said: Hear, O Israel, the decrees and laws I declare in your hearing today. Learn them and be sure to follow them. (*instruction*)

²The LORD our God made a covenant with us at Horeb.

³It was not with our fathers that the LORD made this covenant, but with us, with all of us who are alive here today.

⁴The LORD spoke to you face to face out of the fire on the mountain.

⁵(At that time I stood between the LORD and you to declare to you the word of the LORD, because you were afraid of the fire and did not go up the mountain.) And he said:

⁶'I am the LORD your God, who brought you out of Egypt, out of the land of slavery. (*explanation*)

⁷'You shall have no other gods before me.

⁸'You shall not make for yourself an idol in the form of anything . . .

¹¹'You shall not misuse the name of the LORD your God . . .

¹²'Observe the Sabbath day by keeping it holy, . . .

¹³Six days you shall labor and do all your work, ¹⁴ but the seventh day is a Sabbath to the LORD your God. On it you shall not do any work,

¹⁶'Honor your father and your mother, . . .

¹⁷'You shall not murder.

¹⁸'You shall not commit adultery.

¹⁹'You shall not steal.

²⁰'You shall not give false testimony against your neighbor.

²¹'You shall not covet . . .' (*instruction*) NIV

Moses realized that there was only one way in which the Israelites would be happy in the Promised Land: if they, again, committed themselves to the Ten Commandments. The reason for this was because all the commandments concerned building healthy relationships.

In the same way, we should look for happiness in healthy relationships. The first four commandments concern our relationship with God, while the last six concern our relationship with other people. These guidelines are our freedom, not our constraint. In the same way that a fish is only free in water, a human being is only free within God's 10 guidelines. This *commitment* to the Ten Commandments is indicated in verse 1 by three consecutive actions: hear, learn and follow. Happiness is not embedded in things, but is rather the result of righteous living.

 Thank You, Lord, for allowing me enough space to experience happiness.

Happiness . . . is not a destination: it is a manner of traveling. Happiness is not an end in itself. It is a by-product of working, playing, loving and living.
—Haim Ginott (1922–1973), *American clinical psychologist and child therapist*

GOOD THEOLOGY IS ALWAYS GOOD COUNSELING!

A dentist friend of mine studied part-time for his theology degree. He then wanted to specialize in counseling. He phoned his lecturer (also a good friend of mine) and asked him whether he thought that a different field of study might help him more in counseling. The lecturer's answer was simple: "Good theology is always good counseling." This important section that you are about to read confirms the value of this answer.

Deuteronomy 6 (explanation and instruction)

[4]Hear, O Israel: The LORD our God, the LORD is one. (*explanation*)
[5]Love the LORD your God with all your heart and with all your soul and with all your strength.
[6]These commandments that I give you today are to be upon your hearts.
[7]Impress them on your children. Talk about them when you sit at home and when you walk along the road, when you lie down and when you get up.
[8]Tie them as symbols on your hands and bind them on your foreheads.
[9]Write them on the doorframes of your houses and on your gates. (*instruction*) NIV

One could say that this passage contains the central theme of the book of Deuteronomy. It follows a pattern that could help us to apply God's Word in our daily lives. First, we should love God. Jesus included the words of verse 5 in His answer about the most important commandment (Matt. 22:34–40). What God wants us to learn concerns Him. If we love Him, we will have the desire to learn His commandments.

Second, we should constantly think about His commandments. The sowing of good thoughts usually enables one to reap good deeds. Third, we should impress the lessons and information in the Scripture on our children. It is important for us to realize that we cannot achieve this through Sunday school alone. It is a shame to attend to the lessons in the Scripture haphazardly—the truths that God wants to teach us are too extensive for this. While watching television we can, for example, teach our children what is morally right or wrong. We can show our children the consequences of violence and remind them of the sixth commandment: You shall not murder.

Fourth, it is important to teach by setting the example, because that will make us credible. Deuteronomy 6:8–9 has a figurative meaning: "Your hands" indicate what you do, while "your head" shows what you think. (Unfortunately, the Jews interpreted this literally by wearing phylacteries.) The theory that God wants to teach us is meant to be applied in practice. Sow what you have learned! The saying is true: "Sow a thought, reap an action; sow an action, reap a habit; sow a habit, reap a character; sow a character, reap a destiny."

 Lord, help me to apply Your commandments practically in my life.

Even for practical purposes theory generally turns out the most important thing in the end.
—Oliver Wendell Holmes (1809–1894), *American author and poet*

THE MOST IMPORTANT DECISION TO MAKE EVERY DAY

Choices are part of our daily life. Within the first 10 minutes of waking up, we make a number of decisions. For many of us, the most important decision during those 10 minutes is what to wear! In the hurly-burly of life, we often forget the most important decision. Moses tells us very clearly what this should be.

Deuteronomy 30 (explanation and instruction)

[15]See, I set before you *today* life and prosperity, *death* and destruction. [16]For I command you *today* to love the LORD your God, to walk in his ways, and to keep his commands, decrees and laws; then you will live and increase, and the LORD your God will bless you in the land you are entering to possess. *(instruction)*

[17]But if your heart turns away and you are not obedient, and if you are drawn away to bow down to other gods and worship them, [18] I declare to you this day that you will certainly *be destroyed*. You will not live long in the land you are crossing the Jordan to enter and possess.

[19]This day I call heaven and earth as witnesses against you that I have set before you life and *death*, blessings and curses. *(explanation)*

Now choose life, *(instruction)*

so that you and your children may live [20]and that you may love the LORD your God, listen to his voice, and hold fast to him. For the LORD is your life, and he will give you many years in the land he swore to give to your fathers, Abraham, Isaac and Jacob. *(explanation)* NIV

This passage enables us to draw a few conclusions about decisions and choices. First, the most important choice is to *choose life* (v. 19). We can become so fixated on our dreams and so engulfed by our problems that we forget to choose life when we wake up in the morning. We choose life by saying the following each morning: "Lord, I love You (vv. 16,20). Thank You that I have what many do not have: health, water, family . . ."

Second, choices have *consequences* (vv. 16–18). Moses showed the Israelites the consequences of their choices. These consequences were contrasting: life and death, success and adversity (vv. 15). Third, *we are responsible* for our own choices. Our position today can most likely be attributed to previous choices we made.

Fourth, we should not *procrastinate*. Moses repeats the word "today" three times during his speech. Life is too precious to wait. Finally, our choices *influence others* (v. 19). How many people experience misery because of the choices they and others made? We should also consider others in our choices.

 Lord, I choose life today, tomorrow and every day of my life. I love You!

And in the end, it's not the years in your life that count. It's the life in your years.
—Abraham Lincoln (1809–1865), *Sixteenth President of the United States (1861–65),*
who brought about the emancipation of the slaves

DOES GOD HAVE FRIENDS?

Before we answer this question, I would like to ask another: Do you have a really good friend? The answer many people have to this question is that they have many acquaintances, but not many close friends. Friendships are rare. Let us read about a very special friendship.

Deuteronomy 34 (history)

⁵And Moses the servant of the LORD died there in Moab, as the LORD had said.

⁶He buried him in Moab, in the valley opposite Beth Peor, but to this day no one knows where his grave is.

⁷Moses was a hundred and twenty years old when he died, yet his eyes were not weak nor his strength gone.

⁸The Israelites grieved for Moses in the plains of Moab thirty days, until the time of weeping and mourning was over.

⁹Now Joshua son of Nun was filled with the spirit of wisdom because Moses had laid his hands on him. So the Israelites listened to him and did what the LORD had commanded Moses.

¹⁰Since then, no prophet has risen in Israel like Moses, whom the LORD knew face to face. (NIV)

God and Moses shared a special bond. This is evident from the fact that Moses is called the Lord's servant (v. 5) and that he knew the Lord personally (v. 10). Exodus 33:11 confirms this special bond: "The Lord would speak to Moses face to face, as a man speaks with his friend" (NIV). It is interesting to note that Moses' age of 120 years has symbolic value: 40 years in Egypt, 40 years as a fugitive who fled from Egypt, and 40 years as leader of God's people until they reached the gates of the Promised Land.

Not only was Moses a friend of God, but Matthew also draws a parallel between Moses and Jesus. Matthew viewed Jesus as a kind of second Moses. As children, both Moses and Jesus were threatened by mass murders instigated by the Pharaoh and King Herod, respectively. Both were put to the test in the desert—Moses by the people and Jesus by Satan. Both performed all kinds of miracles.

However, whereas Moses was the go-between between God and His people, Jesus Himself was the mediator. Fortunately, Jesus restored our relationship with God, which enables us to talk to God personally as Moses did. Through Jesus, we too have God as a friend. What is really wonderful is that this friend is also our Savior—a true friend who died to save us. That is why we sing the well-known hymn, "What a Friend We Have in Jesus!"

 Thank You, Lord, that I may call You my friend. Help me to also be a true friend to others.

To the query, "What is a friend?" his reply was "A single soul dwelling in two bodies.
—Aristole (384–322 B.C.),I Greek philosopher

IMAGINE TWO SPIES AND A PROSTITUTE IN ONE ROOM

Spies and prostitutes have dangerous careers. What would happen if two spies visited a prostitute? Read this remarkable story!

Joshua 2 (story)

Tension: Two spies and a prostitute in one room

¹Then Joshua son of Nun secretly sent two spies from Shittim. 'Go, look over the land,' he said, 'especially Jericho.' So they went and entered the house of a prostitute named Rahab and stayed there. ²The king of Jericho was told, 'Look! Some of the Israelites have come here tonight to spy out the land.' ³So the king of Jericho sent this message to Rahab: 'Bring out the men who came to you and entered your house, because they have come to spy out the whole land.'

Relief of tension: The prostitute acts wisely

⁴But the woman had taken the two men and hidden them. She said, 'Yes, the men came to me, but I did not know where they had come from. ⁵At dusk, when it was time to close the city gate, the men left. I don't know which way they went. Go after them quickly. You may catch up with them.' ⁶(But she had taken them up to the roof and hidden them under the stalks of flax she had laid out on the roof.)

Result: An agreement involving mutual trust

⁷So the men set out in pursuit of the spies on the road that leads to the fords of the Jordan, and as soon as the pursuers had gone out, the gate was shut. ⁸Before the spies lay down for the night, she went up on the roof ⁹and said to them, . . . ¹²Now then, please swear to me by the LORD that you will show kindness to my family, because I have shown kindness to you . . . ¹⁵So she let them down by a rope through the window, for the house she lived in was part of the city wall. (NIV)

Mutual trust is the last thing one would expect when two spies and a prostitute end up together. As a prostitute, Rahab was only good enough to be used for the pleasure of others. However, in this instance, she encountered two men who did not lust after her body but instead sought her goodness. She experienced kindness during the invasion of Jericho when the Israelites protected her and her family. It is wondrous that she also experienced God's goodness when she was included in the genealogy of Jesus (Matt. 1:5). She is also honored for her faith (Heb. 11:31) and for her good deeds (Jas. 2:25). Her life changed after she showed kindness. Be kind to others!

 Lord, I have to confess that I am not always kind toward others.

Goodness is the only investment which never fails.
—Henry David Thoreau (1817–1862), *American naturalist, poet and philosopher*

WHAT DO I DO ABOUT MY SORRY PAST?

Unfortunately, it is not always that easy to get rid of a sorry past. We all do things that we are ashamed of and would rather forget, and many of us are tormented by guilt about our past. There is also another factor that we cannot always control: other people's gossip. Gossip is a cruel way to keep the past of others alive. Have we not become masters at this? Yet do not despair. Read the following extract!

Joshua 5 (story)

Tension: The Israelites are uncircumcised

⁴All those who came out of Egypt—all the men of military age—died in the desert on the way after leaving Egypt. ⁵All the people that came out had been circumcised, but all the people born in the desert during the journey from Egypt had not. ⁶ The Israelites had moved about in the desert forty years until all the men who were of military age when they left Egypt had died, since they had not obeyed the LORD.

Relief of tension: The people of Israel are circumcised

⁷So he raised up their sons in their place, and these were the ones Joshua circumcised. They were still uncircumcised because they had not been circumcised on the way. ⁸And after the whole nation had been circumcised, they remained where they were in camp until they were healed.

Result: The dawning of a new era for Israel

⁹Then the LORD said to Joshua, 'Today I have rolled away the reproach of Egypt from you.' So the place has been called Gilgal to this day. (NIV)

After the Israelites had traveled in the desert for a period of about 40 years, they were ready to enter the Promised Land. But one thing remained to be done before they could do this: they had to be circumcised. The previous generation had been circumcised, but the current generation had neglected this practice during their sojourn in the desert.

The previous generation's disobedience caused a short journey of 11 days to turn into one that lasted for 40 years. Their stay in the desert earned them a reputation of shame and embarrassment. The entry of this generation into the Promised Land would now signal the start of a new period for the people of Israel. Because the Lord wanted to start afresh, Joshua was told to circumcise the people at Gilgal to mark the end of their life of reproach. Gilgal means to roll some object away. The reason for naming the place Gilgal is because they obeyed God by literally rolling away the flesh (circumcision).

Many centuries later, the scene at Gilgal changed to the one at Golgotha when God brought an end to our sins and disgrace. Express your shame in prayer, and thank the Lord for the end brought about at Golgotha!

Thank You, Lord, that I can experience the liberation from my past that you brought about at Golgotha.

The sting of a reproach is the truth of it.
—English proverb

GOD AND WAR?

War! War! War! This is how we can summarize the book of Joshua. No other book in the Bible contains more about death, destruction and violence than this book. To some, this is proof of God's cruelty and unfairness. But before we draw all kinds of conclusions, we should pay attention to the next section.

Joshua 6 (story)

Tension: What will happen at dawn?

> [15]On the seventh day, they got up at daybreak and marched around the city seven times in the same manner, except that on that day they circled the city seven times.
> [16]The seventh time around, when the priests sounded the trumpet blast, Joshua commanded the people, 'Shout! For the LORD has given you the city!

Relief of tension: The walls collapse!

> [20]When the trumpets sounded, the people shouted, and at the sound of the trumpet, when the people gave a loud shout, the wall collapsed; so every man charged straight in,

Result: Destroyed city and a prostitute set free

> [20]and they took the city. [21]They devoted the city to the LORD and destroyed with the sword every living thing in it—men and women, young and old, cattle, sheep and donkeys. [25]But Joshua spared Rahab the prostitute, with her family and all who belonged to her, because she hid the men Joshua had sent as spies to Jericho—and she lives among the Israelites to this day. (NIV)

Although war and death are often featured in the book of Joshua, it is the meaning of Joshua's name, "the Lord saves," that triumphs. In this case, it is Rahab and her family who experience the meaning of Joshua's name in that their lives are saved. The book of Joshua does not condone violence but stays in touch with the realities of life. The book is marked by a tension between God's actions of fulfilling His promises on the one hand and his punishment of disobedience on the other. However, the meaning of the name Joshua directs the story throughout.

God keeps His promises to the people in a concrete way. By doing this, He demonstrates His love toward His people. Therefore, we cannot consider Him to be harsh and cruel. Should we not lay the blame for war and cruelty at the door of human beings and their greed?

 Thank You, Lord that the meaning of Joshua's name also rings true for me!

Those who are at war with others are not at peace with themselves.
—William Hazlitt (1778–1830), *British essayist*

A "DOG" THAT TOOK THE PLACE OF A GIANT!

A promise is binding and should not be broken. The following story tells us about a "dog" that took the place of a giant 45 years after a promise was made.

Joshua 14 (story)

Tension: Caleb asks Joshua for land

[6]Now the men of Judah approached Joshua at Gilgal, and Caleb son of Jephunneh the Kenizzite said to him, 'You know what the LORD said to Moses the man of God at Kadesh Barnea about you and me. [7]I was forty years old when Moses . . . sent me from Kadesh Barnea to explore the land. And I brought him back a report according to my convictions, [8]but my brothers who went up with me made the hearts of the people melt with fear. [9]So on that day Moses swore to me, 'The land on which your feet have walked will be your inheritance and that of your children forever, . . .' [11]I am still as strong today as the day Moses sent me out; I'm just as vigorous to go out to battle now as I was then. [12]Now give me this hill country that the LORD promised me that day.

Relief of tension: Joshua blesses Caleb

[13]Then Joshua blessed Caleb son of Jephunneh

Result: Caleb receives his promised land without a fight

and gave him Hebron as his inheritance. [14] So Hebron has belonged to Caleb . . . ever since, because he followed the LORD, the God of Israel, wholeheartedly. [15] (Hebron used to be called Kiriath Arba after Arba, who was the greatest man among the Anakites.) Then the land had rest from war. (NIV)

Where is this dog? Caleb is the "dog," because that is what his name means. He came to Joshua to remind him of a promise that had been made to him 45 years before. At that stage, the Lord had promised Caleb and his offspring the land of Hebron. This promise emanated from the fact that Joshua and Caleb were the only 2 of the 12 spies who believed that the Israelites could conquer Jericho (Num. 13). The other 10 spies had feared the giants (Anakites) and the big cities.

After all these years, Caleb did not lose faith in the Lord. His loyalty was eventually rewarded when Joshua gave him Hebron. It is interesting to note that Hebron was once named after the feared giant Arba—namely Kiriath Arba, or city of Arba (Gen. 23). This was also the giant who struck fear into the hearts of the 10 spies. Ironically, a "dog" would take the place of a dreaded giant—which was only possible because Caleb put his trust in a loyal God.

 Lord, like Caleb I want to put my trust in You, because You are always loyal.

All I have seen teaches me to trust the creator for all I have not seen.
—Ralph Waldo Emerson (1803–1882), *American poet, essayist and lecturer*

THE BIG "J" THAT GOD WOULD LIKE TO SEE ON EARTH!

God's desire is that human life should not be treated indifferently. In order for that to happen, we need God's big "J"!

Joshua 20 (procedure)

[1]Then the LORD said to Joshua: [2]"Tell the Israelites to designate the cities of refuge, as I instructed you through Moses, [3]so that anyone who kills a person accidentally and unintentionally may flee there and find protection from the avenger of blood.
[4]"When he flees to one of these cities, he is to stand in the entrance of the city gate and state his case before the elders of that city. Then they are to admit him into their city and give him a place to live with them. [5]If the avenger of blood pursues him, they must not surrender the one accused, because he killed his neighbor unintentionally and without malice aforethought. [6]He is to stay in that city until he has stood trial before the assembly and until the death of the high priest who is serving at that time. Then he may go back to his own home in the town from which he fled.'
[7] So they set apart Kedesh . . . , Shechem . . ., and Kiriath Arba (that is, Hebron) . . . [8]On the east side of the Jordan of Jericho they designated Bezer . . ., Ramoth . . ., and Golan . . . [9]Any of the Israelites or any alien living among them who killed someone accidentally could flee to these designated cities and not be killed by the avenger of blood prior to standing trial before the assembly. (NIV)

It is a common practice for people to seek asylum at embassies. People ask to be protected from persecution by another authority. This practice is also found in the Bible. After the land was divided between the tribes, God instructed Joshua to identify six cities of refuge. A "city of refuge" was a place where a person who had unintentionally committed a murder could enjoy safety from the acts of revenge by the relatives of the deceased.

It is interesting to note that the three cities of refuge west of the Jordan are mentioned from north to south, whereas the cities east of the Jordan are mentioned from south to north. The cities were, therefore, situated in such a way that everyone could reach them within a day. The cities of refuge were under the control of God's servants, the Levites. By doing this, God ensured that His servants could see to it that justice prevailed.

God seeks justice for everyone. In the Old Testament, after someone had been convicted, he or she could stay on in the city of refuge as an exile. The exile could then go free when the high priest passed away. Justice is of the utmost importance to God, which is why He sent us the High Priest, Jesus Christ, who brought about our final freedom when He died. Believers should do everything possible to create a just society. We should have the courage of our convictions to act against all forms of injustice and inequality.

 Lord, give me the courage to speak out and to act against injustice.

Justice is truth in action.
—Benjamin Disraeli (1804–1881), *British politician and author*

DON'T MISS THIS TRIP!

Joshua delivered his last speech on the eve of a new beginning. The conquest (Josh. 1–12) and division (Josh. 13–22) of the land were complete. Joshua now took the people on a trip down memory lane. At each resting point, he pointed out something special in their past that they had to take with them on their journey into the future. Let's read about this.

Joshua 24 (history)

[1]Then Joshua assembled all the tribes of Israel at Shechem. He summoned the elders, leaders, judges and officials of Israel, and they presented themselves before God.
[2]Joshua said to all the people, 'This is what the LORD, the God of Israel, says: 'Long ago your forefathers, including Terah the father of Abraham and Nahor, lived beyond the River and worshiped other gods. [3]But I took your father Abraham from the land beyond the River and led him throughout Canaan and gave him many descendants. I gave him Isaac, [4]and to Isaac I gave Jacob and Esau. I assigned the hill country of Seir to Esau, but Jacob and his sons went down to Egypt. [5]"Then I sent Moses and Aaron, and I afflicted the Egyptians by what I did there, and I brought you out. [6]When I brought your fathers out of Egypt, you came to the sea, and the Egyptians pursued them with chariots and horsemen as far as the Red Sea. [13]So I gave you a land on which you did not toil and cities you did not build; and you live in them and eat from vineyards and olive groves that you did not plant.' [14]"Now fear the LORD and serve him with all faithfulness . . . [15]But if serving the LORD seems undesirable to you, then choose for yourselves this day whom you will serve, whether the gods your forefathers served beyond the River, or the gods of the Amorites, in whose land you are living. But as for me and my household, we will serve the LORD.' (NIV)

At each halt in their past, the name of God was written in capital letters. Joshua wanted the people to remember that God was with them when their history unfolded. It began when God called Abraham while he was worshipping other gods. From then on, God walked with Isaac, Jacob and their descendants up to where they were right now in the Promised Land. Their past had to be kept alive, because that would help them to be loyal to God.

Joshua feared that the exposure to other gods would affect their loyalty to God. To prevent this from happening, he urged them to choose God without delay. It was the best time because God's care and trust were still fresh in their minds. Joshua unequivocally told them where he and his family made their cross. Joshua realized that taking time to stop and remember the past could help the people keep on believing.

 Thank You, Lord, that Your name is also written in capital letters at my halts.

Memory is the only paradise from which we cannot be driven.
—Jean Paul (1763–1825), *German novelist and humorist*

THE LAST CHAPTERS REVEAL SO MUCH

The last chapters of the book of Joshua end with the deaths and funerals of two prominent figures: Joshua and the high priest Eleazar. The death of Joshua and Eleazar indicated the end of an era in the history of Israel—the period of the patriarchs—and ushered in the next phase in the history of Israel—the time of the judges. It is interesting to note that this period started at the time of Abraham at Shechem (Gen. 12) and ended at Shechem with Joshua. A death notice can hardly be considered pleasant reading, but the last chapters of the book of Joshua contain so much food for thought that it would be worth our while to read it. Let's take a look.

Joshua 24 (story)

[29]After these things, Joshua son of Nun, *the servant of the LORD,* died at the age of a hundred and ten. [30]And they buried him in the land of his inheritance, at Timnath Serah in the hill country of Ephraim, north of Mount Gaash.
[31]Israel served the LORD throughout the lifetime of Joshua and of the elders who outlived him and who had experienced everything the LORD had done for Israel.
[32]And Joseph's bones, which the Israelites had brought up from Egypt, were buried at Shechem in the tract of land that Jacob bought for a hundred pieces of silver from the sons of Hamor, the father of Shechem. This became the inheritance of Joseph's descendants.
[33]And Eleazar son of Aaron died and was buried at Gibeah, which had been allotted to his son Phinehas in the hill country of Ephraim. (NIV)

The book of Joshua starts as follows: "After the death of Moses, *the servant of the Lord,* the Lord said to Joshua, son of Nun, Moses' aide . . ." (NIV). In the last chapters of Joshua, we read that Joshua was also called the servant of the Lord. Through his actions, Joshua ensured that he would grow to the stature of Moses in all spheres. Joshua completed what Moses had started with honors. The exodus from Egypt and the conquest of the Promised Land took place under the leadership of these two great men. During this time, Joshua's actions inspired those around him to trust in God.

Someone once observed that a saint is someone who makes it easy for others to believe. The words "Israel served the LORD throughout the lifetime of Joshua" (v. 31) confirm that Joshua was such a person. May the way we live also make it easier for others to believe in God!

 Lord, help me to live in such a way that my life will make it easier for others to believe in You.

Aspire to inspire before you expire.
—Author unknown

OUR THIRD STOP: JUDGES

(±1200–1020 B.C.)
(JUDGES AND RUTH)

The previous period began with Moses and the exodus from Egypt and ended with Joshua and the Israelites' entry into Canaan, the Promised Land. This period ended with the death of Joshua (the political leader) and Aaron's son (the religious leader). After the death of these leaders, the people had to venture into the future alone with God. This brings us to the time of the judges.

The period of the judges covers the events between the entry into the Promised Land and the establishment of the monarchy in Israel. During this phase, the tribes were not as closely united as they would later become. The tribes also moved to different areas, and God's people were still at the mercy of the hostile nations who lived in and around Canaan (for example, the Syrians, Philistines, Moabites, Edomites, Ammonites and the Amalekites).

The continuous raids and battles were a struggle for possession of the land. Other groupings also wanted to expand their territory. The judges (leaders sent by God) acted timely to restore order in these hostile times. Only one or two Israelite tribes were normally involved in these clashes. The most well-known judges were Othniel, Ehud, Deborah, Gideon, Jephtah and, of course, Samson. The story of Ruth also takes place during the time of the Judges.

This was a dark period in the history of Israel. Whereas the people still worshiped God in the time of Joshua, their faith in Him started to dwindle during this phase. The people began to lead an immoral life and wander off after other gods, and the judges were unable to follow in Joshua's foot-steps and turn Israel back to the Lord. The book of Judges shows a clear pattern whereby the people would sin, show remorse and then again be pardoned by God. However, the time of the judges ends on a note of despair, when even the system of the judges stopped working in Israel and people were left to their own devices to determine what was right or wrong.

The book of Judges sketches specific human inclinations that still hold true today. It is about the rejection of God and the consequences that follow, and it concerns people who ma-nipulate and exploit others. However, this book gives us a different perspective on God. He is not depicted as a stern and heartless judge but rather as a patient and loving God. He is willing to go the extra mile with His children despite their stubbornness and is quick to forgive them if they show remorse. He uses people, despite their shortcomings: the judges Ehud and Jair were assassins, Jephtah was a mercenary, and Samson had a weakness for women. Yet despite all this, God sent His Spirit to them to lead His people. Likewise, God wants to—and is able to—use us despite our shortcomings.

DOES GOD SOMETIMES FORGET ABOUT US?

As time goes by, we often lose contact with people who are not in our daily lives. It is then such a pleasure to receive an unexpected phone call, e-mail or letter from someone whom we have not had contact with for a while. It is wonderful to think that someone else remembers us. Will God ever forget about us? This section will shed some light on this question.

Judges 13 (story)

Tension: Israel disappoints once again and a childless woman

> [1]Again the Israelites did evil in the eyes of the LORD, so the LORD delivered them into the hands of the Philistines for forty years.
> [2]A certain man of Zorah, named Manoah, from the clan of the Danites, had a wife who was sterile and remained childless.

Relief of tension: An angel appears on the scene

> [3]The angel of the LORD appeared to her and said, 'You are sterile and childless, but you are going to conceive and have a son. [4]Now see to it that you drink no wine or other fermented drink and that you do not eat anything unclean, [5]because you will conceive and give birth to a son. No razor may be used on his head, because the boy is to be a Nazirite, set apart to God from birth, and he will begin the deliverance of Israel from the hands of the Philistines.'

Result: Samson is born and is led by the Spirit

> [24]The woman gave birth to a boy and named him Samson. He grew and the LORD blessed him, [25]and the Spirit of the LORD began to stir him while he was in Mahaneh Dan, between Zorah and Eshtaol.
> (NIV)

Israel's apostasy reaches a low point with the story of Samson in Judges. This is affirmed by the refrain: "Again the Israelites did evil in the eyes of the Lord," which is repeated throughout the book and is heard for the last time in this story (Judg. 3:7,12; 4:4; 6:1; 13:1). It is obvious in the last refrain that the Israelites no longer ask the Lord for help. They have absolutely no desire to be freed from the Philistines. The Israelites who initially were so faithful to God chose to marry the Philistines and worship their gods instead. Joshua would most probably have turned over in his grave if he heard about this!

However, God took pity on them and sent His angel to visit a childless woman. She gave birth to Samson, who would later free the Israelites from the Philistines. Samson was set aside to be a Nazirite from birth. A Nazirite was forbidden to consume wine, beer or any product produced from the vine. He also could not shave his beard or cut his hair. He had to remind the people through his dedication that they belonged to God and that God would never forget them.

As this section in Judges proves, it is the way people live that leads them to believe that God has forgotten them, when in actual fact, they are the ones who have forgotten Him. May our conduct bear witness to the fact that God never forgets us.

Lord, thank You that I have the assurance that You will never forget me.

If you find yourself further from God than you were yesterday, you can be sure who has moved.
—Author unknown

SOMETIMES GOD DOES NOT MAKE SENSE!

Sometimes God just does not make sense—especially when bad things happen to good people. This makes one wonder about God's role in our lives. The story of Samson supports this perception that we sometimes have about God.

Judges 14 (story)

Tension: Samson wanted to marry a Philistine girl

> [1]Samson went down to Timnah and saw there a young Philistine woman.
> [2]When he returned, he said to his father and mother, 'I have seen a Philistine woman in Timnah; now get her for me as my wife.'
> [3]His father and mother replied, 'Isn't there an acceptable woman among your relatives or among all our people? Must you go to the uncircumcised Philistines to get a wife?' But Samson said to his father, 'Get her for me. She's the right one for me.'

Relief of tension: God is the director

> [4](His parents did not know that this was from the LORD, who was seeking an occasion to confront the Philistines; for at that time they were ruling over Israel.)

Result: They travel to Timnah

> [5]Samson went down to Timnah together with his father and mother. (NIV)

The story of Samson unfolds in two phases. The first phase starts when Samson goes to Timnah, and the second phase when he goes to Gaza (Judg. 16:1–31). In the first phase, Samson wants to get married, but his parents oppose the marriage. They have a good reason for doing so: Samson's future bride is a Philistine. At his birth, God had promised his parents that he would free the Israelites from the Philistines. Now he chooses to marry a Philistine girl, one of the enemy!

As a Nazirite, Samson had to behave in a way that would remind the Israelites that they belonged to God. Samson's action must have grieved his parents tremendously. They must have been constantly aware of the purpose of Samson's life as announced by the angel. His parents, unlike us, did not know that everything came from God.

One wonders why God would work in this way. It is strange that God would fulfill His promise to Samson's parents in this manner. Yet we have to accept that we cannot explain God's ways within the framework of our own ideas. God's actions here and in our lives are often incomprehensible. We should learn to trust God in everything—no matter how difficult it might be. Perhaps we should also learn to know God in a different way! We can so easily become trapped in an oversimplified way of understanding of God.

 Lord, help me to keep on trusting You even when Your actions do not always make sense to me.

God is subtle, but He is not malicious. I cannot believe that God plays dice with the world.
—Albert Einstein (1879–1955), *German-Swiss-American scientist*

WHEN A YOUNGSTER LOSES IT . . .

The saying goes, "Small children step on your lap, but bigger children step on your heart." Samson's parents, like many other parents, experienced the pain of a child who lost the way.

Judges 14 (story)

Tension: Samson is surprised by a lion

> [5] . . . As they approached the vineyards of Timnah, suddenly a young lion came roaring toward him.

Relief of tension: The Spirit makes him strong

> [6] The Spirit of the LORD came upon him in power so that he tore the lion apart with his bare hands as he might have torn a young goat.

Result: Samson is silent about his deeds

> But he told neither his father nor his mother what he had done. [7] Then he went down and talked with the woman, and he liked her.
> [8] Some time later, when he went back to marry her, he turned aside to look at the lion's carcass. In it was a swarm of bees and some honey, [9] which he scooped out with his hands and ate as he went along. When he rejoined his parents, he gave them some, and they too ate it. But he did not tell them that he had taken the honey from the lion's carcass. (NIV)

On his way to his wedding feast, Samson attacked a lion with his bare hands. He did this with great ease, as if it were a young goat. Now, we would think that someone who had just killed a lion with his bare hands would be proud of his achievement and boast about it. Samson, however, did not say a word about it to his parents, for if he had, they would have known that he (as Nazirite) was unclean because he had touched a dead animal.

This episode with the lion has a sequel. Samson later returns to the carcass and discovers honey in it. He gives his parents some of the honey to eat, but still does not tell them about the dead lion. It is sad to think that Samson kept on deceiving his parents. As a Nazirite, Samson knew exactly what was expected of him. He had to abstain from drinking hard liquor, was not allowed to shave or cut his hair, and was not allowed to touch the dead.

Samson gradually turned his back on being a Nazirite. His parents watched helplessly while their only son went completely off the rails. I once asked a friend of mine what he thought parents should do if this happened to their children. His answer was, "Weather the storm with them. If you choose differently, you take the risk of losing them along the way." Fortunately, Samson's parents did not leave him but weathered the storm with him.

 Lord, I pray that You will give me the strength and forbearance to weather the storms of life.

Children need your presence more than your presents.
—Jesse Jackson (b. 1941), *American politician, civil rights activist and Baptist minister*

DOES GOD WORK "BECAUSE OF" OR "IN SPITE OF"?

The story of Samson gives us a very clear answer to this question, as the following episode illustrates.

Judges 14 (story)

Tension: The riddle

> [10]Now his father went down to see the woman. And Samson made a feast there . . . [11]When he appeared, he was given thirty companions. [12]'Let me tell you a riddle,' Samson said to them. 'If you can give me the answer within the seven days of the feast, I will give you thirty linen garments and thirty sets of clothes. [13]If you can't tell me the answer, you must give me thirty linen garments and thirty sets of clothes.' 'Tell us your riddle,' . . .
> [14] He replied,

'Out of the eater, something to eat;

out of the strong, something sweet.'

> For three days they could not give the answer . . .
> [16]Then Samson's wife threw herself on him, sobbing, 'You hate me! You don't really love me. You've given my people a riddle, but you haven't told me the answer.' . . .
> [17]She cried the whole seven days of the feast. So on the seventh day he finally told her, . . . She in turn explained the riddle to her people. [18] Before sunset on the seventh day the men of the town said to him,

What is sweeter than honey?

What is stronger than a lion?'

> Samson said to them,
> 'If you had not plowed with my heifer, you would not have solved my riddle.'

Relief of tension: The Spirit of the Lord is with him

> [19]Then the Spirit of the LORD came upon him in power. He went down to Ashkelon,

Result: Thirty men die and Samson loses his wife

> struck down thirty of their men, stripped them of their belongings and gave their clothes to those who had explained the riddle. Burning with anger, he went up to his father's house. [20]And Samson's wife was given to the friend who had attended him at his wedding. (NIV)

Before Samson was born, the angel told his parents that he would save the Israelites from domination by the Philistines. To achieve this, Samson had to dedicate his life to the Lord as a Nazirite. His life had to bear testimony to the fact that the people belonged to God. It is tragic that Samson failed as a Nazirite, but wonderful that God uses him to free the Israelites from the Philistines despite his erroneous ways.

Samson's wedding and the fact that he gave away the answer to the riddle eventually lead to the death of 30 Philistines. Despite Samson's wrong deeds, God went about fulfilling the promise of the angel to his parents (Judg. 13:5). God used Samson to show that He can hit a straight blow with a crooked stick.

 Thank You, Lord, for continuing to work in my life despite my disobedience.

So tonight you better stop and rebuild all your ruins, because peace and trust can win
the day despite all your losing.
—Led Zeppelin (formed in 1968), *English rock band that has sold more than*
300 million albums worldwide

WHAT FOLLOWS AFTER REVENGE IS TAKEN?

It is only natural to feel like taking revenge when someone has harmed us. But this is not the answer because—as the following story shows—revenge can lead to something much worse!

Judges 15 (story)

Tension: Samson is in conflict with his father-in-law

> [1]Later on, at the time of wheat harvest, Samson took a young goat and went to visit his wife. He said, 'I'm going to my wife's room.' But her father would not let him go in.
> [2]'I was so sure you thoroughly hated her,' he said, 'that I gave her to your friend. Isn't her younger sister more attractive? Take her instead.'
> [3]Samson said to them, 'This time I have a right to get even with the Philistines; I will really harm them.'

Relief of tension: Samson and the foxes

> [4]So he went out and caught three hundred foxes and tied them tail to tail in pairs. He then fastened a torch to every pair of tails, [5]lit the torches and let the foxes loose in the standing grain of the Philistines. He burned up the shocks and standing grain, together with the vineyards and olive groves. [6]When the Philistines asked, 'Who did this?' they were told, 'Samson, the Timnite's son-in-law, because his wife was given to his friend.'

Result: Murder and massacre

> So the Philistines went up and burned her and her father to death. [7]Samson said to them, 'Since you've acted like this, I won't stop until I get my revenge on you.' [8]He attacked them viciously and slaughtered many of them. Then he went down and stayed in a cave in the rock of Etam. (NIV)

After the episode that involved the riddle (see Day 49), Samson returns to get his wife and is furious to learn that his father-in-law has given his wife to his best man. Samson did not think he had done anything wrong and felt that revenge was justified. So he catches 300 foxes, ties them together and fastens flaming torches to them. (We should not interpret 300 hundred literally, but it does mean that there were many.) Samson drives the foxes with the burning torches into the fields of the Philistines, destroying their food supply. The Philistines then retaliate by burning Samson's wife and his father-in-law. Samson again retaliates and massacres the Philistines. If revenge is not curtailed or managed immediately, it can become an uncontrollable cycle of violent evil. There is only one answer to revenge: Stop it!

 Lord, help me not to turn my anger into revenge and viciousness.

Before you embark on a journey of revenge, dig two graves.
—Confucius (551–479 B.C.), *Chinese philosopher*

DOES GOD EASILY BECOME DISHEARTENED WITH US?

We can easily and quickly become disheartened if we feel that someone else has disappointed us. But does God do the same?

Judges 15 (story)

Tension: The Philistines rush at Samson

> [14]As he approached Lehi, the Philistines came toward him shouting.

Relief of tension: He is strengthened by the Spirit

> The Spirit of the LORD came upon him in power. The ropes on his arms became like charred flax, and the bindings dropped from his hands.

Result: Victory and acknowledgement that it comes from God

> [15]Finding a fresh jawbone of a donkey, he grabbed it and struck down a thousand men. [16]Then Samson said,
> > *'With a donkey's jawbone*
> > *I have made donkeys of them.*
> > *With a donkey's jawbone*
> > *I have killed a thousand men.'*
>
> [17]When he finished speaking, he threw away the jawbone; and the place was called Ramath Lehi. [18]Because he was very thirsty, he cried out to the LORD, 'You have given your servant this great victory. Must I now die of thirst and fall into the hands of the uncircumcised?' [19]Then God opened up the hollow place in Lehi, and water came out of it. When Samson drank, his strength returned and he revived . . . [20]Samson led Israel for twenty years in the days of the Philistines. (NIV)

The Israelites had suffered as a result of Samson's actions (Judg. 9–13), so they handcuffed him and turned him over to the Philistines. He resisted the Philistines' attack with the help of the Spirit by breaking the handcuffs and killing the Philistines with the jawbone of an ass. His conduct, again, did not befit that of a Nazirite, because he touched a dead animal. Yet for the first time, Samson called on the Lord.

Samson acknowledged that the Lord made this victory possible. But nowhere do we read that Israel called out to the Lord for deliverance. In his call, Samson also expressed his tremendous thirst. The Lord listened and gave him water, and in this way Samson regained his strength. The Lord wanted Samson to realize that he was dependent on Him. The wonderful thing is that the almighty God never gave up on Samson, even though he often disappointed Him. Today, God is still prepared to patiently walk alongside us. The story of Samson ends on a high note in verse 20, but this is only the end of the first phase. The next phase begins when Samson sets out for Gaza.

 Thank You, Lord, for not giving up on me—even if You have enough reason to do just that.

The more we depend on God the more dependable we find He is.
—Cliff Richard (b. 1940), *English singer*

THE DESTRUCTIVE POWER OF SEXUAL DESIRES

Sexual desires are an integral part of our lives. These desires can, however, be destructive if they are not managed properly. The following story tells us about a man who had a divine calling but who could not control his sexual urges. Like many people today, he became the victim of his own desires.

Judges 16 (story)

Tension: Samson is surrounded while visiting a prostitute

¹One day Samson went to Gaza, where he saw a prostitute. He went in to spend the night with her. ²The people of Gaza were told, 'Samson is here!' So they surrounded the place and lay in wait for him all night at the city gate. They made no move during the night, saying, 'At dawn we'll kill him.'

Relief of tension: Samson dodges the enemy

³But Samson lay there only until the middle of the night. Then he got up and took hold of the doors of the city gate, together with the two posts, and tore them loose, bar and all.

Result: A city without gates

He lifted them to his shoulders and carried them to the top of the hill that faces Hebron. (NIV)

This episode at Gaza, which begins the second phase of the Samson saga, reveals how Samson eventually became victim to his own sexual desires. Gaza was one of the Philistines' five most important cities. When Samson went there and visited a prostitute, the inhabitants surrounded the house and lay in ambush for him at the city gates—proving that he was the Philistine's enemy number one. By midnight, Samson had miraculously managed to escape, and on his way out of town he pulled the doors of the city gates from their frames. Samson's brute force intimidated the Philistines. What a pity he could not keep his sexual urges in check!

Today, all the exposure to explicit sex and advertisements with sexual undertones makes it difficult for people to control their sexual urges. What can we do about this? I believe we have to look for what Solomon asked for: wisdom. The wise words of the Church father Ambrose come to mind: "Samson had the strength to strangle a lion, but could not restrain his own love. He was able to break the shackles his enemy used to tie him up, but could not break the shackles of his passion."

Samson was a strong man, and his passion was intense. Unfortunately, he used it to ill effects and not to attain what was good. It might be worth our while to reread the story of Joseph (Gen. 39) in order to see how he dealt with sexual temptations. He turned his back on it and did not allow it to get a hold over him.

 Lord, help me to be like Joseph and not like Samson.

Temptation is a woman's weapon and man's excuse.
—Henry Louis Mencken (1880–1956), *American journalist, satirist and social critic*

GOD MOVES TOO SLOWLY AT TIMES!

I often wonder why God does not intervene to avert the evils of the world. I have thought that if I could have acted on His behalf I would have acted faster. This section has, however, helped me to gain more insight in how God intervenes in the world.

Judges 16 (story)

Tension: Delilah is instructed to seduce Samson

⁴Some time later, he fell in love with a woman in the Valley of Sorek whose name was Delilah. ⁵The rulers of the Philistines went to her and said, 'See if you can lure him into showing you the secret of his great strength . . .'
⁶So Delilah said to Samson, 'Tell me the secret of your great strength and how you can be tied up and subdued.' . . . ¹⁵Then she said to him, 'How can you say, 'I love you,' when you won't confide in me? This is the third time you have made a fool of me and haven't told me the secret of your great strength.' ¹⁶With such nagging she prodded him day after day until he was tired to death.

Relief of tension: Samson tells his life secret

¹⁷So he told her everything. 'No razor has ever been used on my head,' he said, 'because I have been a Nazirite set apart to God since birth. If my head were shaved, my strength would leave me, and I would become as weak as any other man.' . . . ¹⁹Having put him to sleep on her lap, she called a man to shave off the seven braids of his hair, and so began to subdue him. And his strength left him.²⁰ Then she called, 'Samson, the Philistines are upon you!'
He awoke from his sleep and thought, 'I'll go out as before and shake myself free.' But he did not know that the LORD had left him.

Result: He loses his power and sight

²¹Then the Philistines seized him, gouged out his eyes and took him down to Gaza. Binding him with bronze shackles, they set him to grinding in the prison. ²² But the hair on his head began to grow again after it had been shaved. (NIV)

Samson did not take his life as a Nazirite seriously and led a reckless life. We can rightly ask, "Should God not have stepped in earlier?" We might feel this way, but the story of Samson wants to reveal something about God. First, God Himself is above the prescriptions He gives to human beings. His plan proceeds *despite* Samson, who does not stick to the prescriptions. Second, the story of Samson tells us something about God's patience with us. We can be grateful that God shows so much patience toward us, because we often harbor something of Samson within us.

 Thank you, Lord, for being patient with us—especially with me!

God delays, but doesn't forget.
—Spanish proverb

HOW DOES GOD CARRY OUT HIS PLANS?

I often hear people (especially preachers) say that God has a plan for our lives. My question concerns the way in which God carries out His plans. The last episode in the story of Samson can perhaps help us to understand this issue better.

Judges 16 (story)

Tension: "god" or "God"?

²³Now the rulers of the Philistines assembled to offer a great sacrifice to Dagon their god and to celebrate, saying, 'Our god has delivered Samson, our enemy, into our hands.' ²⁴When the people saw him, they praised their god, saying, 'Our god has delivered our enemy into our hands, the one who laid waste our land and multiplied our slain.' ²⁵While they were in high spirits, they shouted, 'Bring out Samson to entertain us.' So they called Samson out of the prison, and he performed for them.

Relief of tension: Samson calls on God

²⁸Then Samson prayed to the LORD, 'O Sovereign LORD, remember me. O God, please strengthen me just once more, and let me with one blow get revenge on the Philistines for my two eyes.' ²⁹Then Samson reached toward the two central pillars on which the temple stood. Bracing himself against them, his right hand on the one and his left hand on the other, ³⁰Samson said, 'Let me die with the Philistines!' Then he pushed with all his might, and down came the temple on the rulers and all the people in it.

Result: God executes His plan

Thus he killed many more when he died than while he lived. ³¹Then his brothers and his father's whole family went down to get him. They brought him back and buried him between Zorah and Eshtaol in the tomb of Manoah his father. He had led Israel twenty years. (NIV)

As we've mentioned, before Samson's birth, God's angel told Samson's mother that her child would free the Israelites from the domination of the Philistines (Judg. 13:5). However, in order for this to happen, he had to dedicate his life to God and become a Nazirite. Samson did not succeed in this, and his life deteriorated systematically. He sacrificed his own *values* because he mixed with foreign women. He also lost his *power* by allowing his hair to be cut off. In the end, Samson lost his *eyes* as well as his *freedom* when he was locked up in the enemy's jail and eventually he lost *his life*.

The Philistines believed that their god was stronger than the Israelite's God because their god had handed Samson over to them (v. 23). Samson had to entertain them at the feast. At this point, it seems as if Samson's disobedience jeopardized God's plans. But luckily, this is not the end of Samson's story. He held on to two pillars and called on the Lord to help him one last time. His prayer was answered, and Samson *died* alongside thousands of Philistines. The miracle is that God's plan with Samson was a success—in spite of Samson's faults. God uses people—ordinary people—to execute His plans.

 Thank You, Lord that You want to use me despite my weaknesses.

God is a good worker, but loves to be helped.
—Basque proverb

ESCAPE NEVER BRINGS COMFORT . . .

Not everybody finds it easy to talk about the sorrows and suffering in their lives. People use different mechanisms to escape from the pain and hurt. But can we find comfort if we do this? Naomi's life story tells us no!

Ruth 1 (story)

Tension: Famine

> ¹In the days when the judges ruled, there was a famine in the land,

Relief of tension: Emigration

> and a man from Bethlehem in Judah, together with his wife and two sons, went to live for a while in the country of Moab. ² The man's name was Elimelech, his wife's name Naomi, and the names of his two sons were Mahlon and Kilion. They were Ephrathites from Bethlehem, Judah. And they went to Moab and lived there.

Result: Hopeless situation

> ³Now Elimelech, Naomi's husband, died, and she was left with her two sons.
> ⁴They married Moabite women, one named Orpah and the other Ruth. After they had lived there about ten years, ⁵ both Mahlon and Kilion also died, and Naomi was left without her two sons and her husband.
> ⁶When she heard in Moab that the LORD had come to the aid of his people by providing food for them, Naomi and her daughters-in-law prepared to return home from there. (NIV)

Except for Boaz, we meet all the characters in Ruth early on in the story. Many names are mentioned, which should alert us to the fact that we are dealing with the changes and chances of people. One would normally not attach too much significance to the meaning of names, but the author of the book of Ruth uses names skillfully to add to the tension. This viewpoint is strengthened by the use of sound in the names Mahlon and Kilion, as well as the fact that Naomi wanted to change her name to Mara (meaning "bitter"). Mahlon means "weak" or "sick," while Kilion means "finished" or "end." Add to this the meanings of the names Naomi ("pleasant"), Orpah ("resistant") and Ruth ("friend"), and it becomes clear that this story confronts us with the harsh reality of life.

At the outset, the author sketches the hopeless situation of a defenseless widow who has lost her husband and two sons in a foreign land. This story might link up with our own life story in the sense that we also can find it too difficult and too painful to confront life's realities. It might be comforting for us to know that the Bible is realistic and shares in the pain and comfort of people's lives.

 Lord, like Naomi, I also feel vulnerable at times. May Your Spirit comfort me!

Life is not a problem to be solved, but a reality to be experienced.
—Søren Kierkegaard (1813–1855), *Danish philosopher and theologian,*
generally recognized as the first existentialist philosopher

WHAT SHOULD WE DO IN A CRISIS?

We can sometimes become engulfed by life's problems, pain and sorrow, which causes us to lose direction. The story of Naomi and her daughters-in-law shows us that there is hope even in a hopeless situation.

Ruth 1 (story)

Tension: Naomi says farewell to her daughters-in-law

> [7]With her two daughters-in-law she left the place where she had been living and set out on the road that would take them back to the land of Judah.
> [8]Then Naomi said to her two daughters-in-law, 'Go back, each of you, to your mother's home. May the LORD show kindness to you, as you have shown to your dead and to me . . . [11] But Naomi said, 'Return home, my daughters. Why would you come with me? Am I going to have any more sons, who could become your husbands?

Relief of tension: A Logical and a Remarkable choice

> [14]At this they wept again. Then Orpah kissed her mother-in-law good-by, but Ruth clung to her . . .
> [16]But Ruth replied, 'Don't urge me to leave you or to turn back from you. Where you go I will go, and where you stay I will stay. Your people will be my people and your God my God. [17]Where you die I will die, and there I will be buried. May the LORD deal with me, be it ever so severely, if anything but death separates you and me.'

Result: Naomi notes that Ruth is serious

> [18]When Naomi realized that Ruth was determined to go with her, she stopped urging her. (NIV)

Naomi's life is in a crisis. She has lost her husband and two sons. Without them, she has no inheritance and must contend with people who want to abuse her. Yet this defenseless widow did not rest on her laurels but got out of her comfort zone to plan her life and those of her daughters-in-law. She suggested to the two of them that they remain with their own people in the country of Moab—after all, they were still young and could expect a better future in that country. The farewell was sad and tearful.

In the end, Orpah makes a *logical decision,* namely to remain with her people. Her sister, on the other hand, makes a *remarkable decision.* Ruth's choice signifies her loyalty and love toward her mother-in-law. Ruth becomes God's witness ("your God [will be] my God . . ." vv. 16–17) while Naomi's life is witness to life itself. This episode teaches us to take action when we experience a crisis. It is not wise to wait passively, hoping the crisis will disappear by itself. We need to follow Naomi's example and get active, leave our comfort zone and plan our life. We should also allow those who care for us to tackle the crisis with us.

The emptiness inside Naomi did not disappear immediately. Quick fixes have never been a recipe for success. It all takes time—but what kind of time? The time of the wise.

Lord, give me the courage to take action during times of crises in my life.

When written in Chinese, the word "crisis" is composed of two characters—one represents danger, and the other represents opportunity.
—John F. Kennedy (1917–1963), Thirty-fifth President of the United States

DEALING WITH BITTERNESS

Crises induce negative emotions that we all have to deal with. Bitterness is probably one of the most difficult emotions to control. It stems from deep disappointment and robs us of a zest for life. It also blinds us to positive opportunities; we become critical towards life and might resort to obscene language. This episode from Ruth is riddled with such bitterness and disappointment.

Ruth 1 (story)

Tension: Naomi arrives in Bethlehem

[19]So the two women went on until they came to Bethlehem. When they arrived in Bethlehem, the whole town was stirred because of them, and the women exclaimed, 'Can this be Naomi?'

Relief of tension: Naomi shares her pain

[20]'Don't call me Naomi,' she told them. 'Call me Mara, because the Almighty has made my life very bitter. [21]I went away full, but the LORD has brought me back empty. Why call me Naomi? The LORD has afflicted me; the Almighty has brought misfortune upon me.'

Result: Naomi and Ruth settle in Bethlehem

[22]So Naomi returned from Moab accompanied by Ruth the Moabitess, her daughter-in-law, arriving in Bethlehem as the barley harvest was beginning. (NIV)

The vulnerable widow and her loyal daughter-in-law travel to Bethlehem, where the women of the town are surprised to see Naomi again. They most likely asked her, "Naomi, how are you?" Naomi did not answer in the usual fashion, but shared her pain and disappointment with them. She did not want to be called Naomi ("pleasant") but rather Mara ("bitter"). She blames the Lord because she feels that He has turned against her.

We can easily identify with her struggle. Her reference to God as the "Almighty" and "Lord" in Ruth 1:21–22 express something about her struggle with life. As the Almighty, God is far removed and sublime, but as the Lord he is closer and more involved. Naomi does not understand God's involvement in her life and why things are going so badly for her. Naomi's bitterness has blinded her to the loyal love and support of her daughter-in-law. Likewise, we have to be careful not to allow bitterness and disappointment to blind us to positive opportunities. Fortunately, this was not the end of God's involvement in Naomi's life.

 Lord, forgive me of my rebelliousness and bitterness that blur my vision. Please show me the way out of my difficulty!

Bitterness imprisons life; love releases it. Bitterness paralyzes life; love empowers it. Bitterness sours life; love sweetens it. Bitterness sickens life; love heals it. Bitterness blinds life; love anoints its eyes.
—Harry Emerson Fosdick (1878–1969), *American clergyman*

MERCIFUL COINCIDENCES!

Why are God's workings not always evident in our lives? If we want to answer this question, we first need to know how God works. Without us knowing it, God might be busy in our present situations. This episode will provide more insight into the way God works in our lives.

Ruth 2 (story)

[1]Now Naomi had a relative on her husband's side, from the clan of Elimelech, a man of standing, whose name was Boaz.

Tension: Will Ruth find food?

[2]And Ruth the Moabitess said to Naomi, 'Let me go to the fields and pick up the leftover grain behind anyone in whose eyes I find favor.' Naomi said to her, 'Go ahead, my daughter.'

Relief of tension: Boaz is sympathetic towards Ruth

[8]So Boaz said to Ruth, 'My daughter, listen to me. Don't go and glean in another field and don't go away from here. Stay here with my servant girls. [9]Watch the field where the men are harvesting, and follow along after the girls. I have told the men not to touch you. And whenever you are thirsty, go and get a drink from the water jars the men have filled.'
[10]At this, she bowed down with her face to the ground. She exclaimed, 'Why have I found such favor in your eyes that you notice me—a foreigner?'
[11]Boaz replied, 'I've been told all about what you have done for your mother-in-law since the death of your husband—how you left your father and mother and your homeland and came to live with a people you did not know before. (NIV)

The solution to Naomi's problems lies in ordinary events. Nothing sensational happens. Ruth takes the initiative by asking her mother-in-law if she could glean some grain in the fields of someone who will be sympathetic towards her. She takes the initiative and accepts responsibility for her situation. After this, a few events happen—things that one would normally call "coincidences." She "coincidently" goes to the land that belongs to Boaz, who "coincidently" is Naomi's only relative—and also very rich. It is also a "coincidence" that he is unmarried and shows interest in Ruth, a woman from a foreign land. "Coincidently" Boaz arrives on the day she is harvesting the leftover grain. It is a "coincidence" that he notices her and asks questions about her.

In the next episode, we read that Boaz shows mercy towards her. This episode teaches us that we can solve our problems if we follow Ruth's example, namely to take responsibility for our situation and be willing to do something about it. Without our noticing it, God uses people and ordinary events to bring about relief. We often contribute this to "coincidence," but in actual fact it is God who is working behind the scenes.

 Thank You, Lord, for accompanying me during the dark times of my life.

Coincidence is God's way of staying anonymous.
—Author unknown

WE SOMETIMES HAVE TO TAKE CALCULATED RISKS!

We sometimes have to take risks to deal with the crises of life. This observation is echoed in the saying, "Nothing ventured, nothing gained!" But these risks should be done in a responsible manner—or else the risk might be life threatening to us and our fellow human beings. The following episode serves as a wonderful example of someone who took a calculated risk.

Ruth 3 (story)

[6]So she went down to the threshing floor and did everything her mother-in-law told her to do.

Tension: Ruth's calculated risk

[7]When Boaz had finished eating and drinking and was in good spirits, he went over to lie down at the far end of the grain pile. Ruth approached quietly, uncovered his feet and lay down. [8]In the middle of the night something startled the man, and he turned and discovered a woman lying at his feet. [9]'Who are you?' he asked. 'I am your servant Ruth,' she said. 'Spread the corner of your garment over me, since you are a kinsman-redeemer.'

Relief of tension: The risk bears fruit!

[10]'The LORD bless you, my daughter,' he replied. 'This kindness is greater than that which you showed earlier: You have not run after the younger men, whether rich or poor. [11]And now, my daughter, don't be afraid. I will do for you all you ask . . .

Tension: But, there is another redeemer

[12]Although it is true that I am near of kin, there is a kinsman-redeemer nearer than I.

Relief of tension: Boaz sets Ruth's mind at ease

[13]Stay here for the night, and in the morning if he wants to redeem, good; let him redeem. But if he is not willing, as surely as the LORD lives I will do it. Lie here until morning.' (NIV)

Naomi realized that a marriage between the well-to-do Boaz and Ruth could ensure a new future for them. As the closest male family member, Boaz was the ideal kinsman-redeemer, and he was also rich and eligible. A "redeemer" was a technical term in family law to refer to the person who had responsibility to redeem his family members in a predicament.

Ruth and Naomi carefully planned this romantic rendezvous. They took a risk in organizing a meeting with Boaz. He could have turned his back on Ruth—after all, she was a Moabite, and the Israelites considered them to be foreigners. How would he react? Luckily, Naomi's plan worked out.

Naomi was not alone when she took this calculated risk. The Lord blessed her with His presence all along the way! Boaz later married Ruth, and much was gained by this venture.

Spirit of God, thank You for enabling me to venture through life's challenges with You by my side.

A turtle makes progress when it sticks its neck out.
—Author unknown

THE DEFENSELESS WIDOW
BECOMES A HAPPY GRANDMOTHER

The beginning of Naomi's story is in complete contrast to its end. The story starts when she is a disconsolate and vulnerable widow who has lost her husband and her two sons. By chapter 4, the end of the story, this defenseless widow becomes a happy grandmother holding a baby in her lap. We should pay attention to what lies between the beginning of this story and its end, as we can learn a lot from it.

Ruth 4 (story)

Result: The defenseless widow becomes a happy grandmother

¹³So Boaz took Ruth and she became his wife. Then he went to her, and the LORD enabled her to conceive, and she gave birth to a son. ¹⁴The women said to Naomi: 'Praise be to the LORD, who this day has not left you without a kinsman-redeemer. May he become famous throughout Israel! ¹⁵He will renew your life and sustain you in your old age. For your daughter-in-law, who loves you and who is better to you than seven sons, has given him birth.' ¹⁶Then Naomi took the child, laid him in her lap and cared for him. ¹⁷The women living there said, 'Naomi has a son.' And they named him Obed. He was the father of Jesse, the father of David. ¹⁸This, then, is the family line of Perez: Perez was the father of Hezron, ¹⁹Hezron the father of Ram, Ram the father of Amminadab, ²⁰Amminadab the father of Nahshon, Nahshon the father of Salmon ²¹Salmon the father of Boaz, Boaz the father of Obed, ²²Obed the father of Jesse, and Jesse the father of David. (NIV)

God operated within this story and worked with the deeds of people. How does the grandmother's grandchild come into being? The obvious answer is because Ruth and Boaz had sexual intercourse. Ruth 4:13, however, gives another important perspective: the Lord enabled Ruth to conceive.

This is why the women of Bethlehem could say to Naomi, "Praise be to the Lord." In spite of the initiatives of the people in this story, the author wants to draw our attention to the fact that God had the final say. His blessing does not exclude our initiatives. For this reason, we have to leave our comfort zones in order to plan our lives.

Ruth 4:17–21 was most likely added later on as an epilogue to highlight the *boundless mercy* of God. Ruth, the girl from Moab, became part of David's genealogy. God has no preferences. He surprises us by using people we never would have considered as possible candidates. The Lord uses a stranger who gave sense and meaning to a desperate widow by being loyal and loving. However, this is not the end of the story. Ruth was totally unaware that her offspring would pave the way for a new chapter in world history—she became part of the genealogy of Jesus (Matt. 1:5).

 Thank You, Lord for Your boundless and amazing mercy.

Through many dangers, toils and snares, I have already come;
This grace has brought me save thus far, and grace will lead me home.
—John Newton (1725–1807), *English author and composer*

OUR FOURTH STOP: THE UNITED KINGDOM

(±1020–925 B.C.)
(1–2 SAMUEL, 1 KINGS 1–11, 1 CHRONICLES—2 CHRONICLES 9, JOB, PSALMS, PROVERBS, ECCLESIASTES AND SONG OF SOLOMON)

The previous period in Israel's history ended on a note of despair, because there were no judges left in Israel and the people were left to act according to what was right and wrong in their own sight. Idolatry and lawlessness prevailed. The guidance of a king therefore became a matter of urgency. Judges paved the way for the period of the kings.

Samuel anointed the first two kings, namely Saul and David. Initially, Samuel warned the people that they did not need an earthly king because God was their king (1 Sam. 8:5,20). God regarded their request as a rejection of Him as their king (1 Sam. 8:7). However, Israel ignored the warnings about the consequences of having an earthly king (1 Sam. 8:10–19).

The three kings of this period were Saul, David and Solomon. Saul became king in ±1020 B.C. He had a lot of potential, but he did not have God at heart. He disobeyed God on three occasions: (1) when he exceeded his powers as king by taking on the function of prophet (1 Sam. 13); (2) when he failed to completely destroy the Amalekites (1 Sam. 15); and (3) when he consulted a medium (1 Sam. 28). Saul also did not interact well with other people.

David became king in ±1000 B.C. The name "David" conjures up images of a shepherd, a poet, a brave soldier, a king and the precursor of Jesus. He is one of the great characters in the Old Testament. But David also had a dark side, which the Bible does not hide. He was a deceiver, a liar, an adulterer and a murderer. Yet David is still called a man after God's own heart (Acts 13:22) because he was prepared to admit and confess his sins. David united Israel and led them during the most blessed time in its history. Through everything, God always kept His promise to Abraham that He would multiply the children of Israel (1 Kings 4:20–21).

Solomon became king in 965 B.C. and led his people to great heights. The completion of the Temple is a testimony to his reign. But below the surface, things were deteriorating. Solomon's trust in his military power, his many wives and their idols, and his wealth drove a wedge between himself and God. However, God continued to systematically execute His plan of salvation and His promise to Abraham. God's promise to Abraham manifested in David's line of descent:

Land: Genesis 12:7; 2 Samuel 7:10
Offspring: Genesis 12:2; 2 Samuel 7:12

God promised that David's kingdom would last forever (2 Sam. 7:14–16).

WHY ARE THE MINISTER'S CHILDREN SO NAUGHTY?

The answer I most often receive to this question is "because they play with the kids in the congregation." This answer is intended to raise a laugh. In this episode, we read about a minister's two sons whose conduct caused their father (and God) great pain.

1 Samuel 2 (story)

Tension: A worried minister

²²Now Eli, who was very old, heard about everything his sons were doing to all Israel and how they slept with the women who served at the entrance to the Tent of Meeting. ²³So he said to them,

Relief of tension: Eli "preaches" to his sons

'Why do you do such things? I hear from all the people about these wicked deeds of yours. ²⁴No, my sons; it is not a good report that I hear spreading among the LORD's people. ²⁵If a man sins against another man, God may mediate for him; but if a man sins against the LORD, who will intercede for him?'

Result: They turn a deaf ear to their father's "sermon"

His sons, however, did not listen to their father's rebuke, for it was the LORD's will to put them to death. (NIV)

Eli was a well-known minister (high priest) of Israel who had two notorious sons—Hophni and Phinehas. These two men were philanderers and guilty of malpractices concerning the handling of the sacrifices (1 Sam. 2:15–17). Negative reports about these two sons of the minister spread like wildfire through the nation.

These must have been very trying times for Eli. Like any good father, he had a heart to heart talk with his sons, but they took no notice of his "sermons." Eli should have acted more wisely and stopped his sons from working with the offerings. Eventually, their disobedience and the fact that Eli was not strict enough with them lead to tragedy. The two brothers died in war. When Eli heard the report about their death, he fell over backwards, broke his neck and died (4:18).

Why do children, including those who are believers, lose their way? There are numerous answers to this question. It is a fact that good parents do not always have exemplary children. The opposite is also true, namely that bad parents can have exemplary children. To brood over this can drive one "round the bend," resulting in feelings of unnecessary guilt and remorse. Children should realize that they are responsible for their own conduct despite their upbringing. All of us—including believers—should seek wisdom and pray for it.

 Lord, help me to seek wisdom and do my part to achieve it.

Don't be discouraged if your children reject your advice.
Years later they will offer it to their own offspring.
—Author unknown

HOW SHOULD WE SEE THINGS?

Crisis situations can rob us of something very precious: perspective. This section sheds some light on this fact.

1 Samuel 8 (story)

Tension: Samuel's sons disappoint the people of Israel and they start complaining

[1]When Samuel grew old, he appointed his sons as judges for Israel. [2]The name of his firstborn was Joel and the name of his second was Abijah, and they served at Beersheba. [3]But his sons did not walk in his ways. They turned aside after dishonest gain and accepted bribes and perverted justice. [4]So all the elders of Israel gathered together and came to Samuel at Ramah. [5]They said to him, 'You are old, and your sons do not walk in your ways; now appoint a king to lead us, such as all the other nations have.' [6]But when they said, 'Give us a king to lead us,' this displeased Samuel;

Relief of tension: Samuel prays

so he prayed to the LORD.

Result: God grants their request

[7]And the LORD told him: 'Listen to all that the people are saying to you; it is not you they have rejected, but they have rejected me as their king. [8]As they have done from the day I brought them up out of Egypt until this day, forsaking me and serving other gods, so they are doing to you. [9]Now listen to them. (NIV)

Samuel was Israel's leader. He had two sons and, like any other father, had high aspirations for them. The names he gave to them reflect his desire that they would follow in his footsteps. The one son's name was Joel ("the Lord is God"), and the other one was called Abijah ("the Lord is father"). Samuel appointed them as leaders in the southern part of the land. Unfortunately, they disappointed everyone by being guilty of all kinds of misconduct.

The people of Israel also disappointed Samuel by asking for a king. The reason for their request was Samuel's age and the fact that his two sons were incompetent. Samuel took their request personally and interpreted it as rejection of him. For many years, he was a good leader to his people, but now they longed for someone else to lead them. The Lord comforted Samuel by pointing out that they had, in fact, rejected the Lord Himself. Samuel was merely an instrument in the hands of God.

Looking at the situation from this perspective, Samuel need not have felt rejected. Like Eli, it must have been difficult for him to witness that his children had lost the way. It is important for us to keep the right perspective by realizing that good parents can have children who are a disappointment. Parents should not always be blamed if their children misbehave. We should learn to always see things in perspective.

Lord, help me to see things in perspective and to evaluate them objectively.

Perspective is not what we see, but the way we see it.
—Kent Crockett, *"I Once Was Blind, But Now I Squint,"* Chattanooga, TN: AMG Publishers, 2004

FROM "ZERO" TO "HERO"

The story of David and Goliath is surely one of the most famous stories in the Bible. Even people who have never read the Bible know this story. David was the youngest of several brothers and had to look after his father's cattle while his brothers fought in the war against the Philistines. One day, his father sent him to find out how his brothers were doing (1 Sam. 17:17–18). When David arrived at the place where his brothers were fighting, he saw how terrified the Israelites were of Goliath and offered to fight against the giant. His brothers were dismissive of their youngest brother's abilities (17:28–29). They—and even Saul—saw him as a loser, a nobody, a zero. Why, then, is this such a remarkable story?

1 Samuel 17 (story)

Tension: Saul wants to prevent David from fighting Goliath

³¹What David said was overheard and reported to Saul, and Saul sent for him.
³²David said to Saul, 'Let no one lose heart on account of this Philistine; your servant will go and fight him.' ³³Saul replied, 'You are not able to go out against this Philistine and fight him; you are only a boy, and he has been a fighting man from his youth.'
³⁴But David said to Saul, 'Your servant has been keeping his father's sheep. When a lion or a bear came and carried off a sheep from the flock, ³⁵I went after it, struck it and rescued the sheep from its mouth. When it turned on me, I seized it by its hair, struck it and killed it. ³⁶Your servant has killed both the lion and the bear; this uncircumcised Philistine will be like one of them, because he has defied the armies of the living God.
³⁷The LORD who delivered me from the paw of the lion and the paw of the bear will deliver me from the hand of this Philistine.'

Relief of tension: Saul gives David his blessing

Saul said to David, 'Go, and the LORD be with you.'

Result: Saul's clothes do not fit

³⁸Then Saul dressed David in his own tunic. He put a coat of armor on him and a bronze helmet on his head. ³⁹David fastened on his sword over the tunic and tried walking around, because he was not used to them. 'I cannot go in these,' he said to Saul, 'because I am not used to them.' So he took them off. (NIV)

David's decisive victory over Goliath was impressive. But it was the example he set by his faith and his courage that has inspired people through the ages. While Saul saw an enormous giant, David saw a mere mortal who dared to challenge the living God. Saul was concerned about survival, while David was concerned about God's honor. David's triumph made him an international hero—even today.

 Oh Spirit, help me to also act bravely to honor Your name.

It all depends on how we look at things and not how they are in themselves.
Carl Gustav Jung (1875–1961), *Swiss psychologist and psychiatrist*

AN IMPRESSIVE BEGINNING, BUT . . .

Many people's lives can be likened to an athlete who starts off well but gets tired during the race or gives up completely. In the race of life, an impressive start is just as important as its end. How many new undertakings—such as a business partnership or a marriage—start off well, only to end up on the rocks.

First Samuel contains the stories of people who had impressive beginnings but unfortunate endings. The book starts with the impressive Eli, the high priest of Israel. Unfortunately, he could not control his ungodly sons, and during his time the Ark was stolen and the priests' influence over the people waned.

Then there was Samuel, a man who was dedicated to God even before his birth. What a beginning! He was simultaneously the last judge, a prophet and a Levite who performed priestly duties. But later, like Eli, he had problems with his two sons. Consequently, the people rejected the leadership of the priests and the judges and asked for an earthly king. Then the prophets became prominent. This concluding episode tells us about the sad ending of Saul, his sons and his armor-bearer.

1 Samuel 31 (story)

Tension: Saul is in deadly danger

[1]Now the Philistines fought against Israel; the Israelites fled before them, and many fell slain on Mount Gilboa. [2]The Philistines pressed hard after Saul and his sons, and they killed his sons Jonathan, Abinadab and Malki-Shua. [3]The fighting grew fierce around Saul, and when the archers overtook him, they wounded him critically. [4]Saul said to his armor-bearer, 'Draw your sword and run me through, or these uncircumcised fellows will come and run me through and abuse me.' But his armor-bearer was terrified and would not do it;

Relief of tension: Saul and his armor-bearer die

so Saul took his own sword and fell on it. [5]When the armor-bearer saw that Saul was dead, he too fell on his sword and died with him. [6]So Saul and his three sons and his armor-bearer and all his men died together that same day.

Result: The Israelites flee

[7]When the Israelites along the valley and those across the Jordan saw that the Israelite army had fled and that Saul and his sons had died, they abandoned their towns and fled. (NIV)

This episode moves one to tears as the master writer involves us, the readers, in the stories. These stories become mirrors that make each of us see something of the biblical characters in ourselves. We are forced to decide for ourselves whether we want to run the race of life with the finishing line as our ultimate goal.

 Lord, not only do I want to start off well, I also want to persevere. Please give me the strength!

I hope you will go out and let stories happen to you, and that you will work them, water them with your blood and tears and your laughter till they bloom, till you yourself burst into bloom.
—Author unknown

THE DAY WHEN A DISABLED PERSON'S LIFE CHANGED

I have no idea what disabled people and their families have to endure. The next story describes the day when the life of a disabled person changed radically because he was treated with kindness.

2 Samuel 9 (story)

Tension: Mephibosheth goes down on his knees

⁶When Mephibosheth son of Jonathan, the son of Saul, came to David, he bowed down to pay him honor. David said, 'Mephibosheth!' 'Your servant,' he replied.

Relief of tension: David puts Mephibosheth's mind at rest

⁷'Don't be afraid,' David said to him, 'for I will surely show you kindness for the sake of your father Jonathan. I will restore to you all the land that belonged to your grandfather Saul, and you will always eat at my table.' ⁸Mephibosheth bowed down and said, 'What is your servant, that you should notice a dead dog like me?' ⁹Then the king summoned Ziba, Saul's servant, and said to him, 'I have given your master's grandson everything that belonged to Saul and his family. ¹⁰You and your sons and your servants are to farm the land for him and bring in the crops, so that your master's grandson may be provided for. And Mephibosheth, grandson of your master, will always eat at my table.'

Result: Mephibosheth receives royal treatment

¹³And Mephibosheth lived in Jerusalem, because he always ate at the king's table, and he was crippled in both feet. (NIV)

Mephibosheth's father was Jonathan, and his grandfather was Saul. When he was five years old, his nurse fled with him after hearing that Jonathan and Saul had died in war. In her haste, the nurse dropped the heir to the throne, and he was crippled (2 Sam. 4:4). It was custom in those times for the future king to kill all the possible contenders to the throne. The nurse was afraid that David, the designated king, would kill Mephibosheth.

This is why Mephibosheth lived in fear of David for many years. David only heard about his existence much later. What Mephibosheth did not know, was that David did not want to kill him but instead show him a favor. He had promised Jonathan (1 Sam. 20) and Saul (1 Sam. 24) that he would not wipe out their descendants.

David's generosity came as a surprise to the 20-year-old man. This is surprising, because David was not particularly fond of the disabled (1 Sam. 5:6–8). However, David kept his promise and took Mephibosheth into the royal house. Being disabled does not make one a lesser person! Those of us who are not disabled should learn to be more sensitive toward those who are.

Thank You, Lord, that this story helps me to understand that a disabled person is not a lesser person and that those who are not disabled should be more sensitive toward those who are!

I thank God for many handicaps, for, through them, I have found myself, my work, and my God.
—Helen Keller (1880–1968), American author and educator who was blind and deaf

THE THREE WORDS
THAT CHANGE YOUR LIFE!

The words "I am pregnant" can express great joy—and perhaps the answer to prayer! However, these words can also be an expression of dismay and disillusionment if they come as a result of a passionate fling. These three words, "I am pregnant," completely changed the lives of a soldier's wife and David, one of the most popular figures in the Bible.

2 Samuel 11 (story)

¹In the spring, at the time when kings go off to war, David sent Joab out with the king's men and the whole Israelite army. They destroyed the Ammonites and besieged Rabbah. But David remained in Jerusalem.

Tension: David's eyes wander off

²One evening David got up from his bed and walked around on the roof of the palace. From the roof he saw a woman bathing. The woman was very beautiful, ³and David sent someone to find out about her. The man said, 'Isn't this Bathsheba, the daughter of Eliam and the wife of Uriah the Hittite?' ⁴Then David sent messengers to get her.

Relief of tension: David gets what he wants (she too, maybe)

She came to him, and he slept with her. (She had purified herself from her uncleanness.) Then she went back home.

Result: Trouble

⁵The woman conceived and sent word to David, saying, 'I am pregnant. (NIV)

The stories in the Bible are wonderful because they relate to real life. The story of David and Bathsheba is no exception. This story has stirred people's imagination through the ages. The author uses the "empty spaces" in the story to involve us as readers. Did Bathsheba's husband know what was going on between her and David? Was the adulterous deed rape, or did Bathsheba try to seduce David? Did Bathsheba perhaps exploit the situation in an attempt to become queen? Or Did David fall victim to circumstances?

We will never know the answers to these questions for sure, but we do know that David's (and Bathsheba's) fling had an unhappy ending. David most likely wished that he could turn back the clock when he heard those three words from Bathsheba: "I am pregnant." This episode teaches us that when we make choices, we should always be aware of the consequences—and always prepared to bear them.

 Lord, help me to make level-headed choices under all circumstances.

It's choice—not chance—that determines your destiny.
—Jean Nidetch (b. 1923), *Founder and consultant of Weight Watchers International*

GOD ALSO HAS A MIRROR!

Our mirrors have limited use: they only reflect what is on the outside. But God is also interested in what goes on inside us. He wants us to also look at our lives so that we can make the necessary changes if things are not in order. For this reason, He has a "mirror" that He would like us to look into. What does God's mirror look like?

2 Samuel 12 (parable)

¹The LORD sent Nathan to David. When he came to him, he said, 'There were two men in a certain town, one rich and the other poor. ²The rich man had a very large number of sheep and cattle, ³but the poor man had nothing except one little ewe lamb he had bought. He raised it, and it grew up with him and his children. It shared his food, drank from his cup and even slept in his arms. It was like a daughter to him.

Tension: David is on the red carpet

⁴'Now a traveler came to the rich man, but the rich man refrained from taking one of his own sheep or cattle to prepare a meal for the traveler who had come to him. Instead, he took the ewe lamb that belonged to the poor man and prepared it for the one who had come to him.' ⁵David burned with anger against the man and said to Nathan, 'As surely as the LORD lives, the man who did this deserves to die! ⁶He must pay for that lamb four times over, because he did such a thing and had no pity.' ⁷Then Nathan said to David, 'You are the man . . . ⁹Why did you despise the word of the LORD by doing what is evil in his eyes? You struck down Uriah the Hittite with the sword and took his wife to be your own. You killed him with the sword of the Ammonites.

Relief of tension: David confesses

¹³Then David said to Nathan, 'I have sinned against the LORD.'

Result: David is forgiven

Nathan replied, 'The LORD has taken away your sin. You are not going to die.
¹⁴But because by doing this you have made the enemies of the LORD show utter contempt, the son born to you will die.' (NIV)

David could hide the fact that he had committed adultery with Bathsheba from everybody but God. The Lord took out His "mirror" so that David could see his inner self. The mirror was in the form of a parable of a rich man who took away a poor man's only lamb and slaughtered it. At first David reacted to the parable with fury, but then the prophet pointed out that he was the guilty one. David recognized himself in the mirror and did not try to refute what he saw. He confessed his sins! God expects us to do just that! David writes about this in Psalm 51:6 "You desire truth in the inner parts" (NIV).

 Lord, I confess that I am not always honest and that I do not always want to confess my guilt!

When looking for faults use a mirror, not a telescope.
—Author unknown

BREAK THE SILENCE!

We all have problems. But how do we deal with our problems? The following episode concerning David's domestic woes might help us to answer this question. The first sentence reminds one of a soap opera: "In the course of time Amnon son of David fell in love with Tamar, the beautiful sister of Absalom son of David . . ."

2 Samuel 13 (story)

Tension: The brother who could not keep his hormones in check

[1]In the course of time, Amnon son of David fell in love with Tamar, the beautiful sister of Absalom son of David. [2]Amnon became frustrated to the point of illness on account of his sister Tamar, for she was a virgin, and it seemed impossible for him to do anything to her. [6]So Amnon lay down and pretended to be ill. When the king came to see him, Amnon said to him, 'I would like my sister Tamar to come and make some special bread in my sight, so I may eat from her hand.' [8]So Tamar went to the house of her brother Amnon, who was lying down. She took some dough, kneaded it, made the bread in his sight and baked it. [11]But when she took it to him to eat, he grabbed her and said, 'Come to bed with me, my sister.' [12]'Don't, my brother!' she said to him.

Relief of tension: A brother who rapes his younger sister

[14]But he refused to listen to her, and since he was stronger than she, he raped her.

Result: A devastated family with an inept father

[15]Then Amnon hated her with intense hatred. In fact, he hated her more than he had loved her. Amnon said to her, 'Get up and get out!' [16]'No!' she said to him. 'Sending me away would be a greater wrong than what you have already done to me.' But he refused to listen to her. [17]He called his personal servant and said, 'Get this woman out of here and bolt the door after her.' [20]Her brother Absalom said to her, 'Has that Amnon, your brother, been with you? Be quiet now, my sister; he is your brother. Don't take this thing to heart.' And Tamar lived in her brother Absalom's house, a desolate woman. [21]When King David heard all this, he was furious. [22]Absalom never said a word to Amnon, either good or bad; he hated Amnon because he had disgraced his sister Tamar. (NIV)

Up to this day, similar events are commonplace in many homes. We are not always aware that these events are occurring because people think that they are best kept secret. I want to be crude and put it bluntly—bull^#*%! Silence breeds more anger and feelings of guilt and reproach. The only way for the emotional wounds of innocent victims to heal, for parents to be brought to book, and for all the Amnons around us to confess is to break the silence. Life is too precious to keep quiet! Go and speak to someone today! Please!!

 Lord, please give me the courage to break the silence!

Silence implies consent.
—Author unknown

PARENTS DO NOT HAVE CHILDREN, BUT CHILDREN HAVE PARENTS!

Do parents "own" their children? The following episode of a case that was brought before Solomon can shed some light on this issue.

1 Kings 3 (story)

Tension: Two prostitutes fight over a baby

[16]Now two prostitutes came to the king and stood before him. [17]One of them said, 'My Lord, this woman and I live in the same house. I had a baby while she was there with me. [18]The third day after my child was born, this woman also had a baby. We were alone; there was no one in the house but the two of us. [19]During the night this woman's son died because she lay on him. [20]So she got up in the middle of the night and took my son from my side while I your servant was asleep. She put him by her breast and put her dead son by my breast. [21]The next morning, I got up to nurse my son—and he was dead! But when I looked at him closely in the morning light, I saw that it wasn't the son I had borne.' [22]The other woman said, 'No! The living one is my son; the dead one is yours.' But the first one insisted, 'No! The dead one is yours; the living one is mine.' And so they argued before the king. [23]The king said, 'This one says, 'My son is alive and your son is dead,' while that one says, 'No! Your son is dead and mine is alive.'' [24]Then the king said, 'Bring me a sword.' So they brought a sword for the king. [25]He then gave an order: 'Cut the living child in two and give half to one and half to the other.' [26]The woman whose son was alive was filled with compassion for her son and said to the king, 'Please, my lord, give her the living baby! Don't kill him!' But the other said, 'Neither I nor you shall have him. Cut him in two!'

Relief of tension: Solomon shows who the real mother is

[27]Then the king gave his ruling: 'Give the living baby to the first woman. Do not kill him; she is his mother.'

Result: Solomon's decision is met with admiration

[28]When all Israel heard the verdict the king had given, they held the king in awe. (NIV)

The two prostitutes in this story made the mistake of thinking that parents own children. As we read in 1 Kings 3:22, "The other woman said, 'No! The living one is *my* son; the dead one *is yours*.' But the first one insisted, 'No! The dead one is *yours*; the living one is *mine*.' And so they argued before the king." The perspective changes at the end of the trial when Solomon refers to the baby as the *child of* the mother (v. 27). The two prostitutes made the same mistake parents often make: Parents do not have children, but children have parents. When a baby is born, we often tell the parents, "May your baby give you much joy." Instead we should say, "May you bring joy to your baby."

 Lord, I would like to bring joy to my children.

Before I got married, I had six theories about bringing up children;
now I have six children, and no theories.
—John Wilmot (1647–1680), *English poet*

IN WHAT WAY IS GOD INVOLVED IN OUR LIVES AND IN HISTORY?

The author(s) of 1 Kings seek to answer this question. They look back on Israel's sad past and wonder why events went so wrong for God's people. The majority of the kings of Israel disappointed God, the kingdom was divided, and the destruction of Jerusalem in 586 B.C. was followed by a time of exile. Where did things go wrong?

1 Kings 11 (conversation)

[9]The LORD became angry with Solomon because his heart had turned away from the LORD, the God of Israel, who had appeared to him twice.

[10]Although he had forbidden Solomon to follow other gods, Solomon did not keep the LORD's command.

[11]So the LORD said to Solomon, 'Since this is your attitude and you have not kept my covenant and my decrees, which I commanded you, I will most certainly tear the kingdom away from you and give it to one of your subordinates.

[12]Nevertheless, for the sake of David your father, I will not do it during your lifetime. I will tear it out of the hand of your son.

[13]Yet I will not tear the whole kingdom from him, but will give him one tribe for the sake of David my servant and for the sake of Jerusalem, which I have chosen.' (NIV)

Israel's history follows a repeating pattern. The pattern starts with God, who makes a covenant with the people, but then the people sin and God has to punish them. Solomon is a classic example of this pattern. God made a covenant with Solomon (1 Kings 3:10–13). God committed Himself to bless Solomon if he obeyed the instructions of the covenant. It was, therefore, Solomon's responsibility to adhere to the instructions of the covenant. Solomon started off well, but he completely went off the rails after a while. His life is summed up very well in 1 Kings 11:4: "As Solomon grew old, his wives turned his heart after other gods, and his heart was not fully devoted to the LORD his God, as the heart of David his father had been" (NIV).

God's subsequent punishment was the division of the kingdom. The author(s) of 1 Kings realize that God is indeed involved in history. God gives us *privileges* but also *responsibilities*. If we do not meet our responsibilities, we will eventually lose our privileges. Misery is, therefore, not God's fault but the result of the wrong choices people make—like those choices Solomon made. God's involvement is manifested in the privileges He gives us. We are involved when we use those privileges responsibly.

 Lord, help me not to forfeit my privileges by making the wrong choices.

It is easy to dodge our responsibilities, but we cannot dodge the consequences of dodging our responsibilities.
—Josiah Charles Stamp (1880–1941), *English economist and president of the Bank of England in the 1920s.*
He was the second richest man in Great Britain at the time.

DO WE REALLY NEED TO READ THESE GENEALOGIES? THEY ARE SO BORING!

I have always found the genealogical registers in the Bible utterly boring. They just do not make sense, and some of the names are so difficult to pronounce. In fact, I often wonder whether it is necessary to read the first nine chapters of Chronicles, as they only consist of such registers. Yet the Chronicler (author of the book of Chronicles) would have been affronted if we skipped the first nine chapters of his book. Why did these genealogical registers thrill him so much?

1 Chronicles 1 (history)

From Adam to Noah's Sons

¹The descendants of Adam were Seth, Enosh, ²Kenan, Mahalalel, Jared, ³Enoch, Methuselah, Lamech, ⁴and Noah.
The sons of Noah were Shem, Ham, and Japheth.

Descendants of Japheth

⁵The descendants of Japheth were Gomer, Magog, Madai, Javan, Tubal, Meshech, and Tiras.
⁶The descendants of Gomer were Ashkenaz, Riphath, and Togarmah.
⁷The descendants of Javan were Elishah, Tarshish, Kittim, and Rodanim.

Descendants of Ham

⁸The descendants of Ham were Cush, Mizraim, Put, and Canaan.
⁹The descendants of Cush were Seba, Havilah, Sabtah, Raamah, and Sabteca. The descendants of Raamah were Sheba and Dedan. ¹⁰Cush was also the ancestor of Nimrod, who was the first heroic warrior on earth.
¹¹Mizraim was the ancestor of the Ludites, Anamites, Lehabites, Naphtuhites, ¹²Pathrusites, Casluhites, and the Caphtorites, from whom the Philistines came.
¹³Canaan's oldest son was Sidon, the ancestor of the Sidonians. Canaan was also the ancestor of the Hittites, ¹⁴Jebusites, Amorites, Girgashites, ¹⁵Hivites, Arkites, Sinites, ¹⁶Arvadites, Zemarites, and Hamathites. (NLT)

The Chronicler wrote to the Jews who had returned to the land of Israel after the exile. They were unsure of where they fit in and felt stripped of their identity. The Chronicler used the long genealogical registers to help them establish their place in the land of their forefathers. The lists could help a returnee to discover, for example, that he or she was from the lineage of Judah or Simeon. This gave the returned exiles a new identity and helped them to regain their self-respect.

These genealogical lists helped the post-exilic community realize that they were a continuation of old Israel. They were still part of God's chosen people who had to dedicate their lives to Him. It is for this reason that the New Testament also starts with a genealogical register—the genealogy of Jesus. Our faith makes us part of the genealogy of Christ. It helps us to know that we belong somewhere and fit in somewhere. These seemingly boring lists should, therefore, fill us with wonder—wonder about God, who really cares for us.

Thank You, Lord, that I can know that I am part of Your genealogy.

A family tree can wither if nobody tends its roots.
—Author unknown

WHAT PROOF IS THERE THAT GOD IS INVOLVED IN OUR LIVES?

It would be comforting to know that God is involved in our lives. But how can we truly know this? The long lists of names in 1 Chronicles might seem boring and uninteresting reading, but they can help us discover that God is indeed involved in our lives. We have to read very carefully because, between the lines, we will discover something very special about God.

1 Chronicles 1 (history)

Descendants of Abraham

[28]The sons of Abraham were Isaac and Ishmael. [29]These are their genealogical records: The sons of Ishmael were Nebaioth (the oldest), Kedar, Adbeel, Mibsam, [30] Mishma, Dumah, Massa, Hadad, Tema,

Descendants of Isaac

[34]Abraham was the father of Isaac. The sons of Isaac were Esau and Israel.

Descendants of Esau

[35]The sons of Esau were Eliphaz, Reuel, Jeush, Jalam, and Korah.
[36]The sons of Eliphaz were Teman, Omar, Zepho, Gatam, Kenaz, and Amalek, who was born to Timna.
[37]The sons of Reuel were Nahath, Zerah, Shammah, and Mizzah.

1 Chronicles 2 (history)

Descendants of Israel

[1]The sons of Israel were Reuben, Simeon, Levi, Judah, Issachar, Zebulun, [2]Dan, Joseph, Benjamin, Naphtali, Gad, and Asher.

Descendants of Judah

[3]Judah had three sons from Bathshua, a Canaanite woman. Their names were Er, Onan, and Shelah. But the Lord saw that the oldest son, Er, was a wicked man, so he killed him. (NLT)

The names of three important figures are mentioned in the beginning of Chronicles: Abraham, Isaac and Israel (the name the Chronicler gives to Jacob). These three characters represent a story of pain, humiliation and frustration. All three of them had infertile wives.

People made fun of Abraham's wife, *Sarah*, because she failed to produce a child despite the fact that she was promised many offspring (Gen. 11:30). She helplessly watched the years pass by without having the joy of a child. God saw her helplessness and despair and answered her prayers with the birth of Isaac (Gen. 21:1–6). Isaac's wife, *Rebecca*, also could not become pregnant, which frustrated Isaac tremendously. What would come of the promise of descendants in abundance? God took note of Isaac's pain and answered his prayers with the birth of Jacob (Gen. 25:21). Jacob's wife,

Rachel, was also childless. She was jealous of her sister, who was able to give Jacob children. So she prayed, and her prayers were answered when Joseph was born.

What we read between the lines is that God kept His promise to Abraham even though there were infertile women in Abraham's family. If we look closely at our own history, we will discover the wonder of God's involvement in our lives—even though this might not always appear to be the case.

 Thank You, Lord, that I can know You are always involved in my life.

God is more anxious to bestow his blessings on us than we are to receive them.
—Saint Augustine (354–386), *Christian theologian, rhetor, North African bishop and doctor of the Roman Catholic Church*

WHERE GOD OFTEN SURPRISES US

The *Guinness Book of Records* lists a number of exceptional achievements that people have accomplished. We can easily get so carried away by these types of extraordinary achievements. Consequently, we often overlook and underestimate the ordinary things in life. This is a pity, because that is exactly where God often surprises us with His presence.

1 Chronicles 11 (history) David Captures Jerusalem

[4]Then David and all Israel went to Jerusalem (or Jebus, as it used to be called), where the Jebusites, the original inhabitants of the land, were living. [5]The people of Jebus taunted David, saying, 'You'll never get in here!' But David captured the fortress of Zion, which is now called the City of David. [6]David had said to his troops, 'Whoever is first to attack the Jebusites will become the commander of my armies!' And Joab, the son of David's sister Zeruiah, was first to attack, so he became the commander of David's armies.
[7]David made the fortress his home, and that is why it is called the City of David. [8]He extended the city from the supporting terraces to the surrounding area, while Joab rebuilt the rest of Jerusalem. [9]And David became more and more powerful, because the Lord of Heaven's Armies was with him. (NLT)

Several ordinary events happen in this section. In the previous verses, David was anointed king, and here he advances to Jebus to turn it into his capital city. This was an ordinary action because all kings were entitled to a capital. It was an ordinary act to rebuild the city and to extend its boundaries. However, through this ordinary deed, the people of Israel were rebuilding a city that would later become much bigger than the future capital of the kingdom of David. They were, in fact, building a city that would become very important in the religious life of all Jews and Christians.

To David's descendants, the city of Jerusalem was the place where the Temple stood and where God's presence was felt in a special way. Jerusalem was the place where, according to the Lord's promise, the house of David would rule for centuries to come. To Christians, Jerusalem became the place where Jesus was crucified and resurrected to give them new life. The importance of the city was later reflected in the figure of speech "the new Jerusalem," which indicated the newness of God with His children.

Could David, Joab and all the other communities have foreseen this? David experienced God in the ordinary things (v. 9). We should not underestimate the ordinary things in life, because we never know what their outcome will be. In fact, God often performs His greatest miracles in the ordinary things of life.

 Lord, help me not to underestimate the ordinary things in life!

God never wrought miracles to convince atheism, because his ordinary works convince it.
—Francis Bacon, Sr. (1561–1626), *English lawyer and philosopher*

HOW SHOULD WE REACT TO GOD'S CARE?

We constantly react to other people's actions. Words such as "thank you," "please" and "you're welcome" are only a few examples of the ones we use to react to the deeds of others. But how should we react to God's grace, goodness and favor? The following section, like many other sections in the Bible, gives us the answers.

1 Chronicles 25 (history)—Duties of the Musicians

¹David and the army commanders then appointed men from the families of Asaph, Heman, and Jeduthun to proclaim God's messages to the accompaniment of lyres, harps, and cymbals. Here is a list of their names and their work:
²From the sons of Asaph, there were Zaccur, Joseph, Nethaniah, and Asarelah. They worked under the direction of their father, Asaph, who proclaimed God's messages by the king's orders.
³From the sons of Jeduthun, there were Gedaliah, Zeri, Jeshaiah, Shimei, Hashabiah, and Mattithiah, six in all. They worked under the direction of their father, Jeduthun, who proclaimed God's messages to the accompaniment of the lyre, offering thanks and praise to the Lord.
⁴From the sons of Heman, there were Bukkiah, Mattaniah, Uzziel, Shubael, Jerimoth, Hananiah, Hanani, Eliathah, Giddalti, Romamti-ezer, Joshbekashah, Mallothi, Hothir, and Mahazioth. ⁵All these were the sons of Heman, the king's seer, for God had honored him with fourteen sons and three daughters. ⁷They and their families were all trained in making music before the Lord, and each of them—288 in all—was an accomplished musician. (NLT)

King David arranged the Temple service in such a way that songs of praise could be heard in the Temple every day. David knew that praise was a true reaction to the great deeds of God. The Levites praised the Lord for His great deeds on behalf of Israel. God's great love made Israel a great kingdom where peace prevailed and where the Temple was rebuilt after the time of exile.

Songs of praise were so much a part of the Levites' lives that some of them were named after words from a psalm or a song. For example, each name of the last nine sons of Heman (v. 4) was a word from an unknown song. Together, the names made up a complete song: "Be gracious, oh Lord [sixth son], be gracious unto me! [seventh], My God, Thou [eighth]; I've praised [ninth] and exalted for helping [tenth]; though sitting forlorn [eleventh], I've proclaimed [twelfth] highest [thirteenth] visions [fourteenth]."

Let us join Heman's sons in praising the Lord every day. This is the best response to God's care for us—in the small things as well as in the big things in life. Praise the Lord! Hallelujah!!!

 Lord, I want to praise and glorify You for Your kindness and goodwill toward me.

Whether the angels play only Bach praising God, I am not quite sure. I am sure, however,
that en famille they play Mozart.
—Karl Barth (1886–1968), *Swiss theologian, among the most influential of the twentieth century*

IS EVIL TAKING OVER?

I have often heard people say that life is just not the same anymore and that we are living in evil times. It seems as if evil has started to get the upper hand over the kingdom of God. This is a disturbing thought. But is this really happening?

2 Chronicles 1 (history)

³Then he led the entire assembly to the place of worship in Gibeon, for God's Tabernacle was located there. (This was the Tabernacle that Moses, the Lord's servant, had made in the wilderness.)
⁴David had already moved the Ark of God from Kiriath-jearim to the tent he had prepared for it in Jerusalem. ⁵But the bronze altar made by Bezalel son of Uri and grandson of Hur was there at Gibeon in front of the Tabernacle of the Lord. So Solomon and the people gathered in front of it to consult the Lord. ⁶There in front of the Tabernacle, Solomon went up to the bronze altar in the Lord's presence and sacrificed 1,000 burnt offerings on it. (NLT)

As you read these verses, you are probably wondering how they could possibly shed light on this complex issue. The connection is that the Chronicler also felt that evil was gaining the upper hand in his time. He thought about all the godless kings, the divided kingdom and the exile. To make sense of God's actions, he explored the long history of Israel and tried to fit in the pieces like a jigsaw puzzle.

Life is like a puzzle with many different pieces that seemingly do not fit. What is frustrating is that only God sees the overall picture. But sometimes—and only sometimes—it seems as if God wants to bring the pieces of the puzzle a bit closer so that a picture starts emerging. These verses represent something of this. The Chronicler uses three "puzzle pieces" to open up the old world and fit it into the new world of David and Solomon:

1. Solomon stands at the same tent (the Tent of Meeting or Tabernacle) where Moses stood centuries before. Like Moses, Solomon experiences the closeness of the Lord.
2. Solomon's plan for the Temple follows the pattern and content of the Tabernacle. Something of the old would, therefore, be in the new.
3. Solomon follows the example of Bezalel, who built the bronze altar with great skill (Exod. 31:2–5; 35:30–33; 36:1–39:31), by building the Temple with great skill. Like Bezalel, Solomon is also filled with the Spirit.

The Chronicler looks back and realizes that evil does not have the upper hand in the kingdom—and this also applies to today. God sees the overall picture. Let us accept this!

 Thank You, Lord, that I can know that evil is not taking over.

The only thing necessary for the triumph of evil is for good men to do nothing.
—Edmund Burke (1729–1797), *British political writer*

HOW DO WE MAKE SENSE OF LIFE?

As we mentioned in yesterday's reading, life resembles different pieces of a jigsaw puzzle that do not always seem to fit. This can be frustrating, because we do not always have the overall picture that could help us to fit together the pieces and make sense of life. Only God has the overall picture. Yet the Chronicler shows us a simple but effective way to match some of the pieces together.

2 Chronicles 3 (history)—Solomon Builds the Temple

[1]So Solomon began to build the Temple of the Lord in Jerusalem on Mount Moriah, where the Lord had appeared to David, his father. The Temple was built on the threshing floor of Araunah the Jebusite, the site that David had selected. [2]The construction began in midspring, during the fourth year of Solomon's reign.

[3]These are the dimensions Solomon used for the foundation of the Temple of God (using the old standard of measurement). It was 90 feet long and 30 feet wide.[4]The entry room at the front of the Temple was 30 feet wide, running across the entire width of the Temple, and 30 feet high. He overlaid the inside with pure gold. (NLT)

The Chronicler uses history to make sense of life. He looks back to the building of the Temple and relates that event to other events. He uses two symbolic places in verse 1: Mount Moriah and the threshing floor of Araunah. Mount Moriah, where Solomon would build the Temple, was the same location where the Lord appeared to David, Solomon's father. On this exact spot, Solomon was to build a temple where daily sacrifices could be offered to the Lord.

However, the location had a deeper meaning: Mount Moriah was also the place where God provides! For it was here on Moriah, more than eight centuries before, where Abraham was to sacrifice his son, Isaac, but the Lord saved the boy's life by providing Abraham with a ram to sacrifice instead of Isaac (Gen 22:1–19). Likewise, Solomon's Temple would also become a place where God would, in a wondrous way, provide for the sick, the poor and the careworn. This is why the Chronicler could link the building of the Temple to Abraham.

There might be another deeper meaning of which the Chronicler did not even know—for by then he had been dead a long time. Not far from this place, and many centuries later, another Son of David would die for His people on Golgotha. When this happened, the lambs, the offerings and the Temple became redundant. Jesus was the perfect lamb who died once and for all for our sins. Because His Spirit came to live within us, we are the Temple of the Lord.

May you, in your search for meaning in life, also discover how the different pieces of your life fit together. May you make sense of life!

 Thank You, Lord, for still providing in wonderful ways.

If there is a meaning in life at all, then there must be a meaning in suffering. Suffering is an ineradicable part of life, even as fate and death. Without suffering and death, human life cannot be complete.
—Viktor Emil Frankl (1905–1997), *Austrian neurologist and psychiatrist who survived the Holocaust, although his wife, father and mother were murdered in concentration camps*

WISDOM THAT SHOWS, WORKS!

Wisdom is not some abstract theory. When wisdom works, people notice it and are amazed by it. It can even take people's breath away. In the following episode, a woman was filled with amazement by the wisdom she saw.

2 Chronicles 9 (story)—Visit of the Queen of Sheba

Tension: The test of wisdom

¹When the queen of Sheba heard of Solomon's fame, she came to Jerusalem to test him with hard questions. She arrived with a large group of attendants and a great caravan of camels loaded with spices, large quantities of gold, and precious jewels. When she met with Solomon, she talked with him about everything she had on her mind.

Relief of tension: Solomon's wisdom impresses

²Solomon had answers for all her questions; nothing was too hard for him to explain to her.

Result: amazement

³When the queen of Sheba realized how wise Solomon was, and when she saw the palace he had built, ⁴she was overwhelmed. She was also amazed at the food on his tables, the organization of his officials and their splendid clothing, the cup-bearers and their robes, and the burnt offerings Solomon made at the Temple of the Lord. ⁵She exclaimed to the king, 'Everything I heard in my country about your achievements and wisdom is true! ⁶I didn't believe what was said until I arrived here and saw it with my own eyes. In fact, I had not heard the half of your great wisdom! It is far beyond what I was told. ⁷How happy your people must be! What a privilege for your officials to stand here day after day, listening to your wisdom! ⁸Praise the Lord your God, who delights in you and has placed you on the throne as king to rule for him. Because God loves Israel and desires this kingdom to last forever, he has made you king over them so you can rule with justice and righteousness.' (NLT)

Solomon's wisdom impacted all the facets of his life and his government. The queen of Sheba had heard so much about Solomon and his wisdom that she decided to go and see for herself. When she arrived in Jerusalem, she was overwhelmed by what she saw and found much more than she expected. She discovered God's love (v. 8) in ordinary things, such as clothing, table manners and in the attitude of the people toward attending the Temple services (v. 4). It is, therefore, not always necessary to do something extraordinary to make a difference. The challenge is to live an ordinary life but to live in such a way that it bears testimony to God's love and mercy. Wisdom that shows, works!

 Lord, I realize once again that it is wise to perform my daily duties in a way that will bear testimony to Your love and mercy.

Excellence is doing ordinary things extraordinarily well.
—John W. Gardner (1912–2002), *American Writer and Secretary of Health, Education and Welfare*

AN IMPORTANT STEP AWAY FROM THE DUMPS OF DESPAIR!

Life's pain and heartache can so easily strip us of our purpose in life. During the next few days, we will ponder the reality of life's pain and hurt as it is reflected in the life of Job. The whole book of Job (except 1–2 and 42:7–17) is a wonderful poetic story. The repetitions (something to always consider when reading poetry) emphasize how important it was to Job to make sense of his suffering. Job teaches us to take an important step away from the dumps of despair in which we might find ourselves.

Job 3

> ²⁰*Oh, why give light* to those in misery,
> *and life* to those who are bitter?
> ²¹They long for death, *and it won't come.*
> They search for death *more eagerly than for hidden treasure.*
> ²²*They're filled with joy* when they finally die,
> *and rejoice* when they find the grave. (NLT)

Job is completely honest with God and not afraid to reveal his true feelings to Him. His suffering becomes unbearable. Materially, the once wealthy Job loses everything. In addition to this, the community begins to treat this well-known and respected man as an outcast. Emotionally, Job struggles with depression and heartache. Spiritually, Job feels that God has turned His back on him. Job has nothing left to live for. Death would come as a relief.

We know that Job made it through this dark period of his life. Although his feelings and protest against God were honest, he did not blaspheme the Lord. And although he longed for death, he did not commit suicide. We can follow Job's example by verbalizing and uttering our cries of fear and protest against God. Protest against God does not mean we stop believing—it is a religious battle to keep on believing or to believe anew. Protest says, "Lord, I want to keep on believing, but I am battling to do so!" Absolute honesty is an important step away from the dumps of despair.

 Thank You, Lord, for allowing me to protest against You. Thank You for listening!

Despair is the only genuine atheism.
—Jean Paul (1763–1825), *German novelist and humorist*

HOW DO WE DEAL WITH HEARTACHE?

So many people do not know how to deal with their heartache and prefer not to discuss it with anybody. Yet Job teaches us the right way to deal with heartache.

Job 7

²⁰If I have sinned, what have I done to you,
    O watcher of all humanity?
Why make me your target?
    Am I a burden to you?
²¹Why not just forgive *my sin*
    and take away *my guilt?*
For soon I will lie down in the dust and die.
    When you look for me, I will be gone.' (NLT)

Job's physical and emotional suffering became more intense by the day. His "why" questions as well as the repetition in the poetry reinforce the intensity of his frustration. To Job, it appears as if God wants to punish him and make him the bearer of the brunt of His anger. During the time of Job, it was generally accepted that suffering was the result of sin. Therefore, Job pleads with God to forgive his sins in order to stop the hurt.

Job's outburst against God sounds shocking—shocking because a human being dares to speak with such brutal honesty to his Creator. Looking back, however, we see that these honest outbursts against God helped Job to escape from the depths of his misery. It is important for us to express our heartache and emotions. It helps us to gain clarity into our situation. *Honest confession* is a way of declaring to God and ourselves that we are in the process of moving away from despair toward hope.

Lord, I want to be honest with You about my heartache and emotions. The heartache I feel is _____ and the emotions it creates are _____. Amen!

It is not the criminal things that are hardest to confess, but the ridiculous and the shameful.
—Jean Jacques Rousseau (1712–1778), *Swiss political philosopher, educationist and essayist*

HOW DO WE SUPPORT SOMEONE IN TIMES OF HEARTACHE?

If we look around and listen carefully to what people have to say, we will soon discover that people are wrestling with pain. It is not necessary for them to do this alone. We can help them! How?

Job 11

¹Then Zophar the Naamathite replied to Job:
²"Shouldn't someone answer this torrent of words?
Is a person proved innocent just by a lot of talking?
³Should I remain silent while you babble on?
When you mock God, shouldn't someone make you ashamed?
⁴You claim, 'My beliefs are pure,'
and 'I am clean in the sight of God.'
⁵If only God would speak;
if only he would tell you what he thinks! (NLT)

Zophar was the third friend who talked to Job about his hurt. Zophar differs from the other two friends in the sense that he was the most undiplomatic of the three. The rhetorical questions that he puts to Job are abrupt and aggressive. He interprets Job's honest quest for comfort as slanderous (v. 3). He does not realize that Job's protest is an honest attempt to carry on believing. Zophar aggravates Job's pain because he does not understand Job but condemns him anyway. In verse 4, Zophar accuses Job of being someone who thinks he is right and God is wrong. Zophar's friendship does nothing to help Job.

When you try to support others in their heartache, you need to avoid having the mentality of Zophar. Here are three practical hints that will help you to be a good friend:

1. Ask yourself how you would feel if you were in that person's shoes. How would you deal with such a painful experience?
2. Be there to listen, and keep on listening with an attitude of, "I want to understand what you are saying—feel free to talk or to cry." Remember: If people feel that nobody is listening to them, it only adds frustration, anger and loneliness to their pain. Not being heard is hurtful and causes loneliness.
3. Realize that the person who is hurting would like you not to be a person who stands in front of them but one who stands beside them and accompanies them.

All the best!

 Lord, help me to be a good friend to others who are experiencing heartache and pain.

Friendship is love with understanding.
—Author unknown

CAN WE PROTEST AGAINST GOD?

Sometimes when we hurt and it feels as if the world has turned against us, bitterness and anger can easily overpower us. This makes us want to protest against God. But are we allowed to do this? Will not God turn his back on us if we protest against Him?

Job 13

¹³'Be silent now and leave me alone.
Let me speak, and I will face the consequences.
¹⁴Yes, I will take my life in my hands
and say what I really think.
¹⁵God might kill me, but I have no other hope.
I am going to argue my case with him.
¹⁶But this is what will save me—I am not godless.
If I were, I could not stand before him.
¹⁷'Listen closely to what I am about to say.
Hear me out.
¹⁸I have prepared my case;
I will be proved innocent. (NLT)

Job is busy preparing himself thoroughly for his trial. He will appear before God to prove his innocence. He knows it is a risky thing to do (v. 14) because it could mean his death (Exod. 33:20). However, he also knows it is the only way to prove that he is innocent, because his friends do not believe this to be the case.

As we mentioned yesterday, in Job's time people believed that one's suffering was the result of a life of sin. Job realizes that his misery must be a mistake, because it cannot be traced to sinfulness in his life. So Job dares to protest against God. However, he does it in style. He says exactly how he feels without being disdainful of God or rejecting Him.

We may express our cries of protest against God in the finest detail, but this does not mean that we reject Him or that we are disdainful of Him. God welcomes our protest, for by protesting we say, "Lord, I'm struggling to believe. Help me to believe again!" God allows us to bother Him with our prayers and wishes. The good news is that we do not sigh alone: "And the Holy Spirit helps us in our weakness. For example, we don't know what God wants us to pray for. But the Holy Spirit prays for us with groanings that cannot be expressed in words" (Rom. 8:26, NLT).

 Thank You, Lord, that I may feel free to voice my protest against You. It is wonderful to know that Your Spirit supports me in this.

I have not lost faith in God. I have moments of anger and protest.
Sometimes I've been closer to him for that reason.
—Elie Wiesel (b.1928), Romanian-born American writer and
winner of the Nobel Prize for Peace in 1986

SO MANY QUESTIONS ABOUT GOD . . .

Children ask the most difficult questions about God. For example, "Who created God?" Adults also have questions about God. This section might help us to gain better insight into our questions about God.

Job 38

¹Then the Lord answered Job from the whirlwind:
²"Who is this that questions my wisdom
with such ignorant words?
³Brace yourself like a man,
because I have some questions for you,
and you must answer them.
⁴"Where were you when I laid the foundations of the earth?
Tell me, if you know so much. (NLT)

The fact that Job was hurt made him ask many "why" questions. He could not understand why God had treated him the way He did. Why did he have to suffer so much? His friends who came to speak to him could not stop him from questioning God or from wrestling over his situation. But then in Job 38, God breaks His silence and begins to answer Job with His own rhetorical questions.

God did not answer any of Job's questions, because that was not the crux of the problem. The crux of the problem was that Job dared to question God as one would an equal. God shows Job that he lacks insight in presuming to know how God's spiritual order works (v. 2). Job and his friends thought that suffering was the punishment for sin, but Job finds that this order has been turned upside down.

God reveals this lack of understanding in Job by asking him rhetorical questions about creation—something that Job can see. By doing this, God implies to Job that he does not even understand the order of creation, which is visible, so how can he possibly understand the spiritual order, which is not visible? It is fine for us to ask questions. However, we should realize that we are not God's equals. The Lord is more interested in restoring relationships than in answering our questions.

 Thank You, Lord, that I may ask questions. Help me to realize that my relationship with You is more important than all the questions that bother me.

The word question is derived from the Latin quarrier (to seek) which is the same root as the word for quest. A creative life is a continued quest, and good questions can be very useful guides. Most useful are open-ended questions; they allow for fresh unanticipated answers to reveal themselves.
—Author unknown

HOW GREAT IS GOD?

The Lord showed Job His creation in order to give him a glimpse of His greatness. Let's join Job and see what God wants to show him.

Job 39

[26]'Is it your wisdom that makes the hawk soar
and spread its wings toward the south?
[27]Is it at your command that the eagle rises
to the heights to make its nest?
[28]It lives on the cliffs,
making its home on a distant, rocky crag.
[29]From there it hunts its prey,
keeping watch with piercing eyes.
[30]Its young gulp down blood.
Where there's a carcass, there you'll find it.' (NLT)

Job has many questions about the spiritual aspects of life and wants insight into the reasons for his suffering—specifically why he has to suffer so much if he leads such a good life. God answers Job's difficult questions by showing him creation. In verse 26, God shows Job that He—and not Job—endowed the hawk with instinct to migrate south during the winter and return north in the summer. God also draws Job's attention to the fact that He—and not Job—enables the eagles to build their nests high above the ground, where their sharp eyes can watch everything.

Job does not see the usefulness of death, but in nature death can have a useful function—dead animals become food for other animals. God shows Job that even animals have insight, so why, then, does he lack it? Animals do not ask questions; they just live life the way they have received it from God. God teaches Job that if one is able to live with the secrets of creation, one should also be able to live with the secrets and riddles of human life. Both the secrets of life and of creation are encircled by the all-knowing God who has insight into everything. God is truly great. Knowing this helps us to live with confidence.

 Lord, I worship You as the God who is greater than anything I can think of or dream of. I am amazed!

Any fool can count the seeds in an apple. Only God can count all the apples in one seed.
—Dr. Robert H. Schuller (b. 1926), *Founder of the Crystal Cathedral in Garden Grove, California*

THE STRUGGLE TO FIND ANSWERS TO OUR QUESTIONS

Many questions about life can drive us crazy—questions such as, "Why did this happen to me?" or "Couldn't the Lord have intervened?" The book of Job teaches us to look beyond our questions.

Job 42

¹Then Job replied to the Lord:
²'I know that you can do anything,
and no one can stop you.
³You asked, 'Who is this that questions my wisdom
with such ignorance?'
It is I—and I was talking about things I knew nothing about,
things far too wonderful for me.
⁴You said, 'Listen and I will speak!
I have some questions for you,
and you must answer them.'
⁵*I had only heard about you before,*
but now I have seen you with my own eyes.
⁶'I take back everything I said,
and I sit in dust and ashes to show my repentance.' (NLT)

Job realizes that God is too great to understand. He realizes that it is impossible for him to fully understand God and His creation. Previously, Job reacted to God as if he knew exactly what life entailed, but now he realizes that he was arrogant in trying to compete with God on an equal footing. The words of verse 6 show Job's intense remorse. The insignificant Job is overwhelmed by God's greatness when he says, "I sit in dust and ashes to show my repentance."

Job does not get clear answers, but he realizes that God is greater than his questions. Our questions about life are often questions about God Himself. Job is not disappointed in this, because his dream in life, to see God (Job 19:27), comes true (v. 5). To "see" God in this case means to meet Him. Job's meeting with God enables him to accept his situation. Instead of finding answers, he finds God.

 Lord, help me to realize like Job that I will not find the answers to all of life's questions. Help me to accept my situation, because You are greater than all my questions.

Young man, young man, your arm's too short to box with God.
—James Weldon Johnson (1871–1938), *Leading American author, poet and early civil rights activist*

WE CANNOT ASPIRE TO HAPPINESS!

Wouldn't we all like to be happy? Sadly, so many people are never truly happy. In fact, we might be making a mistake in thinking that we can aspire to happiness. Psalm 1 states very clearly that although happiness is possible, it is not something to which we necessarily can aspire.

Psalm 1

¹Oh, the joys of those who do not
follow *the advice of the wicked,*
or stand *around with sinners,*
or join *in with mockers.*
²But they delight in the law of the Lord,
meditating on it day and night.
³They are like trees planted along the riverbank,
bearing fruit each season.
Their leaves never wither,
and they prosper in all they do.
⁶For the Lord watches over the path of the godly,
but the path of the wicked leads to destruction. (NLT)

Psalm 1 is the introduction to the book of Psalms. In this passage, we are introduced to the main characters of this book: the righteous, the wicked, and God. According to this psalm, we cannot aspire to happiness. Happiness is rather the result or byproduct of doing what is right. In verse 1, three verbs (follow, stand and join) are used to warn us about what not to do. It is interesting to note that verse 1 indicates a process of deterioration in the life of the wicked. Verse 2 confirms that a believer's happiness rests with God. Happiness is the consequence of leading a life to please God. A godless person's path of life is a dead-end street, while the righteous is God's companion.

Before he was converted, Augustine (345–430), a well-known theologian from Africa, sought happiness in parties, drink, sex and violent fights . . . but his life remained empty, aimless and desolate. His mother, Monica, kept on praying for him. Everything changed when God walked into his life and he became a great man of God. Today, he is considered to be one of the greatest theologians in history. In his autobiography, *The Confessions of Augustine,* he writes the following striking and fitting words: "You have made us for yourself, O Lord, and our hearts are restless till they find their rest in you."

 Lord, thank You for letting me know that happiness is the result of living according to Your will!

Happiness is not a goal; it is a by-product.
—Eleanor Roosevelt (1884–1962), *American columnist, lecturer and humanitarian*

HOW TO COPE WITH ALL THE VIOLENCE!

Every day, we witness some form of injustice. If injustice depresses you, Psalm 37 should calm you.

Psalm 37

¹Don't worry *about the wicked*
or envy those *who do wrong.*
²*For like grass,* they soon fade away.
Like spring flowers, they soon wither.
³Trust in the Lord and do good.
Then you will live safely in the land and prosper.
⁴Take delight in the Lord,
and he will give you your heart's desires.
⁵Commit everything you do to the Lord.
Trust him, and he will help you. (NLT)

Psalm 37:1 stresses that we should not focus on the actions of evildoers, because this will not hearten us but cause bitterness. The repetition in verse 2 emphasizes that the lives of those who do evil end in tragedy and that God has the final word. Why should we allow our thoughts to be dominated by mortals who are only interested in wrongdoing? This only pollutes our thoughts and upsets us. In the end, the people who are closest to us have to bear the brunt of this frustration.

The alternative to this is to change our focus on doing what is good (v. 3), such as getting involved in a neighborhood watch or forming one when crime is high in our neighborhood. Such actions might comfort us to know that we are working toward a solution in a concrete way. We should not merely depend on God in all matters (v. 5) if we are not prepared to do good. May the Lord help us to do good and to find our happiness in Him!

 Lord Jesus, help me to focus on You in the midst of all the danger that surrounds me.

If you want happiness for an hour, take a nap. If you want happiness for a day, go fishing.
If you want happiness for a month, get married. If you want happiness for a year, inherit a fortune.
If you want happiness for a lifetime, help someone else.
—Chinese proverb

I DO NOT WANT TO TELL ANYBODY

Not all of us find it easy to open our hearts to others. Sharing our hurt and shame with other people makes us very vulnerable, and once we have done this, we will have no control over what others will do with the information. People often disappoint us because they tell others about something we told them in confidentiality, which is precisely why we are hesitant to talk to others. But we cannot keep quiet and bottle up our feelings all the time. It is not good for our health. Fortunately, there is someone we can trust!

Psalm 51

¹Have mercy on me, O God,
because of your unfailing love.
Because of your great compassion,
blot out the stain of my sins.
²*Wash me clean* from my guilt.
Purify me from my sin.
³For I recognize my rebellion;
it haunts me day and night.
⁴*Against you, and you alone,* have I sinned;
I have done what is evil *in your sight.*
You will be proved right in what you say,
and your judgment against me is just.
⁵For I was born a sinner—
yes, from the moment my mother conceived me. (NLT)

This poet, who could very well have been David after his adultery with Bathsheba, is prepared to open his heart to God. He does not try to find excuses for his transgressions but confesses that what he did was wrong. He is prepared to reveal his inner feelings because he knows that God is merciful. Unlike our fellow human beings, to whom we are often afraid to reveal our feelings because experience has shown us that they might reject us or think badly of us, God will never turn His back on us when we open our hearts to Him.

It is unnecessary for you to be burdened with a sense of guilt. Instead, open your heart to someone you can trust—not just anybody.

 Thank You, Lord, that I can open my heart to You. Thank You that You will never reject me. Let Your Spirit help me to listen to the sorrows of others.

We're never so vulnerable than when we trust someone—but paradoxically,
if we cannot trust, neither can we find love or joy.
—Walter Anderson (1885–1962), *German ethnologist (folklorist)*

ARE WE BEING HONEST WITH OURSELVES?

We are not always honest with ourselves. Often, we are quick to find excuses for our mistakes and blame others for what goes wrong in our lives. Yet in this psalm, the poet is prepared to face his mistakes.

Psalm 51

⁶But you desire honesty from the womb,
teaching me wisdom even there.
⁷*Purify me from my sins,* and I will be clean;
wash me, and I will be whiter than snow.
⁸Oh, give me back my joy again;
you have broken me—
now let me rejoice. (NLT)

This poet (probably David after he committed adultery) uses repetition to emphasize the honesty with which he looks at himself. He realizes that his sin robbed him of his happiness and that God expects him to be honest with himself. He has a desire to know how God wants him to live his life.

So many of us have a smile on our face while our heart is being torn apart by our battle with sin. We are so concerned about how others want us to live that we follow a lifestyle that fits others' expectations. By doing this, however, we are merely maintaining an image.

If you want to live the way God wants you to live, you need to have integrity. Integrity means that your deeds reflect what is in your heart of hearts. Are you really a happy person? Truly? Are there things that bother you? Try to be honest with yourself when answering these questions. It might just be the beginning of the journey towards happiness and joy (v. 8) that you have been looking for.

 Lord, help me to be honest with myself. Thank You that I am able to talk to You. Help me to find a companion who can walk with me.

Honesty is the best policy. If I lose mine honor, I lose myself.
—William Shakespeare (1564–1616), *British poet and playwright*

DO WE SEE TOO LITTLE OF THIS?

There is something that we see very little of in today's complex life. This poet draws our attention to it.

Psalm 51

[11]Do not banish me from your presence,
and don't take your Holy Spirit from me.
[12]Restore to me the joy of your salvation,
and make me willing to obey you.
[13]Then I will teach your ways to rebels,
and they will return to you.
[14]Forgive me for shedding blood, O God who saves;
then I will joyfully sing of your forgiveness.
[15]Unseal my lips, O Lord,
that my mouth may praise you. (NLT)

The writer of Psalm 51 is greatly concerned about the lack of happiness he has experienced in his life. He turns to God in honesty and expresses his longings in prayer. There are many reasons why so many of us share this lack of happiness. Perhaps it is because we think that happiness is the result of the absence of pain and suffering. Perhaps we think that we will find happiness in worldly things. However, this poet realizes very well that happiness should be found elsewhere. He realizes that happiness is the result of living one's life in the presence of God. This is why he prays that the Holy Spirit should not be taken away from him (v. 13). He begs for salvation (v. 14), for deliverance and for triumph over his sins so that he can do what brings him happiness—praise the Lord (v. 15) because those who praise the Lord live!

 Thank You, Lord, that I can know that happiness comes from living in Your presence.

Happiness is not a state to arrive at, rather, a manner of traveling.
—Samuel Johnson (1709–1784), *British author*

THE UNGODLY LOOK SO HAPPY!

Christians should be happy and joyful people. However, sometimes it seems as if the people who are outside the Church are happier than those who are inside the Church. Where does the fault lie?

Psalm 73

[1]Truly God is good to Israel,
to those whose hearts are pure.
[2]But as for me, I almost lost my footing.
My feet were slipping, and I was almost gone.
[3]For I envied the proud
when I saw them prosper despite their wickedness.
[4]They seem to live such painless lives;
their bodies are so healthy and strong.
[16]So I tried to understand why the wicked prosper.
But what a difficult task it is!
[17]Then I went into your sanctuary, O God,
and I finally understood the destiny of the wicked.
[19]In an instant they are destroyed,
completely swept away by terrors. (NLT)

The writer of this psalm is very honest about his feelings. He cannot understand why things sometimes go well for the ungodly and so badly for the righteous. This causes tremendous religious doubt in him. It seems to him as if it is not worth his while to lead a pure life (v. 1). There is too much misfortune in his life.

We do not know what heartache this poet had to endure, but it bothers him that things do not go as well for him, a believer, as it does for those who lead an ungodly life. It seems as if the poet wants to trade places with the ungodly and that he has thought about this a lot in an attempt to reach an answer. Fortunately, the poem has a turning point (v. 17). The poet's questions are not answered, but he gains insight. He comes to the conclusion that the lives of the ungodly end in tragedy. He realizes that his happiness should not lie in earthly possessions, which are temporal, but in God.

A king from the East had a sentence engraved on his ring that would motivate him in all situations—whether he was walking through his treasure chambers or experiencing a bout of depression. The sentence was, "This too shall end." We should, therefore, look for happiness in God's goodness (v. 1), for His goodness will never come to an end.

 Father, forgive me for trying to find my happiness in earthly wealth. Thank You that I can look at life differently.

The search for happiness is one of the chief sources of unhappiness.
—Eric Hoffer (1902–1983), *American philosopher and author*

WHEN LIFE IS TOO HARD TO FACE

The poet of Psalm 73 writes about something we see around us each day and of which we all may have had firsthand experience: suffering! However, for this poet, suffering did not lead to his destruction but to his spiritual enrichment!

Psalm 73

¹³*Did I keep my heart pure* for nothing?
Did I keep myself innocent for no reason?
¹⁴I get nothing but *trouble all day long;*
every morning brings me pain.
¹⁵If I had really spoken this way to others,
I would have been a traitor to your people.
¹⁶So I tried to understand why the wicked prosper.
But what a difficult task it is!
¹⁷Then I went into your sanctuary, O God,
and I finally understood the destiny of the wicked.
¹⁸Truly, you put them on a slippery path
and send them sliding over the cliff to destruction.
²⁸But as for me, how good it is to be near God!
I have made the Sovereign Lord my shelter,
and I will tell everyone about the wonderful things you do. (NLT)

This poet did not look forward to getting up in the mornings. Life was just too terrible to face. Perhaps he lay awake at night because he could not take his mind off his suffering. His thoughts were preoccupied because he felt that his religion did not benefit him. He just could not understand why he, as a believer, had to suffer the way he did.

The repetition in verses 13 and 14 emphasizes this. Then in verse 17, we read about the turning point in his life. He stopped trying to understand why he was suffering and decided to start praying. By using prayer as a vehicle to express his feelings, he gained perspective about life. He realized that the ways of the ungodly were not worth his while, as their lives ended in tragedy. He shifted his focus from the prosperity of the ungodly to his relationship with God.

This is why, at the end of his struggle, he could confess that it was good for him to be near God. This insight and confession helped him to move forward with his life. The valuable experience of God's presence is often all we need.

 Thank You, Lord, that I can reveal my feelings and struggles to You in prayer. Thank You that Your valuable presence is a source of strength to me.

When you turn to God, you discover He has been facing you all the time.
—Zig Ziglar, *American motivational speaker and author*

WILL GOD REALLY FORGIVE US?

People can be so mean to each other and hurt each other by raking up things that happened in the past. Fortunately, God acts differently.

Psalm 103

[8]The Lord is compassionate and merciful,
slow to get angry and filled with unfailing love.
[9]He will not constantly accuse us,
nor remain angry forever.
[10]He does not punish us for all our sins;
he does not deal harshly with us, as we deserve.
[11]For his unfailing love toward those who fear him
is as great as the height of the heavens above the earth.
[12]He has removed our sins as far from us
as the east is from the west. (NLT)

Verses 8–9 of this psalm contain a wonderful description of God's nature—He does not hold our sins against us. When God is part of our lives, He is not concerned about our previous wrongdoings, nor does He hold it against us. In other words, God does not act the same way people would. People would easily say, "Watch out for that person. He/she has a bad past." Instead, God looks at our lives today without holding what we did in the past against us. He does not even think about our past sins, because He has forgotten them.

Verses 11–12 use two wonderful figures of speech to support this thought. God's total forgiveness and removal of our sins is like the distance between heaven and earth and between east and west—they will never meet. Therefore, we need not worry about the sins we have confessed. People may be cruel and keep on reminding us of them (and may even hold them against us), but not God. May the Lord help us to forgive others to such an extent that we will never use their sins and shortcomings against them, especially during an argument.

 Thank You, Father, for completely forgiving my sins and even forgetting them. I want to praise You for enabling me to free myself from my past. Help me to forgive others.

We pardon to the extent that we love.
—François de La Rochefoucauld (1613–1680), *French writer*

THE MANY QUESTIONS OF LIFE

We grapple with many questions about life on a daily basis. The book of Proverbs was written precisely to help us with this.

Proverbs 1 (wisdom literature)

²Their purpose is to teach people wisdom and discipline,
to help them understand the insights of the wise.
³Their purpose is to teach people to live disciplined
and successful lives,
to help them do what is right, just, and fair.
⁴*These proverbs will give insight* to the simple,
knowledge and discernment to the young.
⁷Fear of the Lord is the foundation of true knowledge,
but fools despise wisdom and discipline. (NLT)

A proverb is a short sentence that conveys a profound truth about life. According to Proverbs 1:2, its purpose is to teach us wisdom. What is wisdom? Wisdom is to live out the truth about life. Or, to put it differently, wisdom is faith in practice. All of us have, at one time or another, made wrong choices for which we have paid dearly. Normally, we react by saying, "I've learned my lesson. Next time I'll do differently." Wisdom teaches us to act correctly from the outset so that we need not make mistakes.

Mistakes cause so much chaos and disruption in one's life. The Israelites believed that everything in creation stood in relation to each other and that disruption of these relationships caused chaos. Compare this to the disturbance that occurs in nature when trees are felled or the pain and chaos caused when a marriage breaks apart. The order in creation came from God. This is why we read in verse 7 that knowledge starts with fearing (honoring) the Lord. To honor the Lord with our life will enable us to deal with the questions of life and make good choices. We will learn on our life journey that wisdom is not to have all the right answers but rather to ask the right questions.

 Lord, help me to always remember that wisdom begins in worshipping You.

One who asks a question is a fool for five minutes;
one who does not ask a question remains a fool forever.
—Chinese proverb

A COMPANION WHO WILL NEVER LET YOU DOWN!

Our companions will often let us down on life's journey. However, this section in Proverbs tells us about a companion who will never leave us in the lurch.

Proverbs 4 (wisdom literature)

⁴My father taught me,
Take my words to heart.
Follow my commands, and you will live.
⁵Get wisdom; develop good judgment.
Don't forget my words or turn away from them.
⁶*Don't turn your back on wisdom,* for she will protect you.
Love her, and she will guard you.
⁷Getting wisdom is the wisest thing you can do!
And whatever else you do, develop good judgment. (NLT)

In this passage, we read about a father who encourages his son to make wisdom his companion on life's journey. His father knows that wisdom will never let him down, for it will always be there to protect and keep him safe (v. 6). This is why his father has an earnest talk with him and urges him to make wisdom his companion. The young man's father knows what he is talking about. The truths of life that he teaches his son are what he tried and tested during his own life. He knows that this wisdom will help his son to truly live (v. 4).

We often cause our own sorrow. Why? Simply because we make the wrong decisions. We often speak too hastily, and once the words are uttered, we cannot retrieve them. It is like toothpaste that has been squeezed from its tube. Once it has been squeezed out, it can't be pushed back in. The sayings "It is no use crying over spilt milk" or "What's done is done" then ring true.

Wisdom will help you to be cautious about whom you share something confidential. It will enable you to think before you act and not be hasty in your actions. Who can teach you about this wisdom? It might be a good book, a friend or your parents. Regardless, do not wait another moment to make wisdom your companion.

 Lord, help me to act wisely in order to avoid getting hurt unnecessarily.

The next best thing to being wise oneself is to live in a circle of those who are.
—C.S. Lewis (1898–1963), *High-powered Oxford and Cambridge professor and perhaps the twentieth century's most famous convert to Christianity. Lewis was the creator of the Narnia series.*

IS WISDOM AGE-RELATED?

Are only those with grey hair wise? Can young people also be wise? The most important question to consider, however, is whether or not *we* are wise. The following section will help us to answer this question.

Proverbs 9 (wisdom literature)

[10]*Fear of the Lord* is the foundation of wisdom.
Knowledge of the Holy One results in good judgment.
[11]Wisdom *will multiply your days*
and add years to your life.
[12]If you become wise, *you will be the one to benefit.*
If you scorn wisdom, *you will be the one to suffer.* (NLT)

Wisdom is not the same as knowledge. Knowledge is merely knowing facts, such as two plus two equals four. Wisdom, on the other hand, helps us to apply that knowledge practically. But where do we start? Proverbs 9:10 states very clearly that wisdom starts with "the fear of the Lord."

It is evident from this that wisdom was a religious matter to ancient Israel. Wisdom was meant to clarify God's intentions in the world and in life. One could not see it spontaneously, because sin blinded humankind from seeing God's intentions for life. People become wise when they gain insight into God's intentions for life and give expression to it in their daily life.

One of my colleagues told the following endearing story about his granddaughter. After a visit from his children and grandchildren, he went to say farewell to them at the airport. He asked his granddaughter if he could pray that Jesus would accompany them on their journey. The four-year-old replied, "You don't need to pray, Grandpa, because the Spirit of Jesus is in my heart and is always with me." The young girl most likely did not understand completely what she said, but she had peace in her heart.

Such wisdom from a four-year-old gives one goosebumps. She could claim to be wise because she served the Lord. Wisdom, therefore, is not necessarily age-related. The important question is not are we wise, but rather do we serve the Lord. It is from there that wisdom flows.

 Thank You, Lord, that I can be wise by serving You. Lord, help me to live daily according to Your purpose. Thank You that it is possible for me to do this, even though I am still young.

Science is organized knowledge. Wisdom is organized life.
—Immanuel Kant (1724–1804), *German philosopher, widely regarded as one of the most influential thinkers of modern Europe*

WHAT IS OUR MOST PRECIOUS POSSESSION?

There are many diverse answers to this question. The next section teaches us what our most precious possession should be.

Proverbs 22 (wisdom literature)

¹Choose a good reputation *over great riches;*
being held in high esteem *is better than silver or gold.* (NLT)

There is nothing wrong with being rich and making money. Unfortunately, money has become an obsession to many people. There are different reasons for this, such as the following:

- People think that by having more money, others will think better of them.
- Many people experience a sense of worth when they accumulate wealth and find security in their wealth.
- Many grew up poor and are afraid of having to deal with that situation again.
- Others think that they can only be happy if they become rich.
- Some people have more honorable reasons—such as paying for their children's studies, helping missionaries or visiting family and friends who live far away.

The sad part is that people often neglect other important things in their pursuit of wealth and then have regrets later on. Many parents realize too late that they did not spend enough time with their children. This is often the cause of bad feelings (v. 1) and broken relationships in families. I once read something that had a great impact on me: "Success at work can never make up for failure at home." Children do not only need their parents' money but also their time and love.

People are also often prepared to sacrifice their principles in order to obtain wealth. It is sad to hear about all the dishonesty that exists in the world. So many honest people have been tempted to be dishonest in their drive for more money. One can easily get a reputation that is difficult to shed.

Wisdom teaches us that some things in life are more important than money. This truth is emphasized in verse 1. Our good name is our most precious possession. Look after it! If we live wisely, we need not worry about what people think of us.

 Lord, help me to always remember that my good name is more precious than great riches.

The legacy of heroes is the memory of a great name and the inheritance of a great example.
—Benjamin Disraeli (1804–1881), *British Prime Minister and novelist*

EVERY DOG HAS HIS OR HER DAY!

Many people tend to think that they are better than other people. One's pride can easily lead to one's fall. The following proverbs affirm this.

Proverbs (wisdom literature)

16 [18]First pride, *then the crash—*
the bigger the ego, *the harder the fall.*
18 [12]*Pride first,* then the crash,
but humility is precursor to honor.
29 [23]Pride *lands you flat on your face;*
humility *prepares you for honors.* (MSG)

Pride is the one trait that Proverbs highlights as something that should be avoided at all cost. The consequences of being arrogant are not very pleasant, as the repetition in the above verses above emphasizes.

We see these consequences very clearly in the life of Joseph. As a young man, he was full of pride. He also transgressed in other ways Proverbs warns us against: He was a conceited talebearer (Gen. 37:2; c.f. Prov. 25:9); he showed no discretion about when to talk and when to keep quiet (Gen. 37:2,5,9; c.f. Prov. 15:23); his words greatly angered his brothers (Gen 37:8; c.f. Prov 15:1); and he thought himself better than his brothers and told them that they would one day bow before him (Gen. 37:7,9; c.f. Prov. 27:2). But then the arrogant Joseph came to a fall. His brothers threw him in a well and later sold him as a slave to the Ishmaelites. He did not live according to the instructions of Proverbs, and his day of reckoning soon came.

But is this how the story ends? Fortunately not! Joseph reached great heights in Egypt. The secret is that he started living according to the instructions of Proverbs. He resisted the advances of Potiphar's immoral wife (Gen. 39:7–9; c.f. Prov. 23:27), spoke at the right time (Gen. 40:12, 8; 41:25; c.f. Prov 15:23), exercised self-control (Gen. 42:24; 43:30–31; c.f. Prov 16:32) and, in time, made plans for the provision of food (Gen. 41:36; c.f. Prov 20:4). Wisdom was the reason for having life after his downfall!

 Lord, help me to be humble. Forgive me if I am arrogant.

The doors of wisdom are never shut.
—Benjamin Franklin (1706–1790), *American statesman, scientist and philosopher*

SMALL IN STATURE BUT BIG AT HEART!

We often hear extraordinary stories of people who had success because they used the opportunities that came their way and were creative in exceptional ways. We sometimes feel that this only happens to others and not to us. We feel small and insignificant. This section in Proverbs will help us to think differently.

Proverbs 30 (wisdom literature)

²⁴ Four things on earth are small,
yet they are exceedingly wise:
²⁵ the ants are a people without strength,
yet they provide their food in the summer;
²⁶ the badgers are a people without power,
yet they make their homes in the rocks;
²⁷ the locusts have no king,
yet all of them march in rank;
²⁸ the lizard can be grasped in the hand,
yet it is found in kings' palaces. (NRSV)

The four types of small animals listed in this passage have one thing in common: they are small and insignificant but nevertheless successful. The secret of their success does not lie in their strength or importance—they are not the kind of animals that will attract people to game parks to see them—but in the fact that they are wise and sensible.

Ants plan according to the seasons. They gather enough food before the onset of the cold winters. Ants can teach us about planning and to prepare thoroughly so that we will have enough when we need it. *Badgers* dance on the cliffs. They are defenseless but wise enough to realize that they can reach places that the mighty elephant cannot reach. The badger can teach us to position ourselves correctly in relation to what is stronger and more influential than us. *Locusts* are perfect team members. No one takes the lead among them, but—like a well organized army—they fearlessly proceed en masse. They can teach us that cooperation leads to great success. *Lizards* inhabit palaces. They know that they can get through small openings to reach important places. We can learn from lizards to spot the gaps and opportunities life has to offer and use them.

If you feel small and insignificant, the secret is to live wisely!

 Thank You, Lord, that wisdom can help me to live successfully.

The sublimity of wisdom is to do those things living that are desired when dying.
—Author unknown

WHAT DOES A DREAM WOMAN LOOK LIKE?

For many men, a dream woman is a beautiful woman who is well proportioned. Others think that the ideal woman (as portrayed in the Bible) is one who remains in the background and keeps herself busy with domestic duties and activities. Let's have a look at what Proverbs says.

Proverbs 31 (wisdom literature)

²⁸Her children stand *and bless her.*
Her husband *praises her:*
²⁹ 'There are many virtuous and capable women in the world,
but you surpass them all!'
³⁰Charm is deceptive, and beauty does not last;
but a woman who fears the Lord will be greatly praised.
³¹ Reward her for all she has done.
Let her deeds publicly declare her praise. (NLT)

The book of Proverbs contains a lot about women. It is, therefore, appropriate that the book should conclude with a description of the ideal woman—the dream woman. According to Proverbs, the dream woman is not necessarily the one with the right vital statistics (verse 30 emphasizes this by saying that looks do not last forever). Rather, the dream woman is a producer, an importer, a manager, a landowner, a farmer, a seamstress, an upholsterer and a trader. She is more than a housewife. Her strength and skills stem from her devotion to the Lord (v. 30).

It is interesting to note that her looks are not mentioned anywhere. Today, a lot of emphasis is placed on a woman's appearance, but according to Proverbs, beauty comes from inside. Also, note that this woman in Proverbs 31 is most probably a compound image of a dream woman. You should, therefore, not try to imitate all her glory—your day will be too short to do this. Instead, this woman should be seen as an inspiration to reach your full potential.

 Lord, thank You that the Bible describes the dream woman in such refreshing and exciting terms.

The strength of women comes from the fact that psychology cannot explain us.
Men can be analyzed, women merely adored.
—Oscar Wilde (1854–1900), *Irish poet and dramatist*

EVERYTHING SEEMS SO MEANINGLESS!

Today's society is characterized by an increasing amount of people who are depressed and desperate. Many people fail to see the meaning of life. People who feel this way have a kindred spirit in the Bible in the book of Ecclesiastes. Twenty-two centuries ago, the author of Ecclesiastes came to the conclusion that everything is utterly meaningless. Can we learn something from him?

Ecclesiastes 1 (wisdom literature)

²'Meaningless! Everything is meaningless!'
says the Teacher.
'Everything is completely meaningless!
Nothing has any meaning.'
³What does a man get for all of his work?
Why does he work so hard on this earth?
⁴People come and people go.
But the earth remains forever.
⁵The sun rises. Then it sets.
And then it hurries back to where it rises.
⁶The wind blows to the south.
Then it turns to the north.
Around and around it goes.
It always returns to where it started.
⁷Every stream flows into the ocean.
But the ocean never gets full.
The streams return
to the place they came from. (NIRV)

"Everything is meaningless" is a main theme of the book that weaves through each chapter like a golden thread. These are the words of a man who apparently "had it all." He had every reason to feel good about his life, but pessimism reigns as he asks, "What does a man get for all of his work?" (v. 3). His conclusion is that everything is a senseless chasing after wind.

The author feels that even nature shows signs of meaninglessness. The sun, the wind and rivers follow the same pattern day after day in a senseless cycle of events. The question we need to ask is whether we should read such a cynical book in a time that already reflects so much despair. The answer is yes, we should, because the author challenges us to think about life—our own lives. The wisdom he gives us is something he only came to realize late in life: we need to "fear God and obey his commands, for this is everyone's duty" (12:13, NLT).

Although the writer of Ecclesiastes was very cynical, he was honest with himself. He realized that the things we so readily pursue (money and possessions) often boils down to chasing after the wind. Is there perhaps truth in this?

 Lord, teach me to be honest with myself and not to stop seeking an honest life with You.

Ever more people today have the means to live, but no meaning to live for.
—Victor Frankl (1905–1997), *Austrian psychiatrist and psychotherapist*

ARE WE LEFT TO OUR OWN FATE?

Slogans can be very motivating. One of the most well known is "carpe diem," which means "seize the opportunity." This piece of wisdom tells us that we can determine our own destiny. Is this true? Let us see!

Ecclesiastes 3 (wisdom literature)

¹For everything there is a season,
a time for every activity under heaven.
²A time to be born +
and a time to die.-
A time to plant and a time to harvest. +
³A time to kill-
and a time to heal. +
A time to tear down-
and a time to build up. +
⁴A time to cry-
and a time to laugh. +
A time to grieve-
and a time to dance. +
⁹What does the worker get for his hard work? (NLT)

This must be one of the most well known—yet also the most misunderstood—sections in Ecclesiastes. According to the wisdom of the time, this section would have been interpreted as carpe diem—seize the opportunity! This is also the popular interpretation of this section. However, this is not what the author intended. In fact, he meant exactly the opposite: We are unable to seize the opportunities because they are too unpredictable. Instead, the opportunities seize us and upset our lives.

The artful composition of the poem emphasizes precisely this fact. The poem moves between the positive (+) and the negative (-) aspects of life that we cannot control (e.g., death). Opportunities do come our way, but they can be completely ruined by unfortunate events such as injury, illness or even death. This is why Ecclesiastes concludes with the rhetorical question in verse 9: "What does the worker get for his hard work?" The answer to this question is nothing at all!

Through these verses, the author showed the wise people of his time that their wisdom of carpe diem was not the only slogan about life. Much more was at stake! He was much too realistic about faith. Perhaps the following prayer by Niebuhr, an American theologian, would have been meaningful to him:

> *God, grant me the serenity to accept the things I cannot change, the courage to change the things I can, and the wisdom to know the difference.*
> —Reinhold Niebuhr (1892–1971), *American theologian*

IS THE AUTHOR OF ECCLESIASTES TOO PESSIMISTIC?

The main theme of Ecclesiastes (everything is meaningless) indicates that the author was very pessimistic. He was very honest with himself and did not hesitate to question the prevalent beliefs of his time. He can teach us to be honest with ourselves. But was he not perhaps too pessimistic? Let's take a look.

Ecclesiastes 3 (wisdom literature-explanation)

[18]I also thought about the human condition—how God proves to people that they are like animals. [19]For people and animals share the same fate—both breathe and both must die. So people have no real advantage over the animals. How meaningless! [20]Both go to the same place—they came from dust and they return to dust. [21]For who can prove that the human spirit goes up and the spirit of animals goes down into the earth? (NLT)

This section reaffirms the author's pessimism. He is pessimistic because he feels that the destiny of good and bad people is the same as that of the animals. We can gather from his rhetorical question (v. 19) that the breath of both human beings and animals go to the same place: downwards.

From this, you might think the author is manic-depressive and in need of an antidepressant, but if you understand where he comes from, you might be more sympathetic. He lived during a period when God's relationship with humankind was seen in a negative light. God was a remote and superior God, removed from human beings and their daily lot. For this reason, he felt that human beings were exposed to an uncertain and unfair life (Eccles. 11:1–6).

Fortunately, we see things differently. We know that God is not remote but that He became human in Christ. Although the author of Ecclesiastes does not think much of being human, we know that many other biblical writers thought differently (Gen. 1:26; Ps. 8:6; Prov. 4:7–9). Indeed, God became human in Christ to change our Ecclesiastes experiences of hopeless ends to endless hope. Yes, the author of Ecclesiastes might have been too pessimistic, but he never turned his back on God. How did this help him? He believed that God was the creator and giver of life.

 Thank You, Lord, that I can know that You have a high regard for human life and that You are with us!

Pessimism is an excuse for not trying and a guarantee to a personal failure.
—Bill Clinton (b. 1946), *Forty-second President of the United States (1993–2001)*

IS MONEY THE KEY TO HAPPINESS?

We all strive to be happy, but judging by all the sadness around us, it seems that we are not very successful in attaining it. Many people believe that money leads to happiness. But is this the case? Let's see what the author of Ecclesiastes says.

Ecclesiastes 5 (wisdom literature)

¹⁰*Anyone who loves money* never has enough.
Anyone who loves wealth is never satisfied with what he gets.
That doesn't have any meaning either.
¹¹As more and more goods are made,
more and more people use them up.
So how can those goods benefit their owner?
All he can do is look at them with longing.
¹²The sleep of a worker is sweet.
It doesn't matter whether he eats a little or a lot.
But the wealth of a rich man
keeps him awake at night. (NIRV)

As we discussed yesterday, the theme of the book of Ecclesiastes (that everything is meaningless) gave the author the reputation of being a pessimist. But in this case, we have to concede that his judgment of money is realistic. He warns us in these three proverbs that the pursuit of money does not lead to happiness—in fact, the contrary is more often true.

The author gives us several reasons why he believes this to be the case. First, we will never reach the point in which we will feel that we have enough money (v. 9). Second, others (such as family and friends) will normally use up our money (v. 10). Third, it is often the very rich who will have sleepless nights about money (v. 11).

When you chase after money, you become like money—cold and clinical. Those who do not have money are normally the ones who think that money will bring them happiness. However, happiness does not reside in things, but in good human relations—everywhere you go and belong! At most, money can bring comfort, but not true happiness.

 "O God, I beg two favors from you; let me have them before I die. First, help me never to tell a lie. Second, give me neither poverty nor riches! Give me just enough to satisfy my needs. For if I grow rich, I may deny you and say, 'Who is the Lord?' And if I am too poor, I may steal and thus insult God's holy name"

—Prov. 30:7–9, NLT

True happiness brings more richness than all the money in the world.
—Author unknown

DON'T TALK ABOUT DEATH!

Understandably, most of us would rather attend a wedding than a funeral. A funeral confronts us with a reality that we often do not want to talk about: death. However, the author of Ecclesiastes likes to talk about death, although some of the conclusions he draws will make us frown. Let's look at what he writes.

Ecclesiastes 7 (wisdom literature)

[1]A good reputation *is more valuable than costly perfume.*
And the day you die *is better than the day you are born.*
[2]Better to spend your time at funerals than at parties.
After all, everyone dies—
so the living should take this to heart.
[3]Sorrow is better than laughter,
for sadness has a refining influence on us.
[4]A wise person *thinks a lot about death,*
while a fool *thinks only about having a good time.* (NLT)

In this section, the author's pessimism again reigns supreme. Four times he uses the words "better than" to affirm that for him, death is better than life. In verse 1, he uses parallels to represent life and death: "A good reputation" and "the day you die" are metaphors for death, while "fine perfume" and "the day of birth" are metaphors for life. He uses poetry to say that death (a good name and the day of death) is better than life (perfume and the day of birth). He therefore prefers the day of death to the day of birth, the house of mourning to the house of feasting, and sorrow to laughter.

Why would this author choose death above life? First, he sees death as a certainty in an uncertain world. Second, he knows that death will free him from life's pain and sorrow, although in no way does he encourage suicide or romanticize death. Basically, he wants to say two things about death: (1) death is a certainty in this life; and (2) the dead have the advantage in that they are freed from the toil of a senseless existence.

During the time of this author, people believed that there was no life after death. Fortunately, we know that these proverbs are not the final or only word about death in the Bible. However, these verses teach us to speak about death with honesty and respect.

 Lord, thank You that the author of Ecclesiastes helps me to speak about death in an honest way.

If a man hasn't discovered something that he will die for, he isn't fit to live.
—Martin Luther King, Jr. (1929–1968), *American Baptist minister, civil rights leader and winner of the Nobel Prize in 1964*

LIFE DOESN'T MAKE SENSE!

Many of us have uttered the words, "I don't understand life." It often seems that bad things happen to good people and good things happen to those who do not deserve it. During the time of the author of Ecclesiastes, the sages always had answers to all of life's questions—as if they understood God completely. The author of Ecclesiastes had a problem with this. You might agree with him!

Ecclesiastes 8 (wisdom literature-explanation)

[16]In my search for wisdom and in my observation of people's burdens here on earth, I discovered that there is ceaseless activity, day and night. [17]I realized that no one can discover everything God is doing under the sun. Not even the wisest people discover everything, no matter what they claim. (NLT)

The author struggled for a long time to understand the meaning of true wisdom. What did he discover? Human beings are unable to fully understand life. He emphasizes this insight in verse 17.

The author comes to the conclusion that one cannot understand everything. First, one cannot understand everything that happens in the world (for example, why innocent people are brutally murdered). Second, one has to admit that all of his efforts to understand things better are fruitless. Third, although one can say that he understands everything (like the sages of the time), one can never truly know everything. The author realizes that he himself can never know everything.

This insight thrills me. We always think that we must have the answers to all of life's questions, but this is not the case! Unfortunately, many believers sometimes create the impression that they know everything. They tend to give people who are in need easy solutions and answers. Instant answers seldom comfort those in need—in fact, they immerse others in more gloom and doom.

People often find believers who thrive on instant answers cold and unsympathetic. People who are in need do not always look for answers but rather for someone who will lend them an ear. Although they do not understand everything, it helps them if someone listens to them carefully and sympathetically.

 Thank You, Lord, that the author of Ecclesiastes makes me aware of the fact that I do not have to understand everything in life. Help me to listen more instead of trying to provide all the answers.

Confidence, like art, never comes from having all the answers;
it comes from being open to all the questions.
—Author unknown

AGING IS NOT FOR COWARDS!

I have the privilege to work with senior citizens quite often. After each discussion, I realize anew that getting old poses many difficulties. After you have read the next section, you will realize that aging is not for cowards.

Ecclesiastes 12 (wisdom literature)

[1]Remember your Creator
in the days of your youth,
before the days of trouble come
and the years approach when you will say,
'I find no pleasure in them'—
[2]before the sun and the light
and the moon and the stars grow dark,
and the clouds return after the rain;
[3]when the keepers of the house tremble,
and the strong men stoop,
when the grinders cease because they are few,
and those looking through the windows grow dim;
[4]when the doors to the street are closed
and the sound of grinding fades;
when people rise up at the sound of birds,
but all their songs grow faint; (TNIV)

In the above passage, the author uses vivid imagery in writing about aging. In verse 2, he describes the winter rains of Palestine: wet and depressing. This is what aging means to him. In verse 3, he describes how a person's limbs deteriorate one after the other. The "keepers" refer to the arms and hands, which previously protected the person when he fell but have now become shaky. The "strong men" refer to the legs, which walked tall and upright but now start to stagger. The "grinders" describe the teeth that chewed all the food but now, because there are few of them left, are no longer able to do that properly. The "windows" are the eyes that can no longer see as well and as far as before, making the world seem as if it has become a dark place. Verse 4 tells us about the ears: they can no longer hear distinctly what goes on in the streets. The "sound of grinding" is the voice, which has become old and faint. Aging is not easy. For this reason, the author suggests in verse 1 that the best time to establish our relationship with God is in our youth.

 Thank You, Lord, for all the young people who know You. Thank You for all the senior citizens who have known You since their childhood.

When I was young I felt I had to carry the gospel; now that I am old
I know that the gospel carries me.
—Martin Niemoeller (1892–1984), *A prominent German anti-Nazi theologian and Lutheran pastor*

IS DEATH THE END OF EVERYTHING?

Nothing is more *certain* than death, and nothing is more *uncertain* than the exact time when death will occur. Death shows no mercy toward the poor and does not respect the rich. Death spares no one. Let's read what the author of Ecclesiastes says about death.

Ecclesiastes 12 (wisdom literature)

¹Remember the One who created you.
Remember him while you are still young.
Think about him before your times of trouble come.
The years will come when you will say,
'I don't find any pleasure in them.'
⁶Remember your Creator before the silver cord is cut.
That's when the golden bowl will be broken.
The wheel will be broken at the well.
The pitcher will be smashed at the spring.
⁷Remember your Creator before you return to the dust you came from.
That's when your spirit will go back to God who gave it.
⁸'Meaningless! Everything is meaningless!'
says the Teacher.
'Nothing has any meaning.' (NIRV)

In the last verse of Ecclesiastes, the author sketches death. To him, the death of a person is like the breaking of a precious silver cord or an irreplaceable golden bowl. The "golden bowl" that breaks at the fountain and the "broken wheel" at the well paint a sad picture of worthlessness. The broken bowl cannot carry water, and the broken wheel cannot draw the water. The silver cord, the bowl, the pitcher and the wheel are symbols of life's transience and frailty. Once these items are broken, they become useless and without meaning. This is what happens to human life when a person dies.

The author sees death as an affirmation that life is meaningless. Death is merely the completion of a cycle. When death arrives, dust becomes dust again, and the spirit returns to God—meaning that God, as creator, gives life (Eccles. 11:5) and receives it back again at the end. This is why the author ends his letter with the same theme he started it with: "Everything is meaningless."

To the author of Ecclesiastes, there was no life after death. He lived before the resurrection of Jesus and his vision was limited. Fortunately, we do not believe that everything is meaningless, because the resurrection of Jesus has conquered death. "Since, then, you have been raised with Christ, set your hearts on things above, where Christ is seated at the right hand of God" (Col. 3:1, TNIV).

 Thank You, Lord, that I can know that everything is not meaningless and that You give life.

I'm not afraid to die, I just don't want to be there when it happens.
—Woody Allen (b. 1935), *American director, actor and comedian*

HOW CAN OUR HAPPINESS IN LOVE GROW?

Most songs are about love—specifically, about love that has suffered loss. We all seek after love but often stumble in our search. The pain of love that has failed can be a bitter pill to swallow. So, how can our happiness in love blossom to maturity? There are many answers to this question. This section in Song of Solomon contains a handy tip.

Song of Solomon 2 (wisdom literature)

³Like the finest apple tree in the orchard
is my lover among other young men.
I sit in his delightful shade
and taste his delicious fruit.
⁴ He escorts me to the banquet hall;
it's obvious how much he loves me.
⁵ *Strengthen me* with raisin cakes,
refresh me with apples,
for I am weak with love.
⁶ *His left arm* is under my head,
and his right arm embraces me.
⁷Promise me, O women of Jerusalem,
by the gazelles and wild deer,
not to awaken love until the time is right. (NLT)

In this passage, the poet tells us about a passionate encounter between two lovers. The woman describes how her lover stands out above all the other men (v. 3). She feels safe with him ("I sit in his delightful shade") and enjoys his caresses ("and taste his delicious fruit."). She finds this experience of love so overwhelming that she needs sustenance (raisins and apples). Her romantic encounter culminates in the warm embrace (v. 6).

The woman interrupts her description of the encounter by asking the women of Jerusalem, her imaginary interlocutors, for a favor. Her earnest request contains an important tip for relationships: "not to awaken love until the time is right." These words mean that happiness that flows from love should develop spontaneously. It should not be forced, nor should it ripen prematurely.

Love ripens prematurely when the *passion* of the embrace/caress is stronger than the *union* and commitment to each other. Our emotions and union have to develop in unison. This will let the happiness of love grow!

 Lord, help me to create space for love's happiness to grow.

The sound of a kiss is not so loud as a cannon, but its echo lasts a great deal longer!
—Author unknown

RELATIONSHIPS ON AUTOPILOT

When relationships become routine, loved ones tend to stop appreciating each other. The spark of the relationship is just not there anymore, and it seems as if the relationship has switched on autopilot. What can be done about this? Let's read the following section.

Song of Solomon 4 (wisdom literature)

¹You are beautiful, my darling,
beautiful beyond words.
Your eyes are like doves
behind your veil.
Your hair falls in waves,
like a flock of goats winding down the slopes of Gilead.
²*Your teeth* are as white as sheep,
recently shorn and freshly washed.
Your smile is flawless,
each tooth matched with its twin.
³*Your lips* are like scarlet ribbon;
your mouth is inviting.
Your cheeks are like rosy pomegranates
behind your veil.
⁴*Your neck* is as beautiful as the tower of David,
jeweled with the shields of a thousand heroes.
⁵*Your breasts* are like two fawns,
twin fawns of a gazelle grazing among the lilies.
⁶Before the dawn breezes blow
and the night shadows flee,
I will hurry to the mountain of myrrh
and to the hill of frankincense.
⁷You are altogether beautiful, my darling,
beautiful in every way. (NLT)

In this passage, the man's relationship has spark. He compares his lover's body to objects that were indisputably beautiful to the people of that time. He starts with the eyes, and then gradually moves down to her lips, neck and her breasts. He takes pleasure in her body without becoming perverse. He admires her in minute detail and draws the conclusion that everything about her is beautiful. His lover felt his *admiration and appreciation*. This is the best medicine for a relationship that is on autopilot.

 Lord, help me to express my appreciation for my beloved.

Appreciation is a wonderful thing. It makes what is excellent in others belong to us as well.
—Voltaire (1694–1778), *French philosopher and writer—one of the greatest of all French authors*

WHY DOES LOVE FADE SO EASILY?

In this world of violence and hate, it is wonderful to witness the love between two people. It is like an oasis in the desert. But the excitement, the romance and the love can easily fade. She notices that there are fewer flowers and text messages, and he finds that the sparkle in her eyes has disappeared. He no longer opens the car door for her, and she does not sit on his lap anymore. Why does this happen? This section might give us an answer.

Song of Solomon 6 (wisdom literature)

> ¹¹I went down to the grove of walnut trees
> and out to the valley to see the new spring growth,
> to see whether the grapevines had budded
> or the pomegranates were in bloom.
> ¹²Before I realized it,
> I found myself in the royal chariot with my beloved. (NLT)

After the man's ode to his beloved (Song of Sol. 6:4–10), he longs to be near her. The grove of walnut trees represents a grove of love. In those days, nuts were considered the food of love. Like trees that blossom and grow, he wants to experience the growth of their relationship in his grove of love. When he meets his lover, he is overwhelmed by the ecstasy of love and is beside himself with joy. He feels as exited as a hero who rides on a chariot in a procession.

It is God's intention that we experience this excitement in our lives. This excitement should be nurtured, because it can fade so easily after the initial excitement of marriage. Perhaps this is why many people see marriage as the ultimate destination rather than the gateway to a new life. Lovers spend so much time and money on a wedding feast, planning every detail, but then quickly forget that this is merely the first step on a new journey. They easily spend money on a wedding but are reluctant to spend money on an enrichment seminar.

Marriage often means the end of our consideration for each other: we no longer give flowers, open the car door or watch our weight (someone once remarked that she was illegally married to a part of her husband—the 66 pounds he gained after they got married!). However, marriage is really the gateway to a new life that should be lived one step at a time. On this road, we will encounter challenges, new bridges that we will have to cross and new pitfalls. This journey, with all its surprising experiences, should not be taken for granted. It entails more work than the wedding feast. May we experience the sparkle of love!

 Lord, help me to work hard at my relationship so that I can prevent it from weakening.

Love, like a river, will cut a new path whenever it meets an obstacle.
—Crystal Middlemas

WHERE DOES SEX FIT IN?

Nowadays, people write and speak openly about sex. However, I believe that if we want to talk about sex in a meaningful way, we need to have clarity about the following question: Where does sex fit in? Let's have a look!

Song of Solomon 7 (wisdom literature)

⁶Oh, how beautiful you are!
How pleasing, my love, how full of delights!
⁷You are slender like a palm tree,
and your breasts are like its clusters of fruit.
⁸I said, 'I will climb the palm tree
and take hold of its fruit.'
May your breasts be like grape clusters,
and the fragrance of your breath like apples.
⁹May your kisses be as exciting as the best wine,
flowing gently over lips and teeth.
¹⁰I am my lover's,
and he claims me as his own. (NLT)

In this section, the lover makes it very clear that he wants to have sex with his partner. He yearns for her body and wants to caress her breasts. When she kisses him, it resembles the smell of apples and the taste of good wine—too wonderful! This union of love is exciting and special because it is exclusive. He is the only one who has the privilege to enjoy his lover's body. She does not hold back anything, because she experiences love and feels excited because he desires her and nobody else (v. 10).

Three words sum up their feelings on sex: *love*, *trust* and *longevity*. If either of these three is absent, sexuality cannot really flourish. How many people have not regretted the fact that they had sex when they were too young? So many people have been disillusioned because they thought that sex would guarantee their happiness.

Sex is intimate and should be protected, and love, trust and longevity create the ideal environment in which this can occur. Although this passage does not mention marriage, common sense tells us that marriage creates the best situation in which love, trust and longevity can be guaranteed. Sex was a wonderful experience for the couple in the Song of Solomon because love, trust and longevity were featured in their relationship. Where do you stand on this?

 Lord, help me to focus on love, trust and longevity in my own relationship.

Love knows no limit to its longevity, no end to its trust, no fading of its hope; it can outlast anything.
Love still stands when all else has fallen.
—The Apostle Paul, *1 Corinthians 13:7–8 (Phillips)*

WHO SHOULD TAKE THE INITIATIVE IN LOVEMAKING?

Many couples experience frustration in who should take the initiative in lovemaking, which can lead to immense tension in their relationships. Complaints such as the following often reflect this frustration:

- You only think about sex.
- You think I am only good for sex.
- Sometimes, I just want to be embraced.
- You always say, "I'm just too tired tonight."
- I always have to take the initiative.

Let's focus on the last complaint. Who should take the initiative? Taking a look at the couple in the Song of Solomon might help us to find the answer to this question.

Song of Solomon 7 (wisdom literature)

[10]I am my lover's,
and he claims me as his own.
[11]Come, my love, let us go out to the fields
and spend the night among the wildflowers.
[12]Let us get up early and go to the vineyards
to see if the grapevines have budded,
if the blossoms have opened,
and if the pomegranates have bloomed.
There I will give you my love.
[13]There the mandrakes give off their fragrance,
and the finest fruits are at our door,
new delights as well as old,
which I have saved for you, my lover. (NLT)

In this section, the woman takes the initiative in lovemaking because she feels that she is being appreciated. In the previous section, her lover told her how beautiful she was and that she was very special to him. In this passage, the poet does not suggest who should take the initiative but instead shows that appreciation for each other should never fade. The vineyards, pomegranate trees, mandrakes and fruit are metaphors for the act of lovemaking. It must have been a wonderful experience for the man to know that he was the only person who could eat of the fruit of his beloved (v. 13). Love, trust and longevity ensure that both lovers will feel free to take the initiative.

 Lord, teach me to be more appreciative of my beloved.

There is more hunger for love and appreciation in this world than for bread.
—Mother Teresa of Calcutta (1910–1997), *Albanian born Indian missionary, founder of the Order of the Missionaries of Charity and winner of the Nobel Prize for Peace in 1979*

HOW DO WE ENSURE INTIMACY?

We all yearn for intimacy. Knowing that we are loved and feeling that we are appreciated and cherished gives meaning to our lives. Yet in reality, many people experience rejection and loneliness. This is so unnecessary! Why did the couple in the Song of Solomon experience intimacy? Let's read and find out.

Song of Solomon 8 (wisdom literature)

[5]Who is this sweeping in from the desert,
leaning on her lover?
I aroused you under the apple tree,
where your mother gave you birth,
where in great pain she delivered you.
[6]*Place me like a seal* over your heart,
like a seal on your arm.
For love is as strong *as death*,
its jealousy as enduring *as the grave*.
Love flashes like fire,
the brightest kind of flame.
[7]*Many waters* cannot quench love,
nor can rivers drown it.
If a man tried to buy love
with all his wealth,
his offer would be utterly scorned. (NLT)

The love of the couple described in the Song of Solomon blossoms to full maturity. As they come in from the desert, she leans on him and experiences his support. Then the focus shifts to the woman, who thinks back to the awakening of his love for her. The phrase "your mother gave you birth" implies that it started in his home. She continues by asking her bridegroom a big favor: "*Place me like a seal* over your heart, *like a seal* on your arm." (v. 6).

In the ancient world, a man's signet ring was like a signature. It belonged to him exclusively and was, therefore, his most precious possession. The woman's request implies that she wants to feel safe with him, which requires his trust. Why would she ask this if things were going so well in their relationship? Because intimacy between two people has the potential that someone will get hurt.

True intimacy will make you vulnerable because the other person will know everything about you. This vulnerability should be protected, but you can only protect this vulnerability if there is mutual trust. This is why you should not rush into a relationship. You have to make sure that the degree of intimacy coincides with the degree of commitment to the relationship. You will only get hurt if you allow the other person to take you to a level of intimacy for which he or she is not prepared. Protect yourself by following the degree of commitment.

 Lord, help me to protect intimacy through commitment.

Stay committed to your decisions, but stay flexible in your approach.
—Tom Robbins (b. 1936), *American novelist*

DOES SEX HAVE TO WAIT FOR MARRIAGE?

In the past, sex was not discussed openly, but today the subject is discussed with ease. A lot of focus is placed on sexual matters in today's society. Films and magazines are flooded with it. It is disturbing to see how many young people become sexually active at a very early age. Premature sex can be harmful. Young people tend to confuse sex and love, and sexually transmitted diseases are on the increase worldwide. To be a virgin in modern times means to be a bit out of date. So, is it still worthwhile to wait until marriage to have sex? This section will help you find out.

Song of Solomon 8 (wisdom literature)

⁸We have a little sister
too young to have breasts.
What will we do for our sister
if someone asks to marry her?
⁹*If she is a virgin, like a wall,*
we will protect her with a silver tower.
But if she is promiscuous, like a swinging door,
we will block her door with a cedar bar.
¹⁰I was a virgin, like a wall;
now my breasts are like towers.
When my lover looks at me,
he is delighted with what he sees. (NLT)

The woman in the Song of Solomon remembers how her brothers watched out for her when she was young (when her breasts were still undeveloped). Two opposing images symbolize what her brothers did for her. If she remained pure and like a wall protected herself from lustful men, her brothers would honor her by decorating the wall with towers of silver. However, if she was like a door that allowed men entry, her brothers would board up the door with panels of cedar wood.

This woman had wonderful brothers to keep such a watchful eye on her. She sets their minds at ease in verse 10 when she tells them that she is like a wall. She is a grown woman (her breasts are like towers) who has lived a sexually pure life. This bears fruit, because she is able to give herself wholeheartedly to her bridegroom.

It is rewarding to follow her example. A young girl who was under peer pressure to give up her virginity once defended herself by saying to her friends, "I can become like you at any time, but you can never be like me again." Naturally, the same applies to men! Sexual impurity has caused so much pain. Wait to have sex until you are married—you are worth it!

 Lord, please give the strength to live a sexually pure life.

Sex within marriage is the only kind that's truly fun and exciting—
the kind that lasts for a lifetime. I'm glad I waited.
—Kirk Cameron (b. 1970), *American actor*

OUR FIFTH STOP: THE DIVIDED KINGDOM

(925–586 B.C.)
(1 Kings 12–2 Kings 25, 2 Chronicles 10–36, Jonah, Amos, Hosea, Isaiah 1–39, Micah, Nahum, Zephaniah, Jeremiah, Lamentations, Habakkuk, Obadiah, Isaiah 40–66)

Unfortunately, the once-united kingdom of Israel split into two. How did this happen? It all started with Solomon. On the surface, his kingdom appeared to be very prosperous. Unlike David, he did not engage in battle to enlarge his territory but used trade and marriages to wives from other nations to increase his power. His accumulated wealth contributed to his fame. Even the Queen of Sheba paid him a visit and was overwhelmed by his wealth and wisdom.

For tax purposes, Solomon divided his land into different administrative regions, each with its own governor. Sad to say, his wisdom did not prevent him from making basic mistakes. The people became embittered because of all the hard labor Solomon enforced and the heavy taxes he imposed on them to generate money for his building projects. He even began worshipping the foreign gods that his wives worshiped. The Bible states that because of this, "The Lord was very angry with Solomon, for his heart had turned away from the Lord, the God of Israel, who had appeared to him twice" (1 Kings 11:9, NLT).

THE KINGDOM IS DIVIDED (925 B.C.)

After Solomon's death, a delegation from the people went to visit his son Rehoboam to ask him whether he was prepared to relieve their burden. After discussing it with his advisors, he answered, "My father laid heavy burdens on you, but I'm going to make them even heavier! My father beat you with whips, but I will beat you with scorpions!" (1 Kings 12:14, NLT).

The southern tribes, whom Solomon had treated better, remained loyal to Rehoboam. However, Rehoboam's threats became too much for the northern tribes, and they broke away in 925 B.C. to form an independent kingdom under the reign of Jeroboam, an official in Solomon's court. The Northern Kingdom retained the name "Israel," while the Southern Kingdom became known as

"Judah." Israel had more territory and wealth, but it was situated on an important trade route and was therefore exposed to attacks from other nations.

In short, Solomon's disobedience caused the division of the kingdom. The Northern Kingdom (Israel) consisted of 10 tribes and had 19 kings before they were taken into exile by Assyria. All 19 kings committed evil. The Southern Kingdom (Judah) consisted of 2 tribes and had 20 kings before they were taken into exile by Babylon. Eight of the 20 kings were good, while 12 were bad.

THE END OF THE NORTHERN KINGDOM (722 B.C.)

The Assyrians lived in the region between the Tigris and the Euphrates rivers (modern-day Iraq) during most of the Old Testament period. The Assyrian kingdom came into being in 900 B.C. and soon blossomed into a mighty empire. The Assyrians were cruel and relentless in war. In 722 B.C. they invaded Israel, which had slowly been declining politically and socially, and conquered the capital city of Samaria.

The reason why God allowed this to happen is set out in detail in 2 Kings 17: they continued to sin against God and ignored the warnings of the prophets. After the Assyrians conquered them, the Israelites of the Northern Kingdom were taken into exile, never to return. After the Israelites were exiled, the Assyrians sent foreigners from different parts of the kingdom to inhabit the land (2 Kings 17:24), a practice that was meant to prevent uprisings in the conquered territories. The foreigners married the few Israelites who were not displaced, and this mixed race of Israelites and foreigners became known as the Samaritans. The Israelites were whisked off not because God was powerless but because they were stubborn.

THE END OF THE SOUTHERN KINGDOM (586 B.C.)

The Assyrian kingdom collapsed suddenly and unexpectedly in 622 B.C. when Media and Babylon (modern-day southern Iraq) conquered Nineveh, the capital of Assyria. Babylon then became the new world power. More than a century after the fall of Israel, Jehoiakim, the king of Judah, acted foolishly and rose up against Babylon. Nebuchadnezzar, the king of Babylon, struck back forcefully against Jerusalem in 598 B.C.

Jehoiakim's 18-year-old son, Jehoiachin, succeeded his father. He, too, was unable to offer resistance to Nebuchadnezzar and eventually had to surrender. After he and his supporters were taken to Babylon, the Babylonians appointed Zedekiah to reign in Judah. Zedekiah, Judah's last king, was under the impression that Jerusalem could never be destroyed and dared to revolt against the king of Babylon. Then the unthinkable happened: Jerusalem, the capital of Judah, was invaded and destroyed by Babylon in 586 B.C.

Nobody ever expected such a tragedy to happen. Jerusalem was the city God Himself had chosen. The Temple was in the city. But even this special status could not save Jerusalem. The beautiful city, with its Temple, was completely destroyed. The people's persistent sins, despite all the warnings by the prophets, had caused the Lord to allow Jerusalem and the Temple to be destroyed (2 Kings 24:8–25:1). God's people were then taken to Babylon as exiles. In the next stop, we will see what happened during their time in exile.

WHAT CAN WE EXPECT TO FOLLOW AFTER A HIGH POINT?

A small girl tried for months to fasten her own shoelaces. Eventually, she succeeded. Her parents thought that she would be overjoyed with this accomplishment, but they were surprised by the disappointed look on her face.

"Why are you unhappy?" her father asked her.

"I have just learned to fasten my shoelaces," she answered.

"But that is marvelous!" he replied. "Why are you crying?"

She answered him, "Because now I will have to do it all by myself for the rest of my life!"

It seems as if it is one of life's unwritten rules to expect an emotional low point to follow after a high point. It is as if a high point is followed by emptiness. We have longed so much to achieve something that the success of attaining it turns into an anticlimax. Elijah had a similar experience after a spiritual victory he had attained over the 450 prophets of Baal.

1 Kings 19 (story)

Tension: A prophet who no longer wants to live

[1]Ahab told Jezebel all that Elijah had done, and how he had killed all the prophets with the sword. [2]Then Jezebel sent a messenger to Elijah, saying, 'So may the gods do to me, and more also, if I do not make your life like the life of one of them by this time tomorrow.' [3]Then he was afraid; he got up and fled for his life, and came to Beer-sheba, which belongs to Judah; he left his servant there. [4]But he himself went a day's journey into the wilderness, and came and sat down under a solitary broom tree. He asked that he might die: 'It is enough; now, O Lord, take away my life, for I am no better than my ancestors.'

Relief of tension: An angel intervenes

[5]Then he lay down under the broom tree and fell asleep. Suddenly an angel touched him and said to him, 'Get up and eat.' [6]He looked, and there at his head was a cake baked on hot stones, and a jar of water. He ate and drank, and lay down again. [7]The angel of the Lord came a second time, touched him, and said, 'Get up and eat, otherwise the journey will be too much for you.'

Result: Elijah gets new strength and courage

[8]He got up, and ate and drank; then he went in the strength of that food for forty days and forty nights to Horeb the mount of God. (NRSV)

After high points, one should be realistic and expect to feel depressed during the next day or week. This is normal. Unfortunately, Elijah allowed this to affect him negatively. Beware of this!

 Lord, thank You for teaching me to be realistic about life.

I always like to look on the optimistic side of life, but I am realistic enough to know that life is a complex matter.
—Walt Disney (1901–1966), *American motion picture producer and pioneer of animated cartoon films*

THE DAY A LITTLE GIRL MADE A DIFFERENCE

The faith of children should never be underestimated. The following gripping story starts with a little girl's faith in God.

2 Kings 5 (story)

Tension: A respected man falls seriously ill

¹Naaman, commander of the army of the king of Aram, was a great man and in high favour with his master, because by him the Lord had given victory to Aram. The man, though a mighty warrior, suffered from leprosy.

Relief of tension: A little girl gives advice

²Now the Arameans on one of their raids had taken a young girl captive from the land of Israel, and she served Naaman's wife. ³She said to her mistress, 'If only my lord were with the prophet who is in Samaria! He would cure him of his leprosy.' ⁴So Naaman went in and told his lord just what the girl from the land of Israel had said. ⁵And the king of Aram said, 'Go then, and I will send along a letter to the king of Israel.' He went, taking with him ten talents of silver, six thousand shekels of gold, and ten sets of garments. ⁶He brought the letter to the king of Israel, which read, 'When this letter reaches you, know that I have sent to you my servant Naaman, that you may cure him of his leprosy.' ⁷When the king of Israel read the letter, he tore his clothes and said, 'Am I God, to give death or life, that this man sends word to me to cure a man of his leprosy? Just look and see how he is trying to pick a quarrel with me.'

Result: Elisha steps in

⁸But when Elisha the man of God heard that the king of Israel had torn his clothes, he sent a message to the king, 'Why have you torn your clothes? Let him come to me, that he may learn that there is a prophet in Israel.' (NRSV)

In this story, the distraught king of Israel stands in sharp contrast to the slave girl's advice. Naaman, an Armenian, was so desperate to be cured that he listened to the kidnapped girl. He was also willing to turn his back on his own gods. After Naaman arrived in Israel full of expectations, the king of Israel tore up his clothes in distress because he knew that he could not fulfill the promise of curing Naaman. The king knew that leprosy was incurable and that when he failed to cure Naaman, the stronger Armenians would raid the Israelites. Fortunately, Elisha intervened and saw this as an opportunity to demonstrate God's power to the foreigner. Naaman was eventually cured, and he praised the Lord for it. This all started with the childlike faith of a little girl. We should never underestimate children's faith.

 Lord, thank You for the wonderful example of this girl's faith!

You can learn many things from children. How much patience you have, for instance.
—Franklin P. Adams (1881–1960), *American journalist*

IS GOD REALLY INTERESTED IN US?

Celebrities are often featured on the front covers of magazines and written and spoken about. Ordinary people, however, do not have this honor, because the doings of ordinary people do not excite society. It is for this reason that some people have a passion to be important. Many are even prepared to give up their principles in order to attain fame and popularity. But what about God? Is He interested in the lives of ordinary people? The following short story, consisting of only seven verses, gives us a lot of insight into this.

2 Kings 6 (story)

Tension: A borrowed axe falls in the water

> [1]Now the company of prophets said to Elisha, 'As you see, the place where we live under your charge is too small for us. [2]Let us go to the Jordan, and let us collect logs there, one for each of us, and build a place there for us to live.' He answered, 'Do so.'
> [3]Then one of them said, 'Please come with your servants.' And he answered, 'I will.' [4]So he went with them. When they came to the Jordan, they cut down trees. [5]But as one was felling a log, his axehead fell into the water; he cried out, 'Alas, master! It was borrowed.'

Relief of tension: Elisha intervenes

> [6]Then the man of God said, 'Where did it fall?' When he showed him the place, he cut off a stick, and threw it in there, and made the iron float.

Result: The axe is safe

> [7]He said, 'Pick it up.' So he reached out his hand and took it. (NRSV)

A very ordinary individual experiences a crisis when his borrowed axe falls into the water. God uses his prophet, Elisha, to help him solve his crisis. With this deed, God shows us that ordinary people can depend on Him. This theme is emphasized very strongly in 2 Kings. Simple people like the poor widow (4:1–7), and even the mighty ones like Naaman (5:1–27), could take their problems to Elisha. Stories such as these in the Bible illustrate that no one is too insignificant for God. Our comings and our goings are front-page news to God.

 Thank You, Lord, that You are interested in everything I do. For that I praise You!

The self-assured believer is a greater sinner in the eyes of God than the troubled disbeliever.
—Søren Kierkegaard (1813–1855), *Danish philosopher and theologian,*
generally recognized as the first existentialist philosopher

DOES GOD ALLOW US TO MESS WITH HIM?

God's patience toward people is endless. We learn this from his relationship with Israel. However, the day came when God said enough was enough.

2 Kings 17 (story)

Tension: The Israelites defy God

[7]This occurred because the people of Israel had sinned against the Lord their God, who had brought them up out of the land of Egypt from under the hand of Pharaoh king of Egypt. They had worshiped other gods [8]and walked in the customs of the nations whom the Lord drove out before the people of Israel, and in the customs that the kings of Israel had introduced.

[12]they served idols, of which the Lord had said to them, 'You shall not do this.' [13]Yet the Lord warned Israel and Judah by every prophet and every seer, saying, 'Turn from your evil ways and keep my commandments and my statutes, in accordance with all the law that I commanded your ancestors and that I sent to you by my servants the prophets.' [14]They would not listen but were stubborn, as their ancestors had been, who did not believe in the Lord their God.

[16]They rejected all the commandments of the Lord their God and made for themselves cast images of two calves; they made a sacred pole, worshiped all the host of heaven, and served Baal. [17]They made their sons and their daughters pass through fire; *they used divination and augury; and they sold themselves to do evil in the sight of the Lord, provoking him to anger.*

Relief of tension: God turns his back on Israel

[18]Therefore the Lord was very angry with Israel and removed them out of his sight; none was left but the tribe of Judah alone.

Result: Exile

[22]The people of Israel continued in all the sins that Jeroboam committed; they did not depart from them [23]until the Lord removed Israel out of his sight, as he had foretold through all his servants the prophets. So Israel was exiled from their own land to Assyria until this day. (NRSV)

In this passage, the author looks back on the history of Israel and realizes that one cannot mess with God. Over a long period of time, the Northern Empire (Israel) did not adhere to the covenant with God. They continued to disobey His commands and turn to other gods despite His repeated warnings. So the fall of Samaria in 722 B.C. and the Israelites' exile to Assyria did not come as a surprise.

Israel's decline can be attributed to the unfaithfulness of the people, not to God's inability. They never returned, but simply disappeared from the pages of history. They wanted to enjoy God's privileges without honoring Him. So remember: It is a privilege to be a Christian, but it is also a responsibility. God's honor is at stake.

 Lord, help me to be responsible in my faith!

Ease and honor are seldom bedfellows.
—Proverb

IS GOD THREATENED BY HISTORY?

Through the ages, God has made covenants with His children. A "covenant" is a binding promise or agreement. For example, God made covenants with Noah (Gen. 9:8–17), Abraham (Gen. 15) and with his people on Mount Sinai (Exod. 19). Later, He made a covenant with David (2 Sam. 7:11–16), whereby He promised that one of David's descendants would always occupy the throne. However, the truth is that the descendents of king David and Jehoiachin were taken into exile by the Babylonians. Does this history and today's current events threaten God's promise?

2 Kings 25 (history)

[27]In the thirty-seventh year of the exile of King Jehoiachin of Judah, in the twelfth month, on the twenty-seventh day of the month, King Evil-merodach of Babylon, in the year that he began to reign, released King Jehoiachin of Judah from prison; [28]he spoke kindly to him, and gave him a seat above the other seats of the kings who were with him in Babylon. [29]So Jehoiachin put aside his prison clothes. Every day of his life he dined regularly in the king's presence. [30]For his allowance, a regular allowance was given him by the king, a portion every day, as long as he lived. (NRSV)

At the end of the book of Kings, the narrator describes how the kingdom of Judah came to an infamous end when it was taken to Babylon by Nebuchadnezzar. The narrator is not very encouraging. He does not mention the future, but does say that the new king of Babel, Evil-Merodach, set Jehoiachin free. This did not, however, mean that the king could return to Jerusalem. He was merely released from prison, had freedom of movement and enjoyed a higher status than the other conquered princedoms. In actual fact, no one occupied David's throne.

As readers, we can rightly ask whether Jehoiachin's release was a sign of a new beginning. The answer is not to be found in Kings. Fortunately, there is an affirmative answer on the first few pages of the New Testament when Jehoiachin's name appears in the genealogy of Jesus. The last entry in the Bible (Rev. 22:16) confirms this when Jesus tells the congregations that He is David's descendent. The promise made to David comes true in Jesus, who will always reign as king!

Neither the murderous plans of Herod nor the crucifixion could prevent the fulfillment of God's promise to David. It is also comforting to know that history will not be able to prevent the promise of Jesus' return. So keep up your courage!

 Lord, thank You that You give me the courage to face the future.

The biblical prophet doesn't predict the future, but bears witness to the presence of God in history.
—Nicolás Gómez Dávila (1913–1994), *Colombian philosopher*

EVER LISTEN TO A SERMON FROM CHRONICLES?

The author of the Chronicles would be quite disappointed to learn that his book is not used much in sermons these days. He used the seemingly boring genealogies and facts to get a very clear message across: *God never stops His involvement with people!* God stays involved in people's lives even though they might have acted wrongly. God stays involved even though they might have trampled on His love. Chronicles ends on a wonderfully high point.

2 Chronicles 36 (history)

[22]In the first year of King Cyrus of Persia, in fulfilment of the word of the Lord spoken by Jeremiah, the Lord stirred up the spirit of King Cyrus of Persia so that he sent a herald throughout all his kingdom and also declared in a written edict: [23]'Thus says King Cyrus of Persia: The Lord, the God of heaven, has given me all the kingdoms of the earth, and he has charged me to build him a house at Jerusalem, which is in Judah. Whoever is among you of all his people, may the Lord his God be with him! Let him go up.' (NRSV)

Chronicles ends in the triumph of God's mercy. When the Babylonians destroyed Jerusalem in 586 B.C., the extent of the destruction was so great that no one believed the Judeans would survive it. It seemed Judah would follow only one course—namely, to disappear from the history books. But then the opposite happened. While in exile, the people started to plan the rebuilding of Judah. The prophet Ezekiel told them that the Temple would once again be the center point of the nation.

Slowly but surely, a small flame of hope started burning. Another prophet, the author of Isaiah 40–55, told of a time when a person—not a ram—would die for the sins of others. People's expectations were raised. The big question was whether it could be true. Then in 539 B.C., the Persian king Cyrus destroyed the Babylonians. Cyrus' policy was not to keep the conquered Judeans in exile but to return them to their country of origin. They would be turned into a loyal Persian nation that would serve as buffers against hostile powers.

Judah's day of glory came when Cyrus commanded in 538 B.C. that the Judean exiles be allowed to return to Judah. Wow! God's mercy amazed the Chronicler. He used history to share his excitement about God's mercy. History is not that bad after all! We see the golden thread of God's grace triumph!

 Lord, I want to praise and honor You for your indescribable mercy—also towards me!

I thank God I had the opportunity to be there then, and I'm thankful to be here now.
Everyone uses stamps sometimes, and look at what they will have—a history.
—Johnnie Carr (b. 1912), *American civil rights leader*

GOD'S MERCY IS NOT FLAT

Centuries ago, seafarers were afraid to undertake long sea voyages because they believed that the earth was flat. This restricted them, as they were afraid they would fall off the edge of the world. Our problem is that we view God's mercy in the same way as the seafarers viewed the earth. Centuries before Christopher Columbus (1451–1506) came across the new world on his voyages, heathen sailors discovered that God's mercy is not flat but round. What does this mean?

Jonah 1 (story)

Tension: The sea gets more stormy

> [11]The sea was getting rougher and rougher. So they asked him, 'What should we do to you to make the sea calm down for us?'

Relief of tension: Jonah's solution

> [13]Instead, the men did their best to row back to land. But they could not, for the sea grew even wilder than before. [14]Then they cried out to the LORD, 'Please, LORD, do not let us die for taking this man's life. Do not hold us accountable for killing an innocent man, for you, LORD, have done as you pleased.' [15]Then they took Jonah and threw him overboard,

Result: The storm subsides and Jonah is swallowed by a fish

> and the raging sea grew calm. [16]At this the men greatly feared the LORD, and they offered a sacrifice to the LORD and made vows to him.
> [17]Now the LORD provided a huge fish to swallow Jonah, and Jonah was in the belly of the fish three days and three nights. (TNIV)

Jonah did not want to be a prophet in Nineveh and therefore fled in the opposite direction to Tarshish. However, during the sea voyage to Tarshish, a heavy storm erupted. Jonah told the sailors that if they threw him overboard, the sea would calm down. These heathen sailors at first tried to row harder, but when this did not help, they prayed to Jonah's God instead.

It is ironic that heathens recognized God's absolute power with their prayers while Jonah denied it by fleeing. The actions of these heathens affirmed that God's mercy is not flat but round. Something that is round does not have a beginning or an end. It cannot, therefore, be restricted. God's mercy is exactly like this! He saved the lives of the heathen seafarers and also that of the disobedient Jonah. His mercy also encircles us on all sides.

 Thank you, Lord, that Your mercy encircles us on all sides.

> *Our prayer and God's mercy are like two buckets in a well;*
> *while the one ascends the other descends.*
> —Mark Hopkins

WAS JONAH REALLY SWALLOWED BY A FISH?

The answer is a definite *yes!* Jonah 1:17 states very clearly that a fish swallowed Jonah. The real problem is in deciding whether we should read this story as fiction or nonfiction (an historical story). We could continue arguing about this until the Second Coming. I personally choose to read the book of Jonah as fiction and not as a factual account, as too many things in the story are not consistent with history. But the *good news* is that regardless of whether we view the story as fact or fiction, we will get the same message—that God is sovereign and His mercy is available to all people. His mercy means that people get a second chance.

Jonah 2

¹From inside the fish Jonah prayed to the LORD his God. ² He said:
'In my distress I called to the LORD, (PHRASE 1 = salvation)
and he answered me.
From deep in the realm of the dead I called for help,
and you listened to my cry.
³You hurled me into the deep, (PHRASE 2 = need)
into the very heart of the seas,
and the currents swirled about me;
all your waves and breakers swept over me.
⁴I said, 'I have been banished (PHRASE 3 = salvation)
from your sight;
yet I will look again
toward your holy temple.'
⁵*The engulfing waters* threatened me, (PHRASE 4 = need)
the deep surrounded me;
seaweed was wrapped around my head.
⁶To the roots of the mountains I sank down;
the earth beneath barred me in forever.
But you, LORD my God, PHRASE 5 = salvation)
brought my life up from the pit.
⁷'When my life was ebbing away,
I remembered you, LORD,
and my prayer rose to you,
to your holy temple.
⁸'Those who cling to worthless idols (PHRASE 6 = song of praise)
forfeit God's love for them.
⁹But I, with shouts of grateful praise,
will sacrifice to you.
What I have vowed I will make good.
I will say, 'Salvation comes from the LORD.' '
¹⁰And the LORD commanded the fish,
and it vomited Jonah onto dry land. (TNIV)

Jonah expresses his gratitude for getting a second chance in this prayer. The prayer alternates between the themes of *salvation and need* and then explodes in praise. We can use Jonah's prayer as our prayer about the second chance we received. This is exactly what we should see in the book of Jonah!

 Thank you, Lord, that Your mercy means that You give us a second chance.

> *The God I believe in is a god of second chances.*
> —Bill Clinton (b. 1946), *Forty-second President of the United States (1993–2001)*

CAN GOD CHANGE HIS PLANS?

We are not always sure about God's plans. The faithful often struggle with this question: What is God's plan with my life? Today's reading does not attempt to answer this question but instead answers whether God can change His plans—which might comfort you.

Jonah 3 (story)

¹Then the word of the LORD came to Jonah a second time: ²'Go to the great city of Nineveh and proclaim to it the message I give you.'
³Jonah obeyed the word of the LORD and went to Nineveh. Now Nineveh was a very large city; it took three days to go through it.

Tension: Panic in the terrible city

Jonah began by going a day's journey into the city, proclaiming, *'Forty more days and Nineveh will be overthrown.'*

Relief of tension: The Ninevites show remorse

⁵The Ninevites believed God. They declared a fast, and all of them, from the greatest to the least, put on sackcloth.
⁶When the news reached the king of Nineveh, he rose from his throne, took off his royal robes, covered himself with sackcloth and sat down in the dust. ⁷ Then he issued a proclamation in Nineveh:
'By the decree of the king and his nobles:
Do not let people or animals, herds or flocks, taste anything; do not let them eat or drink. ⁸But let people and animals be covered with sackcloth. Let everyone call urgently on God. Let them give up their evil ways and their violence. ⁹Who knows? God may yet relent and with compassion turn from his fierce anger so that we will not perish.'

Result: God changes his plan

¹⁰When God saw what they did and how they turned from their evil ways, he relented and did not bring on them the destruction he had threatened. (TNIV)

Jonah's sermon consisted of one short sentence, but its effect was overwhelming. His sermon explained God's plan for Nineveh very clearly: *"Forty more days and Nineveh will be overthrown."* Nineveh was the capital of Assyria, the superpower at the time (935–612 B.C.). This judgment did not materialize. Instead, the wishes of the Ninevites came true: God relented and with compassion turned from his fierce anger so that they did not perish (v. 9). God saw that the cruel Ninevites truly regretted all their wrongdoings. God can change His plans because His mercy is not flat but round. For this reason it could include the Ninevites—and also us!

 Thank You, Lord, that You can change Your plans because of Your wonderful mercy!

I have always found that mercy bears richer fruits than strict justice.
—Abraham Lincoln (1809–1865), *Sixteenth President of the United States (1861–1865), who brought about the emancipation of the slaves*

WE MUST NOT KEEP THIS TO OURSELVES!

Although Jonah's sermon to the Ninevites consisted of only one short sentence, it had the desired effect. However, Jonah was unhappy about the effect of his sermon. He was unhappy because he wanted to keep something wonderful to himself!

Jonah 4 (story)

Tension: Jonah is angry about the consequences

¹But Jonah was very upset. He became angry.

Relief of tension: Jonah opens up his heart

²He prayed to the Lord and said, 'Lord, isn't this exactly what I thought would happen when I was still at home? That's why I was so quick to run away to Tarshish. I knew that you are gracious. You are tender and kind. You are slow to get angry. You are full of love. You are a God who takes pity on people. You don't want to destroy them.
³Lord, take away my life. I'd rather die than live.'
⁴But the Lord replied, *'Do you have any right to be angry?'*

Result: Jonah leaves the city

⁵Jonah left the city. He sat down at a place east of it. There he put some branches over his head. He sat in their shade. He waited to see what would happen to the city.
⁶Then the Lord God sent a vine and made it grow up over Jonah. It gave him more shade for his head. It made him more comfortable. Jonah was very happy he had the vine.

Tension 2: Jonah's concern about his vine

⁷But before sunrise the next day, God sent a worm. It chewed the vine so much that it dried up. ⁹But God said to Jonah, 'Do you have any right to be angry about what happened to the vine?' 'I do,' he said. 'In fact, I'm angry enough to die.'

Relief of tension 2: God opens up His heart

¹⁰But the Lord said, 'You have been concerned about this vine. But you did not take care of it. You did not make it grow. It grew up in one night and died the next. ¹¹Nineveh has more than 120,000 people. They can't tell right from wrong. Nineveh also has a lot of cattle. So shouldn't I show concern for that great city?' (NIRV)

Jonah became angry because God saved the lives of Israel's enemies. Jonah's problem was so ironic: He was glad because of his own salvation, but he became angry when God saved Nineveh. Jonah wanted to die while all the heathens in the book—the sailors and the Ninevites—wanted to live. Jonah was concerned about a vine, yet he grew angry when God took pity on a whole city. He did not understand that God's mercy is for everybody. It cannot be kept for ourselves. The story of Jonah ends without providing an answer to God's question (v. 4). This engages every reader to provide his or her own answer.

 Lord, save me from prejudice and selfishness. Let me not keep Your mercy all to myself!

Where Mercy, Love, and Pity dwell, there God is dwelling too.
—William Blake (1757–1827), *English visionary mystic, poet, painter and engraver*

TO READ ONE'S OWN OBITUARY IN THE NEWSPAPER . . .

It would be upsetting to read your own obituary in the newspaper, but Israel had this very experience after the prophet Amos (c. 760 B.C.) announced the death of Israel in a lamentation. During the next four days, we will focus on the fifth chapter of Amos, the theological high point and structural center of the book. Amos 5 is compiled artistically. The following is a schematic representation of the chapter:

A5:1–3	Death and burial
B5:4–6	Search for the Lord and live
C5:7	The legal system
D5:8–9	Honor to the Almighty
C'5:10:13	The legal system
B'5:14–15	Look for the good and live
A'5:16–17	Death and burial

Amos 5

A) ¹Hear this word that I take up over you in lamentation, O house of Israel:
²Fallen, no more to rise,
is maiden Israel;
forsaken on her land,
 with no one to raise her up.
³For thus says the Lord God:
The city that marched out a thousand
shall have a hundred left,
and that which marched out a hundred
shall have ten left.
A') ¹⁶Therefore thus says the LORD, the God of hosts, the Lord:
In all the squares there shall be wailing;
and in all the streets they shall say, 'Alas! alas!'
They shall call the farmers *to mourning,*
and those skilled *in lamentation, to wailing;*
¹⁷in all the vineyards there shall be wailing,
for I will pass through the midst of you,
says the LORD. (NRSV)

The Israelites regularly visited the Temple but did injustice on a daily basis. This is the reason why their demise was imminent. Israel would not rise again (v. 2), and only 10 percent of its army would remain (v. 3). Lamentations would be heard everywhere in Israel, even in the vineyards (places of joy). God despises believers who piously attend church services but are guilty of injustice during the rest of the week!

Lord, please do not permit me to sit piously in church on Sundays and do injustice during the rest of the week.

Injustice anywhere is a threat to justice everywhere.
—Martin Luther King, Jr. (1929–1968), *American Baptist minister, Civil Rights leader and winner of the Nobel Prize in 1964*

WHEN SHOULD A CHURCH SERVICE END?

Not all denominations have the same duration of church services. Some will tell you that they like their services long, while others like to complete a service in less than an hour. When should a church service end?

Amos 5

B) [4]For thus says the LORD to the house of Israel:
Seek me and live;
[5]*but do not seek* Bethel,
and do not enter into Gilgal
or cross over to Beer-sheba;
for Gilgal shall surely go *into exile*
and Bethel shall come *to nothing.*
[6]Seek the LORD and live,
or he will break out against the house of Joseph like fire,
and it will devour Bethel, with no one to quench it.
B') [14]Seek good and not evil,
that you may live;
and so the Lord, the God of hosts, will be with you,
just as you have said.
[15]Hate evil and love good,
and establish justice in the gate;
it may be that the Lord, the God of hosts,
will be gracious to the remnant of Joseph. (NRSV)

One day, a child went to the morning service without his parents and returned earlier than usual. The father's reaction was, "My, the service ended early!" The child answered, "I listened to only half of the service, because I have to live out the other half." Israel did not do this. They went to the Temple but did not live according to God's will. Their legal system was corrupt, and they exploited the poor. This is why it all ended in death (A).

However, this section (B) shows that there was still hope for them. They had to seek God's will (vv. 5–6) and then live it out (vv. 14–15). The result of this asking and doing would give life back to them. They had to realize that sanctuaries (Bethel, Gilgal and Beersheba) could not bestow life. They had to replace those places with the Person who is the Source of life. He asks us to honor His name every day, not only on Sundays!

 Lord, let my whole life be a service to You!

A Sunday well spent brings a week of content.
—Author unknown

WHAT MAKES SOCIETY LIVABLE?

Two words feature very prominently in the book of Amos. If these words find expression in people's lives, society will be a livable and safe place.

Amos 5

C) ⁷Ah, you that turn justice *to wormwood,*
and bring righteousness *to the ground!*
C') ¹⁰*They hate the one* who reproves in the gate,
and they abhor the one who speaks the truth.
¹¹Therefore, because you trample on the poor
and take from them levies of grain,
you have built houses of hewn stone,
but you shall not live in them;
you have planted pleasant vineyards,
but you shall not drink their wine.
¹²*For I know how many are your transgressions,*
and how great are your sins—
you who afflict the righteous, who take a bribe,
and push aside the needy in the gate.
¹³Therefore the prudent will keep silent in such a time;
for it is an evil time. (NRSV)

The two words that make a society livable and safe are "judiciary" and "law." The laws of a country ensure peace within a community and the justice system is the practical application thereof. Law and order make a society a habitable, safe and happy place in which to live. Laws and the justice system are especially meant to protect the weak, the poor and those who need help. Unfortunately, the leaders of Israel trampled on these very important institutions. Consequently, Israelite society was marked by exploitation and corruption. No corrupt society welcomes the truth, because the truth exposes injustice. Christians should uphold the truth at all times, because this will ensure that justice prevails. We should not be afraid to let our voice be heard!

 Lord, give me the courage to speak up against any form of injustice.

Peace is not the absence of war but the presence of justice.
—Harrison Ford (b. 1942), *American actor*

GOD HAS MESSENGERS IN SPACE!

The following two verses (D) form the focal point of chapter 5 and, therefore, also of the book of Amos. It is a song of praise about God's greatness and unlimited power, although there seems to be no apparent link between the preceding verses (1–7) and the following verses (10–17). The prophet used these two verses to tell Israel that the terrible judgment that awaited them was not just the scary tales of a prophet but that it came from Almighty God Himself. Israel, therefore, had to heed the warning. God used messengers in space to remind His people of His unlimited power.

Amos 5

D) [8]The one who made the Pleiades and Orion,
and turns deep darkness into the morning,
and darkens the day into night,
who calls for the waters of the sea,
and pours them out on the surface of the earth,
the Lord is his name,
[9]who makes destruction flash out against the strong,
so that destruction comes upon the fortress. (NRSV)

The first messengers in space that had to remind Israel of God's unlimited power were the Pleiades and Orion, which He made. The Pleiades, which appears in May, heralds in the beginning of summer, while the constellation of Orion, which appears in November, indicates the beginning of winter in the Northern Hemisphere. The fact that God made the Pleiades and Orion serves as proof that He controls the seasons. Furthermore, the Lord also controls the succession of day and night. He is, therefore, in control of life in all its totality. And that is not all: He also provides the rain. His unlimited power is not only evident in space and in nature but also in history (v. 9). God Almighty has the power to demolish all human opposition and dwellings. When the vastness of creation tells us about God's greatness, it is very foolish not to take notice of God.

 Lord, I simply have to take You seriously. I praise You!

The artist must be in his work as God is in creation, invisible and all-powerful;
one must sense him everywhere but never see him.
—Gustave Flaubert (1821–1880), *French Novelist regarded as the prime mover of the realist school of*
French literature. He is best known for his masterpiece, Madame Bovary.

GOD IS NO COWBOY!

We easily say, "Cowboys don't cry," because we think tears are a sign of weakness. Could we say this about God?

Hosea 1 (conversation)

[2]When the Lord first spoke through Hosea, *the Lord said to Hosea,* 'Go, take for yourself a wife of whoredom and have children of whoredom, *for* the land commits great whoredom by forsaking the Lord.' [3]So he went and took Gomer daughter of Diblaim, and she conceived and bore him a son.
[4]And *the Lord said to him,* 'Name him Jezreel; *for* in a little while I will punish the house of Jehu for the blood of Jezreel, and I will put an end to the kingdom of the house of Israel. [5]On that day I will break the bow of Israel in the valley of Jezreel.'
[6]She conceived again and bore a daughter. *Then the Lord said to him,* 'Name her Lo-ruhamah, *for* I will no longer have pity on the house of Israel or forgive them. [7]But I will have pity on the house of Judah, and I will save them by the Lord their God; I will not save them by bow, or by sword, or by war, or by horses, or by horsemen.'
[8]When she had weaned Lo-ruhamah, she conceived and bore a son.
[9]*Then the Lord said,* 'Name him Lo-ammi, *for* you are not my people and I am not your God.'
[10]Yet the number of the people of Israel shall be like the sand of the sea, which can be neither measured nor numbered; and in the place where it was said to them, 'You are not my people', it shall be said to them, 'Children of the living God.' (NRSV)

The Lord called Hosea to be a prophet in order to show His people exactly why He was so sad. Hosea's call entailed frightening assignments. It is interesting to note that all four of his assignments follow the same pattern: an introductory formula ("Then the Lord said"), a directive and an explanation of the directive (which always starts with "for").

The Lord ordered Hosea to marry Gomer, knowing full well that she would be unfaithful to him. One has the feeling that God's assignments to Hosea were a bit unreasonable and strange. However, Hosea had to understand that his unhappy marriage and the names of his children were a reflection, a living gospel, of the relationship between the Lord and His people.

Hosea's pain, heartache and rejection that Gomer's extra-marital affairs caused him contained a message to the people that the Lord was hurt by their extra-marital affair with Baal, the rain god. God's wrath caused Him to want to divorce His people. Fortunately, His love was stronger than His wrath (vv. 7,10). God is terribly hurt when people push Him aside and thereby relinquish their only hope for life itself.

 Thank You, Lord, that Your love is stronger than Your wrath. I never want to relegate You to an inferior position!

God is closest to those with broken hearts.
—Jewish proverb

WHERE IS GOD'S TRAINING SCHOOL?

God wants us to always remember that we are dependent on Him. When we forget this, He has a way of taking us to His training school. Often, we do not recognize it as a school but rather see it as a place from which we want to escape. Where is this place?

Hosea 2

⁸She did not know
that it was I who gave her
the grain, the wine, and the oil,
and who lavished upon her silver
and gold that they used for Baal.
¹²I will lay waste her vines and her fig trees,
of which she said,
'These are my pay,
which my lovers have given me.'
I will make them a forest,
and the wild animals shall devour them.
¹³I will punish her for the festival days of the Baals,
when she offered incense to them
and decked herself with her ring and jewellery,
and went after her lovers,
and forgot me, says the Lord.
¹⁴Therefore, I will now persuade her,
and bring her into the wilderness,
and speak tenderly to her.
¹⁵From there I will give her her vineyards,
and make the Valley of Achor a door of hope.
There she shall respond as in the days of her youth,
as at the time when she came out of the land of Egypt.
¹⁶On that day, says the Lord, you will call me, 'My husband', and no longer will you call me, 'My Baal'.
(NRSV)

Two words in verse 13, "forgot me," sum up the Lord's complaint against His people. He blessed them with good harvests and wealth, but Israel attributed these gifts to the rain god, Baal (v. 8). The Lord was hurt because His people had pushed Him aside and were following other gods. How did God react to this enormous insult?

The Lord decided to take away everything that was important to His people in an effort to teach them that no one but God was in a position to provide for them (vv. 9–12). He would send them out into the desert. This might sound as harsh as the death penalty (v. 14), but there is a sudden turning point, a surprise. They did go to the wilderness/desert, but not to be punished. They went there to learn that they were dependent on God.

Your own experience in the figurative desert might be a painful one, but it could be God's training school for you. The very first lesson the disciples learned from Jesus was that those who realize that they are dependent on God (like a baby on his or her parents) are blessed. May you be one of the blessed ones!

 Lord, I want to profess my dependence on You once more.

> *In the deserts of the heart let the healing fountain start, in the prison of his*
> *days teach the free man how to praise.*
> —W.H. Auden (1907–1973), *English-born American poet, dramatist and editor who achieved early*
> *fame during the Great Depression of the 1930s as a hero of the left*

AN EMOTION WE NEED NEVER FEEL
TOWARD GOD . . .

In this section, we read about an emotion the Israelites felt for the golden calf. You, however, will never have to feel this way about God.

Hosea 10

¹Israel is a luxuriant vine
that yields its fruit.
The more his fruit increased
the more altars he built;
as his country improved,
he improved his pillars.
²Their heart is false;
now they must bear their guilt.
The Lord *will break down their altars,*
and destroy their pillars.
³For now they will say:
'We have no king,
for we do not fear the Lord,
and a king—what could he do for us?'
⁴They utter mere words;
with empty oaths they make covenants;
so litigation springs up like poisonous weeds
in the furrows of the field.
⁵The inhabitants of Samaria tremble
for the calf of Beth-aven.
Its people shall mourn for it,
and its idolatrous priests shall wail over it,
over its glory that has departed from it. (NRSV)

Israel's prosperous relationship with the Lord is compared to a luxuriant vine (v. 1). Sadly, they thanked Baal and not the Lord for this. As they became increasingly prosperous, they built more altars and stone pillars for Baal. It hurt God immensely to see how His people did not trust in Him anymore. They found security in the king and the golden calf.

The Northern Kingdom (Israel) saw the golden calf as a personification of Baal. To them, it was a symbol of godly presence—much like the Ark in Jerusalem (the capital of the Southern Kingdom) was to Judah. So the Lord used Assyria, the superpower at the time, to plunge the Northern Kingdom into a crisis. The threat Assyria posed made them realize that their securities were worthless.

The inhabitants of Samaria were under the impression that the golden calf would protect them against the Assyrians, but the irony is that they ended up having to protect the golden calf. They mourned for the calf (v. 5), because the calf had been stripped of its gold (glory). Yet we will never need to mourn for God, because He cannot be stripped of His glory. This is very comforting to know.

Lord, it is comforting to know that nobody can strip You of Your glory.

A man can no more diminish God's glory by refusing to worship Him than a lunatic
can put out the sun by scribbling the word "darkness" on the walls of his cell.
—C.S. Lewis (1898–1963), *High-powered Oxford and Cambridge professor and perhaps the twentieth*
century's most famous convert to Christianity. Lewis was the creator of the Narnia series.

THE DAY GOD YIELDED!

The following moving poem tells us of a court case in which a father (God) accuses his son (Israel) of rebelliousness. However, there is a twist to the story!

Hosea 11

The charge

> [1]When Israel was a child, I loved him,
> and out of Egypt I called my son.
> [2]The more I called them,
> the more they went from me;
> *they kept sacrificing* to the Baals,
> *and offering incense* to idols.

The judgment

> [6]The sword rages in their cities,
> it consumes their oracle-priests,
> and devours because of their schemes.

The turning point

> [8]How can I give you up, *Ephraim?*
> How can I hand you over, *O Israel?*
> *How can I make you* like Admah?
> *How can I treat you* like Zeboiim?
> My heart *recoils within me;*
> my compassion *grows warm and tender.*
> [9]I will not execute my fierce anger;
> I will not again destroy Ephraim;
> for I am God and no mortal,
> the Holy One in your midst,
> and I will not come in wrath.

The new beginning

> [10]They shall go after the Lord,
> who roars like a lion;
> when he roars,
> his children shall come trembling from the west.
> [11]They shall come trembling like birds from Egypt,
> and like doves from the land of Assyria;
> and I will return them to their homes, says the Lord. (NRSV)

In the past, the Lord had laid His hand on the young slave boy (Israel) and bought back his freedom. In the desert, the Father had taught the Israelites the first steps of nationhood, protected them and cared for them. However, once in Canaan, they had chosen to follow the gods of Baal and pretend that God wanted nothing to do with them. Baal, as a symbol of materialism and sexuality, was very enticing.

Even today, people are lured away from God by such attractions. The court sentenced the rebellious son to death. But then there is a twist: before the final judgment, God realizes that His love is stronger than His wrath. If Israel would not yield, God Himself would do so and turn the judgment into mercy. His love was too strong! God is a Holy God, but not one who is distant and uninvolved. He is among us!

 Father, I yield myself to You today as Your child who is overwhelmed by Your love.

The minister's speech was like God's wisdom—it surpassed all understanding,
and like God's mercy, it was everlasting.
—Author unknown

LOW POINTS BECOME THE BACKDROP FOR HIGH POINTS

The book of Hosea seemingly ends on a low point. Nobody likes reading a book that ends on a low point. However, the wonderful fact is that Israel's sorrow was not the low point but rather the décor, the backdrop, for the high point of the book. Hosea ends with a love song from God's heart. Let's read it.

Hosea 14

¹Return, O Israel, to the Lord your God,
for you have stumbled because of your iniquity.
²Take words with you
and return to the Lord;
say to him,
'Take away all guilt;
accept that which is good,
and we will offer the fruit of our lips.
³Assyria shall not save us;
we will not ride upon horses;
we will say no more, 'Our God',
to the work of our hands.
In you the orphan finds mercy.'
⁴I will heal their disloyalty;
I will love them freely,
for my anger has turned from them.
⁵I will be like the dew to Israel;
he shall blossom like the lily,
he shall strike root like the forests of Lebanon.
⁶His shoots shall spread out;
his beauty shall be like the olive tree,
and his fragrance like that of Lebanon.
⁷They shall again live beneath my shadow,
they shall flourish as a garden;
they shall blossom like the vine,
their fragrance shall be like the wine of Lebanon.
⁸O Ephraim, what have I to do with idols?
It is I who answer and look after you.
I am like an evergreen cypress;
your faithfulness comes from me.
⁹*Those who are wise*
understand these things;
those who are discerning know them.
For the ways of the Lord are right,
and the upright walk in them,
but transgressors stumble in them. (NRSV)

Verses 1 to 3 of this passage are in the form of a song of penance that sets out the only solution to Israel's misery: come back! But how? The people had to turn back and repent of their sins. Their confession was not to be vague and general. They had to call their sins by name: their flirtation with the enemy (Assyria), their dependence on their own ability (weapons) and their idolatry (own handiwork). They would then discover that forgiveness could turn their low points into the backdrop for a high point: God's love song (vv. 5–9)!

God affirms His forgiveness and healing in this love song ("I will be like," v. 5). God's love triumphs over His wrath. This high point of God's love forces each of us to heed a very important call: return to God (v. 1). May you also discover that your low points are merely the backdrop for God's love!

 Thank You, Lord, that Your forgiveness turns my low points into the backdrop for Your love!

> *No child of God sins to that degree as to make himself incapable of forgiveness.*
> —John Bunyan (1628–1688), *English minister and author*

RELIGION CAN BECOME SIN!

Isaiah was a prophet in Jerusalem during the latter part of the eighth century. Assyria was the great world power and posed a threat to Israel. During that time, the prophet earnestly reprimanded the leaders by telling them that their religion had become sinful.

Isaiah 1

[10]*Hear the word of the Lord,*
you rulers of Sodom!
Listen to the teaching of our God,
you people of Gomorrah!
[11]What to me is the multitude of your sacrifices?
says the Lord;
I have had enough of burnt-offerings of rams
and the fat of fed beasts;
I do not delight in the blood of bulls,
or of lambs, or of goats.
[12]When you come to appear before me,
who asked this from your hand?
Trample my courts no more;
[13]bringing offerings is futile;
incense is an abomination to me.
New moon and sabbath and calling of convocation—
I cannot endure solemn assemblies with iniquity.
[14]Your new moons and your appointed festivals
my soul hates;
they have become a burden to me,
I am weary of bearing them.
[15]*When you stretch out your hands,*
I will hide my eyes from you;
even though you make many prayers,
I will not listen;
your hands are full of blood. (NRSV)

Isaiah flatly told the religious leaders that the Lord despised their religion. This is not to say that the Lord rejects religious acts per se—only that He rejects them if they are not accompanied by an honest life. Religion should encompass a person's whole life. The leaders of Israel put up a front of being religious, but then did wrong during the week. Their hands were full of blood (v. 15). The worst part is that they thought they could fool the Lord.

When someone plays games with God, the terrible result is that God turns his back on that person. Henry David Thoreau, the well-known American writer, poet and philosopher who lived in the nineteenth century, preferred jail to paying "poll" taxes that supported slavery. His good friend Ralph Waldo Emerson rushed to visit him. As he peeped through the bars and called out, "Why are you here, Henry?" Thoreau answered, "No, Ralph, the question is: What are you doing out there?"

Lord, I realize anew that religion can become sin.

I must ever believe that religion is substantially good which produces an honest life, and we have been
authorized by One whom you and I equally respect, to judge of the tree by its fruit.
—Thomas Jefferson (1762–1826), *Third President of the United States (1801–1809)*

WHAT IF WE HAD THE PRIVILEGE OF ASKING GOD FOR A SIGN?

What would you do if you had the privilege to ask the Lord for a sign that would prove His words true? In this section, we see how Ahaz turned down such an opportunity. Why would he be so stupid?

Isaiah 7 (conversation)

[10]Again the Lord spoke to Ahaz, saying, [11]Ask a sign of the Lord your God; let it be deep as Sheol or high as heaven. [12]But Ahaz said, I will not ask, and I will not put the Lord to the test. [13]Then Isaiah said: 'Hear then, O house of David! Is it too little for you to weary mortals, that you weary my God also? [14]Therefore the Lord himself will give you a sign. Look, the young woman is with child and shall bear a son, and shall name him Immanuel. [15]He shall eat curds and honey by the time he knows how to refuse the evil and choose the good. [16]For before the child knows how to refuse the evil and choose the good, the land before whose two kings you are in dread will be deserted.
[17]The Lord will bring on you and on your people and on your ancestral house such days as have not come since the day that Ephraim departed from Judah—the king of Assyria.' (NRSV)

Ahaz, king of Judah, was threatened by his neighbors to the north (Aram and Israel) because he refused to join Peka (leader of Israel/Ephraim) and Resin (leader of Syria/Aram) in a coalition against Assyria, the superpower at the time. For this reason, they wanted to topple Ahaz's government. The Lord used Isaiah to encourage Ahaz, saying, "Stay calm . . . it will not take place" (Isa. 7:4–7).

Ahaz was also given the privilege to ask the Lord for a sign as confirmation. But he refused to do it. His excuse was that he would not "put the Lord to the test." He appeared to be pious, but this was only a front to hide his lack of faith. Ahaz preferred to trust in his own plans. A sign would have forced him to trust God, so therefore he refused to ask for one under the pretence of faith.

God saw through the king's façade and decided to give him a sign anyway. Isaiah told him, "Look, the young woman is with child and shall bear a son, and shall name him Immanuel . . . for before the child knows how to refuse the evil and choose the good, the land before whose two kings you are in dread will be deserted" (vv. 14–16). The woman would call her son Immanuel, which means "God is with us," and the birth of this son would be a confirmation that God keeps His promises. He did not do it because of Israel, but despite Israel. Unlike Ahaz, we must trust God! We do not need a sign to do this.

 Thank You, Lord, that You do not act because of our deeds but despite them.

My dear child, you must believe in God despite what the clergy tells you.
—Benjamin Jowett (1817–1893), *British classical scholar*

WHAT WILL HAPPEN
IF WE CAN NO LONGER DREAM?

Dreams can spur us on to great heights and can help us to persevere in troubled times. It is difficult to live a meaningful life in the absence of dreams. Israel also had dreams. In the Promised Land, they dreamed of the day when God would wipe all their enemies from the face of the earth and live among them. They thought that it would only be a matter of time before all their dreams would come true. After all, God was on their side and nothing could go wrong for them. But then everything changed. Their dreams turned into a nightmare when Isaiah passed judgment on Israel instead of their enemies. But then, Isaiah 35 came as sunshine after the rain.

Isaiah 35

¹*The wilderness and the dry land* shall be glad,
the desert shall rejoice and blossom;
like the crocus ² it shall blossom abundantly,
and rejoice with joy and singing.
The glory of Lebanon shall be given to it,
the majesty of Carmel and Sharon.
They shall see the glory of the Lord,
the majesty of our God.
³*Strengthen* the weak hands,
and make firm the feeble knees.
⁴Say to those who are of a fearful heart,
'Be strong, do not fear!
Here is your God.
He will come with vengeance,
with terrible recompense.
He will come and save you.' (NRSV)

Isaiah here pronounces that Israel would once again become a blooming garden (vv. 1–2). God wanted them to dream again! Just as with Israel, the suffering of our day should not destroy our dreams but rather give us a new dream. God wants to purify our dreams so that we can dream His dream. God's dream for us is that we love Him and our neighbors. However, our dreams are often selfish and at the expense of others.

The fact is that many people have lost the ability to dream because life has too often been a disillusion for them. Isaiah gives us an important and clear instruction in this regard: Encourage them! Those who have been hurt should, however, learn to allow others to reach out to them and not let pride and arrogance prevent them from allowing others into their lives. God's dream is that we will take hold of each other's hands and live life in abundance (John 10:10).

 Lord, I want to dream again and reach out with love to those who find it difficult to dream.

A house is made of walls and beams; a home is built with love and dreams.
—Author unknown

SERMONS PEOPLE LIKE TO HEAR

A church member once told his minister that he liked to listen to sermons on the radio. The minister was curious and asked him why. The man replied, "Because I can switch off the radio whenever I don't like what I hear." Which sermons do churchgoers not like to listen to?

Micah 2

6'Do not prophesy,' their prophets say.
'Do not prophesy about these things;
disgrace will not overtake us.'
7House of Jacob, should it be said,
'Does the LORD become impatient?
Does he do such things?'
'Do not my words do good
to those whose ways are upright?
8Lately my people have risen up
like an enemy.
You strip off the rich robe
from those who pass by without a care,
like men returning from battle.
9You drive the women of my people
from their pleasant homes.
You take away my blessing
from their children forever.
10Get up, go away!
For this is not your resting place,
because it is defiled,
it is ruined, beyond all remedy.
11If liars and deceivers come and say,
'We will prophesy for you plenty of wine and beer,'
they would be just the prophets for this people! (TNIV)

Micah's message to the Israelites was not something they wanted to hear, which is why the other prophets tried to silence him (vv. 6–7). These prophets gave the people a message they did want: they would not suffer any misery. The Lord was not angered. The Lord did not consider sin in such a serious light as Micah wanted them to believe. They were God's people, and therefore nothing could go wrong. Sermons such as these are popular because they reassure people. But Micah's message was disturbing. Micah called those who thought that they lived close to God the enemies of God. You cannot be unkind to your neighbor (vv. 8–9) and still entertain the idea that you are in a loving relationship with God. This does not make sense!

 Lord, make me more sensitive in my interaction with other people.

A good sermon should be like a woman's skirt: short enough to arouse interest but long enough to cover the essentials.
—Ronald Knox (1888–1957), *English writer and theologian*

RELIGION CAN BE DANGEROUS!

So many wars have been fought in the name of religion. People's religious convictions are sometimes so strong that it blinds them to the true purpose of it all. This section in Micah is a telling example.

Micah 3

[9]Hear this, *you leaders of the house of Jacob,*
you rulers of the house of Israel,
who despise *justice*
and distort *all that is right;*
[10]*who build Zion* with bloodshed,
and Jerusalem with wickedness.
[11]Her leaders judge *for a bribe,*
her priests teach *for a price,*
and her prophets tell fortunes *for money.*
Yet they lean upon the LORD and say,
'Is not the LORD among us?
No disaster will come upon us.'
[12]Therefore because of you,
Zion will be plowed like a field,
Jerusalem will become a heap of rubble,
the temple hill a mound overgrown with thickets. (TNIV)

Micah put the leaders of God's people under the spotlight. He revealed a hidden motive beneath the surface of the judges' unfair judgments, the comforting prophecies of the prophets and the religious advice of the priests, namely, materialism. He stated that they abused their positions in order to enrich themselves.

It is very sad that everything was measured in terms of money—even those things that were too precious to be measured in monetary value; namely, a good judiciary, true religion and high moral values. Worst of all, the leaders thought they were living a good and righteous life (v. 11). They laid claim to the Lord's presence and blessings. Unbelievable! They were under the impression that the Lord was with them and therefore nothing could go wrong for them. In the meantime, everything had already gone wrong.

How could people think that God was present in the midst of such injustice? If love is absent in your relationship with your neighbor, you cannot expect to have a loving relationship with God. God's presence and people's injustice are incompatible. False motives in the sphere of religion always have tragic consequences.

 Lord, I want to be sincere in all my doings.

The tendency to turn human judgments into divine commands makes
religion one of the most dangerous forces in the world.
—Georgia Elma Harkness (1891–1974), *Christian theologian in the American Methodist tradition*

THE ONE THING
GOD DOES NOT BOTHER ABOUT . . .

Reputation often determines what others think of us and how they behave toward us. Fortunately, as this section shows, God does not bother much about reputation.

Micah 5

2'But you, Bethlehem Ephrathah,
though you are small among the clans of Judah,
out of you will come for me
one who will be ruler over Israel,
whose origins are from of old,
from ancient times.'
3Therefore Israel will be abandoned
until the time when she who is in labor gives birth
and the rest of his brothers return
to join the Israelites.
4He will stand and shepherd his flock
in the strength of the LORD,
in the majesty of the name of the LORD his God.
And they will live securely, for then his greatness
will reach to the ends of the earth.
5And he will be our peace(TNIV)

The kings of Israel and Judah were a bitter disappointment. Fortunately, Micah was the bearer of good news. The people would have a king who would not disappoint. He would lead them like a good shepherd (v. 3) and would bring peace (v. 4). The king's background was noticeably simple. He would come from Bethlehem—an insignificant hamlet in Judah.

At the time, Bethlehem Ephrathah was one of the smallest and most unimportant places in Israel and Judah. If God considered reputation important, this king would have come from a prominent tribe and city. God's approach tells us something: He can perform great and important things by using the most improbable things. What we see as small and insignificant becomes big and important in God's hands.

Centuries later, Jesus was the embodiment of this new king (Matt 2:6). Jesus was born in the small town of Bethlehem. He came from the line of David (Matt. 1). When Jesus was born, He became King. He is also the Good Shepherd (John 10) who does not disappoint. He brought about peace. And during His life on earth He, like His father, did not consider reputation. This enabled Him to lovingly reach out to the vulnerable and those considered unimportant in society. May we also learn to look beyond a person's reputation.

Lord, let me care for others—for everybody—in all sincerity.

Reputation is what men and women think of us; character is what God and angels know of us.
—Thomas Paine (1737–1809), *English-born writer and political pamphleteer whose "Common Sense"
and "Crisis" papers were important influences on the American Revolution*

GOD IS ALSO PRESENT
WHERE THE CASH REGISTERS RING!

"Corruption" is a word that sullies the front pages of our newspapers and magazines. However, corruption was also part and parcel of Israel of old. What does God say about corruption? Let's find out.

Micah 6

⁹Listen! The LORD is calling to the city—
and to fear your name is wisdom—
'Heed the rod and the One who appointed it.
¹⁰Am I still to forget your ill-gotten treasures, you wicked house,
and the short ephah, which is accursed?
¹¹Shall I acquit a person with dishonest scales,
with a bag of false weights?
¹²*Her rich people* are violent;
her inhabitants are liars
and their tongues speak deceitfully.
¹³Therefore, I have begun to destroy you,
to ruin you because of your sins.
¹⁴You will eat but not be satisfied;
your stomach will still be empty.
You will store up but save nothing,
because what you save I will give to the sword.
¹⁵*You will plant* but not harvest;
you will press olives but not use the oil on yourselves,
you will crush grapes but not drink the wine. (TNIV)

Corruption means to pretend that you are selling a meter of material when in actual fact you are only giving the client 980 centimeters. Corruption is to pretend that you are selling one kilogram of corn when you are actually giving less than that. Corruption is to lie about your income on your tax return. Corruption is to over utilize the cash register. Corruption is to steal from your neighbor and to be violent toward them. The Lord condemns this in no uncertain terms.

The Lord exposed one corruption scandal after the other in Israel of old, and this is why the Lord said He would punish them (vv. 13–15). This is emphasized by the parallels (v. 15) in the text. The Israelites had to realize that the ordinary things in their lives had a direct bearing on their spiritual lives. They had to realize, as do we, that ordinary things are also spiritual things.

We cannot lead a corrupt life during the week and then go and praise the Lord on Sundays. God is not only present during the church service on a Sunday but also where the cash registers ring! In a nutshell, money must ring in with God!

 Lord, I want to be honest under all circumstances.

A Christian can never serve God and Money, but they must learn to serve God WITH money.
—Brian Kluth (b. 1955), *Pastor and speaker-author on generosity*

WHAT MAKES GOD SO UNIQUE AND UNEQUALLED?

Christians believe that the God they worship is unique and unequalled. Micah uses wonderful poetry to explain why the God of the Bible is this way.

Micah 7

[18]Who is a God like you,
who pardons sin and forgives the transgression
of the remnant of his inheritance?
You do not stay angry forever
but delight to show mercy.
[19]*You will again have compassion on us;*
you will tread our sins underfoot
and hurl all our iniquities into the depths of the sea.
[20]You will be faithful *to Jacob,*
and show love *to Abraham,*
as you pledged on oath to our ancestors
in days long ago. (TNIV)

The book of Micah begins on a low point with God accusing His people of sinning but ends on a high point: a song of praise to God! What happens between these two points? God forgives the people of their sins! He does not stay angry forever but shows love and mercy—which lets the author rejoice with a song of praise!

The fact that God can act in this way makes Him unique and unequalled. That is why verse 18 starts with a rhetorical question: "Who is a God like You?" The question is a wonderful wordplay on Micah's name, which is an abbreviation of "Micaiah," meaning, "Who is like the Lord?" Micah's name thus proclaims that no one is like the Lord.

Forgiveness always opens up a new beginning. God's forgiveness meant that sin was eliminated—it was thrown into the deep sea and would not count against the people. They need not suffer from the burden of guilt. In the same way that the Lord started out anew with Abraham and Jacob, the Lord would make a fresh start with His people. They would be taken into exile, but God will make a fresh start with them.

By forgiving each other, we create an opportunity for a fresh start among ourselves. The fact that God is willing to forgive does not make sin insignificant. Like Micah, we can also ask with joy in our hearts, "Who is a God like You?"

 Thank You, Lord, that Your forgiveness heralds in a new beginning for me.

To err is human, to forgive is divine.
—Alexander Pope (1688–1744), *English poet and satirist*

GOD IS MORE THAN WHO WE THINK HE IS!

Abuse of power is not a new phenomenon and usually goes hand in hand with violence. The more violence is displayed, the more insensitive and arrogant the powers that be become. Victims of violence often lose all hope because they feel vulnerable against such powers. The Israelites and other nations suffered at the hands of Assyria, the superpower at the time. The book of Nahum is a prophecy about what will happen to Nineveh, the capital of Assyria. The name Nahum means "comfort," which is precisely what this book is about.

Nahum 1

²*The LORD* is a jealous and avenging God;
the LORD takes vengeance and is filled with wrath.
The LORD takes vengeance *on his foes*
and vents his wrath *against his enemies.*
³The LORD is slow to anger but great in power;
the LORD will not leave the guilty unpunished.
His way is in the whirlwind and the storm,
and clouds are the dust of his feet.
⁴*He rebukes* the sea and dries it up;
he makes all the rivers run dry.
Bashan and Carmel *wither*
and the blossoms of Lebanon *fade.*
⁵*The mountains* quake before him
and the hills melt away.
The earth trembles at his presence,
the world and all who live in it. (TNIV)

We sometimes focus helplessly on our situation and look past God. What does Nahum teach us about God? A contradictory picture emerges. God is concerned about His people and takes revenge on the enemy. The same God who is full of *wrath* is also *patient.* This does not make sense. Nahum wants his readers to realize that God is much bigger than we think.

Nahum makes us intensely aware of God's inconceivable majesty—especially where nature is concerned (vv. 4–5). Judah needed to know that God Almighty did not condone everything in the name of love—especially not the abuse of power the mighty Assyrians were guilty of committing. It must have comforted Judah immensely to know that God was still in control and that He would punish the cruel Assyrians. May God's majesty also be a comfort to you!

 Lord, it is comforting to know that You are still in control.

I believe God is managing affairs and that He doesn't need any advice from me. With God in charge, I believe everything will work out for the best in the end. So what is there to worry about.
—Henry Ford (1863–1947), *American industrialist and founder of the Ford Motor Company*

THIS LION IS KING NO MORE . . .

In this section in Nahum, a mighty lion is ridiculed because he had been rendered harmless. This lion is no longer king. What happened?

Nahum 2

¹¹ Where now is the lions' den,
the place where they fed their young,
where the lion and lioness went,
and the cubs, with nothing to fear?
¹² The lion killed enough *for his cubs*
and strangled *the prey for his mate,*
filling his lairs with the kill
and his dens with the prey.
¹³ 'I am against you,'
declares the LORD Almighty.
'I will burn up your chariots in smoke,
and the sword will devour your young lions.
I will leave you no prey on the earth.
The voices of your messengers
will no longer be heard.' (TNIV)

The rhetorical question in verse 11 is used to apply the image of the lion as king to Nineveh. The image of the lion describes the Assyrians' fierce conduct. Although Nineveh was regarded as a safe stronghold for the king (a lion) and his subjects (the cubs), this would no longer be the case after the forthcoming judgment. This is why the mighty lion (Nineveh) is ridiculed—he would no longer be able to instill fear in his enemy. The once mighty lion would become harmless. The lion would no longer have a den (a palace and a capital; v. 12), and his hunting days would be over.

The Lord Himself speaks in verse 13 to seal Nineveh's doom. The repetition of "I" emphasizes that the Lord would be responsible for Nineveh's downfall. Its military power (chariots), its financial power (young lions) and its diplomatic power (your messengers) would come to their final end. It is hard to believe that this was the same city that 150 years previously had experienced a rebirth after Jonah had preached there. All those years ago they had received God's mercy, but now they would experience His wrath. God does not tolerate the abuse of power. If you happen to be in a position of power, how will you use it?

 Lord, forgive me if I have exploited my neighbor in any way.

The property of power is to protect.
—Blaise Pascal (1623–1662), *French mathematician, physicist and philosopher*

HOW DO WE TEST CHARACTER?

Jonah preached in Nineveh 150 years before Nahum (c. 633–612 B.C.) came on the scene. Jonah's message brought about a renewal in the nation. Now, many years later, Nahum announces the destruction of the very same Nineveh. What went wrong? Nineveh became mighty and unfortunately failed the test of character. What was this test of character? Abraham Lincoln put it very well when he said, "Nearly all men can stand adversity, but if you want to test a man's character, give him power."

After their spiritual revival, Assyria went from strength to strength and obtained the status of a super power. But unfortunately, they did not pass the test of character. Let us read Nahum's prophecy about Nineveh's end.

Nahum 3

¹⁸ *King of Assyria, your shepherds* slumber;
your nobles lie down to rest.
Your people are scattered on the mountains
with no one to gather them.
¹⁹ Nothing can heal you;
your wound is fatal.
All who hear the news about you
clap their hands at your fall,
for who has not felt
your endless cruelty? (TNIV)

Nahum ends with a satire about Nineveh. Nineveh would be destroyed to the extent that it would never recover. The last line in the book serves as summary of the divine judgment on Nineveh: their cruelty was the reason for their demise. When power becomes evil and cruel, it exceeds the bounds God set for it.

We need to remember that this is a prophecy. The words of Nahum only proved to be true much later in 612 B.C., when Nineveh was completely destroyed, never to be a factor in world history again. Nahum shows us the cruelty of the abuse of power, but it also shows us the salvation of God because, in actual fact, all power belongs to him. In a sense, we are all in a position of power and authority. Our character will be determined by the way we handle it. Since power can easily lead us astray, we need to be responsible with it.

 Lord, I realize anew that power goes hand in hand with responsibility.

Nearly all men can stand adversity, but if you want to test a man's character, give him power.
—Abraham Lincoln (1809–1865), *Sixteenth President of the United States (1861–65), who brought about the emancipation of the slaves*

THEORETICALLY BELIEVERS, BUT IN PRACTICE ATHEISTS

The name "Zephaniah" means "the Lord hides" (protects). Zephaniah was a brilliantly creative writer who lived in Judah round about 630 B.C., during the last years of the mighty Assyrian kingdom. During this time, God's people practiced idolatrous customs in secret. The perception of this hypocrisy stirred the young prophet to action. As a word artist, he paints a very strange picture.

Zephaniah 1

[7]Be silent before the Sovereign LORD,
for the day of the LORD is near.
The LORD has prepared a sacrifice;
he has consecrated those he has invited.
[8]"On the day of the LORD's sacrifice
I will punish the officials
and the king's sons
and all those clad
in foreign clothes.
[9]On that day I will punish
all who avoid stepping on the threshold,
who fill the temple of their gods
with violence and deceit.
[10]'On that day,'
declares the LORD,
'a cry will go up from the Fish Gate,
wailing from the New Quarter,
and a loud crash from the hills.
[11]Wail, you who live in the market district;
all your merchants will be wiped out,
all who trade with silver will be destroyed.
[12]At that time I will search Jerusalem with lamps
and punish those who are complacent,
who are like wine left on its dregs,
who think, 'The LORD will do nothing,
either good or bad.'
[13] *Their wealth* will be plundered,
their houses demolished.
Though they build houses,
they will not live in them;
though they plant vineyards,
they will not drink the wine.' (TNIV)

Zephaniah paints a picture of a strange religious service with a disturbing sermon. The members of the congregation (Judah) had been invited to a sacrificial feast, only to discover that they were the sacrifice. The meal turned into a massacre. Those who thought they were saved rudely discovered that they were actually lost. The problem was that they attended religious services on the holy day but exploited people during the week.

The people were smug because they believed that the Lord did not do good or evil. God was inactive and uninvolved. These worshipers were, therefore, under the impression that God could not really make a difference. Theoretically, they were believers, but in practice they were atheists. This does not make sense! Where do you stand on this?

 Lord, let me live my words.

> *I once wanted to become an atheist, but I gave up—they have no holidays.*
> —Henny Youngman (1906–1998), *English-born American comedian and violinist*

ONE MINUTE TO MIDNIGHT

Zephaniah paints a very morbid picture. It seems as if there is no way out for Judah. The Lord's judgment seems to be a foregone conclusion. Zephaniah announces Judah's judgment, and although it has not yet happened, it is close to fulfillment. It is one minute to midnight for Judah. Yet if we look closely, it seems as if there was a hint of sunshine. This is confirmed by a specific word—a stroke of the paintbrush.

Zephaniah 2

¹ Gather together, gather yourselves together,
you shameful nation,
² before the decree takes effect
and that day passes like windblown chaff,
before the LORD's fierce anger
comes upon you,
before the day of the LORD's wrath
comes upon you.
³ Seek the LORD, all you humble of the land,
you who do what he commands.
Seek righteousness, seek humility;
perhaps you will be sheltered
on the day of the LORD's anger. (TNIV)

Commands such as "gather together," "seek the Lord" and "seek righteousness" indicate the seriousness of Judah's situation. However, these commands declare that the Lord's judgment can be averted. The word "perhaps" in verse 3 clears away any form of doubt about this. It is the perhaps of God's mercy. This is the stroke of the sun that might rise for Judah. Deliverance is a possibility.

Nahum not only paints the red glow of God's wrath but also the shades of His love. Even though judgment has been announced, it has not yet been executed. The Lord postpones it for as long as possible. For Judah, it is one minute to midnight. It is a time of grace. During this very important minute, they are called on to convert and seek the Lord (v. 3). More than a vertical repentance is required: Judah's relationship with its neighbors would also have to change, and they were told to seek righteousness and humility (v. 3b).

According to the New Testament, we also find ourselves in the last minute before the wheat will be separated from the chaff (Rev. 22:10). Fortunately, we have time to convert; time to become wheat. Let us use this last minute properly! "Perhaps" is embraced by God's mercy to be a picture of sunshine!

 Thank You, Lord, that Your mercy shows so much patience towards us.

Teach me to feel another's woe. To hide the fault I see: That the mercy I show to others;
that mercy also show to me.
—Alexander Pope (1688–1744), *English poet and satirist*

SOMETHING OF THE FUTURE
IN THE PRESENT!

Good prospects for the future put a smile on our faces. Without a future and without hope, no one can live a meaningful life. Our own lives should also bring something of the future into the present in order to give others hope. But how do we do this?

Zephaniah 3

⁹'Then I will purify the lips of the peoples,
that all of them may call on the name of the LORD
and serve him shoulder to shoulder.
¹⁰From beyond the rivers of Cush
my worshipers, my scattered people,
will bring me offerings.
¹¹On that day you, Jerusalem, will not be put to shame
for all the wrongs you have done to me,
because I will remove from you
those who revel in your glory.
Never again will you be haughty
on my holy hill.
¹²But I will leave within you the meek and humble.
The remnant of Israel will trust in the name of the LORD.
¹³*They will do* no wrong;
they will tell no lies.
A deceitful tongue will not be found in their mouths.
They will eat and lie down
and no one will make them afraid.' (TNIV)

Zephaniah, in this fourth and last section of the book, paints a bright picture of the future. Judgment does not have the final say. God's love triumphs! It is the Lord who brings about the change. He changes nations (v. 9), removes the haughty (v. 11) and establishes the humble (v. 12). Zephaniah uses language that belongs to the future.

The wonderful part is that the future is already unfolding. Those who did not know Him previously can now worship Him. Where there are no lies and deception and we can trust the Lord, something of the future emerges (vv. 12–13). In this way, we can also use the way we live to bring something of the future into the present. The present in which we live desperately needs it!

 Lord, I want to use my way of living to let a bit of the future shine through!

Tomorrow belongs to the people who prepare for it today.
—African proverb

THE IMPOSSIBLE POSSIBILITY!

Can a bride forget her bridegroom? Surely this is impossible. Yet this is the impossible possibility that became a reality in this next section.

Jeremiah 2

¹ The word of the Lord came to me, saying:
² Go and proclaim in the hearing of Jerusalem, Thus says the Lord:
I remember the devotion of your youth,
your love as a bride,
how you followed me in the wilderness,
in a land not sown.
⁵ Thus says the Lord:
What wrong did your ancestors find in me
that they went far from me,
and went after worthless things, and became worthless themselves?
⁸ The priests did not say, 'Where is the Lord?'
Those who handle the law did not know me;
the rulers* transgressed against me;
 the prophets prophesied by Baal,
 and went after things that do not profit.
¹⁰ . . . see if there has ever been such a thing.
¹¹ Has a nation changed its gods,
even though they are no gods?
But my people have changed their glory
for something that does not profit. (NRSV)

In this passage, Jeremiah uses the metaphor of a wife who is unfaithful to her husband to sketch the relationship between Judah and the Lord. The marriage had a happy beginning: Judah loved her Groom during the honeymoon and was faithful to Him. But then something dreadful happened. As time went by, Judah started to forget about God. The word "forget" is actually a bit too innocent here. We all sometimes forget things, but what the Lord actually means is that His people (His Bride) preferred idols to Him. Worse than this, they blamed the Lord for their unfaithfulness by asking in what way they had failed. God did not fail. The people thought they made the right choice and were oblivious to their mistake. This was the reason why the Lord had to use prophets to wake them up, because the impossible possibility became possible. We should be careful not to become too complacent in our relationship with God.

 Lord, forgive me for also often replacing You with earthly gods.

Complacency is a state of mind that exists only in retrospective:
it has to be shattered before being ascertained.
—Vladimir Nabokov (1899–1977), *Russian-born novelist and poet*

IT CAN BE DANGEROUS TO ATTEND CHURCH SERVICES!

Church services can uplift and empower us. But after attending a church service, we should guard against a big danger. This section paints a very clear picture of this danger.

Jeremiah 7 (conversation)

¹The word that came to Jeremiah from the Lord: ²Stand in the gate of the Lord's house, and proclaim there this word, and say, Hear the word of the Lord, all you people of Judah, you that enter these gates to worship the Lord. ³ Thus says the Lord of hosts, the God of Israel: Amend your ways and your doings, and let me dwell with you* in this place. ⁴Do not trust in these deceptive words: 'This is the temple of the Lord, the temple of the Lord, the temple of the Lord.'
⁵For if you truly amend your ways and your doings, if you truly act justly one with another, ⁶if you do not oppress the alien, the orphan, and the widow, or shed innocent blood in this place, and if you do not go after other gods to your own hurt, ⁷then I will dwell with you in this place, in the land that I gave of old to your ancestors for ever and ever.
⁸Here you are, trusting in deceptive words to no avail. ⁹Will you steal, murder, commit adultery, swear falsely, make offerings to Baal, and go after other gods that you have not known, ¹⁰and then come and stand before me in this house, which is called by my name, and say, 'We are safe!'—only to go on doing all these abominations? ¹¹Has this house, which is called by my name, become a den of robbers in your sight? You know, I too am watching, says the Lord. (NRSV)

When the people of Israel attended religious services, they developed a false sense of security. They were under the impression that as long as the Temple stood, they would be safe. This religious ease caused them to lose their admiration for God, because they took His love and care for granted. They exploited those who were vulnerable: the foreigners, the orphans and the widows. They were also guilty of theft, murder, adultery and deceit (v. 9).

The worst part is that this lifestyle did not bother them. After all, they went to the Temple. Because of this, Jeremiah had to speak to them (and to us) clearly. His message to them was that service to their neighbor was just as important as attending a religious service. The two cannot be separated. If they did not do good to their neighbors, they were hypocrites. The danger is that we can easily pacify our conscience by thinking, *At least I attended the church service.* Being a Christian entails a way of life that lasts all week.

 Lord, I want to commit myself anew to serving You and serving my neighbor!

Better to be known as a sinner than a hypocrite.
—Author unknown

WHAT MAKES RELIGION DANGEROUS?

It is upsetting to think that religion can be dangerous. However, this section from Jeremiah shows us very clearly that this can happen.

Jeremiah 8

[4] You shall say to them, Thus says the Lord:
When people fall, do they not get up again?
If they go astray, do they not turn back?
[5] Why then has this people turned away
in perpetual backsliding?
They have held fast to deceit,
they have refused to return.
[6] I have given heed and listened,
but they do not speak honestly;
no one repents of wickedness,
saying, 'What have I done!'
All of them turn to their own course,
like a horse plunging headlong into battle.
[11] They have treated the wound of my people carelessly,
saying, 'Peace, peace',
when there is no peace. (ESV)

Jeremiah 9

[1] *O that my head* were a spring of water,
and my eyes a fountain of tears,
so that I might weep day and night
for the slain of my poor people! (NRSV)

Israel displayed unbridled recklessness by breaking away from God like a horse charging into battle (v. 6). Up to this day, people sometimes break away from God to recklessly explore the other side of life. One is reminded of the parable of the prodigal son who broke away from his father (Luke 15).

How does God react when we break away? One would expect judgment and damnation. However, according to Jeremiah 8, God responds to our actions with sadness and incomprehension. Furthermore, those who break away set out on an unknown path that ends in misery.

Because the Lord knows all this, He sent Jeremiah to warn the people. However, they did not take him seriously, because they thought everything was in order (v. 11). After they broke away from God, they foolishly kept on going to the Temple. By acting in this way, they became immune to God's call for them to convert. We can easily fall into the same trap as Israel when we say to ourselves, *At least I went to church!* People easily liken church attendance to being religious. This is precisely why religion can be dangerous.

 Lord, save me from thinking that I need not be converted.

> *Many come to bring their clothes to church rather than themselves.*
> —Thomas Fuller *(1608–1661), British clergyman and author*

THE DAY WHEN GOD WAS NOT MOVED BY PRAYER

We believe that prayer is powerful and can change things. In this section, Jeremiah approached the Lord with a sincere lamentation on behalf of the people. Although his lamentation contained all the elements of a prayer, the Lord was not moved by it. Why?

Jeremiah 14

[20] We acknowledge our wickedness, O Lord,
the iniquity of our ancestors,
for we have sinned against you.
[21] Do not spurn us, for your name's sake;
do not dishonour your glorious throne;
remember and do not break your covenant with us. (poetry)ESV

Jeremiah 15 (conversation)

[1] Then the Lord said to me: Though Moses and Samuel stood before me, yet my heart would not turn towards this people. Send them out of my sight, and let them go! [2] And when they say to you, 'Where shall we go?' you shall say to them: Thus says the Lord: (prose)
Those destined for pestilence, to pestilence,
and those destined for the sword, to the sword;
those destined for famine, to famine,
and those destined for captivity, to captivity. (poetry)
[3] And I will appoint over them four kinds of destroyers, says the Lord: the sword to kill, the dogs to drag away, and the birds of the air and the wild animals of the earth to devour and destroy. [4] I will make them a horror to all the kingdoms of the earth because of what King Manasseh son of Hezekiah of Judah did in Jerusalem. (prose) NRSV

The people were in the midst of a severe drought. With sincere lamentation, Jeremiah pleaded with the Lord for deliverance on behalf of the people. However, his prayer was flawed. Its weakness was not in the words he used but in the people's deeds. Their words were not consistent with their deeds.

It is of no use to rend your clothes and not your heart (Joel 2:13). If repentance lacks sincerity, nothing will help—not even the pleas of two of the greatest prophets, Moses and Samuel. The only option that remained was judgment (Jer. 15:2). Prayer should, therefore, never be taken lightly. We have to be sincere in our prayers and make sure that our prayers are always consistent with our deeds. Sincere prayers—in which deeds and words link up—move God's heart!

 Lord, I confess that I am often not serious enough about prayer.

A lot of kneeling will keep you in good standing.
—Author unknown

A POINT THAT MAKES THE LORD INTOLERANT!

The Bible teaches us that God is a compassionate God and Father who is tolerant towards human beings. However, one thing makes the Lord intolerant. This section sheds light on what this is.

Jeremiah 17

⁵Thus says the LORD:
Cursed are those who trust in mere mortals
and make mere flesh their strength,
whose hearts turn away from the LORD.
⁶They shall be like a shrub in the desert,
and shall not see when relief comes.
They shall live in the parched places of the wilderness,
in an uninhabited salt land.
⁷Blessed are those *who trust in the LORD,*
whose trust is the LORD.
⁸They shall be like a tree planted by water,
sending out its roots by the stream.
It shall not fear when heat comes,
and its leaves shall stay green;
in the year of drought it is not anxious,
and it does not cease to bear fruit.
⁹The heart *is devious above all else;*
it *is perverse*—
who can understand it?
¹⁰I the LORD *test the mind*
and search the heart,
to give to all *according to their ways,*
according to the fruit of their doings. (NRSV)

According to this text, there are two kinds of people: Those who trust people (vv. 5–6) and those who trust the Lord (vv. 7–8). The difference between the two groups of people is illustrated by means of an elaborate parable. Those who trust in people are similar to a bush in the wastelands that is deprived of water (v. 6). Those who trust in the Lord are like a tree that grows near the water and can survive droughts.

Trust in God and trust in human beings are two mutually exclusive options. Trusting people in the "ordinary" sense of the word is certainly in order—we cannot live without it. But here, the author means that our ultimate trust should be in God and only in Him! Our trust in God should not be "by the way," as if it is just another option. He is the only One we should trust to take charge of our life. Not doing this makes the Lord intolerant. He expects our undivided trust in Him.

To entrust our lives to people is dangerous because the heart can be very deceitful (v. 9). Our hearts often have the tendency to tell us only what we want to hear. Those who trust in the Lord will be blessed (v. 7), but it is not always easy to completely trust God. The Lord's path is not an easy one. Being blessed does not necessarily imply prosperity, but it does mean that we can persevere through difficulties in the same way the tree planted next to the water does. In whom do you put your trust?

 Lord, I want to entrust my life to You anew.

> *He that takes truth for his guide, and duty for his end, may safely trust to God's*
> *providence to lead him aright.*
> —Blaise Pascal (1623–1662), *French mathematician, philosopher and physicist*

WHAT IS THE DIFFERENCE BETWEEN A TRUE AND A FALSE PROPHET?

The next section in Jeremiah tells us about a discussion between two prophets. The problem is that they had different messages. How can we know for sure who is sent by the Lord and genuinely speaks His words?

Jeremiah 28 (conversation)

⁵Then the prophet Jeremiah spoke to the prophet Hananiah in the presence of the priests and all the people who were standing in the house of the Lord; ⁶and the prophet Jeremiah said, 'Amen! May the Lord do so; may the Lord fulfil the words that you have prophesied, and bring back to this place from Babylon the vessels of the house of the Lord, and all the exiles. ⁷But listen now to this word that I speak in your hearing and in the hearing of all the people. ⁸The prophets who preceded you and me from ancient times prophesied war, famine, and pestilence against many countries and great kingdoms. ⁹As for the prophet who prophesies peace, when the word of that prophet comes true, then it will be known that the Lord has truly sent the prophet.'

¹⁰Then the prophet Hananiah took the yoke from the neck of the prophet Jeremiah, and broke it. ¹¹And Hananiah spoke in the presence of all the people, saying, 'Thus says the Lord: This is how I will break the yoke of King Nebuchadnezzar of Babylon from the neck of all the nations within two years.' At this, the prophet Jeremiah went his way. ¹²Some time after the prophet Hananiah had broken the yoke from the neck of the prophet Jeremiah, the word of the Lord came to Jeremiah: ¹³Go, tell Hananiah, Thus says the Lord: You have broken wooden bars only to forge iron bars in place of them! ¹⁴For thus says the Lord of hosts, the God of Israel: I have put an iron yoke on the neck of all these nations so that they may serve King Nebuchadnezzar of Babylon, and they shall indeed serve him; I have even given him the wild animals. ¹⁵And the prophet Jeremiah said to the prophet Hananiah, 'Listen, Hananiah, the Lord has not sent you, and you made this people trust in a lie. ¹⁶Therefore thus says the Lord: I am going to send you off the face of the earth. Within this year you will be dead, because you have spoken rebellion against the Lord.'

¹⁷In that same year, in the seventh month, the prophet Hananiah died. (NRSV)

Jeremiah and Hananiah were two prophets with different messages. Hananiah told the people that they would return from exile after 2 years and not 70 years as Jeremiah said. Hananiah's message was merciful and reflected the meaning of his name: "The Lord is merciful."

Who was right? We should remember that false prophets are often serious and sincere. Hananiah was so convinced of his message that Jeremiah left (v. 11) because he could not convince the people to listen to him instead. False prophets are often successful because they bring a message people like to hear. Hananiah's message of peace was not unbiblical, but it was inappropriate for the time. God wanted to punish His people. Jeremiah *understood the specific hour* and realized that it was a time of judgment and not mercy. This distinguished him from the false prophet.

A well-known story about a church council that called a new minister to lead their congregation sums this up. They told the minister never to preach about compassion, justice, missionary work, alcohol abuse or infidelity but only about the Jews, "because where we live there are no Jews." Hananiah's message was popular and an easy way out for the Israelites without them having to show remorse. Beware of popular messages that only serve to ease your conscience!

Lord, help me not to believe everything blindly.

*Fear prophets and those prepared to die for the truth, for as a rule they make many others die
with them, often before them, at times instead of them.*
—Umberto Eco (b. 1929), *Italian novelist and critic*

GOD IS FULL OF SURPRISES!

Some people say that to live with God is rather boring, but in actual fact, God is full of surprises. Jeremiah 31:31–34 tells us about one such surprise. Jeremiah 31 is about a broken relationship: the relationship between God and His people, Israel. This relationship was meant to be sincere and strong—the word "covenant" (an agreement) is used to describe it. Sadly, the relationship between God and His people ended on the rocks. The question is whether or not this relationship can be restored.

Jeremiah 31 (conversation)

[31] The days are surely coming, says the Lord, when I will make a new covenant with the house of Israel and the house of Judah. [32] It will not be like the covenant that I made with their ancestors when I took them by the hand to bring them out of the land of Egypt—a covenant that they broke, though I was their husband, says the Lord. [33] But this is the covenant that I will make with the house of Israel after those days, says the Lord: I will put my law within them, and I will write it on their hearts; and I will be their God, and they shall be my people.

[34] No longer shall they teach one another, or say to each other, 'Know the Lord', for they shall all know me, from the least of them to the greatest, says the Lord; for I will forgive their iniquity, and remember their sin no more. (NRSV)

God was part of a relationship that did not work out. He was the innocent party and could freely walk out of it. The surprise is that despite this fact, He decided to pursue His relationship with Israel. Why would He do that? God wanted to be Israel's God (v. 33). This need was greater than the desire to walk away from the relationship. He remained part of the relationship because He had forgiven their transgressions and no longer thought about their sins (v. 34).

However, the Lord could not continue with the covenant Israel broke. So He decided to make a new covenant with them. Once again, He took the risk with humanity. What guarantee was there that the new covenant would be better than the old one? The answer lies in the nature of the covenant: God would enshrine it in their hearts. The old covenant was written on stone, but this time it would be written in their hearts and minds.

The people could not say that this new covenant was forced on them. What was demanded from them in the previous covenant was now given to them. This would enable each one to instinctively know the requirements of the covenant. Because God is loving and merciful, we can be sure that He is full of surprises.

 Thank You, Lord, that You are my God and that I may be Your child. I praise You for this!

We may be surprised at the people we find in heaven. God has a soft spot for sinners. His standards are quite low.
—Archbishop Desmond Tutu (b. 1931), *South African religious leader and winner of the Nobel Peace Prize in 1984*

THE DAY WHEN GOD CRIED!

It is not strange to see people cry, but it is strange to think that God can cry. After all, God is the almighty. However, the next section confirms that God can indeed cry. But what would cause God to cry?

Jeremiah 48

29 We have heard of the pride of Moab—
he is very proud—
of his loftiness, his pride, and his arrogance,
and the haughtiness of his heart.
30 I myself know his insolence, says the Lord;
his boasts are false,
his deeds are false.
31 Therefore I wail *for Moab*;
I cry out *for all Moab*;
for the people of Kir-heres I mourn. (NRSV)

Arrogance does something to God—it makes Him cry. Why would God cry about arrogance? Arrogance is human beings' way of saying to God that they can do without Him and their neighbors. It destroys people's lives, and God finds it distasteful. After all, He is our Father and is not cold and aloof about what happens to us.

Jeremiah 28:29 is very clear about the effects that arrogance can have on us: we become arrogant, foolhardy and complacent. Arrogance is an indication that we do not need anybody or anything and is probably one of the greatest stumbling blocks that prevent us from responding to God's call. This is the reason why God hates arrogance.

Many people are too proud to admit that they need God and others. What causes this arrogance? It is a quest for freedom, but a freedom away from God, without any need to have Him in their lives. To be arrogant is to be foolish, because it leads to self-destruction. It would be wise to take the following wisdom to heart: "The fear of the Lord is hatred of evil. Pride and arrogance and the way of evil and perverted speech I hate" (Prov. 8:13, NLT). "First pride, then the crash—the bigger the ego, the harder the fall" (Prov. 16:18, MSG).

Lord, I realize again how dangerous arrogance is and that it causes You so much pain.

Arrogance and snobbism live in adjoining rooms and use a common currency.
—Morley Safer (b. 1931), *Reporter and correspondent for CBS News*

HOW DO WE ESCAPE
THE DEPTHS OF SORROW?

It was the custom in the Old East to sing lamentations when someone died or during serious illness or a major tragedy. The book of Lamentations mourns the destruction of Jerusalem by the Babylonians in 586 B.C. What can one do to escape from the depths of one's own sorrow?

Lamentations 1

¹How lonely sits the city
that once was full of people!
How like a widow she has become,
she that was great among the nations!
She that was a princess among the provinces
has become a vassal.
²She weeps bitterly in the night,
with tears on her cheeks;
among all her lovers
she has no one to comfort her;
all her friends have dealt treacherously with her,
they have become her enemies.
¹²Is it nothing to you, all you who pass by?
Look and see
if there is any sorrow like my sorrow,
which was brought upon me,
which the Lord inflicted
on the day of his fierce anger.
¹³From on high he sent fire;
it went deep into my bones;
he spread a net for my feet;
he turned me back;
he has left me stunned. (NRSV)

In this passage, Jerusalem is portrayed as a woman who once enjoyed prestige but now cries bitterly over her misery. She has been stripped of her dignity. Her pain is aggravated because there is no one to comfort her. The fall of Jerusalem led to the collapse of the people's religious life. Had the Lord forgotten them?

Verses 12 and 13 are the focal point in the song: The Lord made the woman suffer. It sounds shocking to think that a loving God would do this. Why did she have to suffer so much? Yet the people would discover soon enough that their suffering did not imply God's rejection.

This song is an invitation to you to bemoan your own pain to the Lord. Honesty toward God opens the way to lifting your sorrow.

 Thank You, Lord, that I can bring my sorrow to You.

Honesty prospers in every condition of life.
—Johann Friedrich Von Schiller (1759–1805), *German dramatist, poet and historian*

THE DAY IT BECAME IMPOSSIBLE TO SERVE THE LORD

Is it true that God will prevent people from worshipping and serving Him?

Lamentations 2

⁵The Lord has become like an enemy;
he has destroyed Israel.
He has destroyed all its palaces,
laid in ruins its strongholds,
and multiplied in daughter Judah
mourning and lamentation.
⁶He has broken down his booth like a garden,
he has destroyed his tabernacle;
the LORD has abolished in Zion
festival and sabbath,
and in his fierce indignation has spurned
king and priest.
⁷*The Lord has scorned* his altar,
disowned his sanctuary;
he has delivered into the hand of the enemy
the walls of her palaces;
a clamour was raised in the house of the LORD
as on a day of festival. (NRSV)

In this very intense song that is packed with emotion, the poet tells the Lord to look at what He had done! In a way, the Lord had become an enemy to him, because He put a stop to the services in the Temple. God was sick and tired of witnessing how the people's faith was not reflected in their daily life.

The poet expresses his emotions in very strong terms: "laid in ruins," "destroyed," "abolished" and "scorned." By destroying the Temple, God had made it impossible for the people to continue celebrating the Sabbath and the other feasts. They could not even bring an offering to the Lord, because the altar had been abandoned. This led to the collapse of the foundations of their religious life.

The Israelites always believed that the Lord lived among them (in the Temple in Jerusalem) and that He would protect His house and city. But then Jerusalem came to a fall, and they were taken into exile. To crown it all, the enemy rejoiced in the house of the Lord, as if they were His people who were rejoicing there. The people asked all sorts of questions: Had God forgotten them? Was He still the almighty King? Was He dead? What of the promises of a House of David that would reign over them forever?

The people would discover soon enough (and admit) that they were the cause of their own misery. Lamentations 2 teaches us that we should feel free to share our deepest emotions with God. We can tell the Lord that we think He treated us too harshly.

 Thank You, Lord, that I can be frank with You about how I feel.

Shared joy is a double joy; shared sorrow is half a sorrow.
—Swedish proverb

WHERE DOES HOPE BEGIN?

We do not look for hope in the light, when things are going well. That is not the place where we became hopeless. Instead, we look for hope where we lost it—where it is dark. Yet in his darkest hour, this poet experienced a change of mind.

Lamentations 3

[18]so I say, 'Gone is my glory,
and all that I had hoped for from the Lord.'
[19]The thought of my affliction and my homelessness
is wormwood and gall!
[20]My soul continually thinks of it
and is bowed down within me.
[21]But this I call to mind,
and therefore I have hope:
[22]*The steadfast love of the Lord* never ceases,
his mercies never come to an end;
[23]they are new every morning;
great is your faithfulness.
[24]'The Lord is my portion,' says my soul,
'therefore I will hope in him.'
[25] The Lord is good to those who wait for him,
to the soul that seeks him.
[26]It is good that one should wait quietly
for the salvation of the Lord.
[27]It is good for one to bear
the yoke in youth, (NRSV)

The word "but" in verse 21 indicates that the poet's state of mind has changed. This happened when he shifted his focus away from himself on to God. He realizes that he is still alive and that he did not perish because of God's love. He also realizes that his suffering does not imply rejection. His hope becomes more obvious when he takes hold of the old confessions of faith. He uses three words to expand on the concept of hope: "morning" and "wait quietly."

Hope begins when we realize that the least we can do in our hour of need is to say, "I'm still alive!" Hope means that we have a tomorrow (morning), and those who have a tomorrow also have a today. If we know that we will still have a job tomorrow, we can live with hope today. Hope helps us to wait and to do it in style. It helps us to wait quietly (patiently) on God. For this reason, we can call on Him with hope when we are in need. "For I cried out to him for help, praising him as I spoke." (Ps. 66:17, NLT). We can rejoice because we have a tomorrow!

 Lord, thank You that I am assured that You are part of my life even in my darkest hour.

Hope begins in the dark, the stubborn hope that if you just show up and try to do the right thing, the dawn will come. You wait and watch and work: you don't give up.
—Anne Lamott (b. 1954), *American best-selling author*

A LIFE WITHOUT JOY

Life's suffering can deprive us of our joy and sometimes also of our faith. This is precisely what happened to the Lord's people. Fortunately, hope broke through in their suffering.

Lamentations 5

¹⁵*The joy of our hearts* has ceased;
our dancing has been turned to mourning.
¹⁶The crown has fallen from our head;
woe to us, for we have sinned!
¹⁷*Because of this* our hearts are sick,
because of these things our eyes have grown dim:
¹⁸because of Mount Zion, which lies desolate;
jackals prowl over it.
¹⁹*But you, O Lord,* reign for ever;
your throne endures to all generations.
²⁰Why have you forgotten us *completely?*
Why have you forsaken us *these many days?*
²¹Restore us to yourself, O Lord, that we may be restored;
renew our days as of old—
²²unless you have utterly rejected us,
and are angry with us beyond measure. (NRSV)

The Lord's people were dismayed that Mount Zion, the place where they once gathered in great numbers to worship the Lord, was now inhabited by jackal. They realized and admitted that their disobedience was the cause of their misery (v. 16). The words "But you, O LORD" at the beginning of verse 19, however, highlight the contrast with the previous verses. Jerusalem had suffered a severe blow, but the Lord's reign was certain.

The poet realizes that the Lord is not an earthly monarch who will go under with His city. He is not tied to one nation, country or temple. His reign is not affected by catastrophic events. This gave the poet hope. This belief is the reason why the poet is able to ask the Lord why He had forgotten His people and why He had forsaken them for so long (v. 20). This is a rhetorical question. The answer is implied: He will not forget or forsake them.

The poet asks God to take the initiative to convert the people. This request affirms that he is dependent on God. The questions at the end of the book are not questions of doubt, but reflect his knowledge of the certainty that the Lord did not reject His people completely. This certainty helped them to move forward even when they experienced pain.

 Thank You, Lord, that You do not reject me and that You are what You are: merciful!

God is the brave man's hope, and not the coward's excuse.
—Plutarch (46–119), *Ancient Greek biographer and author*

LORD, WHY DO YOU NOT HEAR US?

Why do good people have to suffer so much? Why do bad things happen to us? Why does the Lord not hear our cry? How long will we still have to wait? All of us wrestle with these questions at one point or another. Habakkuk wrestled with the same questions. It would, therefore, do us good to read this book.

Habakkuk 1

¹The prophecy that Habakkuk the prophet received.
²How long, LORD, must I call for help,
but you do not listen?
Or cry out to you, 'Violence!'
but you do not save?
³Why do you make me look at *injustice?*
Why do you tolerate *wrongdoing?*
Destruction and violence are before me;
there is strife, and conflict abounds.
⁴Therefore the law *is paralyzed,*
and justice *never prevails.*
The wicked hem in the righteous,
so that justice is perverted. (TNIV)

Habakkuk experienced a religious crisis when the Babylonians destroyed Jerusalem (568 B.C.). Everything on which the people depended collapsed with the fall of Jerusalem: the kingdom of David, the Temple in Jerusalem and the belief that they were God's special people. Was God really still in control? Was He really still interested? Had He not perhaps died? Habakkuk tried to find the answers to these questions. He complained about his lot to God. He felt that God had disassociated Himself from the injustice, the violence and the oppression that existed. Chaos reigned because there was no respect for the law.

Today, the picture has not changed much. Habakkuk grappled with God about real-life issues. He experienced tension between reality and faith. What he saw and experienced made it difficult for him to cling to God's promises and maintain his faith. His questions reflected bewilderment, but not unbelief. That is why he put his questions to God. We are invited to join Habakkuk in his struggle, because by struggling, we discover the extent of God's mercy. Habakkuk would discover this later.

 Thank You, Lord, that I can approach You with all the questions that bother me.

Judge a person by their questions, rather than their answers.
—Voltaire (1694–1778), *French writer and historian*

GOD'S FINGER

Our breaking point is often the same place where God provides a turning point. This is what Habakkuk experienced when God provided an answer to all the questions that bothered him. What was the answer?

Habakkuk 2

[2]Then the LORD replied:
'Write down the revelation
and make it plain on tablets
so that a herald may run with it.
[3]For the revelation awaits an appointed time;
it speaks of the end
and will not prove false.
Though it linger, wait for it;
it will certainly come
and will not delay.
[4]*See, he is puffed up;*
his desires are not upright—
but the righteous will live by their faithfulness—
[5]indeed, wine betrays him;
he is arrogant and never at rest.
Because he is as greedy as the grave
and like death is never satisfied,
he gathers to himself all the nations
and takes captive all the peoples. (TNIV)

The Lord's answer to Habakkuk's questions was accompanied by an order. Habakkuk had to write down the answer and place it in a public place so that people could read it. In the source text, the intention is that whoever reads it should respond to it by *running*. God's answer was intended to get people moving. The answer Habakkuk had to write down (vv. 4–5) did not answer his questions directly, but it did cause movement. God's answer meant that He accompanies human beings on their journey toward an end—an end that means salvation to the righteous but misfortune to the high and mighty. God sees beyond what we see; He sees His destination.

It can be compared to a dog owner who uses his finger to point out the spot where his dog should fetch the ball. Where does the dog look? The dog usually keeps his eyes on the owner's finger. The owner wants the dog to start moving in the direction he is pointing, but the dog does not grasp this. Our questions can be compared to looking at God's "finger"—that is all we see. We do not understand where it is pointing. But in this passage, the Lord showed Habakkuk where His finger was pointing, which set everything in motion. Habakkuk did not get direct answers to his questions, but he did gain perspective. In the meantime, he had to learn to run the race of life patiently (v. 3), as do we.

Lord, thank You for wanting to move me in order to gain perspective on my circumstances.

The reason many persons don't see things in the right perspective is that they
are always looking for an angle.
—Author unknown

FAITH NEVER EXISTS WITHOUT THIS WORD!

Daily realities sometimes dishearten us and deprive us of all our joy. It often seems as if evil has taken over the world. The ungodly enjoy life, while things do not go well for those who believe. Furthermore, the reality of pain and sorrow has a way of creating tension in our religious life. This tension leads us to question why things happen to us and whether God is still in control.

This is precisely what Habakkuk experienced. He begins by asking questions full of doubt (Hab. 1), but he ends on a moving note with a confession of faith. Chapter 2 brings about a turning point when God's answer (vv. 4–5) gives him a glimpse of the future. He realizes that the end of the ungodly will be tragic, while the believers will live. He learns that faith helps one to live today with the end of all things in sight. He learns that faith never exists without the word "yet" (v. 18).

Habakkuk 3

¹⁶I heard and my heart pounded,
my lips quivered at the sound;
decay crept into my bones,
and my legs trembled.
Yet I will wait patiently for the day of calamity
to come on the nation invading us.
¹⁷Though the fig tree does not bud
and there are no grapes on the vines,
though the olive crop fails
and the fields produce no food,
though there are no sheep in the pen
and no cattle in the stalls,
¹⁸yet I will rejoice in the LORD,
I will be joyful in God my Savior.
¹⁹The Sovereign LORD is my strength;
he makes my feet like the feet of a deer,
he enables me to tread on the heights.
For the director of music. On my stringed instruments. (TNIV)

Habakkuk's circumstances remained desperate—the fig tree did not bud and the olive crop failed—but his faith helped him to say the word "yet," and beyond that, he could rejoice. He could rejoice because, in a remarkable way, God had given him the strength to go on—toward a wonderful end!

 Lord, today I will make this confession mine, even though it may sometimes be difficult!

I will love the light for it shows me the way, yet I will endure the darkness because it shows me the stars.
—Og Mandino (1923–1996), *American essayist and psychologist*

TWO EVILS WE SHOULD GUARD AGAINST!

With only 21 verses, Obadiah is the shortest book in the Old Testament. Verse 15 seems to join the parts of the book together. The first half of the verse forecasts what will be said in verses 16 to 21, while the second half summarizes the first 14 verses. The first part, verses 1–14, describes two evils that we should guard against.

Obadiah 1

²"See, I will make you small among the nations;
you will be utterly despised.
³The pride of your heart has deceived you,
you who live in the clefts of the rocks
and make your home on the heights,
you who say to yourself,
'Who can bring me down to the ground?'
¹²*You should not gloat over your brother*
in the day of his misfortune,
nor rejoice over the people of Judah
in the day of their destruction,
nor boast so much
in the day of their trouble.
¹³*You should not march through the gates of my people*
in the day of their disaster,
nor gloat over them in their calamity
in the day of their disaster,
nor seize their wealth
in the day of their disaster.
¹⁵"The day of the LORD is near for all nations.
As you have done, it will be done to you;
your deeds will return upon your own head. (TNIV)

The Edomites were descendants of Esau, Jacob's twin brother, and were therefore considered in the Israelites' family (v. 12). The Edomites offended God in two ways. First, they were *arrogant*. They thought that they were invincible because of their protected geographical setting (vv. 2–3). Their arrogance grieved God intensely, because they looked down on other people.

Second, Edom was condemned because they *betrayed* their brother, Israel. The Edomites were in cahoots with Israel's enemy and contributed to the downfall of their brother. When Babylon invaded Israel and destroyed Jerusalem in 586 B.C., the Edomites rejoiced in their misfortune (v. 12). Because Judah was disobedient their punishment was justified, but Edom's arrogance and betrayal went against God's sense of justice and honor. He therefore passed judgment on them (v. 15).

We should never take pleasure in other people's misfortune, because it will upset our relationships with others—yes, even with the God of mercy!

Lord, make me humble and help me never to take pleasure in the misfortune of others.

> *Betrayal is the only truth that sticks.*
> —Arthur Miller (1915–2005), *American playwright*

WHAT IS GOD'S ULTIMATE AIM?

As we mentioned yesterday, the fifteenth verse in Obadiah connects the book together. It shows God's ultimate aim in everything.

Obadiah 1

16Just as you drank on my holy hill,
so all the nations will drink continually;
they will drink and drink
and be as if they had never been.
17But on Mount Zion will be deliverance;
it will be holy,
and the house of Jacob
will possess its inheritance.
18*The house of Jacob will be a fire*
and the house of Joseph a flame;
the house of Esau will be stubble,
and they will set it on fire and consume it.
There will be no survivors
from the house of Esau.'
The LORD has spoken.
19*People from the Negev will occupy*
the mountains of Esau,
and people from the foothills will possess
the land of the Philistines.
They will occupy the fields of Ephraim and Samaria,
and Benjamin will possess Gilead.
20This company of Israelite exiles who are in Canaan
will possess [the land] as far as Zarephath;
the exiles from Jerusalem who are in Sepharad
will possess the towns of the Negev.
21Deliverers will go up on Mount Zion
to govern the mountains of Esau.
And the kingdom will be the LORD's. (TNIV)

Obadiah first describes how God punished Edom (1–14), and then verse 15 connects God's punishment to Judah's recovery (16–21). However, Judah's recovery is not the book's climax—rather, it is God's honor and supremacy (v. 21). God's honor was closely linked to the lot of His people. The behavior of the Israelites defiled God's honor. God was willing to harm His honor by sending His people into exile as a punishment for their disobedience. But because God values His honor, He would allow His people to return from exile.

Judah merely became the instrument through which God would restore His honor on earth. God's honor is His ultimate aim in everything. Our lives are instruments that God wants to use to restore

His honor on earth. We do this by reflecting the meaning of Obadiah's name (servant/worshiper of the Lord) in our daily lives.

 Lord, I realize anew that Your honor is at stake in everything I do.

Honor has not to be won; it must only not be lost.
—Arthur Schopenhauer (1788–1860), *German philosopher*

SHOULD WE TAKE A CHANCE WITH GOD?

Relationships cannot flourish without trust. Trust creates a safe environment in which we can reveal our true feelings. It is sad that so many relationships suffer because of a breach of trust. God wants us to have a relationship with Him in our lives. This section in Isaiah gives us two good reasons why we can take the chance of trusting God.

Isaiah 40

¹Comfort, O comfort my people,
says your God.
²Speak tenderly to Jerusalem,
and cry to her
that she has served her term,
that her penalty is paid,
that she has received from the Lord's hand
double for all her sins.
³A voice cries out:
'In the wilderness prepare *the way of the Lord,*
make straight in the desert *a highway for our God.*
⁴*Every valley* shall be lifted up,
and every mountain and hill be made low;
the uneven ground *shall become level,*
and the rough places *a plain.*
⁵Then the glory of the Lord shall be revealed,
and all people shall see it together,
for the mouth of the Lord has spoken.' (NRSV)

The first reason why we can trust God is that He forgives (vv. 1–2). The first part of Isaiah (1–39) ends in a dead end—the Lord's people are in exile in Babylon. However, the second part of Isaiah (40–55) begins with a surprising message: *Salvation is close at hand!* The people's suffering had come to an end. They had paid the penalty for their sins (vv. 1–2). It is not the fact that the exile—the punishment—had come to an end that is comforting, but rather that God's forgiveness had been obtained.

The second reason why we can trust God is that He is present (vv. 3–5). He did not forget the Israelites when they were in Babylon. He decided to lead them from their exile Himself. It's like the minister who visited his uncle in Colorado Springs one summer vacation. On the very first day, he asked his uncle, "Where is Pike's Peak?" His uncle answered, "You are standing on it!" The minister could not believe it. This is often true of our relationship with God. We look for Him in distant places when, in actual fact, He is right there with us. That is reason enough why you should take a chance trusting God!

 Thank You, Lord, that I have enough reasons to trust You. Please forgive me my unbelief!

To put one's trust in God is only a longer way of saying that one will chance it.
—Samuel Butler (1835–1902), *English novelist, essayist and critic*

WHEN WE'RE AFRAID . . .

After I put the kids to bed and switch off the lights, I look at them and sometimes feel afraid. What will become of them? I have traveled further than they have on life's journey, and I know that life can sometimes be cruel. I become fearful when I think that they might fall prey to life's cruelty. Once, after having looked at them while they were sleeping without a care in the world, I paged through the Bible and stopped at Isaiah 43. This chapter comforted me and helped me to sleep peacefully.

Isaiah 43

[1]But now thus says the Lord,
he who created you, O Jacob,
he who formed you, O Israel:
Do not fear, for I have redeemed you;
I have called you by name, you are mine.
[2]*When you pass through the waters,* I will be with you;
and through the rivers, they shall not overwhelm you;
when you walk through fire *you shall not be burned,*
and the flame *shall not consume you.*
[3]*For I am the Lord* your God,
the Holy One of Israel, your Saviour.
I give Egypt *as your ransom,*
Ethiopia and Seba *in exchange for you.*
[4]Because you are precious in my sight,
and honoured, and I love you,
I give people in return for you,
nations in exchange for your life.
[5]Do not fear, for I am with you;
I will bring your offspring from the east,
and from the west I will gather you. (NRSV)

The exiles in Babylon were afraid and disheartened. But the Lord comforted them with the beautiful poetic words in Isaiah 43:1: "Do not fear, for I have redeemed you; I have called you by name, you are mine." The Lord called Israel by name, just as He calls all of His children by name. And He calls my children—Cara-Mari, Elsjé and James—by name! They belong to Him. Their christening confirms that truth. The Lord will provide even when they have to weather the storms of life.

 Thank You, Lord, that You know my name and that I can belong to You. I thank You!

Let me assert my firm belief that the only thing we have to fear is fear itself.
—Franklin D. Roosevelt (1882–1945), *Thirty-second President of the United States*

A "MESSIAH" WHO DID NOT KNOW THE LORD!

In the second (40–55) and third (56–66) parts of Isaiah, the Israelites are in exile in Babylon and the fall of Babylon is predicted. But that is not all. These sections also tell us that the Israelites will be freed and will return to Jerusalem. God put a unique plan in motion to achieve this. This unique plan must have shocked those who first heard about it. Why?

Isaiah 45

[1]Thus says the Lord to his anointed, to Cyrus,
whose right hand I have grasped
to subdue nations before him
and strip kings of their robes,
to open doors before him—
and the gates shall not be closed:
[2]I will go before you
and level the mountains,
I will break in pieces the doors of bronze
and cut through the bars of iron,
[3]I will give you the treasures of darkness
and riches hidden in secret places,
so that you may know that it is I, the Lord,
the God of Israel, who call you by your name.
[4]For the sake of my servant Jacob,
and Israel my chosen,
I call you by your name,
I surname you, though you do not know me. (NRSV)

The Israelites heard that the Lord would use someone who was anointed to free them from exile. They must have been shocked to hear that it would be Cyrus, the Persian king. He did not know the Lord and was not an Israelite. This was the first and only time that a non-Israelite received the title of the anointed—the "messiah." Like us, the Israelites had to realize that the Lord cannot be limited. He works in unexpected ways. This confirms that He alone is God and that He determines the cause of events. The Lord enabled Cyrus to be extremely successful. Cyrus conquered Babylonia and allowed the Israelites to return to Jerusalem. Today, God still works in ways we do not understand because *He alone is God!*

 Lord, it is liberating to know that You are in control in a unique way.

A religion without mystery must be a religion without God.
—Jeremy Taylor (613–1667), *English Anglican clergyman, writer and bishop*

HOW CAN WE KNOW
THAT OUR FAITH IS REAL?

Faith has many names and angles, but it always means to trust God and His promises. The best definition of faith is found in Hebrews 11:1: "Now faith is being sure of what we hope for and certain of what we do not see" (NIV). How can we know whether our faith complies with this definition? This section may help us!

Isaiah 55

[6]*Seek the Lord* while he may be found,
call upon him while he is near;
[7]let the wicked *forsake their way,*
and the unrighteous *their thoughts;*
let them return to the Lord, that he may have mercy on them,
and to our God, for he will abundantly pardon.
[8]For my thoughts *are not your thoughts,*
nor are your ways my ways, says the Lord.
[10]For as the rain and the snow come down from heaven,
and do not return there until they have watered the earth,
making it bring forth and sprout,
giving seed to the sower and bread to the eater,
[11] so shall my word be that goes out from my mouth;
it shall not return to me empty,
but it shall accomplish that which I purpose,
and succeed in the thing for which I sent it. (NRSV)

In this passage in Isaiah, the exiles are invited to become part of God's plan of salvation. For this, they need faith. According to the text, "faith" means to accept God's Word.

Is our faith strong enough to trust God and His Word? This does not always seem to be the case, as our faith often relies on God's blessings. We are often faithful because God is good to us, not because we trust Him and His Word. Fortunately, we can put ourselves to the test. Can we be like Job and maintain our faith despite being stripped of God's blessings?

Of course, we do not have to wait for a similar experience as the one Job went through. According to Isaiah 55:7, faith also means conversion. The test is whether we are prepared to give up our ways and replace it with God's ways. This is risky! But we should take the risk because God is different: He is more patient with us than we are with Him. That is why He gives us so many chances. We should try not to overplay our chances, because the period of grace might pass (v. 6). We must accept God's Word and follow Him—despite our circumstances. That is the test!

 Thank You, Lord, for having so much patience with me!

A faith that hasn't been tested can't be trusted.
—Adrian Rogers (1931–2005), *American pastor, author and three-term president of the*
Southern Baptist Convention

SEEING IS NOT ALWAYS BELIEVING!

A well-known Jewish legend tells about two rabbis who sat and argued whether the Messiah had already come to earth. They quoted the Scriptures and the sages and peppered each other with arguments. In an attempt to settle the argument, one of them walked to the window and said to the other, "Look outside! Look at the state of the world. If the Messiah had already come, it would not look the way it does." How would you have responded to the rabbi's words? Isaiah 60 will help you!

Isaiah 60

¹Arise, shine; for your light has come,
and the glory of the Lord has risen upon you.
²*For darkness* shall cover the earth,
and thick darkness the peoples;
but the Lord *will arise upon you,*
and his glory *will appear over you.*
³*Nations* shall come to your light,
and kings to the brightness of your dawn.
⁴Lift up your eyes and look around;
they all gather together, they come to you;
your sons shall come from far away,
and your daughters shall be carried on their nurses' arms. (NRSV)

The returning exiles were completely disillusioned and despondent. All they could see through their windows were ruins, suffering and misery. Most of us are able to identify with the fears and frustrations of the Israelites. Their fears form part of the reality in which we find ourselves. But Isaiah wanted to teach them to look beyond the ruins of Jerusalem. They had to see that God was once again committed to them.

God's task concerning them had not been completed. His light shone through the ruins so that the different nations could flock to Jerusalem. Isaiah wanted to teach his people that "seeing is not always believing." Today, we can look through the window, past the misery and know that God came to live in this world. Furthermore, His Spirit lives in us to provide the world with light in the same way as Jerusalem (Matt 5:14).

How should we then respond to the words of the rabbi in the above story? By explaining that seeing is not always believing!

 Thank You, Lord, that today I can look outside and know that You came to live in this world.

You must understand that seeing is believing, but also know that believing is seeing.
—Denis Waitley (b. 1933), *American motivational speaker and author of self-help books*

OUR SIXTH STOP: EXILE

(597–538 B.C.)
(EZEKIEL AND DANIEL)

People interpreted the events of the exile in two ways. First, those who saw the exile as a sign of God's weakness interpreted it negatively. During those times, people believed that if a nation won a war, it indicated that their god was mightier than the god of the enemy. Second, those who saw the exiles as God's punishment for sins the people committed interpreted it positively. Although God was not powerless, he let His people be punished.

According to the covenant God made with His people, disobedience would be punished (Deut. 30:15–18). The Lord did not turn His back on His people. After all, He made a covenant with them to be their God. He continued to educate and encourage them through prophets such as Ezekiel and Daniel (who were prophets in Babylon) and Jeremiah (a prophet in Jerusalem and Egypt).

The exile changed the people's way of worshipping. Because they were now far away from Jerusalem, the Temple and sacrifices could no longer be the focal point of their worship. Instead, prayer, confession and teaching became the focus of their worship. The gatherings in their homes preceded the assemblies in the synagogues. The Temple priests who were also taken into exile acted as interpreters of the Law.

"LORD, CAN'T YOU SEE MY SUFFERING?"

It is especially during dark times that we want to call out in anguish, "Lord, where are You? Can't You see my suffering?" The exiles felt exactly the same. They thought that God resided in the Temple in Jerusalem, but they were in Babylon—about 500 miles (804 kilometers) away. They felt that this was their darkest hour. Yet it was during this darkest period of the Old Testament that something surprising happened.

Ezekiel 1 (apocalypse)

[3]the word of the LORD came to Ezekiel the priest, the son of Buzi, by the Kebar River in the land of the Babylonians. There the hand of the LORD was on him.

[4]I looked, and I saw a windstorm coming out of the north—an immense cloud with flashing lightning and surrounded by brilliant light. The center of the fire looked like glowing metal, [5] and in the fire was what looked like four living creatures. In appearance their form was human, [6]but each of them had four faces and four wings.

[7]Their legs were straight; their feet were like those of a calf and gleamed like burnished bronze. [8]Under their wings on their four sides they had human hands. All four of them had faces and wings, [9]and the wings of one touched the wings of another. Each one went straight ahead; they did not turn as they moved.

[10]Their faces looked like this: Each of the four had the face of a human being, and on the right side each had the face of a lion, and on the left the face of an ox; each also had the face of an eagle. (TNIV)

More than 500 miles away from Jerusalem, in the enemy's territory, God appeared to Ezekiel in a vision. This vision made Ezekiel realize that God was not restricted to the four walls of a Temple and confirmed the Lord's omnipotence (unlimited power). The four living creatures were cherubs who protected God's glory. Their four faces represented the strongest species in the animal and bird kingdom. There, in the enemy's territory, God used this vision to say to Ezekiel, "I am not far from you." While the people had their doubts about God, He was the One who went to call on them. Where is God? A rabbi once answered this question by saying that He is where people look for Him, because He is already looking for them.

 Lord, I thank You that you are with me all the time!

Shipwrecked on God, stranded on omnipotence.
—Vance Havner (1901–1986), *American Baptist preacher*

CAN GOD BE HURT?

Each day, we are exposed to the hurt others experience. But did you ever think whether God can hurt? This section reveals something about God.

Ezekiel 5 (conversation)

¹⁴"I will make you a ruin and a reproach among the nations around you, in the sight of all who pass by. ¹⁵You will be a reproach and a taunt, a warning and an object of horror to the nations around you when I inflict punishment on you in anger and in wrath and with stinging rebuke. I the LORD have spoken. ¹⁶When I shoot at you with my deadly and destructive arrows of famine, I will shoot to destroy you. I will bring more and more famine upon you and cut off your supply of food. ¹⁷I will send famine and wild beasts against you, and they will leave you childless. Plague and bloodshed will sweep through you, and I will bring the sword against you. I the LORD have spoken.' (TNIV)

The prophecy of Jerusalem's destruction was disturbing news to the exiles who were taken away shortly before the city fell. As we have seen, they firmly believed that Jerusalem would never be destroyed because God's Temple stood there. Yet Jerusalem, the place that portrayed God's love so clearly, became a place where God's judgment hung dark and ominous.

Ezekiel prophesied that what was about to happen in Jerusalem would not take place in some hidden corner but in the public eye—where everyone could see. God wanted to show His people and the world that the fall of Jerusalem was more than a historical event. He wanted to tell everyone: I have been hurt! God was hurt because His beloved people worshiped other gods. His wrath toward Jerusalem was enormous because His love for Israel was so big. People whom you love the most are usually the ones who hurt you the most.

As early as the sixth chapter in the Bible, God stated that He regretted having made human beings (Gen 6:6) because they caused Him such pain. Our actions have an influence on God's emotions. Yes, He can hurt—and very badly. This is a frightening thought. It must have caused God great pain to punish Jerusalem the way He did. But God did not punish His people in order to destroy them. More than five centuries later, God would stand in the barrage of His own wrath when His only Son died on their behalf. His love for them was greater than His wrath. Nobody states this better than John: "For God so loved the world that he gave His one and only Son, that whoever believes in Him shall not perish but have eternal life" (John 3:16, NIV). He wanted to restore His relationship with them and show them His mercy and love.

 Father, thank You for loving me even though I often hurt You!

Mercy should make us ashamed, wrath afraid to sin.
—William Gurnall (1617–1679), *English author*

THE BIBLE'S TITANIC ALSO SANK!

On Thursday, April 11, 1912, the most famous passenger liner in the world at the time, the Titanic, left Queenstown harbor on its maiden voyage across the ocean to New York. Four days later, the *New York Times* carried the heading: "Titanic Sinks Four Hours After Hitting Iceberg." More than 1,500 people died in that disaster, among them the world's richest man. These events were relived in the successful 1997 movie called *Titanic*. The Bible had its own Titanic. Unfortunately, it also sank. Not a movie, but a sad song describes the end of the Bible's Titanic.

Ezekiel 27

[1]The word of the LORD came to me: [2] 'Son of man, take up a lament concerning Tyre.
[32]As they wail and mourn over you,
they will take up a lament concerning you:
'Who was ever silenced like Tyre,
surrounded by the sea?
[33] *When your merchandise went out on the seas,*
you satisfied many nations;
with your great wealth and your wares
you enriched the kings of the earth.
[34]Now you are shattered by the sea
in the depths of the waters;
your wares and all your company
have gone down with you.
[35]All who live in the coastlands
are appalled at you;
their kings shudder with horror
and their faces are distorted with fear. (TNIV)

Here we have the picture of a mighty ship sailing through the waters. The prosperous trading city of Tyre is represented by a luxury ship. Tyre was the Bible's Titanic. Like the Titanic, it had no equal. It played a leading naval role in the region, had partners everywhere, and was significant in the world market. Unfortunately, the people of Tyre used Jerusalem's destruction to their own advantage. Moving imagery in this passage predicts their end. God does not tolerate enrichment at the expense of others. The story of Tyre lets us see, once again, that sin always has the opposite effect of what we originally intended. May God help us not to exploit others!

 Lord, I once again realize life's Titanics can easily sink.

Professionals built the Titanic, amateurs the ark.
—Frank Pepper (1913–2003), *Merchant seaman who sailed around the world 14 times*

THE MIGHTY PHARAOH WAS NAILED!

People and sports teams are often compared to animals in order to highlight their positive or negative traits. Just think about *Tiger* Woods or the *Blue Bulls*. In the Bible, the mighty Pharaoh is called a crocodile. This comparison is appropriate, because the Nile crocodile is the biggest crocodile species in the world. Before the fall of Jerusalem in 586 B.C., God predicted that this mighty crocodile of a Pharaoh's power would be destroyed. Why would God want to do this?

Ezekiel 29

²'Son of man, set your face against Pharaoh king of Egypt and prophesy against him and against all Egypt. ³ Speak to him and say: 'This is what the Sovereign LORD says: *(instruction)*
' 'I am against you, Pharaoh king of Egypt,
you great monster lying among your streams.
You say, 'The Nile belongs to me;
I made it for myself.'
⁴*But I will put hooks in your jaws*
and make the fish of your streams stick to your scales.
I will pull you out from among your streams,
with all the fish sticking to your scales.
⁵I will leave you in the desert,
you and all the fish of your streams.
You will fall on the open field
and not be gathered or picked up.
I will give you as food
to the beasts of the earth and the birds of the sky. *(poetry)*
⁶Then all who live in Egypt will know that I am the LORD.
' 'You have been a staff of reed for the house of Israel.
⁷When they grasped you with their hands, you splintered and you tore open their shoulders; when they leaned on you, you broke and their backs were wrenched. *(conversation)* TNIV

The Lord had many problems with Pharaoh, the leader of Egypt. For one, Pharaoh had the audacity to place himself on par with God by saying, "The Nile is mine; I made it for myself!" (v. 3b). The Lord also had big problems with the Israelites because they trusted Pharaoh instead of God. For this reason, the Lord proclaimed by way of prophecy that he would "nail" Pharaoh. God sent a clear message: I am the Lord! (v. 6). The Israelites wanted to use the mighty Pharaoh as a crutch, but they had to discover, to their disappointment, that the crutch was merely a reed that would break easily. How often do we not mistake broken reeds for mighty crocodiles? We will have to improve our judgment!

 Lord, forgive me for often wanting to trust the crocodiles in my life.

Everyone complains of the badness of his memory, but nobody of his judgment.
—François de La Rochefoucauld (1613–1680), *French writer*

IF WE SHARE OUR EXPECTATIONS, OUR PROBLEMS WILL BE LESS!

We become very upset when other people do not respond as we expect them to. The big question, however, is whether or not we shared our expectations with them. We should learn to tell others what we want; for instance, "I would like it if you could come home early." God is willing to share His expectations with us. What are these expectations?

Ezekiel 33 (explanation and instruction)

[10]"Son of man, say to the house of Israel, 'This is what you are saying: "Our offenses and sins weigh us down, and we are wasting away because of them. How then can we live?" ' [11]Say to them, 'As surely as I live, declares the Sovereign LORD, I take no pleasure in the death of the wicked, but rather that they turn from their ways and live. *(explanation)*
Turn! Turn from your evil ways! *(instruction)*
Why will you die, house of Israel? ' [12]"Therefore, son of man, say to your people, 'If someone who is righteous disobeys, that person's former righteousness will count for nothing. And if someone who is wicked repents, that person's former wickedness will not bring condemnation. The righteous, if they sin, will not be allowed to live because of their former righteousness.' [13]If I tell the righteous that they will surely live, but then they trust in their righteousness and do evil, none of the righteous things they have done will be remembered; they will die for the evil they have done. [14]And if I say to the wicked, 'You will surely die,' but they then turn away from their sins and do what is just and right—[15]if they give back what they took in pledge for a loan, return what they have stolen, follow the decrees that give life, and do no evil, they will surely live; they will not die. [16]None of the sins they have committed will be remembered against them. They have done what is just and right; they will surely live. [20]Yet you say, house of Israel, 'The way of the Lord is not just.' But I will judge each of you according to your own ways." *(explanation)* TNIV

The Israelites eventually realized that their sins were the cause of their misery (v. 10). They saw a bleak future. It was then that God was willing to talk to them and to open up His heart to them. In verse 11, God tells them exactly what He expects. Two words sum up God's request: "turn" and "live."

Christoph Blumhardt, a German theologian, said that every person should be converted twice: first, from the world to Christ; and second, from Christ to the world. We have to make a difference in this life, and we can do this by rectifying our mistakes (v. 15). We should, therefore, take note of what we do and also of what we neglect to do (v. 20). Life implies having a relationship with the Lord. This should start right now, not sometime in the future.

In the above passage, the author does not distinguish between eternal life and daily life. Our behavior, here and now, has to reveal something about God's kingdom. God's heartbeat is very clear: Turn (convert) and live!

Thank You, Lord, for enabling me to know what Your wishes are. I choose life!

I believe that a man is converted when first he hears the low, vast murmur of life,
of human life, troubling his hitherto unconscious self.
—D. H. Lawrence (1885–1930), *English novelist*

A FRIGHTENING THOUGHT THAT IS ALSO COMFORTING

Most of us dread the thought of performing for an audience. But that is what believers do on a daily basis, because the world is the audience who watches us. Our actions display what God is like—a frightening thought, but also a great comfort. Let us read!

Ezekiel 39 (conversation)

²³And the nations will know that the people of Israel went into exile for their sin, because they were unfaithful to me. So I hid my face from them and handed them over to their enemies, and they all fell by the sword. ²⁴I dealt with them according to their uncleanness and their offenses, and I hid my face from them.

²⁵'Therefore this is what the Sovereign LORD says: I will now restore the fortunes of Jacob and will have *compassion* on all the people of Israel, and I will be zealous for my holy name. ²⁶They will forget their shame and all the unfaithfulness they showed toward me when they lived in safety in their land with no one to make them afraid.

²⁷When I have brought them back from the nations and have gathered them from the countries of their enemies, I will be proved holy through them in the sight of many nations. ²⁸Then they will know that I am the LORD their God, for though I sent them into exile among the nations, I will gather them to their own land, not leaving any behind. ²⁹I will no longer hide my face from them, for I will pour out my Spirit on the house of Israel, declares the Sovereign LORD.' (TNIV)

In this section, God wants the world to realize that the exile of Israel was not mere coincidence. God rejected the Israelites because, as God's people, they no longer showcased His holiness. They became unfaithful to Him. Yet God could not reject them totally, because His honor was at stake. For this reason, God decided to change His people's destiny (v. 25). God's rejection made way for His mercy. He did this because He wanted the world to realize that He was God.

Israel need never again fear rejection, because God's mercy went hand in hand with a promise: He would never again drive them away. This is the same promise Jesus gave to us (John 6:37). What a great comfort it is to know that God will not reject us. People are prepared to forsake their principles to prevent the rejection of others, but it is different with God. Even if we fail to perform on His stage, we can be comforted because we know that God's care and comfort surpasses His rejection! Best of all, God does not forsake us, but His Spirit (and fellow believers) joins us on life's stage. Be strong!

 Spirit of God, thank You for helping me to reflect God's image!

The world's a theater, the earth a stage, which God and nature do with actors fill.
—Author unknown

WHAT DO I NEED IN DARK TIMES?

We have all encountered dark times in our lives. Dark times tend to rob us of something we cannot do without, namely, *hope*. God used Ezekiel in a wonderful way to give His exiled people new hope.

Ezekiel 40 (apocalypse)

[1]In the twenty-fifth year of our exile, at the beginning of the year, on the tenth of the month, in the fourteenth year after the fall of the city—on that very day the hand of the LORD was on me and he took me there. [2]In visions of God he took me to the land of Israel and set me on a very high mountain, on whose south side were some buildings that looked like a city. [3]He took me there, and I saw a man whose appearance was like bronze; he was standing in the gateway with a linen cord and a measuring rod in his hand. [4]The man said to me, 'Son of man, look carefully and listen closely and pay attention to everything I am going to show you, for that is why you have been brought here. Tell the house of Israel everything you see.'
[5]I saw a wall completely surrounding the temple area. The length of the measuring rod in the man's hand was six long cubits, each of which was a cubit and a handbreadth. He measured the wall; it was one measuring rod thick and one rod high. (TNIV)

Fourteen years after the destruction of Jerusalem, God took Ezekiel there in a vision. Ezekiel was ordered to look and listen well—and to tell Israel what he saw and heard. Ezekiel saw the Temple and was overwhelmed by its greatness. The Temple of the Lord outshone all previous buildings. It is described as inconceivable.

The description of the Temple reflects much more than the description of a building—it reflects how the prophet experienced the greatness, steadfastness, majesty and trustworthiness of God. God used this vision to let Ezekiel know that even though the exiles were in an hour of great darkness, *He was still the Lord!* This expression is repeated 54 times in the book. God used this vision to tell His people that their misery would come to an end.

It is therefore no wonder that the scroll of Ezekiel was found at the site of one of the greatest heroic deeds in Jewish history. In A.D. 73, during the Jewish revolt against the Romans, a group of Jews were trapped in the fortress of Masada on the west bank of the Dead Sea. According to the historian Josephus, before the Roman troops reached the Jews, the Jews killed themselves in a mass suicide. They would rather die than give up. When the Romans eventually found the Jews, they discovered Ezekiel's scroll among the corpses. Thus, Ezekiel conveyed everything he saw, because years later those who were trapped in Masada died in hope with the message of Ezekiel in their hearts. They knew that the Lord is God!

 Thank You, Lord, that I can join Ezekiel in confessing that You are God.

Our hopes are but memories reversed.
—Author unknown

WHAT IS GOD'S ADDRESS?

A woman once complained to a minister that after all the years she had spent seeking the Lord, she was still unable to find Him. She told the minister that she had looked for Him everywhere. The minister asked her, "Have you looked for Him at His address?" What is God's address? The last section of the book of Ezekiel will help us to find the answer.

Ezekiel 48 (apocalypse)

30"These will be the exits of the city: Beginning on the north side, which is 4,500 cubits long, 31the gates of the city will be named after the tribes of Israel. The three gates on the north side will be the gate of Reuben, the gate of Judah and the gate of Levi.

32"On the east side, which is 4,500 cubits long, will be three gates: the gate of Joseph, the gate of Benjamin and the gate of Dan.

33"On the south side, which measures 4,500 cubits, will be three gates: the gate of Simeon, the gate of Issachar and the gate of Zebulun.

34"On the west side, which is 4,500 cubits long, will be three gates: the gate of Gad, the gate of Asher and the gate of Naphtali.

35"The distance all around will be 18,000 cubits.

'And the name of the city from that time on will be:

THE LORD IS THERE.' (TNIV)

In Ezekiel's time, the question about God's whereabouts was very topical. One view held that God resided in the Temple of Jerusalem. When the exiles found themselves far away from Jerusalem and the destroyed Temple, like Ezekiel, they wondered, *Did God stay behind in Jerusalem? Are we now without God in Babylon?*

This concluding section in Ezekiel tells us how God used a vision to comfort His people. God looked up His people and prophet in their place of exile, far away from Jerusalem. In this vision, Ezekiel saw a new city. This city had 12 gates that connected it to the rest of Israel. We have to remember that the 10 Northern tribes had been carried off to Assyria in 722 B.C. and had never returned. The new city was renamed Jehovah-Shammah, which is Hebrew for "the Lord is there." Thus, this book begins with judgment and ends with an unsurpassed climax: The Lord is there! The exiles need not ever doubt again. God used visions to confirm that His presence would lay the foundation for their future.

Many centuries later, this was again confirmed by the birth of Jesus: "The virgin will conceive and give birth to a son, and they will call him Immanuel (which means 'God with us')" (Matt. 1:23, TNIV). What a great comfort and privilege! God's address is where believers are. Matthew confirmed this by writing that where two or three of them are together in His name, He will be there (Matt. 18:20). This text also serves as a test: Are our homes and cities places of which people can say that the Lord is there?

 Lord, thank You for the comfort of knowing that You are where I am!

It boggles my mind that someone can see life breathed into a baby, watch the grass die and then come to life again, see leaves fall and watch the rebirth of a tree, or gaze on any of the majestic splendor that is this earth and not be overpowered by the presence of an Almighty God!
—Bill McCartney (b. 1940), *Football coach at the University of Colorado and president of Promise Keepers*

HOW FAR DOES OUR LOYALTY REACH?

A young soldier who had a steady girlfriend in the town where he lived admitted to his chaplain that he would never date any other girl if he were within a radius of 50 miles (80 kilometers) from his home. His loyalty had a reach of only 50 miles! How far does your loyalty reach, especially where God is concerned?

Daniel 3 (story)

Tension: *A charge is brought against Shadrach, Meshach and Abednego*

[8]At this time some astrologers came forward and denounced the Jews. [9]They said to King Nebuchadnezzar, 'May the king live forever! [10]Your Majesty has issued a decree that everyone who hears the sound of the horn, flute, zither, lyre, harp, pipe and all kinds of music must fall down and worship the image of gold, [11]and that whoever does not fall down and worship will be thrown into a blazing furnace. [12]But there are some Jews whom you have set over the affairs of the province of Babylon—Shadrach, Meshach and Abednego—who pay no attention to you, Your Majesty. They neither serve your gods nor worship the image of gold you have set up.'

Tension: *Nebuchadnezzar explodes with anger and uses a threat*

[13]Furious with rage, Nebuchadnezzar summoned Shadrach, Meshach and Abednego. So these men were brought before the king,
[14]and Nebuchadnezzar said to them, 'Is it true, Shadrach, Meshach and Abednego, that you do not serve my gods or worship the image of gold I have set up? [15]Now when you hear the sound of the horn, flute, zither, lyre, harp, pipe and all kinds of music, if you are ready to fall down and worship the image I made, very good. But if you do not worship it, you will be thrown immediately into a blazing furnace. Then what god will be able to rescue you from my hand?'

Tension: *the three friends refuse to worship God*

[16]Shadrach, Meshach and Abednego replied to him, 'King Nebuchadnezzar, we do not need to defend ourselves before you in this matter. [17]If the God we serve is able to deliver us, then he will deliver us from the blazing furnace and from Your Majesty's hand. [18]But even if he does not, we want you to know, Your Majesty, that we will not serve your gods or worship the image of gold you have set up.' (TNIV)

When reading the stories of the three friends in the furnace and Daniel in the lion's den, we cannot help but wonder why God would save them but not the believers in Hitler's gas chambers and furnaces. We will never know for sure. It is interesting to note that the three friends did consider the fact that they could die. "But even if he does not, we want you to know, Your Majesty, that we will not serve your gods" (v. 18). Let us join the prophet Habakkuk in expressing our loyalty in prayer:

[17]Though the fig tree does not bud
and there are no grapes on the vines,
though the olive crop fails
and the fields produce no food,
though there are no sheep in the pen
and no cattle in the stalls,
[18]yet I will rejoice *in the LORD,*
I will be joyful *in God my Savior.*

—Habakkuk 3, TNIV

Loyalty means nothing unless it has at its heart the absolute principle of self-sacrifice.
—Woodrow T. Wilson (1856–1924), *Twenty-eighth President of the United States*

WE CANNOT GLORIFY AND PRAISE GOD WITHOUT THIS!

God wants us to glorify and praise Him as the almighty God. However, there is one characteristic—a vice—that prevents us from doing this wholeheartedly. This is a vice that prevented the mighty Nebuchadnezzar from glorifying and praising God. But when he discovered his shortcomings from the interpretation of a dream and confessed, the mighty king erupted in praise. Nebuchadnezzar's whole experience is told in Daniel 4 in the form of a letter he sent throughout his kingdom. Let's join Nebuchadnezzar in this final section to explore the result of his experience—in other words, what is needed to glorify and praise God.

Daniel 4

Result: Nebuchadnezzar recognized the greatness of God

> [34]At the end of that time, I, Nebuchadnezzar, raised my eyes toward heaven, and my sanity was restored.
> Then I praised the Most High; I honored and glorified him who lives forever. *(story)*
> *His dominion* is an eternal dominion;
> *his kingdom* endures from generation to generation.
> [35]All the peoples of the earth
> are regarded as nothing.
> He does as he pleases
> with the powers of heaven
> and the peoples of the earth.
> No one can hold back his hand
> or say to him: 'What have you done?' *(poetry)*
> [36]At the same time that my sanity was restored, my honor and splendor were returned to me for the glory of my kingdom. My advisers and nobles sought me out, and I was restored to my throne and became even greater than before. [37]Now I, Nebuchadnezzar, praise and exalt and glorify the King of heaven, because everything he does is right and all his ways are just. And those who walk in pride he is able to humble. *(story)* TNIV

Arrogance prevents us from glorifying and praising God, because when we are arrogant, we only praise ourselves. The arrogant Nebuchadnezzar was humiliated, but later on his honor was restored after he humbled himself to acknowledge God's greatness—and he then glorified and praised God.

Some scholars maintain that the book of Daniel was concluded during the time of the arrogant Greek king Antiochus IV Epiphanes (175–164 B.C.), who made the Jews' lives very unpleasant. It must have been very comforting for them to know that God could do the same to Antiochus IV Epiphanes as He did to Nebuchadnezzar. In a subtle way, the author emphasizes that the great and mighty Nebuchadnezzar, who controlled the Jews, was in actual fact himself controlled by God.

We live in totally different times from those who first read the book, but we should remember that none of the writers of the Bible considered arrogance a virtue. As Proverbs 29:23 states, "*Pride brings a person low, but the lowly in spirit gain honor*" (*TNIV*).

Lord, save me from arrogance. I always want to praise and honor You!

A proud man is always looking down on things and people; and, of course, as long as you're looking down, you can't see something that's above you.
—C.S. Lewis (1898–1963), *High-powered Oxford and Cambridge professor and perhaps the twentieth century's most famous convert to Christianity. Lewis was the creator of the Narnia series.*

IS THERE A LESSON TO LEARN FROM HISTORY?

Someone gave a short and sweet answer to this question: "Nobody learns from history." Do you agree? Let's read the next section in Daniel!

Daniel 5 (story)

Relief of tension: Daniel interprets Belshazzar's dream

[1]King Belshazzar gave a great banquet for a thousand of his nobles and drank wine with them. [20]But when his heart became arrogant and hardened with pride, he was deposed from his royal throne and stripped of his glory. [21]He was driven away from people and given the mind of an animal; he lived with the wild donkeys and ate grass like the ox; and his body was drenched with the dew of heaven, until he acknowledged that the Most High God is sovereign over the kingdoms on earth and sets over them anyone he wishes.
[22]"But you, Belshazzar, his son, have not humbled yourself, though you knew all this.
[23]Instead, you have set yourself up against the Lord of heaven. You had the goblets from his temple brought to you, and you and your nobles, your wives and your concubines drank wine from them. You praised the gods of silver and gold, of bronze, iron, wood and stone, which cannot see or hear or understand. But you did not honor the God who holds in his hand your life and all your ways.
[24]Therefore he sent the hand that wrote the inscription.
[25]"This is the inscription that was written:
MENE, MENE, TEKEL, PARSIN
[26]"This is what these words mean:
Mene: God has numbered the days of your reign and brought it to an end.
[27]*Tekel*: You have been weighed on the scales and found wanting.
[28]*Peres*: Your kingdom is divided and given to the Medes and Persians.'

Result: Daniel is honored and the king murdered

[29]Then at Belshazzar's command, Daniel was clothed in purple, a gold chain was placed around his neck, and he was proclaimed the third highest ruler in the kingdom.
[30]That very night Belshazzar, king of the Babylonians, was slain,
[31]and Darius the Mede took over the kingdom, at the age of sixty-two. (TNIV)

Daniel 5 starts with Belshazzar's feast and ends tragically at his deathbed. During the feast, a message from God—only four words in length—appears on the wall. Just before Daniel interprets this message in four sentences, he tells Belshazzar about his predecessor's (Nebuchadnezzar's) experiences. Daniel wanted to show Belshazzar that he had not learned from the terrible mistakes of Nebuchadnezzar and that he was even more arrogant than Nebuchadnezzar (v. 23). The four words on the wall spelled out Belshazzar's tragic end: "You have been weighed on the scales and found wanting." The king was murdered that very same night, and his kingdom was divided. May we learn from the lessons of history!

Lord, from today on, I want to learn from my mistakes and from those of others.

History doesn't repeat itself—at best it sometimes rhymes.
—Mark Twain (1835–1910), *American humorist, writer and lecturer*

WHAT GIVES THE WEARY AND DEPRESSED NEW HOPE . . .

It is not always easy to face life and lead a meaningful life. Life, with all of its storms, has the ability to tire us out and leave us feeling depressed. The authors in the Bible often had to give their readers hope in sad and depressing times. They realized that much the same way people needed food to survive physically they also needed stories to lead a sensible life. Stories have the wonderful ability to help us to consider our situation from a different angle. The story of Daniel is very telling in this regard!

Daniel 6 (story)

Tension: The king goes to see if Daniel is still alive

¹⁸Then the king returned to his palace and spent the night without eating and without any entertainment being brought to him. And he could not sleep.
¹⁹At the first light of dawn, the king got up and hurried to the lions' den. ²⁰When he came near the den, he called to Daniel in an anguished voice, 'Daniel, servant of the living God, has your God, whom you serve continually, been able to rescue you from the lions?'

Relief of tension: Daniel lives!

²¹Daniel answered, 'May the king live forever! ²²My God sent his angel, and he shut the mouths of the lions. They have not hurt me, because I was found innocent in his sight. Nor have I ever done any wrong before you, Your Majesty.'

Result: Daniel's conspirators become food for the lions.

²³The king was overjoyed and gave orders to lift Daniel out of the den. And when Daniel was lifted from the den, no wound was found on him, because he had trusted in his God.
²⁴At the king's command, the men who had falsely accused Daniel were brought in and thrown into the lions' den, along with their wives and children. And before they reached the floor of the den, the lions overpowered them and crushed all their bones. (TNIV)

Daniel was thrown into the lion's den because he refused to worship the king. It is there in the midst of all those hungry lions that his name gets its real meaning: "Daniel" means "God is my judge." God protected Daniel and proved Daniel's innocence to the king.

The author of this story wants to open up our eyes to the fact that God has the power to save people and that He is involved in what happens in the world. Between the lines, the refrain echoes: He is a living God! He wants to use people—much like He used Daniel—to bring about change. And he wants us to recognize the importance of sticking to our values in times of despair. Daniel refused to give up his principles. May this story give you new hope!

 Thank You, Lord, that stories can teach me there is hope!

The fact of storytelling hints at a fundamental human unease, hints at human imperfection.
Where there is perfection there is no story to tell.
—Ben Okri (b. 1959), *Nigerian author who uses magic realism to convey the social and*
political chaos in his country

HOW SHOULD WE UNDERSTAND BIBLICAL VISIONS?

In Daniel 7–12 and in the book of Revelation, a godly message is received by means of visions or dreams. These visions are filled with imagery and symbols. Visions reveal things about the future, which is why these two books are considered apocalyptic prose. "Apocalyptic" is the Greek word for revelation or exposure. Apocalyptic writing was used mainly during the two centuries before and the first century after the birth of Christ.

The first readers of the books of Daniel and Revelation lived under severe persecution. Scholars maintain that the book of Daniel was concluded centuries after Daniel's time during the time of the cruel reign of Antiochus IV Epiphanes (175–164 B.C.), while the book of Revelation was concluded during the reign of the Roman emperor Domitian (A.D. 81–96). In apocalyptic prose, a well-known character from the past "sees" the future. The apocalyptic writing provided readers with hope, because it gave them a glimpse into the future and enabled them to interpret the present from the perspective of the future.

Daniel 7 (apocalypse)

¹In the first year of Belshazzar king of Babylon, Daniel had a dream, and visions passed through his mind as he was lying in bed. He wrote down the substance of his dream.

²Daniel said: 'In my vision at night I looked, and there before me were the four winds of heaven churning up the great sea. ³Four great beasts, each different from the others, came up out of the sea.

⁴'The first was like a lion, and it had the wings of an eagle. I watched until its wings were torn off and it was lifted from the ground so that it stood on two feet like a human being, and a human mind was given to it.

⁵'And there before me was a second beast, which looked like a bear. It was raised up on one of its sides, and it had three ribs in its mouth between its teeth. It was told, 'Get up and eat your fill of flesh!'

⁶'After that, I looked, and there before me was another beast, one that looked like a leopard. And on its back it had four wings like those of a bird. This beast had four heads, and it was given authority to rule.

⁷'After that, in my vision at night I looked, and there before me was a fourth beast—terrifying and frightening and very powerful. It had large iron teeth; it crushed and devoured its victims and trampled underfoot whatever was left. It was different from all the former beasts, and it had ten horns.

⁸'While I was thinking about the horns, there before me was another horn, a little one, which came up among them; and three of the first horns were uprooted before it. This horn had eyes like the eyes of a human being and a mouth that spoke boastfully. (TNIV)

In the above passage, an angel explained this vision to Daniel (7:17). The four large animals represented four successive empires. The readers of the time would have known that these were the empires of Babylonia (lion), Media (bear), Persia (leopard) and Greek-Macedonia (the frightful beast). The small horn represented the cruel Antiochus IV Epiphanes, who forced the Greek culture on the Jews. The rest of the vision contains good news (v. 26), namely that all this would come to an end—a vision of *hope!*

Lord, I beg that the cruelty of people toward each other comes to an end. May Your glory come!

What until recently seemed to be only the apocalyptic fantasies of the Christian faith has today entered the sphere of the soberest scientific calculations; the sudden end of history.
—Emil Brunner (1889–1966), Eminent and highly influential Swiss theologian

WHAT CAN BIBLICAL VISIONS TEACH US?

Biblical visions conveyed messages to the people of the time in which they were recorded, but we can still learn from them today.

Daniel 8 (apocalypse)

[2]In my vision I saw myself in the citadel of Susa in the province of Elam; in the vision I was beside the Ulai Canal. [3]I looked up, and there before me was a ram with two horns, standing beside the canal, . . . [4]I watched the ram as it charged toward the west and the north and the south. No animal could stand against it . . . [5]As I was thinking about this, suddenly a goat with a prominent horn between its eyes came from the west, crossing the whole earth without touching the ground. [7]. . . The ram was powerless to stand against it; the goat knocked it to the ground and trampled on it . . . [8]The goat became very great, but at the height of its power the large horn was broken off, and in its place four prominent horns grew up toward the four winds of heaven. [20]The two-horned ram that you saw represents the kings of Media and Persia. [21]The shaggy goat is the king of Greece, and the large horn between its eyes is the first king. [22]The four horns that replaced the one that was broken off represent four kingdoms that will emerge from his nation but will not have the same power.
[23]In the latter part of their reign, when rebels have become completely wicked, a fierce-looking king, a master of intrigue, will arise. [24]He will become very strong, but not by his own power. He will cause astounding devastation and will succeed in whatever he does. He will destroy the mighty warriors, the holy people. [25]He will cause deceit to prosper, and he will consider himself superior. When they feel secure, he will destroy many and take his stand against the Prince of princes. Yet he will be destroyed, but not by human power. (TNIV)

The ram represented the kingdom of Media and Persia, while the goat represented the Greek kingdom (vv. 20–21). The great horn between the eyes of the goat represented the mighty Alexander the Great (336–333 B.C.), who conquered the Persian Empire. The four horns that replaced the single horn represented the four kingdoms that were formed when the Greek Empire was divided after Alexander's death.

As mentioned previously, the book of Daniel was concluded during the reign of king Antiochus IV Epiphanes. This vision gave the suppressed Jews hope because it foresaw Antiochius' downfall (v. 25) and teaches us that we should not be blinded by the events around us. Life will injure and bruise us, but we must always remember that God's creation leads to an ultimate goal.

 Lord, thank You for leading me to an ultimate goal.

The most pathetic person in the world is someone who has sight, but has no vision.
—Helen Keller (1880–1968), *American author and educator who was blind and deaf*

HOW DO WE BELIEVE DESPITE DESPAIR?

Life is not always easy. It has a way of robbing us of all joy. We often feel like giving up because we are just too weary to face life's hardships. God knew this, which is why He used visions to talk to His people who were suffering at the hand of Antiochus IV Epiphanes. He used these visions for a specific purpose.

Daniel 12 (apocalypse)

⁵Then I, Daniel, looked, and there before me stood two others, one on this bank of the river and one on the opposite bank. ⁶One of them said to the man clothed in linen, who was above the waters of the river, *'How long will it be before these astonishing things are fulfilled?'*
⁷The man clothed in linen, who was above the waters of the river, lifted his right hand and his left hand toward heaven, and I heard him swear by him who lives forever, saying, *'It will be for a time, times and half a time. When the power of the holy people has been finally broken, all these things will be completed.'*
⁸I heard, but I did not understand. So I asked, 'My lord, what will the outcome of all this be?'
⁹He replied, 'Go your way, Daniel, because the words are closed up and sealed until the time of the end. ¹⁰Many will be purified, made spotless and refined, but the wicked will continue to be wicked. None of the wicked will understand, but those who are wise will understand.
¹¹'From the time that the daily sacrifice is abolished and the abomination that causes desolation is set up, there will be 1,290 days.
¹²Blessed is the one who waits for and reaches the end of the 1,335 days.
¹³'As for you, go your way till the end. You will rest, and then at the end of the days you will rise to receive your allotted inheritance.'*
Daniel saw two angels on both sides of the river. He then heard one of them ask: *'How long will it be before these astonishing things are fulfilled?'*
Daniel heard how a third angel, who stood above the water, answered the question: *'It will be for a time, times and half a time. When the power of the holy people has been finally broken, all these things will be completed.'* (TNIV)

Daniel did not understand what the outcome of this vision would be (v. 8). He tried to find out, but the angel reminded him that the end of time is a secret (v. 9). The angel's directive to Daniel in the closing verse inspired many of the Jews during the reign of Antiochus to strive toward the future: "As for you, go your way till the end. You will rest, and then at the end of the days you will rise to receive your allotted inheritance" (v. 13, TNIV). Visions helped these sorrowful Jews to look beyond their situation and to see God as the one who was in control. May this also help us to keep on believing despite despair.

 Thank You, Lord that Your Word helps me to look further—to notice You!

If you look for truth, you may find comfort in the end; if you look for comfort you will not get either comfort or truth only soft soap and wishful thinking to begin, and in the end, despair.
—C.S. Lewis (1898–1963), *High-powered Oxford and Cambridge professor and perhaps the twentieth century's most famous convert to Christianity. Lewis was the creator of the Narnia series.*

OUR SEVENTH STOP: RETURN FROM EXILE

(538—420 B.C.)
(HAGGAI, ZECHARIAH, JOEL, ESTHER, EZRA, NEHEMIAH, AND MALACHI)

We saw that the Northern Kingdom (Israel) was taken away in 722 B.C. by Assyria, while the Southern Kingdom (Judah) was taken into exile by Babylon in 597 B.C. In 549 B.C., Cyrus the Great founded the Persian Empire, and he eventually conquered Babylon. Persia was now the new world power. Cyrus allowed those who were exiled to Babylon to return to their homelands, as he believed that it was in his best interest to have loyal followers all over the world. Cyrus also showed a great deal of tolerance toward the religions of those he conquered.

In 530 B.C., Cyrus was killed in a war and his son, Cambyses, succeeded him. Cambyses was a different kind of man than his father. He murdered his brother to safeguard his throne. After his suicide in 522 B.C., there was confusion as to who would succeed him. An army general, Darius, eventually took control of the army and ascended the throne. In 520 B.C., Darius restored order in the kingdom, which was the same year in which Haggai and Zechariah began to act as prophets. During the time of Darius, work in the Temple was resumed (Ezra 5–6). Darius, who ruled from 521 to 486 B.C., was known as one of the mightiest Persian emperors.

Xerxes ruled from 486 to 465 B.C. (Xerxes was his Greek name; his Hebrew name was Ahasuerus.) Artaxerxes I then reigned from 464 to 423 B.C. (the events in Ezra 7 through the end of Nehemiah took place during his reign). Artaxerxes I was succeeded by Darius II (423–404 B.C.), Artaxerxes II (404–359 B.C.) and Artaxerxes III (359–338 B.C.).

The two centuries the Persians reigned were of great importance to God's people, as the Persians encouraged their repatriation and also subsidized it. (We have to bear in mind that not all exiles returned and that the homecoming took place over a long period.) The first group of exiles returned with Sheshbazzar (538 B.C.), an exiled Jewish prince and later governor of a reestablished Jewish state centered in Jerusalem. As a representative of the Persian crown, protocol demanded that it was he who laid the foundation of the house of God. Unfortunately, for a long time nothing was built on that foundation, but at least Sheshbazzar had shown the way.

A little later Zerubabel, the grandson of king Jehoiachin, escorted another group back to the homeland. The next main group returned in 458 B.C. with Ezra, the scribe. Then in 444 B.C., Nehemiah returned with another group. It was during this time that the exiles who returned home were called "Jews" for the first time. This word derives from the Hebrew word *Yehudi*, which is related to Judah, the tribe in which Jesus was born.

EXCUSES, EXCUSES, EXCUSES!

Haggai was the first prophet to appear on the scene after the Lord's people began to return to Judah from exile (August 29, 520 B.C.–December 18, 520 B.C.). During this time, the people were making all kinds of excuses for not completing the Temple. People can be very inventive when conjuring up excuses. Haggai's message exposes the reason behind many of them.

Haggai 1 (conversation)

²This is what the LORD Almighty says: 'These people say, 'The time has not yet come to rebuild the LORD's house.' '

³Then the word of the LORD came through the prophet Haggai: ⁴'Is it a time for you yourselves to be living in your paneled houses, while this house remains a ruin?'

⁵Now this is what the LORD Almighty says: 'Give careful thought to your ways. ⁶You have planted much, but have harvested little. You eat, but never have enough. You drink, but never have your fill. You put on clothes, but are not warm. You earn wages, only to put them in a purse with holes in it.'

⁷This is what the LORD Almighty says: 'Give careful thought to your ways. ⁸Go up into the mountains and bring down timber and build the house, so that I may take pleasure in it and be honored,' says the LORD. ⁹'You expected much, but see, it turned out to be little. What you brought home, I blew away. Why?' declares the LORD Almighty. 'Because of my house, which remains a ruin, while each of you is busy with his own house. ¹⁰Therefore, because of you the heavens have withheld their dew and the earth its crops. ¹¹I called for a drought on the fields and the mountains, on the grain, the new wine, the olive oil and everything else the ground produces, on people and livestock, and on all the labor of your hands.' (TNIV)

As the story goes, the captain of the Titanic at some stage told his crew, "Now it is every man for himself!" This is often people's reaction when things get tough. Self-interest becomes the highest priority. This is exactly what Haggai exposed as the reason behind all the people's excuses. They took the trouble to look after their own houses but had neglected the house of the Lord (v. 4). They had put their own interests before God's interests. We can be very inventive when we conjure up excuses, but perhaps we should learn to be honest with ourselves. As someone once said, "An excuse is a skin of a reason stuffed with a lie."

 Lord, I confess that self-interest often lies behind my excuses.

An excuse is worse than a lie, for an excuse is a lie, guarded.
—Alexander Pope (1688–1744), *English poet and satirist*

HOW DO WE TURN PRIORITIES INTO ACTION?

In the previous section, we read how the Israelites had put their own interests before the interests of God. How does one succeed in putting God's interests first? Haggai's sermon in 520 B.C. is precisely about this.

Haggai 2 (conversation)

[10]On the twenty-fourth day of the ninth month, in the second year of Darius, the word of the LORD came to the prophet Haggai: [11]"This is what the LORD Almighty says: 'Ask the priests what the law says: [12] If a person carries consecrated meat in the fold of his garment, and that fold touches some bread or stew, some wine, olive oil or other food, does it become consecrated?' '
The priests answered, 'No.'
[13]Then Haggai said, 'If a person defiled by contact with a dead body touches one of these things, does it become defiled?'
'Yes,' the priests replied, 'it becomes defiled.'
[14]Then Haggai said, ' 'So it is with this people and this nation in my sight,' declares the LORD. 'Whatever they do and whatever they offer there is defiled.
[18]"From this day on, from this twenty-fourth day of the ninth month, give careful thought to the day when the foundation of the LORD's temple was laid. Give careful thought: [19] Is there yet any seed left in the barn? Until now, the vine and the fig tree, the pomegranate and the olive tree have not borne fruit.
' 'From this day on I will bless you.' ' (TNIV)

Haggai asked the priests a two-fold question about how transferable holiness and impurity were. He then applied their answer to the people of the Lord. The first question to the priests and their answer indicated that the purity of the meal offering was not necessarily transferable (v. 12). On the other hand, the second question and its answer revealed that impurity was indeed transferable.

We can think about it in this way: Holiness is like being healthy, while impurity is like being sick. If you are sick and come into contact with people, the chances are good that you will infect them. But if you are healthy, you will not spread your health to those around you. In the same way that illness (and not health) spreads, impurity (and not holiness) spreads.

In the time of Haggai, the people thought that the rebuilding of the Temple would automatically make them holy. But the core of Haggai's message was that *religious acts would not automatically make their lives holy.* Disobedience to the Lord would, however, render their religious actions ineffective. How can we turn the Lord's priorities into action? Through *obedience!* This is something we can choose to do starting today!

 Lord, please forgive my disobedience. I choose to be obedient to You.

Obedience without faith is possible, but not faith without obedience.
—Author unknown

WHAT MAKES A FRESH START POSSIBLE?

People can easily plague our lives because they disappoint us bitterly. It can also happen that we disappoint others—yes, we may even disappoint God. The Israelites disappointed God because they were disobedient, and as a result they were exiled. The Persian king, Cyrus, later allowed the people to return to Jerusalem. The big question was what the relationship between the Lord and His people would be like now that the time of exile had come to an end. Would God attempt a new beginning with them?

The book of Zechariah helps us to answer this question. Zechariah became a prophet in 520 B.C., shortly after Haggai. The first part of the book (1–8) tells us about eight night visions Zechariah had (the night visions were merely visions and should therefore not be interpreted literally). The fourth night vision takes us to a court in heaven where symbols are used to show us very clearly what makes a fresh start possible.

Zechariah 3 (apocalypse)

[1] Then he showed me Joshua the high priest standing before the angel of the LORD, and Satan standing at his right side to accuse him.

[2] The LORD said to Satan, 'The LORD rebuke you, Satan! The LORD, who has chosen Jerusalem, rebuke you! Is not this man a burning stick snatched from the fire?'

[3] Now Joshua was dressed in filthy clothes as he stood before the angel. [4] The angel said to those who were standing before him, 'Take off his filthy clothes.'

Then he said to Joshua, 'See, I have taken away your sin, and I will put fine garments on you.'

[5] Then I said, 'Put a clean turban on his head.' So they put a clean turban on his head and clothed him, while the angel of the LORD stood by.

[6] The angel of the LORD gave this charge to Joshua: [7] 'This is what the LORD Almighty says: 'If you will walk in obedience to me and keep my requirements, then you will govern my house and have charge of my courts, and I will give you a place among these standing here. (TNIV)

Zechariah's fourth vision depicts the angel of God as the judge. Before him appears Joshua, the high priest, whom Satan has accused. We do not know what the accusation against Joshua was—perhaps he was being accused of being impure while in exile. Two symbols confirm that Joshua was forgiven. First, the clean clothes that were given to him to wear are a symbol of forgiveness. Second, the turban that he is given symbolizes his suitability to serve as high priest in the rebuilt Temple. Joshua thus received forgiveness on behalf of the whole nation. This salvation and redress is nothing but mercy. It is like a burning stick that is pulled from the fire (v. 2). By forgiving His people, God made a fresh start with them. By forgiving others, we can also make a fresh start with God and our fellow human beings—and we can do this again and again.

 Thank You, Lord, that Satan's accusations do not outweigh Your mercy.

Forgive or relive.
—Author unknown

BIGGER AND MORE BEAUTIFUL IS NOT ALWAYS BETTER!

Many Jews were disappointed when they realized that the second temple would not be as ostentatious as Solomon's Temple. To them, bigger and more beautiful meant better. They had to learn an important lesson.

Zechariah 4 (apocalypse)

[8]Then the word of the LORD came to me: [9]'The hands of Zerubbabel have laid the foundation of this temple; his hands will also complete it. Then you will know that the LORD Almighty has sent me to you.
[10]*Who dares despise the day of small things,* since the seven eyes of the LORD that range throughout the earth will rejoice when they see the chosen capstone in the hand of Zerubbabel?'
[11]Then I asked the angel, 'What are these two olive trees on the right and the left of the lampstand?'
[12]Again I asked him, 'What are these two olive branches beside the two gold pipes that pour out golden oil?'
[13]He replied, 'Do you not know what these are?'
'No, my lord,' I said.
[14]So he said, 'These are the two who are anointed to serve the Lord of all the earth.' (TNIV)

God is not concerned about what is bigger and more beautiful but rather about what is right. That is why He asks, "Who dares despise the day of small things?" (v.10). God expects us to be faithful in small things, which enables Him to perform great things in our lives. God's way of doing things often starts off small, but the results end up big. The rebuilding of the Temple was a small effort by a small group of people, but its consequences were important.

Although the second Temple was smaller and not as beautiful as that of Solomon, it was more important that the people had a central place of worship after all their years in exile. This is why we should not think little of small things. The two olive trees (v. 11) refer to the *high priest* (Joshua) and the *governor* (Zerubbabel). Here we see that both the king and the priesthood served God. *Politics* and *religion* cannot be separated from each other. Just like Zerrubabel and Joshua, we are servants of the Lord, which requires us to be faithful to God in everything we do—even in the small things. Who knows, it might just be in the small things that God will surprise us.

 Thank You, Lord, that the small things we do are also important to You.

Be faithful in small things because it is in them that your strength lies.
—Mother Teresa of Calcutta (1910–1997), *Albanian born Indian missionary, founder of the Order of the Missionaries of Charity and winner of the Nobel Prize for Peace in 1979*

SHOULD WE CLING TO TRADITION?

This question is very relevant, especially in the Church, where tradition plays a very important role. Although tradition has become a dirty word, many people still see it as something to which they should cling. Should we do this?

Zechariah 7 (conversation)

¹In the fourth year of King Darius, the word of the LORD came to Zechariah on the fourth day of the ninth month, the month of Kislev. ²The people of Bethel had sent Sharezer and Regem-Melek, together with their men, to entreat the LORD ³by asking the priests of the house of the LORD Almighty and the prophets, *'Should I mourn and fast in the fifth month, as I have done for so many years?'*
⁴Then the word of the LORD Almighty came to me: ⁵'Ask all the people of the land and the priests, 'When you fasted and mourned in the fifth and seventh months for the past seventy years, was it really for me that you fasted? ⁶And when you were eating and drinking, were you not just feasting for yourselves? ⁷Are these not the words the LORD proclaimed through the earlier prophets when Jerusalem and its surrounding towns were at rest and prosperous, and the Negev and the western foothills were settled?' '
⁸And the word of the LORD came again to Zechariah: ⁹ 'This is what the LORD Almighty said: 'Administer true justice; show mercy and compassion to one another. ¹⁰ Do not oppress the widow or the fatherless, the foreigner or the poor. Do not plot evil against each other.' (TNIV)

According to the Gregorian calendar's calculation of time, verse 1 refers to December 7, 518 B.C. This was two years after the rebuilding of the Temple began, and two years before it was completed. A delegation from the town of Bet-El, located about 11 miles (18 kilometers) north of Jerusalem, went to Jerusalem with a specific request. They wanted to find out whether it was still significant to commemorate the old Temple's destruction (586 B.C.) by fasting, since the new one was nearly completed.

What the delegation really wanted to know was whether tradition was still relevant in changing times. The Lord answered them with a counter question: "Was it really for me that you fasted?" (v. 5). God did not say that fasting (tradition) was wrong but enquired about the attitude behind it. Whether or not the people fasted was not as important as whether they did it to honor God.

It is easy for us to do things out of habit and forget its original meaning. We should always realize that our traditions should do justice to everyone and that we should show compassion and love to one another (v. 9). It is not wrong to hand down good practices from one generation to another, but it is wrong to consider those traditions as unchangeable values! We need to become known for being transformational rather than being traditional. We need to create the future rather than to preserve the past.

 Lord, I want to honor You in everything I do.

Tradition is the illusion of permanence.
—Woody Allen (b. 1935), *American actor, author, screenwriter and film director*

THE BIBLE'S LIMOUSINE

Royalty and limousines go hand in hand. This means of transport portrays dignity. The Bible tells us about a king who traveled with such dignity.

Zechariah 9

> [9]*Rejoice greatly,* Daughter Zion!
> *Shout,* Daughter Jerusalem!
> See, your king comes to you,
> righteous and having salvation,
> lowly and riding on a donkey,
> on a colt, the foal of a donkey.
> [10]*I will take away the chariots* from Ephraim
> *and the warhorses* from Jerusalem,
> and the battle bow will be broken.
> He will proclaim peace to the nations.
> His rule will extend from sea to sea
> and from the River to the ends of the earth. (TNIV)

A new king often heralds good news. People expect him to govern better than the previous king and not to repeat the mistakes of the previous dispensation. In this section, Zechariah tells us about such a king. This king had three special characteristics: He was *righteous,* he was a *conqueror,* and he was *humble.* These characteristics could only bring about good things.

- **Righteous:** When a king was righteous, it indicated that he had a good relationship with God. Such a king governed in accordance with God's will.
- **Conqueror:** The king was very successful because the Lord helped him to conquer. There would be no further wars during his reign (v. 10). It is remarkable to think that there were such good prospects for peace during the time of the Old Testament, a time noted for its conflict.
- **Humility:** Arrogant kings were removed from their subjects, but this king was different. Although he used a royal means of transport that was common at the time, namely the donkey, he was different. He cared about the poor and the weak.

The empire of the Messiah (which means "the anointed one") would be worldwide. In the New Testament, the prophecy is linked to Jesus' entry into Jerusalem (Matt. 21:5; John 12:15). Jesus is therefore the Messiah king who rode with dignity into Jerusalem on a donkey, the Bible's limousine. He proclaimed peace (Zech 9:10). May we, like this king, also help to make the world a better place by being righteous and humble.

 Thank You, Lord, that Your message is one of peace. I praise You!

I long to accomplish a great and noble task, but it is my chief duty to accomplish humble tasks as though they were great and noble.
—Helen Keller (1880–1968), *American author and educator who was blind and deaf*

SOMETHING MORE IMPORTANT THAN TERRITORIAL ADVANTAGE!

If life is a contest, evil must enjoy a territorial advantage. It seems as though fewer people these days believe in God and that the Church has lost its impact on society. It is therefore no wonder that believers sometimes feel that they are on the losing side. Zechariah 12:1–8, however, shows us that there is something more important than territorial advantage.

Zechariah 12 (apocalypse)

¹A prophecy: The word of the LORD concerning Israel.
The LORD, who stretches out the heavens, who lays the foundation of the earth, and who forms the spirit in human beings, declares: ²'I am going to make Jerusalem *a cup* that sends all the surrounding peoples reeling. Judah will be besieged as well as Jerusalem. ³On that day, when all the nations of the earth are gathered against her, I will make Jerusalem an *immovable rock* for all the nations. All who try to move it will injure themselves. ⁴On that day I will strike every horse with panic and its rider with madness,' declares the LORD. 'I will keep a watchful eye over the house of Judah, but I will blind all the horses of the nations. ⁵Then the clans of Judah will say in their hearts, 'The people of Jerusalem are strong, because the LORD Almighty is their God.'
⁶'On that day I will make the clans of Judah like a firepot in a woodpile, like a flaming torch among sheaves. They will consume right and left all the surrounding peoples, but Jerusalem will remain intact in her place.
⁷'The LORD will save the dwellings of Judah first, so that the honor of the house of David and of Jerusalem's inhabitants may not be greater than that of Judah. ⁸On that day the LORD will shield those who live in Jerusalem, so that the feeblest among them will be like David, and the house of David will be like God, like the angel of the LORD going before them. (TNIV)

Zechariah helped the people to look past their difficult circumstances. The Israelites who returned to Jerusalem from exile experienced many hardships, such as poverty, poor harvests, the hostility of neighboring nations and spiritual decay. They felt that they were on the losing side. However, in Zechariah 12, the prophet uses two images to tell the despondent people that powerful nations would become powerless. The mighty would reel because they drank of the cup of wine (Jerusalem). Furthermore, Jerusalem would become like an immovable rock.

These two images point to something more important than the territorial advantage of evil: the end result! Even though it seems as if evil has the territorial advantage, we know that the end result will turn out in our favor. That is why we don't need to wait for the final whistle to blow to know that we have won. Despite the evil around us, we can live life to the full from this very moment. We can muster up courage and live!

 Thank You, Lord, that I know I am on Your side—the winning side!

Count your smiles instead of your tears; Count your courage instead of your fears.
—Author unknown

A BRIDGE LINKS GOD'S WRATH TO HIS MERCY!

The book of Joel primarily concerns the day of the Lord. This phrase, "day of the Lord," refers to a time in the future when the Lord will intervene in the lives of human beings. Joel indicates that this will be a day in which the Lord punishes those who did not serve Him. His judgment will affect all nations, including Israelites who did not serve Him. According to Joel, this will be a terrible day, and nobody will be able to escape it.

It is interesting to note that the day of the Lord in the New Testament refers to the second coming of Jesus. This is why this section is so relevant. The big question is how we can avoid the wrath of God. This section tells us about a bridge that we can cross to experience God's mercy.

Joel 2

¹¹The LORD utters his voice
at the head of his army;
how vast is his host!
Numberless are those who obey his command.
Truly the day of the LORD is great;
terrible indeed—who can endure it?
¹²Yet even now, says the LORD,
return to me with all your heart,
with fasting, with weeping, and with mourning;
¹³rend your hearts and not your clothing.
Return to the LORD, your God,
for he is gracious and merciful,
slow to anger, and abounding in steadfast love,
and relents from punishing.
¹⁴Who knows whether he will not turn and relent,
and leave a blessing behind him,
a grain-offering and a drink-offering
for the LORD, your God? (NRSV)

God makes it very clear that He will use His wrath to intervene in human history. Luckily, there is hope, which is signified by a four-letter word: "even." This word in verse 12 indicates a turnabout, namely God's invitation to the ungodly to experience His love and mercy. This invitation comes in the form of a series of urgent commands: *return, fast, weep and mourn!* It forms the bridge between God's wrath and His mercy.

If you approach God with genuine remorse, you will find that His wrath turns to love. David had this experience after his adultery with Bathsheba. He wrote, "The sacrifice acceptable to God is a broken spirit; a broken and contrite heart, O God, you will not despise" (Ps. 51:17, NRSV). This invitation is also extended to you!

 Thank You, Lord, that Your invitation includes me.

Remorse is regret that one waited so long to do it.
—Henry Louis Mencken (1880–1956), *American journalist, satirist and social critic*

HOW LIVES TURN TO JOY

The first readers of the book of Joel were probably faithful Jews who around 450 to 350 B.C. returned to Jerusalem from exile in Babylon. The returned exiles experienced a difficult time—they had to share Judah, the land of their ancestors, with hostile people. Furthermore, old enemies such as the Edomites and Egyptians did not leave them in peace. The book of Joel begins with a prophecy about the destruction of the land (a plague of locusts, a draught and the day of the Lord) but has a happy ending: the land is triumphantly restored.

Joel 3

¹⁸*'In that day the mountains* will drip new wine,
and the hills will flow with milk;
all the ravines of Judah *will run with water.*
A fountain *will flow out of the LORD's house*
and will water the valley of acacias.
¹⁹But Egypt *will be desolate,*
Edom *a desert waste,*
because of violence done to the people of Judah,
in whose land they shed innocent blood.
²⁰*Judah will be inhabited* forever
and Jerusalem through all generations.
²¹Shall I leave their innocent blood unpunished?
No, I will not.'
The LORD dwells in Zion! (TNIV)

The book of Joel culminates in the last four verses that contain wonderful parallels. Note how often the word "will" is used: seven times altogether. These parallels emphasize the misfortune that awaits Egypt and Edom while Judah will triumph twice. The use of the word "will" emphasizes that God is reliable and that He will forgive them. These words comfort us even up to this day, because God is still willing to forgive us. Forgiveness makes us share in the joy of a restored relationship with God. It is when God forgives us and we, in turn, forgive others that our lives turn to joy.

 Thank You, Lord, that forgiveness makes it possible for me to experience joy.

The ineffable joy of forgiving and being forgiven forms an ecstasy that might well
arouse the envy of the gods.
—Elbert Hubbard (1856–1915), *American editor, publisher and writer*

A REMARKABLE STORY, YET . . .

Only the books of Ruth and Esther in the Bible are named after women. The main characters of the book of Esther are Esther, Mordecai, Xerxes and Haman. Esther is a remarkable story, and yet the Lord is not mentioned in the original text. Are the events in the story merely coincidental? No, these events prove that God's mercy works in the shadows of our lives. We will regularly see that this is the case during the next few days. The following episode tells us about one of the main characters: Xerxes (486–465 B.C.).

Esther 1 (story)

[10]On the seventh day, when King Xerxes was in high spirits from wine, he commanded the seven eunuchs who served him—Mehuman, Biztha, Harbona, Bigtha, Abagtha, Zethar and Karkas—[11]to bring before him Queen Vashti, wearing her royal crown, in order to display her beauty to the people and nobles, for she was lovely to look at.

Tension: Queen Vashti refuses to entertain men!

[12]But when the attendants delivered the king's command, Queen Vashti refused to come.

Relief of tension: Angry king asks for advice!

Then the king became furious and burned with anger.
[13]Since it was customary for the king to consult experts in matters of law and justice, he spoke with the wise men who understood the times [14]and were closest to the king—Karshena, Shethar, Admatha, Tarshish, Meres, Marsena and Memukan, the seven nobles of Persia and Media who had special access to the king and were highest in the kingdom.
[15]'According to law, what must be done to Queen Vashti?' he asked. 'She has not obeyed the command of King Xerxes that the eunuchs have taken to her.'

Result: Royal decree at the expense of the queen

[19]'Therefore, if it pleases the king, let him issue a royal decree and let it be written in the laws of Persia and Media, which cannot be repealed, that Vashti is never again to enter the presence of King Xerxes. Also let the king give her royal position to someone else who is better than she. (TNIV)

The opening scene (vv. 1–9) describes how Xerxes displayed his power and wealth at two major feasts. What is ironic in this episode is that his own beautiful wife, Vasthi, challenged his power by refusing to be put on display for the drunken men. She maintained her self-respect, and for that we praise her! The king had to call in his advisors to handle the humiliation, and they suggested that he get rid of Vashti. The king was very gullible, which made him a dangerous man. The rest of the story tells us how others manipulated him. The king's power caused the downfall of Vashti, but this power created unexpected opportunities for Esther and her people at a later stage. Human power can make or break others. Let us handle power with care!

Lord, I realize anew that I have to handle power with care!

> *Power doesn't corrupt people; people corrupt power.*
> —William Gaddis (1922–1998), *American novelist*

BEAUTIFUL, MORE BEAUTIFUL, ESTHER

In Esther 1:1–22, the king's banquet ended in humiliation when Vashti, the Persian king's wife, refused to be paraded before the men. The king's advisors suggested that a beauty pageant be held to determine who should be Vasthi's successor. This brings us to the next episode, which also ends at a banquet of the king.

Esther 2 (story)

[7]Mordecai had a cousin named Hadassah, whom he had brought up because she had neither father nor mother. This young woman, who was also known as Esther, had a lovely figure and was beautiful. Mordecai had taken her as his own daughter when her father and mother died.
[8]When the king's order and edict had been proclaimed, many young women were brought to the citadel of Susa and put under the care of Hegai. Esther also was taken to the king's palace and entrusted to Hegai, who had charge of the harem.

Tension: Esther keeps silent about her background

[10]Esther had not revealed her nationality and family background, because Mordecai had forbidden her to do so. [16]She was taken to King Xerxes in the royal residence in the tenth month, the month of Tebeth, in the seventh year of his reign.

Relief of tension: The king likes Esther

[17]Now the king was attracted to Esther more than to any of the other women, and she won his favor and approval more than any of the other virgins.

Result: A Jewess is made queen at a banquet

So he set a royal crown on her head and made her queen instead of Vashti. [18]And the king gave a great banquet, Esther's banquet, for all his nobles and officials. He proclaimed a holiday throughout the provinces and distributed gifts with royal liberality. (TNIV)

Esther's Jewish name was Hadassah. Her Persian name (Esther) can be linked to the goddess Ishtar. Esther was an orphan who was brought up by her cousin, Mordecai. The author makes another important point about Esther, namely, that she was devastatingly beautiful. The king's agents noticed her and entered her in the beauty pageant. They did not know that she was a Jew, as Mordecai had forbidden her to reveal this fact out of fear that it might count against her.

The organizers and the king were completely bowled over by Esther's beauty. At a banquet, she was crowned as the queen who would replace Vashti. It is remarkable to think that an orphan, a Jew, could be crowned queen in a foreign country. Was this mere coincidence? No, God had worked behind the scenes to make her queen. Likewise, God often works in inconspicuous ways in our lives. All those coincidences in our lives could be the result of God's plan for our lives.

Thank You, Lord, that You work with me without me always being aware of it.

A coincidence is a small miracle in which God chooses to remain anonymous.
—Author unknown

BITTERNESS, CONSPIRACY AND COINCIDENCE

Bitterness is a cancer that devours people from the inside and plagues their relationships. It robs people of joy and makes them unpleasant. In this next episode, we see how bitterness had tragic consequences for two palace officials.

Esther 2 (story)

[19]When the virgins were assembled a second time, Mordecai was sitting at the king's gate. [20]But Esther had kept secret her family background and nationality just as Mordecai had told her to do, for she continued to follow Mordecai's instructions as she had done when he was bringing her up.

Tension: *Conspiracy to murder the king*

[21]During the time Mordecai was sitting at the king's gate, Bigthana and Teresh, two of the king's officers who guarded the doorway, became angry and conspired to assassinate King Xerxes.

Relief of tension: *Mordecai reports about the murder plan*

[22]But Mordecai found out about the plot and told Queen Esther, who in turn reported it to the king, giving credit to Mordecai.

Result: *The guilty ones are convicted*

[23]And when the report was investigated and found to be true, the two officials were impaled on poles. All this was recorded in the book of the annals in the presence of the king. (TNIV)

For some reason, the two gatekeepers in this passage were embittered with the king and conspired to murder him. Because they held strategic positions and had easy access to the king, it would have been quite easy for them to perform the assassination.

Mordecai "accidentally" heard of the conspiracy. Since Mordecai was loyal to the king, he told Esther about the conspiracy. After a thorough investigation, the news proved to be true. The two gatekeepers died on the gallows, and in this way, Mordecai saved the king's life. Although all this was recorded in the annals of the kingdom, Mordecai was not rewarded immediately. When his deed was revealed later (6:1–13), the effect was much greater than it would have been if he had been rewarded right after the event.

We are often impatient and unhappy when our good deeds are not acknowledged immediately, but sometimes it is good to let matters take their own course. All these events seemed to be purely coincidental, but that is not how Mordecai saw them. Later, he told Esther, "Who knows but that you have come to royal position for such a time as this?" (4:14, TNIV). Perhaps we should stop using the word "coincidence." God is always working in the shadows of our lives.

 Lord, I realize that all the coincidences point to Your involvement in my life.

Coincidence is the word we use when we can't see the levers and pulleys.
—Emma Bull (b.1954), *Science fiction and fantasy author who is best known for the novel* War for the Oaks

WHAT DO WE DO WHEN OUR PRIDE GETS HURT?

You probably have a story to tell about the day your pride was hurt. It might have been the day when you were sworn at or when someone spread lies about you. It might have been the day the bank manager refused to give you a loan even though you had been a respected client for many years. It might have been the day your authority was disregarded and challenged. In the following episode, we read about the next main character in the book of Esther—a man whose pride was hurt.

Esther 3 (story)

¹After these events, King Xerxes honored Haman son of Hammedatha, the Agagite, elevating him and giving him a seat of honor higher than that of all the other nobles.

Tension: Mordecai does not bow down before Haman

²All the royal officials at the king's gate knelt down and paid honor to Haman, for the king had commanded this concerning him. But Mordecai would not kneel down or pay him honor.
³Then the royal officials at the king's gate asked Mordecai, 'Why do you disobey the king's command?'
⁴Day after day they spoke to him but he refused to comply. Therefore they told Haman about it to see whether Mordecai's behavior would be tolerated, for he had told them he was a Jew.

Relief of tension: Haman is furious

⁵When Haman saw that Mordecai would not kneel down or pay him honor, he was enraged.

Result: Haman wants to destroy the Jews

⁶Yet having learned who Mordecai's people were, he scorned the idea of killing only Mordecai. Instead Haman looked for a way to destroy all Mordecai's people, the Jews, throughout the whole kingdom of Xerxes. (TNIV)

In this episode, Haman is honored by the king and is given a position above all the other nobles in the kingdom. However, his pride was soon hurt when Mordecai refused to bow before him. Mordecai might have been somewhat spiteful, because previously he was willing to honor the king. Haman felt insulted and was furious (v. 5), and his anger soon turned to thoughts of revenge. When he heard that Mordecai was a Jew, he made plans to destroy all the Jews in the kingdom. By doing this, Haman became the Hitler in this story. Ironically, Haman's plans would cause his own downfall later on. Thoughts of revenge bedevil relationships and make reconciliation impossible. Revenge targets the other person, but in the end we only end up destroying ourselves. There is only one answer to revenge: Stop it!

 Lord, I confess that I often harbor thoughts of revenge against others.

An eye for eye only ends up making the whole world blind.
—Mahatma Gandhi (1869–1948), *Preeminent leader of Indian nationalism*

EVEN POWER CANNOT RESIST THIS!

King Xerxes was a powerful man, but because he was so easily influenced, his power was actually controlled by other people. Haman used *underhanded* methods to convince the king to sign a proclamation at the expense of the Jews. Esther was the only one who could come to the Jews' rescue, but she used something else to sway the king's power to her advantage.

Esther 5 (story)

Tension: Esther visits the king without an appointment.

[1]On the third day Esther put on her royal robes and stood in the inner court of the palace, in front of the king's hall. The king was sitting on his royal throne in the hall, facing the entrance.

Relief of tension: The king invites her in.

[2]When he saw Queen Esther standing in the court, he was pleased with her and held out to her the gold scepter that was in his hand. So Esther approached and touched the tip of the scepter.
[3]Then the king asked, 'What is it, Queen Esther? What is your request? Even up to half the kingdom, it will be given you.'

Result: Esther takes control!

[4]'If it pleases the king,' replied Esther, 'let the king, together with Haman, come today to a banquet I have prepared for him.'
[5]'Bring Haman at once,' the king said, 'so that we may do what Esther asks.'
So the king and Haman went to the banquet Esther had prepared. [6]As they were drinking wine, the king again asked Esther, 'Now what is your petition? It will be given you. And what is your request? Even up to half the kingdom, it will be granted.'
[7]Esther replied, 'My petition and my request is this: [8]If the king regards me with favor and if it pleases the king to grant my petition and fulfill my request, let the king and Haman come tomorrow to the banquet I will prepare for them. Then I will answer the king's question.' (TNIV)

Vasthi had been dismissed as queen because she did not want to go to the king when he summoned her (Esther 1:12). The king's advisors suggested he issue a decree that ordered all women to be subservient to their husbands. Is this law not sick? Esther showed unparalleled wisdom for her time by visiting her husband unannounced. Yet the king invited her in, because her beauty totally overwhelmed him. She used her charm to sway the king's power to her advantage. It is wonderful that her *charm* stood in the service of respect toward women. The king was easily influenced, but fortunately this weakness worked to the advantage of the Jews.

 Lord, I realize that I have to be more careful about how I handle power.

Charm is the ability to make someone think that both of you are quite wonderful.
—Author unknown

A WORD THAT CAUSED AN ECLIPSE OF GOD!

We often use a word that prevents us from seeing God's involvement in our lives. This episode illustrates this fact.

Esther 6 (story)

[1]That night the king could not sleep; so he ordered the book of the chronicles, the record of his reign, to be brought in and read to him. [2]It was found recorded there that Mordecai had exposed Bigthana and Teresh, two of the king's officers who guarded the doorway, who had conspired to assassinate King Xerxes.
[3]'What honor and recognition has Mordecai received for this?' the king asked.
'Nothing has been done for him,' his attendants answered.

Tension: Haman's agenda and the king's question

[4]The king said, 'Who is in the court?' Now Haman had just entered the outer court of the palace to speak to the king about impaling Mordecai on the pole he had set up for him. [6]When Haman entered, the king asked him, *'What should be done for the man the king delights to honor?'*
Now Haman thought to himself, 'Who is there that the king would rather honor than me?'
[7]So he answered the king, 'For the man the king delights to honor, [8]have them bring a royal robe the king has worn and a horse the king has ridden, one with a royal crest placed on its head. [9]Then let the robe and horse be entrusted to one of the king's most noble princes. Let them robe the man the king delights to honor, and lead him on the horse through the city streets, proclaiming before him, *'This is what is done for the man the king delights to honor!'* '

Relief of tension: Haman's rude awakening

[10]'Go at once,' the king commanded Haman. 'Get the robe and the horse and do just as you have suggested for Mordecai the Jew, who sits at the king's gate.

Result: Haman honours his enemy

[11]So Haman got the robe and the horse. He robed Mordecai, and led him on horseback through the city streets, proclaiming before him, *'This is what is done for the man the king delights to honor!'* (TNIV)

This episode can be interpreted in the following way: "Coincidently," the king could not sleep that night. "Coincidently," he read that it was Mordecai who had saved his life when the gatekeepers had plotted against him. "Coincidently," Mordecai had not been rewarded at that time and would now be rewarded at this time when the advantages for him would be greater. "Coincidently," Haman arrived at the palace at that stage. "Coincidently," his advice to the king meant that his enemy, Mordecai, was honored, which led to his humiliation. All of these coincidences are just too coincidental to be true coincidences. It is more a case of God working behind the scenes in people's lives. Perhaps we should talk less about coincidences and more about the incidences of God's grace!

Thank You, Lord, for using coincidences to work in my life.

When I pray, coincidences happen, and when I don't, they don't.
—Sir William Temple (1628–99), *English diplomat and author*

A QUALITY THAT CAN CAUSE A DRASTIC CHANGE . . .

It is wonderful to see how hopeless situations can open up new possibilities in our lives. A special quality normally causes this to happen. What could this be?

Esther 8 (story)

Tension: Esther goes to the king uninvited.

³Esther again pleaded with the king, falling at his feet and weeping. She begged him to put an end to the evil plan of Haman the Agagite, which he had devised against the Jews.

Relief of tension: The king invites her.

⁴Then the king extended the gold scepter to Esther and she arose and stood before him.
⁵'If it pleases the king,' she said, 'and if he regards me with favor and thinks it the right thing to do, and if he is pleased with me, let an order be written overruling the dispatches that Haman son of Hammedatha, the Agagite, devised and wrote to destroy the Jews in all the king's provinces. ⁶For how can I bear to see disaster fall on my people? How can I bear to see the destruction of my family?'

Result: A decree in favor of the Jews

⁷King Xerxes replied to Queen Esther and to Mordecai the Jew, 'Because Haman attacked the Jews, I have given his estate to Esther, and they have impaled him on the pole he set up. ⁸Now write another decree in the king's name in behalf of the Jews as seems best to you, and seal it with the king's signet ring—for no document written in the king's name and sealed with his ring can be revoked.' ¹³A copy of the text of the edict was to be issued as law in every province and made known to the people of every nationality so that the Jews would be ready on that day to avenge themselves on their enemies. (TNIV)

The Jews were in a precarious situation. Haman had issued a decree stating that the Jews would be destroyed on the thirteenth day of the twelfth month. Esther realized that she had become queen for a time such as this (Esther 4:14). She was willing to take a risk and appear before the king without an invitation—a risk that could have cost Esther her very life. Fortunately, the king held out his golden scepter to her, which was a sign that she would be allowed to see him. The king granted her request to issue a second decree that would allow the Jews to defend themselves on the thirteenth day of the month, which effectively nullified the first proclamation. Esther's *courage* brought about a drastic change. As the saying goes, nothing ventured, nothing gained! Esther dared to speak to the king—for the sake of good—and won!

 Lord, like Esther, I would like to show more courage in my life.

Man cannot discover new oceans unless he has the courage to lose sight of the shore.
—Andre Gide (1869–1951), *French writer, humanist, moralist and winner of the Nobel Prize for literature in 1947*

GOD WORKS WITHOUT FANFARE

Even though God is not mentioned in the text of Esther, the book contains a remarkable story that helps us to see how God works in our lives.

Esther 9 (history)

[20]Mordecai recorded these events, and he sent letters to all the Jews throughout the provinces of King Xerxes, near and far, [21]to have them celebrate annually the fourteenth and fifteenth days of the month of Adar [22]as the time when the Jews got relief from their enemies, and as the month when their sorrow was turned into joy and their mourning into a day of celebration. He wrote them to observe the days as days of feasting and joy and giving presents of food to one another and gifts to the poor.
[23]So the Jews agreed to continue the celebration they had begun, doing what Mordecai had written to them. [24]For Haman son of Hammedatha, the Agagite, the enemy of all the Jews, had plotted against the Jews to destroy them and had cast the *pur* (that is, the lot) for their ruin and destruction. [25]But when the plot came to the king's attention, he issued written orders that the evil scheme Haman had devised against the Jews should come back onto his own head, and that he and his sons should be impaled on poles.
[26](Therefore these days were called Purim, from the word *pur*.) Because of everything written in this letter and because of what they had seen and what had happened to them, [27]the Jews took it on themselves to establish the custom that they and their descendants and all who join them should without fail observe these two days every year, in the way prescribed and at the time appointed. (TNIV)

The book of Esther begins by describing a tense situation in which Haman, the Hitler of the story, deceived the king into issuing a dangerous decree that would have destroyed the Jews. Haman casts lots to determine the date on which the Jews would be destroyed. But the situation changed drastically. The dangerous Haman was hanged on the gallows he himself erected, Mordecai was installed in the position Haman once occupied, Esther was given Haman's land, and the king issued a second decree in favor of the exiles (the Jews).

To celebrate the change in their *lot* (Hebrew *pur*), the feast of Purim was instituted. Although the Lord's name is not mentioned anywhere in the original text, He worked behind the scenes without fanfare to ensure that an orphan, a Jewess (Esther), became queen; that Mordecai heard about the planned assassination of the king; that the king discovered the documents that related how Mordecai had once saved his life; and that the dangerous Haman suffered defeat. God often works without fanfare—without us noticing it. Perhaps we should learn to trust God more in our lives!

 Thank You, Lord, for being involved in my life. Help me to be able to always trust You.

God buries his workmen, but carries on his work.
—John Wesley (1703–1791), *English Evangelist and founder of Methodism*

WHAT THIS CONGREGATION AND A ROCK CONCERT HAVE IN COMMON?

In A.D. 536, the congregation of Jerusalem achieved something for which rock concerts are famous (or perhaps infamous).

Ezra 3 (history)

[8]In the second month of the second year after their arrival at the house of God in Jerusalem, Zerubbabel son of Shealtiel, Joshua son of Jozadak and the rest of the people (the priests and the Levites and all who had returned from the captivity to Jerusalem) began the work, appointing Levites twenty years old and older to supervise the building of the house of the LORD. [9]Joshua and his sons and brothers and Kadmiel and his sons (descendants of Hodaviah) and the sons of Henadad and their sons and brothers—all Levites—joined together in supervising those working on the house of God.
[10]When the builders laid the foundation of the temple of the LORD, the priests in their vestments and with trumpets, and the Levites (the sons of Asaph) with cymbals, took their places to praise the LORD, as prescribed by David king of Israel. [11]With praise and thanksgiving they sang to the LORD:
'He is good;
his love toward Israel endures forever.'
And all the people gave a great shout of praise to the LORD, because the foundation of the house of the LORD was laid. [12]But many of the older priests and Levites and family heads, who had seen the former temple, wept aloud when they saw the foundation of this temple being laid, while many others shouted for joy. [13]No one could distinguish the sound of the shouts of joy from the sound of weeping, because the people made so much noise. And the sound was heard far away. (TNIV)

The exiles who returned all helped to rebuild the Temple. When the foundation was laid, the people exploded with rejoicing. Like a rock concert, the sounds of rejoicing could be heard from afar—without the aid of loudspeakers! The completion of the foundation was a clear indication to the people that the Lord was faithful and that He had not forgotten them.

The song of praise (Psalm 136) that the people sang was the same one that had been sung when the Ark had been brought to Jerusalem and later when Solomon's Temple had been completed. But some of the older people cried amid the rejoicing. From Haggai 2:3, one can deduce that they cried because the foundation was not as big as that of Solomon's Temple, but their crying was muffled by the loud praise songs! May our praise also be heard from afar!

 Lord, thank You for not forgetting me. I want to explode with rejoicing. Hallelujah!!

I praise loudly, I blame softly.
—Catherine the Great (1729–1796), *Reigned as Empress of Russia for some 34 years*

WHAT IS SIGNIFICANT ABOUT MARCH 12, 515 B.C.?

The twelfth of March 515 B.C. was so long ago that it probably does not ring a bell with anyone except theologians. However, this was a very important day in Israel's history. What happened on that day holds a great deal of meaning for us, even up to this day.

Ezra 6 (history)

[13]Then, because of the decree King Darius had sent, Tattenai, governor of Trans-Euphrates, and Shethar-Bozenai and their associates carried it out with diligence. [14]So the elders of the Jews continued to build and prosper under the preaching of Haggai the prophet and Zechariah, a descendant of Iddo. They finished building the temple according to the command of the God of Israel and the decrees of Cyrus, Darius and Artaxerxes, kings of Persia. [15]The temple was completed on the third day of the month Adar, in the sixth year of the reign of King Darius.
[16]Then the people of Israel—the priests, the Levites and the rest of the exiles—celebrated the dedication of the house of God with joy. [17]For the dedication of this house of God they offered a hundred bulls, two hundred rams, four hundred male lambs and, as a sin offering for all Israel, twelve male goats, one for each of the tribes of Israel. [18]And they installed the priests in their divisions and the Levites in their groups for the service of God at Jerusalem, according to what is written in the Book of Moses.
[19]On the fourteenth day of the first month, the exiles celebrated the Passover. (TNIV)

The third day of the month of Adar in the sixth year of King Darius's rule is March 12, 515 B.C. on our calendar. On that day, after almost 21 years of construction, the Temple was finally completed. The words of gratitude expressed during the inauguration contain so much meaning. The prophets Haggai and Zechariah were thanked for their contribution. They had motivated the people to continue with the building of the Temple. It is interesting to note that the Persian kings Cyrus, Darius and Artaxerxes are also mentioned. They were sympathetic toward the building project and even provided the funding (vv. 6–12).

God does not allow Himself to be restricted! The fact that the name "Israel," the tribes of Israel, the offerings (v. 17) and Moses are mentioned confirms that the inauguration of the Temple was a spiritual continuation of the 12 tribes of old. Much like the Israelites, our lives are empty and lack substance if we do not have a historical base. We therefore continue to celebrate the birth, crucifixion, resurrection and ascension of Jesus every year. The events in the past remind us of God's faithfulness. Because God is *faithful*, we can look forward to the second coming with great joy and anticipation.

 Thank You, Lord, for the wonderful historical base of our religion.

Don't forget your history nor your destiny.
—Bob Marley (1945–1981), *Jamaican singer, composer and guitarist*

HOW IMPORTANT IS TIMING?

Success in life depends heavily on timing. A good decision at the wrong time can be fatal. Sportsmen and sportswomen will agree with the importance of timing. Timing is also important to God. This section in Ezra confirms this fact.

Ezra 7 (history)

[1]After these things, during the reign of Artaxerxes king of Persia, Ezra son of Seraiah, the son of Azariah, the son of Hilkiah, [2]the son of Shallum, the son of Zadok, the son of Ahitub, [3]the son of Amariah, the son of Azariah, the son of Meraioth, [4]the son of Zerahiah, the son of Uzzi, the son of Bukki, [5]the son of Abishua, the son of Phinehas, the son of Eleazar, the son of Aaron the chief priest—[6]this Ezra came up from Babylon. He was a teacher well versed in the Law of Moses, which the LORD, the God of Israel, had given. The king had granted him everything he asked, for the hand of the LORD his God was on him. [7]Some of the Israelites, including priests, Levites, musicians, gatekeepers and temple servants, also came up to Jerusalem in the seventh year of King Artaxerxes.
[8]Ezra arrived in Jerusalem in the fifth month of the seventh year of the king. [9]He had begun his journey from Babylon on the first day of the first month, and he arrived in Jerusalem on the first day of the fifth month, for the gracious hand of his God was on him. [10]For Ezra had devoted himself to the study and observance of the Law of the LORD, and to teaching its decrees and laws in Israel. (TNIV)

The returned exiles needed someone special to teach and encourage them. This is why Ezra appeared on the scene in 458 B.C. During this critical period in Israel's history, he was the right person at the right place for the right reasons.

Ezra had a special ancestry. He was a direct descendent of Aaron and was therefore a priest. However, ancestry alone cannot guarantee success. Fortunately, Ezra was an educated man who was knowledgeable about the Law of Moses. He used his knowledge with an inner conviction and applied it in his daily life. He also had the ability to impart his knowledge to others and to equip them for a better life (v. 10).

Ezra possessed knowledge, character and skills. And to crown it all, he was on good terms with the king. The author makes it very clear that all this was God's doing. God invites us to use all our skills in His service—at the right place and at the right time!

 Thank You, Lord, that Your timing is always to our advantage. I praise You!

Life is about timing.
—Carl Lewis (b. 1961), *American track and field athlete who was one of only four Olympic athletes to win nine gold medals and one of only three to win the same individual event four times*

WHAT TO DO WHEN PEOPLE DISAPPOINT US

We all have a story about how someone disappointed us. It is part of life, but it is not always easy and pleasant to cope with. So how should we cope with it?

Ezra 9 (story)

Tension: Intermarriage

> ¹After these things had been done, the leaders came to me and said, 'The people of Israel, including the priests and the Levites, have not kept themselves separate from the neighboring peoples with their detestable practices, like those of the Canaanites, Hittites, Perizzites, Jebusites, Ammonites, Moabites, Egyptians and Amorites. ²They have taken some of their daughters as wives for themselves and their sons, and have mingled the holy race with the peoples around them. And the leaders and officials have led the way in this unfaithfulness.'

Relief of tension: Dismay

> ³When I heard this, I tore my tunic and cloak, pulled hair from my head and beard and sat down appalled. ⁴Then everyone who trembled at the words of the God of Israel gathered around me because of this unfaithfulness of the exiles. And I sat there appalled until the evening sacrifice.

Result: Prayer

> ⁵Then, at the evening sacrifice, I rose from my self-abasement, with my tunic and cloak torn, and fell on my knees with my hands spread out to the LORD my God ⁶and prayed:
> 'I am too ashamed and disgraced, my God, to lift up my face to you, because our sins are higher than our heads and our guilt has reached to the heavens. (TNIV)

When Ezra arrived in Jerusalem, he discovered that the returned exiles had repeated the sins of their forefathers. They had married non-Jews and were worshipping their gods. Even the priests and the Levites were guilty of this. Ezra coped with this bad news in a very mature manner.

He did this first by showing emotion. As a sign of grief and mourning, he tore his clothes and pulled out his beard. Everyone noticed the dismay on his face. He then poured out these emotions to God in prayer. Ezra could have spoken very harshly to the Israelites, but instead he followed a wonderful principle: talk to God first about people before you talk to people about God.

Ezra also did not reproach the Jews. He did not use the words "you" or "they" when referring to the people in his prayer but rather "us" (v. 6). In this way, Ezra identified himself with the sins of his people. If we have this same kind of attitude, we will understand something of God's mercy—mercy that will help us to cope with disappointment!

 Lord, help me to deal with the heartache in my life in a mature way.

Disappointment to a noble soul is what cold water is to burning metal;
it strengthens tempers, intensifies, but never destroys it.
—Eliza Tabor (1835–1914), *American writer*

TEARS LINK OUR PAIN TO SOMETHING . . .

In this next section, we read about how Nehemiah dealt with the bad news he received. The tears that Nehemiah shed for his people can teach us something precious.

Nehemiah 1 (story)

[1]The words of Nehemiah son of Hakaliah:
In the month of Kislev in the twentieth year, while I was in the citadel of Susa,
[2]Hanani, one of my brothers, came from Judah with some other men, and I questioned them about the Jewish remnant that had survived the exile, and also about Jerusalem.

Tension: The exiles experience misery

[3]They said to me, 'Those who survived the exile and are back in the province are in great trouble and disgrace. The wall of Jerusalem is broken down, and its gates have been burned with fire.'

Relief of tension: Nehemiah prays to God

[4]When I heard these things, I sat down and wept. For some days I mourned and fasted and prayed before the G89od of heaven. [5]Then I said:
'LORD, the God of heaven, the great and awesome God, who keeps his covenant of love with those who love him and keep his commandments, [6]let your ear be attentive and your eyes open to hear the prayer your servant is praying before you day and night for your servants, the people of Israel. I confess the sins we Israelites, including myself and my ancestral family, have committed against you. [7]We have acted very wickedly toward you. We have not obeyed the commands, decrees and laws you gave your servant Moses.
[8]'Remember the instruction you gave your servant Moses, saying, 'If you are unfaithful, I will scatter you among the nations, [9]but if you return to me and obey my commands, then even if your exiled people are at the farthest horizon, I will gather them from there and bring them to the place I have chosen as a dwelling for my Name.'
[10]'They are your servants and your people, whom you redeemed by your great strength and your mighty hand. [11]Lord, let your ear be attentive to the prayer of this your servant and to the prayer of your servants who delight in revering your name. Give your servant success today by granting him favor in the presence of this man.' I was cupbearer to the king. (TNIV)

Nehemiah cried when he received the news about Jerusalem's broken walls. He did not ignore his pain but vented it in prayer and weeping. Tears can be very healing. Nehemiah's tears linked his pain to God's promises. In verse 8, he prays, "Remember the instruction you gave your servant Moses." His tears gave him courage to tackle the future. He decided to get up, wash his face and go and talk to the king (v. 11). Through Nehemiah's example, we learn that we should also struggle through the emotions caused by bad news.

 Thank You, Lord that I can learn from Nehemiah that tears bring healing.

What soap is for the body, tears are for the soul.
—Jewish proverb

THE TEARFUL PLANNER

The name "Nehemiah" means "the Lord has comforted." This is what Nehemiah experienced regarding the promises of God. He was comforted because the Persian king gave him permission to rebuild Jerusalem. This tearful planner can teach us so much.

Nehemiah 2 (story)

Tension: Night expedition

[11]I went to Jerusalem, and after staying there three days [12]I set out during the night with a few others. I had not told anyone what my God had put in my heart to do for Jerusalem. There were no mounts with me except the one I was riding on.
[13]By night I went out through the Valley Gate toward the Jackal Well and the Dung Gate, examining the walls of Jerusalem, which had been broken down, and its gates, which had been destroyed by fire.
[16]The officials did not know where I had gone or what I was doing, because as yet I had said nothing to the Jews or the priests or nobles or officials or any others who would be doing the work.

Relief of tension: The construction work begins

[17]Then I said to them, 'You see the trouble we are in: Jerusalem lies in ruins, and its gates have been burned with fire. Come, let us rebuild the wall of Jerusalem, and we will no longer be in disgrace.'
[18]I also told them about the gracious hand of my God on me and what the king had said to me. They replied, 'Let us start rebuilding.' So they began this good work.

Result: Ridiculing

[19]But when Sanballat the Horonite, Tobiah the Ammonite official and Geshem the Arab heard about it, they mocked and ridiculed us. 'What is this you are doing?' they asked. 'Are you rebelling against the king?'
[20]I answered them by saying, 'The God of heaven will give us success. We his servants will start rebuilding, but as for you, you have no share in Jerusalem or any claim or historic right to it.' (TNIV)

Nehemiah teaches us the importance of teamwork. He realized that the task before him required team effort, and he motivated his people by saying, "Come, let us rebuild the wall of Jerusalem" (v. 17). He was mocked, but he did not despair.

Someone once said, "If you do not believe in yourself, chances are that nobody else will either." Nehemiah believed in what he was doing and could press ahead because he had a dream: to rebuild Jerusalem! Someone once also said, "Keep your head and your heart in the same direction and you'll never have to worry about your feet." In difficult times, we should ask ourselves: "What is my dream?" This is not always easy to do, but it will help us to press ahead with our lives. Nehemiah was a wonderful example of someone who realized that tears are not the end of the road.

 Thank You, Lord, for letting me know that tears are not the end of the road.

The soul would have no rainbow had the eyes no tears.
—John Vance Cheney (1848–1922), *American poet*

SICK AND TIRED OF ALL THE DISCORD?

There is so much discord in this world—and it is so unnecessary. Nehemiah became terribly upset when he heard how the wealthy Jews were exploiting the poor Jews. How did Nehemiah handle this situation?

Nehemiah 5 (story)

Tension: Nehemiah is upset

⁶When I heard their outcry and these charges, I was very angry.

Relief of tension: He deals with the problem

⁷I pondered them in my mind and then accused the nobles and officials. I told them, 'You are charging your own people interest!' So I called together a large meeting to deal with them ⁸and said: 'As far as possible, we have bought back our fellow Jews who were sold to the Gentiles. Now you are selling your own people, only for them to be sold back to us!' They kept quiet, because they could find nothing to say.

⁹So I continued, 'What you are doing is not right. Shouldn't you walk in the fear of our God to avoid the reproach of our Gentile enemies?

¹¹Give back to them immediately their fields, vineyards, olive groves and houses, and also the interest you are charging them . . .

Result: The people cooperate

¹²'We will give it back,' they said. 'And we will not demand anything more from them. We will do as you say.'

Then I summoned the priests and made the nobles and officials take an oath to do what they had promised. ¹³I also shook out the folds of my robe and said, 'In this way may God shake out of their houses and possessions anyone who does not keep this promise. So may such a person be shaken out and emptied!' At this the whole assembly said, 'Amen,' and praised the LORD. And the people did as they had promised. (TNIV)

The way in which Nehemiah handled the discord teaches us the following wonderful principles:

- **Principle 1:** There is a direct correlation between the effectiveness of a mission and the way people are treated. Nehemiah *treated his people decently*, which helped him to rebuild Jerusalem's walls in 52 days.
- **Principle 2:** Every relationship has problems that must be dealt with. To ignore discord is detrimental to any relationship. The longer resolution is postponed, the more difficult it becomes to attain that resolution. Nehemiah immediately *addressed the discord*, which resulted in wonderful cooperation (vv. 12–13).

- **Principle 3**: To restore the relationship, we must *take the initiative* (like Nehemiah did). We cannot wait for the other person to act—if we do, we might have to wait a very long time.
- **Principle 4**: Injustice will not continue because God's reputation is at stake (v. 9). Nehemiah could trust that God would not allow the situation to continue.

May we learn to apply these important principles to our relationships!

 Lord, forgive me for the times when my conduct caused discord.

> *Medicine to produce health must examine disease; and music,*
> *to create harmony must investigate discord.*
> —Plutarch (46–119), *Ancient Greek biographer and author*

A BITTERSWEET ENDING

Isn't it nice when a story or a movie has a wonderful, happy ending? Unfortunately, the wonderful book of Nehemiah does not end on such a good note. Yet this ending contains an important lesson for life.

Nehemiah 13 (history)

[23]Moreover, in those days I saw men of Judah who had married women from Ashdod, Ammon and Moab. [24]Half of their children spoke the language of Ashdod or the language of one of the other peoples, and did not know how to speak the language of Judah. [25]I rebuked them and called curses down on them. I beat some of them and pulled out their hair. I made them take an oath in God's name and said: 'You are not to give your daughters in marriage to their sons, nor are you to take their daughters in marriage for your sons or for yourselves. [26]Was it not because of marriages like these that Solomon king of Israel sinned? Among the many nations there was no king like him. He was loved by his God, and God made him king over all Israel, but even he was led into sin by foreign women. [27]Must we hear now that you too are doing all this terrible wickedness and are being unfaithful to our God by marrying foreign women?'

[28]One of the sons of Joiada son of Eliashib the high priest was son-in-law to Sanballat the Horonite. And I drove him away from me.

[29]Remember them, my God, because they defiled the priestly office and the covenant of the priesthood and of the Levites.

[30]So I purified the priests and the Levites of everything foreign, and assigned them duties, each to his own task. [31]I also made provision for contributions of wood at designated times, and for the firstfruits. Remember me with favor, my God. (TNIV)

One would have expected the book of Nehemiah to end on an encouraging note in which the Israelites took their spiritual life to the next level. After all, in Nehemiah 10 they made four promises concerning their spiritual life. Furthermore, the wall of Jerusalem was completed and had been consecrated.

The end of the book tells us of Nehemiah's return to Persia. When he returned later, he was bitterly disappointed. Within a short period of time, the people had broken all of the promises they had made to God. Nehemiah's behavior toward the guilty ones is somewhat strange, but we should understand that intermarriage with foreign wives was exactly what had caused the Israelites to be exiled. The occurrences of intermarriage had led to the worshipping of the foreign gods.

Nehemiah was bitter because his fellow-citizens had committed the exact same sins that had originally led to their exile. While in exile, he himself witnessed the consequences of those sins. The end of Nehemiah does, however, have a touch of sweetness, as Nehemiah's efforts ensured that the Israelites did what was expected of them. This ending teaches us an important lesson: A good beginning does not necessarily guarantee a happy ending—but a bad ending does not necessarily harm the good that has been done!

 Lord, help me not to repeat the same mistakes.

Though no one can go back and make a brand new start, anyone can start from
now and make a brand new ending.
—Carl Bard

A DIRECT QUESTION TO GOD

The name "Malachi" means "My messenger." The Lord used Malachi (c. 430 B.C.) to deliver a message to Israel. This message took the form of a dialogue between God and His people in Jerusalem. When the people dare to ask a question about God at the beginning of the dialogue, we are immediately kept on the edge of our chairs.

Malachi 1 (conversation)

²'I have loved you,' says the LORD.
'But you ask, 'How have you loved us?'
'Was not Esau Jacob's brother?' declares the LORD. 'Yet I have loved Jacob, ³ but Esau I have hated, and I have turned his hill country into a wasteland and left his inheritance to the desert jackals.'
⁴Edom may say, 'Though we have been crushed, we will rebuild the ruins.'
But this is what the LORD Almighty says: 'They may build, but I will demolish. They will be called the Wicked Land, a people always under the wrath of the LORD. ⁵ You will see it with your own eyes and say, 'Great is the LORD—even beyond the borders of Israel!' (TNIV)

The people ask the Lord, "How have you loved us?" (v. 2.) Why would they ask such a direct question? Probably because things were not going well for them. More than 100 years had passed since their forefathers had returned from exile, but still the bliss and success that the earlier prophets had spoke about eluded them. They had started to doubt God's love for them because their expectations were not met.

Today, this very same question, albeit in a different form, is echoed in our questions about poverty, AIDS orphans and perhaps our own circumstances. In Malachi, the Lord answered this in the form of a declaration of love. His declaration of love took the people back many years to the time of Jacob and Esau. By doing this, He was telling His people that His love for them went back a long way.

God's love for Jacob (Israel) is expressed in a very strong way: "I have *loved* Jacob, but Esau I have *hated*" (vv. 2–3). How is it possible that God could hate? We need to see God's words in this passage in the right perspective—as a declaration of love. God merely wanted to say that His love for Jacob (Israel) was so big that by comparison His relationship with Esau could be described as hate. Another explanation is that God was making a declaration of priority: God gave Jacob a task to perform and chose him to carry it out first. We need never doubt God's love.

 Thank You, Lord, for allowing us to ask questions. Thank You for reminding us of Your love.

You can tell whether a man is clever by his answers. You can tell whether
a man is wise by his questions.
—Naguib Mahfouz (b. 1911), *Nobel-Prize-winning Egyptian novelist*

ONE OF THE BIGGEST PROBLEMS IN THE CHURCH!

One of the biggest problems in the Church (and in society) is dealt with very clearly in this next section in Malachi.

Malachi 2 (conversation)

[7]'For the lips of a priest ought to preserve knowledge, because he is the messenger of the LORD Almighty and people seek instruction from his mouth. [8]But you have turned from the way and by your teaching have caused many to stumble; you have violated the covenant with Levi,' says the LORD Almighty. [9]'So I have caused you to be despised and humiliated before all the people, because you have not followed my ways but have shown partiality in matters of the law.' (TNIV)

The big problem in the Church (and in society) reflected here is a total lack of integrity! The priests in the time of Malachi failed dismally in this regard. Verse 7 clearly spells out what was expected of a priest: he was someone who had knowledge about the will of the Lord. Priests had to share this knowledge with the people, which is why a priest is called a "messenger" (v. 7) of God. Note the wordplay here in the meaning of the prophet's name: "Malachi" means "My messenger."

A priest was in a position to influence people. The use of the word "but" in verse 8 points to an unfortunate situation—the priests in Malachi's time lived in sharp contrast to what was expected of them. Instead of edifying people and equipping them to lead a righteous life, they caused people to stumble. The priests, who were supposed to reflect a true relationship with the Lord based on experience, completely lost their way. Consequently, the people lost all respect for them.

In short, the priests had lost their integrity. People no longer saw them as honest and sincere. We should also be aware of the fact that our words and deeds should consistently be for the good and edification of others.

 Lord, whatever I do, I want to do it for You with all my heart.

A person is not given integrity. It results from the relentless pursuit of honesty at all times.
—Author unknown

GET A GLIMPSE OF GOD'S HEART!

This next section gives us a glimpse of God's heart. God is ready to do something specific for us.

Malachi 3 (conversation)

[10]Bring the whole tithe into the storehouse, that there may be food in my house. Test me in this,' says the LORD Almighty, 'and see if I will not throw open the floodgates of heaven and pour out so much blessing that there will not be room enough to store it. [11]I will prevent pests from devouring your crops, and the vines in your fields will not drop their fruit before it is ripe,' says the LORD Almighty. (TNIV)

We often think that God is ready to punish and curse us, but this is not true. In fact, God would much rather bless us than curse us. But what was Israel's problem? Drought and a plague of locust had tormented the Israelites. As a result, the people had withheld their tithes and offerings because they feared that their economic position would deteriorate even further. But the priests relied on these gifts for their livelihood. Consequently, the priests had nothing to eat (v. 10).

God wanted to teach the people that their donations to Him did not have to be dependent on their personal success. Verse 10 was a challenge to them: Test me! Of course, we should not see verse 10 as a business deal whereby we can buy prosperity from God. God challenged the Israelites (and us) to trust Him. We should remember that the things God wanted to use to bless them were not luxuries. Sufficient rain in the semi-desert in which they lived and pest-free harvests were crucial to their survival.

Even today, the Lord blesses us in many ways. The problem is that we do not always see this as a blessing but as a matter of course. We often confuse blessings with luxuries. Perhaps we should make a list of all our blessings. Our lists will confirm that we can trust Him!

 Lord, today I want to count my blessings one by one—and then I want to praise You!

The proud man counts his newspaper clippings, the humble man his blessings.
—Fulton John Sheen (1895–1979), *American Roman Catholic clergyman*

THE LAST THREE VERSES IN THE OLD TESTAMENT!

In these final three verses of the Old Testament, Malachi ends with a concise, but gripping, message. His message contains three important elements.

Malachi 4 (conversation)

⁴"Remember the law of my servant Moses, the decrees and laws I gave him at Horeb for all Israel. ⁵See, I will send the prophet Elijah to you before that great and dreadful day of the LORD comes. ⁶He will turn the hearts of the parents to their children, and the hearts of the children to their parents; or else I will come and strike the land with total destruction.' (TNIV)

Malachi first points out the importance of the Law of Moses (the first five books of the Old Testament), which is also called the Torah. The word "Torah" means education, teaching or instruction. The people were asked to *remember* this (v. 4). Here, "remember" means to think about it and to live according to it. By doing this, the people would show their respect for God.

Second, Malachi warns that God's judgment would certainly come (v. 5). This judgment would also affect the Lord's people. To the Israelites, the day of the Lord (v. 5) meant that the Lord would destroy Israel's enemies sometime in the future. Malachi corrected this perception by telling them that the Lord would also punish all those in Israel who were unfaithful. In the New Testament, the day of the Lord is seen as the second coming of Jesus.

Third, Malachi told the people that the day of the Lord would not exclude His mercy. Before the time of judgment, the Lord would send someone to bring about reconciliation. It would not actually be Elijah (v. 5), but someone of Elijah's stature. In the New Testament, John the Baptist is seen as the one with the power and stature of Elijah who would prepare the world for the coming of the Lord (Luke 1:17; Matt. 11:14; 17:1–13).

Fortunately, God still offers us the opportunity to mend our relationship with Him and with each other. God wanted to reconcile with His people, and He also wants to reconcile with us. The book of Malachi forms the bridge between the Old Testament and the New Testament, and therefore points to Christ. This bridge leads us on the road of reconciliation!

 Thank You, Lord, that in Your great mercy You still reach out to me.

The number one problem in our world is alienation, rich versus poor, black versus white, labor versus management, conservative versus liberal, East versus West . . . but Christ came to bring about reconciliation and peace.
—Billy Graham (b. 1918), *American evangelist*

OUR EIGHTH STOP:
THE 400 SILENT YEARS

(420–±6 B.C.)

Where does the Old Testament end? The Old Testament ends with the return of the Lord's people from exile in Babylonia. At that time, Persia was the great world power and ruled over the returned exiles. The Israelites did not have their own king, but they knew who the successor should be: Zerubbabel, the grandson of king Jehoiachin. The Persians appointed him as governor in Jerusalem (Ezra 2:2 and Haggai 1:1). During his reign, the rebuilding of the Temple was completed in A.D. 515. The rebuilt Temple was smaller and less ostentatious than the Temple that Solomon had built. The priests, from the line of Aaron, continued to use the system of offerings.

Where does the New Testament start? When we open the New Testament, everything is completely different. Rome is now the world power, and once again a king is on the throne. This king is not from the house of David but is a descendent of Esau. His name is Herod the Great. The priests are also not descendents of Aaron.

The reason for this completely different picture is because 400 years had passed from the time the last book of the Old Testament was written to the start of the New Testament. These years are called the "silent years" because they are not reflected in the Bible. Fortunately, there are sources that tell us what happened during those years.

The 400 years can be compared to a stage scene in which the curtain is drawn and the director (the Lord) gets an opportunity to quickly rearrange the décor of history. When the curtain rises 400 years later, we find ourselves in the time of the New Testament. How did the décor change?

1. Political Shifts

The three great powers during these 400 silent years were first the Persians, then the Greeks, and finally the Romans. Initially, Persia was the major world power, but the empire had to contend with the emerging power of the Greeks. In 333 B.C., Alexander the Great conquered the Persians at the young age of 20 and established Greek rule throughout the land. The center of world power thus shifted from the east to the west.

Alexander was one of the greatest generals of all time. He subjected the whole inhabited world, including Palestine, to his rule during his short life span. He was a student of the renowned Greek philosopher Aristotle. This exposure enabled Alexander to spread Greek culture to all corners of the world he conquered.

Alexander died before his thirty-third birthday. After his death, his empire was divided among his four generals. They shared Alexander's dream and continued to spread Greek culture, Greek thinking and the Greek language everywhere. This process has been called "Hellenization" ("Hellas" is the Greek name for "Greece") since the time of Alexander to describe this implementation of Greek culture.

The Jews in Palestine did not escape Hellenism. During the reign of Antiochus IV Epiphanes (175–164 B.C.), Hellenism was forced upon the Jews. Antiochus considered himself to be godly and was one of the cruelest Greek leaders. He plundered the Temple and declared the Jewish religion null and void. No child was allowed to be circumcised, no one was allowed to have a copy of the Torah, and the Jews were forbidden to keep the Sabbath. In 168 B.C., Antiochus erected an altar of Zeus over the altar of burnt offerings in the Temple court. He even sacrificed pigs (considered unholy animals by the Jews) on the altar. He then instructed the Jews to eat pork and to bring offerings to Zeus. The king's troops ensured that his decrees were implemented. The Jews considered all this to be the religious equivalent of rape. A Jewish uprising was inevitable.

Resistance by the Jews ignited when a Greek officer forced two Jewish priests to bring offerings to Zeus. The one priest was prepared to do this, but the other one, named Mattathias, became angry and murdered his fellow priest and the Greek officer. Mattathias then hid in the mountains with his five sons. The family of Mattathias became known as the Maccabees (Hebrew for "hammer") because they attacked their enemy with hammer blows. They were generally known as the Hasmonaeans, a reference to their forefather, Hasmon.

The Hasmonaeans formed an army with Judas, Mattathias's eldest son. The Maccabees (167–141 B.C.) triumphed despite the superior power of Antiochus IV Epiphanes and enforced a peace treaty. The Temple service was reinstated in 164. The Hasmonaean Empire was established, and the Jews had a taste of independence for the first time since the fall of Jerusalem in 586 B.C. Jews commemorate this event as the Feast of Light, or "Hanukkah," in December.

In Palestine, the Maccabees (Hasmonaeans) gained a century of independence (166–63 B.C.) for the Jews. Unfortunately, the Hasmonaean reign was plagued by intrigues and bloodshed. In the meantime, Rome was rising up as the new world power. By 338 B.C., the Romans already controlled the western section of the Italian peninsula, and within a few years they ruled over the whole area. After Rome conquered Carthage during the second century B.C., the Roman Empire started to spread quickly in all directions.

In 63 B.C., Rome brought the end of the Hasmonaean Empire and began its rule over Palestine. The Romans appointed the rulers in Palestine themselves. One of the most unpopular choices among the Jews was probably the appointment of Herod (37–4 B.C.). Rome appointed him as governor in 37 B.C. and then as king of all Judea in 40 B.C. The Jews saw this as a bitter pill, because Herod was a descendent of Esau (an Edomite) and his mother was of Arabic descent. Rome managed to maintain world peace between 27 B.C. and A.D. 180. This period is known as the *Pax Romana* (Latin for "the Roman peace")

2. Cultural Shifts

The empire of Alexander the Great did not last long politically due to his early death, but it was successful in the cultural sphere. His generals worked very hard to establish Greek thought and the Greek language in the regions they controlled. The next world rulers, the Romans, fully embraced Greek culture.

The Greek dialect used at the time was known as *koine* (general) Greek and flourished in the Roman Empire. Greek architecture dominated, and gymnasiums, theatres and stadiums in the Greek style were soon erected everywhere. Alexandria in Egypt, named after Alexander the Great, was an excellent example of Hellenism. The city had museums and a big library. The mathematician Euclid and the physicist Archimedes lived and studied here. Many Jews also lived in Egypt. The city of Alexandria is also where the Old Testament was translated into Greek during 275 to 100 B.C.—a translation that became known as the "Septuagint." The New Testament was written in Greek during the first century A.D.. The Greek culture also had an impact on the Jews in Palestine.

3. Geographical Shifts

Many of the Jews never returned to their country of birth after the period of exile. Many of them settled in Egypt. In fact, during the time of the New Testament, there were probably more Jews in Alexandria than in Jerusalem. The Roman Empire's extended transport system, the *Pax Romana* and the fact that *koine* Greek was widely spoken made it very easy for the Jews to travel. Consequently, Jewish settlements with synagogues developed across the known world of that time. The Jews who spread from Palestine came to be known as the Jews of the Diaspora (dispersion). They spoke Greek and prayed in synagogues.

During Roman domination, Palestine (formerly known as Canaan) was divided into three areas, namely, Galilee, Samaria and Judea. Previously, Palestine was divided into two areas: Samaria in the north and Judea in the south.

Galilee formed the northern part of Palestine and was the largest of the three areas. Although Jesus was born in Bethlehem in the south, He spent most of His life in Galilee.

Samaria was somewhat smaller than Galilee and was situated in the middle of Palestine. The Jews despised the Samaritans and used their name as a swear word, because they did not regard the Samaritans as "true" Jews. The Samaritans came into existence when Assyria invaded Samaria in 722 B.C. and took the prominent Israelites (Northern Empire) into exile. In order to establish stability in the region, foreigners were deported to Samaria. The Samaritans were the offspring of the foreigners and the Israelites who stayed behind. Today, it is known as the so-called West Bank area, where today much of the conflict in the Middle East occurs. It is currently ruled by Israel and Palestine.

Judea formed the southern part of Palestine, and Jerusalem was its most important city. Before the Babylonian exile, the region was known as the kingdom of Judah, but after the Israelites returned from exile, it became known as Judea. During Roman rule, Judea was ruled by governors, of whom Pontius Pilate was the most well known.

4. Religious Shifts

Alexander the Great's attempts to Hellenize the world led to resistance, and new religious parties were formed among the Jews during the 400 silent years in reaction to the pressure to adopt Greek language and culture. These parties all acknowledged the authority of the Torah (Law of Moses) and the importance of the Temple. These different groups, however, had different ideas about the practical application of the religion in their daily lives.

The Pharisees were known for their rigid adherence to religious prescriptions and traditions of the forefathers. They saw themselves as the official interpreters and defenders of the Law. They believed in the resurrection and in angels. They tried not to mix with sinners. They asked Jesus trick questions about issues such as keeping the Sabbath, eating with sinners and fasting. There were about 6,000 Pharisees during the time of Jesus.

The Sadducees, a smaller group than the Pharisees, were politically more active. They tolerated Roman rule, as it brought about stability. Theologically, they were conservative. For instance, they only accepted the first five books of the Old Testament (the Pentateuch) as Scripture. They did not believe in the resurrection or in angels (they asked Jesus about this). They prosecuted the Early Church and questioned the apostles.

Strictly speaking, *the scribes* were not a party but a group of laymen who studied the Law of Moses. They originate as far back as the period of exile when the Torah was the center of Jewish religion because the Temple lay in ruins. Since the time of Ezra (Neh. 8:9), who by that time was already known as a priest and scribe, they were seen as experts of the Law. By the time of the New Testament, they were considered to be the upholders of the Torah and taught it to groups of pupils. They were versed in the Law and judges in the Jewish Sanhedrin. They acted on behalf of the Romans to maintain law and order. They considered Jesus, who many saw as a political liberator, to be a threat to the Roman law and order.

The Zealots were followers of the Pharisees' faith but were firmly set against domination by the Romans. They tried to get rid of Roman rule.

5. Language Shifts

The language of the inhabitants of Palestine changed from Hebrew to Aramaic (a language related to Hebrew and used by the conquering Assyrians as a language of administration communication, and following them by the Babylonian and Persian empires,) after the period of exile in Babylonia. Hebrew was mainly the language of the Old Testament. During the time of Jesus, Hebrew was only used for religious matters by the priests and rabbis. Latin was spoken in Rome, but *koine* Greek was spoken in the rest of the Roman Empire. The New Testament was also written in Greek. The Jewish Bible was translated into Greek (the Septuagint) because many Jews were fluent in both Greek and Aramaic. Jesus and His disciples spoke Aramaic.

When God raised the curtain after the 400 silent years, the world was prepared for the rapid spread of the gospel. There was now a world language (*koine* Greek), it was easy to travel because of the peace brought about by the Roman Empire, and Jewish settlements and synagogues were present everywhere.

The silent years ended with the birth of Christ 6 B.C. There is now more certainty about the year Christ was born. The Roman monk Dionysius Exiguous, who created our calendar, made a calculation error, which meant that there were six years too many. Herod the Great—the Herod at the time of Christ's birth and the one responsible for the murdering of children in Bethlehem (Matt. 2:1)—ruled between 37 and 4 B.C.

The 27 books that make up the New Testament were nearly all written before the end of A.D. 100. The 27 books can be grouped the following way:

- The four Gospels, which describe the life of Jesus from different perspectives (Matthew, Mark, Luke and John)
- The Acts of the Apostles, which describes the first years of the Christian Church
- The letters of Paul (Romans, 1 and 2 Corinthians, Galatians, Ephesians, Philippians, Colossians, 1 and 2 Thessalonians, 1 and 2 Timothy, Titus and Philemon)
- The general letters (Hebrews, James, 1 and 2 Peter, 1–3 John and Jude)
- John's visions (Revelation)

In remaining sections of this book, we will now turn to the period of events after the 400 silent years had ended, beginning in Matthew with the birth of Christ.

HOW DO WE HANDLE EMBARRASSING RELATIVES?

You can choose many things in life, but (unfortunately) family is the one thing you cannot choose. Not everybody is equally positive about his or her relatives. How do you handle family members whom you do not like and whom are an embarrassment to you?

Matthew 1 (history)

¹This is a record of the family line of Jesus Christ. He is the son of David. He is also the son of Abraham.
²Abraham was the father of Isaac.
Isaac was the father of Jacob.
Jacob was the father of Judah and his brothers.
³Judah was the father of Perez and Zerah. Tamar was their mother.
Perez was the father of Hezron.
Hezron was the father of Ram.
⁴Ram was the father of Amminadab.
Amminadab was the father of Nahshon.
Nahshon was the father of Salmon.
⁵Salmon was the father of Boaz. Rahab was Boaz's mother.
Boaz was the father of Obed. Ruth was Obed's mother.
Obed was the father of Jesse.
⁶And Jesse was the father of King David.
David was the father of Solomon. Solomon's mother had been Uriah's wife. (NIRV)

It is strange that the New Testament begins with a list of names. Yet this was not strange to the Jews to whom Matthew wrote. A person's genealogical register identified who he or she was. If no gentile blood was recorded, you could be regarded as a true Jew. It gave the Jews great pleasure to see that Jesus' bloodline could be traced back to Abraham. In this manner, Matthew linked the Old Testament to the New Testament in a wondrous way.

The Jews would have, however, frowned on the women's names in the register. It was unheard of to find a woman's name in a register, because during those times women where regarded as property. The ladies in the register also did not have good reputations. Tamar behaved like a woman of the streets (Gen. 38); Rahab was a prostitute (Josh. 2:1); Ruth was a Moabite—and by law the Moabites were not allowed to become part of the Jewish people (Deut. 23:3); and Bathseba, the wife of Uriah, committed adultery with David (2 Sam. 12:9–10).

Yet the inclusion of these names had a purpose. Here, at the beginning of the gospel (the good news), the list of names is an indication that Jesus broke down the walls of separation. He broke down the barriers between Jew and non-Jew (heathen) by making Ruth (a Moabite) and Rahab (the woman from Jericho) part of His bloodline. He broke down barriers between men and women and restored women to their rightful position.

The Lord does not allow our reputations to become a barrier between Him and us. He makes us part of His family despite our reputations. How, then, can we turn our backs on certain members of our family? Pray to the Lord that you may have more patience with your family.

Thank You, Lord, that You are not ashamed of me despite my reputation.

You can't build a reputation on what you are going to do.
—Henry Ford (1863–1947), *American industrialist*

THE ONLY WAY TO FIND TRUE HAPPINESS!

Many people seek happiness, but many fail to find it because they are not aware of what true happiness entails. This section reveals the secret to true happiness. Let us discover this secret!

Matthew 5 (explanation)

[3]"Blessed are those who are spiritually needy.
The kingdom of heaven belongs to them.
[4]Blessed are those who are sad.
They will be comforted.
[5]Blessed are those who are free of pride.
They will be given the earth.
[6]Blessed are those who are hungry and thirsty for what is right.
They will be filled.
[7]Blessed are those who show mercy.
They will be shown mercy.
[8]Blessed are those whose hearts are pure.
They will see God.
[9]Blessed are those who make peace.
They will be called sons of God.
[10]Blessed are those who suffer for doing what is right.
The kingdom of heaven belongs to them.
[11]"Blessed are you when people make fun of you and hurt you because of me. You are also blessed when they tell all kinds of evil lies about you because of me. [12]Be joyful and glad. Your reward in heaven is great. In the same way, people hurt the prophets who lived long ago. (NIRV)

Jesus is in the business of happiness. He wants people to be happy. The very first recorded sermon by Jesus starts with how one can find real happiness. On the surface, Jesus' opening words seem contradictory and may initially come across as strange. Each of the blessings tells us how we can be truly happy. Jesus overturns the world's way (and possibly ours) of viewing happiness. According to Christ, we should not seek outward happiness but look for it in a place where most people would not think of looking—in our heart.

Jesus wants us to have the right attitude in our hearts in order to do the right thing. The right attitude is to be poor in spirit (v. 3), to be free of pride (v. 5) and to desire what is right (v. 10). The correct attitude should then manifest itself in good deeds: to mourn over what is wrong (v. 4), to show mercy (v. 7) and to be peacemakers (v. 9). To love God means to live a life that the world will find strange. This is not easy, but such a life makes us part of God's kingdom. This differs so much from the short-lived pleasures the world has to offer. Instead, to be part of God's kingdom means that happiness is guaranteed. According to this section in Matthew, happiness is not gained directly, but it is a byproduct of a specific lifestyle!

Lord, thank You for clearly showing me how to be happy.

There is no way to happiness. Happiness is the way.
—Wayne Dyer (b. 1940), *American psychotherapist, author and lecturer*

HOW CAN WE ADD ZEST TO LIFE?

Life can be so beautiful and exciting. However, despite this fact, many people no longer enjoy life. Jesus knew that we can sometimes feel that some of the zest has gone out of our lives. He used the following parable to explain to us how life could be made more fulfilled.

Matthew 5 (parable)

13"You are the salt of the earth. But suppose the salt loses its saltiness. How can it be made salty again? It is no longer good for anything. It will be thrown out. People will walk all over it. (NIRV)

In this parable, Jesus uses the image of salt. In Jesus' time, people associated salt with the following three qualities:

1. **Purity and virtue.** The Romans regarded salt as pure because it comes from pure sources, namely the sea and the sun. Our lives as Christians should be pure and virtuous even though we are surrounded by so much impurity.
2. **A Preservative.** Salt was used to prevent food spoilage and to preserve dead bodies. In this life, we as Christians should counteract corruption, violence and everything that leaves a bitter taste in our mouths. We should be people of integrity.
3. **Something that gives flavor.** The most important quality that salt gives is taste to food. The faithful should be to each other and the world what salt is to food. We should add flavor to life, which many people feel has lost its taste. Unfortunately, the opposite often happens. Jesus clearly speaks out against such Christians. If we no longer give taste to life, we will become like salt that has been discarded.

May you have such a positive and constructive influence on life that others will compliment you in a wonderful way by saying, "You are truly the salt of the earth." It is wonderful to live again!

 Lord, help me to have a constructive influence on people in the things I do and say. Help me to be passionate about life.

I love you not because of who you are, but because of who I am when I am with you.
—Roy Croft

IN WHAT WAY IS GOD THE LIGHT?

"God is light. There is no darkness in him at all" (1 John 1:5, NIRV). It is sad that this life has so much darkness. You might be experiencing great darkness. How do you pray when you are experiencing such dark times? Perhaps it would suffice to just pray, "Lord, please be my light!" But in what way is God the light? Let us have a look!

Matthew 5 (explanation and instruction)

[14]"You are the light of the world. A city on a hill can't be hidden.
[15]Also, people do not light a lamp and put it under a bowl. Instead, they put it on its stand. Then it gives light to everyone in the house. *(explanation)*
[16]"In the same way, let your light shine in front of others. *(instruction)*
Then they will see the good things you do. And they will praise your Father who is in heaven. *(explanation)* NIRV

The answer to the question, "In what way is God the light?" points to us, the believers. Jesus clearly says that we are the light of the world. How is this possible? The following story might help clarify this point.

A statue of Jesus that had been placed in front of a church was destroyed by a bomb during a war. When it fell, the hands and feet of the statue broke off. The church council decided to move the statue out of sight to the back of the church. They found it very difficult to have such a damaged statue of the Jesus figure in front of the church. However, after they had moved the statue, to their amazement they found the damaged statue back in its place in front of the church the next Sunday! An inscription was carved on the statue: "You are my hands and feet."

God wants us to reflect His light in this world of darkness. It is not our light but the light of God that we reflect. Just as the moon reflects the light of the sun, we should reflect God's light. We do it by performing good deeds—by being His hands and feet! If you pray, "Lord, please be my light!" you should carefully tune in on the hands and the feet that God sends to lighten your dark path. That telephone call, the ear of the person who listens or the hand that holds your own is God's way of letting His light shine.

You might not feel that you can make a difference in somebody's life. You might feel as insignificant as the weak flame of a candle. But just remember that there is not enough darkness in the universe to dim the light of one candle. Together with others, you can ignite God's love and signal the message: *God is light!* By doing so, you will glorify Him (v. 16).

 Lord, forgive me for not always being Your hands and feet to other people. Help me to be the light of the world!

There is not enough darkness in all the world to put out the light of even one small candle.
—Robert Alden

I ALSO LIKE TO PEEP ON THE SLY!

There is a story about a theology student who spoke to his professor about a problem he had. "Professor," he said, "when I look at a girl, I see right through her clothes." The professor looked him straight in the eye, smiled and answered, "Dear fellow, you don't have a problem—you have a gift!" Perhaps the professor was telling the young man that every person struggles with lust. Let us read what Jesus says about this!

Matthew 5 (conversation)

[27]'You have heard that it was said, 'Do not commit adultery.'
[28]But here is what I tell you. Do not even look at a woman in the wrong way. Anyone who does has already committed adultery with her in his heart.
[29]'If your right eye causes you to sin, poke it out and throw it away. Your eye is only one part of your body. It is better to lose it than for your whole body to be thrown into hell.
[30]'If your right hand causes you to sin, cut it off and throw it away. Your hand is only one part of your body. It is better to lose it than for your whole body to go into hell. (NIRV)

Jesus says that a person who struggles with lust should gouge out his or her eye. It is no wonder most people consider the demands set out in the Sermon on the Mount to be unrealistic. We should, however, keep the meaning of the words in mind. Here, Jesus' words primarily concern the sanctity of marriage, which Jesus wanted to protect. The Jews thought that only the outward deed of adultery harmed the sanctity of marriage. But Jesus set different standards. To Him, adultery existed the moment a person had the desire to have sexual intercourse with someone other than his or her marriage partner.

What Jesus was saying in this passage is that when men used their eyes to give free reign to their desires and urges, they were already committing adultery. (Of course, the same applied to women who desired men other than their husbands.) To look at someone and to make remarks about the person's attractive appearance cannot, however, be considered wrong. Simply looking at another person need not turn into a sexual desire. Jesus was condemning fantasies that could lead to sin if they were executed.

Jesus' standard makes a lot of sense. After all, none of us would like it if our partner had sexual thoughts about someone else. In verses 29 and 30, Jesus did not mean that we literally have to get rid of our eye or our hand that caused us to err. Yet this radical statement should tell us that marriage is sacred and that we should not allow anything to harm it. Marriage is the best environment in which to give way to our sexual desires.

 Lord, I want to strive to keep my thoughts pure and to enjoy what is good rather than live in a fantasy world of immorality.

What the eye does not admire the heart does not desire.
—Proverb

HOW SHOULD WE TREAT OUR ENEMIES?

Hostility is part of everyday life. Our natural reaction is to avoid our "enemies" and to push them out of our lives. But what would Jesus say about this? Let us read about it.

Matthew 5 (explanation and instruction)

[43]'You have heard that it was said, 'Love your neighbor. Hate your enemy.' *(explanation)*
[44]But here is what I tell you. Love your enemies. Pray for those who hurt you. *(instruction)*
[45]Then you will be sons of your Father who is in heaven.
'He causes his sun to shine on evil people and good people. He sends rain on those who do right and those who don't.
[46]'If you love those who love you, what reward will you get? Even the tax collectors do that. [47] If you greet only your own people, what more are you doing than others? Even people who are ungodly do that.
(explanation)
[48]So be perfect, just as your Father in heaven is perfect. *(instruction)* NIRV

After reading these verses, our immediate reaction may be that Jesus, by giving these commands, had gone too far. Is it not humanly possible for us to love our enemy (v. 44) or, even more, to be perfect (v. 48). This goes against everything that is natural. However, before we get too upset, we should first gain clarity on what Jesus means.

Love your enemies. To love our enemies is humanly impossible, but this is not primarily what the text is about. Rather, this verse is about the nature of God. Verse 45 describes God's immense greatness. He bestows His gifts (sun and rain) on friend and foe; therefore, He asks us to also love our friend and foe. By doing this, we reflect a bit of His greatness. This is not a spontaneous act (like falling in love), but a choice we make. Prayer makes this possible.

Be perfect. The Jews did not see perfection as perfectionism. To them, perfection involved a certain attitude. If we are focused on loving God and our neighbor, then we are considered "perfect." We prove nothing by loving our family and friends (vv. 46–47), but to extend our love to those who are not that friendly toward us is a challenge. We do not do it to show that we are better than them, but rather how good God is. Pray to the Holy Spirit for strength to obey this command!

 Holy Spirit, give me the strength to truly love my enemies.

We must develop and maintain the capacity to forgive. He who is devoid of the power to forgive is devoid of the power to love. There is some good in the worst of us and some evil in the best of us. When we discover this, we are less prone to hate our enemies.
—Martin Luther King, Jr. (1929–1968), *American Baptist minister, Civil Rights leader and winner of the Nobel Prize in 1964*

THE SECRET OF A SUCCESSFUL INVESTMENT

Money is the one subject that is always on everybody's lips. People's conversations usually center on the fact that they have too little money and could do with another million. Financial advisers will give you good advice (and sometimes the wrong advice) about what to do with your money and where to invest it. Fortunately, the Bible also has a lot to say about money.

Matthew 6 (explanation and instruction)

[19]Don't store up treasures on earth! (*instruction*)
Moths and rust can destroy them, and thieves can break in and steal them. (*explanation*)
[20]Instead, store up your treasures in heaven, (*instruction*)
where moths and rust cannot destroy them, and thieves cannot break in and steal them. [21] Your heart will always be where your treasure is. (*explanation*) CEV

In this section, the best financial consultant, Jesus Christ, advises us on what to do with money. (What a pity that we do not always listen to Him!) He uses two warnings to tell us where to invest.

First, Jesus states that we should not store up treasures on earth. He then goes on to explain what he means. Moths can damage our clothes, rust can eat away our cars (not to mention we can lose them to carjackers), and our houses can be raided by thieves or damaged by storms. Our earthly investments are not safe. We also cannot take them with us when we die. That is why a hearse does not have a trailer!

In His second warning, Jesus reveals the secret of a successful and safe investment: store up your treasures in heaven. There are no moths, rust, carjackers, hurricanes, thieves or robbers in heaven. Of course, the million-dollar question is: Where are these treasures? The Jews were familiar with the phrase "treasures in heaven" and identified it with two things. First, they believed that people's good deeds on earth became their treasures in heaven. During the persecution of Christians in Rome, the Romans broke into a church to steal the treasures. One of the Romans asked a deacon to show him the treasures. The deacon pointed to the widows, the orphans and the poor and said, "They are the church's treasures." Second, the Jews associated treasures with character. They understood that people's character was the one item they could take with them from this world into eternity.

 Lord, help me to accumulate treasures in heaven by doing good deeds and having a good character.

Lay up your treasures in heaven where there is no depreciation.
—Author unknown

DO GOD'S MIRACLES DEPEND ON OUR FAITH?

Someone I knew well once attended the service of a well-known "faith healer." He went there with great expectations because he believed that his illness would be cured. He went to a lot of trouble to attend the service, but he left with great disappointment, as his condition did not improve. The problem with "faith healing" is that many people believe that if they are not immediately healed, there is something wrong with their faith. If only they could believe more, they would be healed. This brings us to a very important question: Do God's miracles depend on our faith?

Matthew 13 (history)

⁵⁴He came to his hometown of Nazareth. There he began teaching the people in their synagogue. They were amazed.

'Where did this man get this wisdom? Where did he get this power to do miracles?' they asked. ⁵⁵'Isn't this the carpenter's son? Isn't his mother's name Mary? Aren't his brothers James, Joseph, Simon and Judas? ⁵⁶Aren't all his sisters with us? Then where did this man get all these things?' ⁵⁷They were not pleased with him at all.

But Jesus said to them, 'A prophet is not honored in his hometown. He doesn't receive any honor in his own home.'

⁵⁸He did only a few miracles there because they had no faith. (NIRV)

When Jesus returned to his hometown, Nazareth, those who knew Him from childhood were amazed at how wise He was and how powerful the miracles were that He performed. To them, Jesus was just the son of Mary—an ordinary person who grew up as the son of a carpenter. They did not realize that He had been sent by God. This might be why they rejected Him. These events in Nazareth mirrored what would happen later in Jesus' life when His own people rejected and eventually crucified Him.

This section ends in a strange way: "He did only a few miracles there because they had no faith" (v. 58). In a sense, God's miracles depend on our faith. God does not want to give more than what we are prepared to accept. However, it is important to note that despite the opposition in Nazareth, Jesus did show His mercy by performing a few miracles. His mercy is indeed incomprehensible. Romans 5:8 describes it wonderfully: "But here is how God has shown his love for us. While we were still sinners, Christ died for us" (NIRV).

 Lord, it is a miracle that You are concerned about me despite my shortcomings.

Don't believe in miracles. Depend on them.
—Laurence J. Peter (1919–1990), *Canadian teacher and writer*

WHAT IS THE SECRET TO A FULFILLED LIFE?

All people seek fulfillment in life. Nobody expresses this better than the author of Proverbs 13 (the parallelisms stress his point of view.):

Hope that is put off
makes one sick at heart.
But a longing that is met
is like a tree of life. . . .
A longing that is met
is like something that tastes sweet (12,19, NIRV)

The question is not whether we are rich or poor but rather whether our lives are fulfilling or boring. What is the secret to a fulfilled life? Peter will help us!

Matthew 14 (story)

²⁵Early in the morning, Jesus went out to the disciples. He walked on the lake.

Tension: The disciples get a fright

²⁶They saw him walking on the lake and were terrified. 'It's a ghost!' they said. And they cried out in fear.

Relief of tension: Jesus comforts them

²⁷Right away Jesus called out to them, 'Be brave! It is I. Don't be afraid.'

Result: Peter gets off the boat

²⁸'Lord, is it you?' Peter asked. 'If it is, tell me to come to you on the water.'
²⁹'Come,' Jesus said.
So Peter got out of the boat. He walked on the water toward Jesus. ³⁰But when Peter saw the wind, he was afraid. He began to sink. He cried out, 'Lord! Save me!'
³¹Right away Jesus reached out his hand and caught him. 'Your faith is so small!' he said. 'Why did you doubt me?'
³²When they climbed into the boat, the wind died down. ³³Then those in the boat worshiped Jesus. They said, 'You really are the Son of God!' (NIRV)

The secret to a fulfilled life is to be like Peter, who moved from his stationary position on the boat (comfort zone) to walking on the water (new terrain). The attitude of those who walk on the water can be distinguished from those who sit in the boat in the following way:

Boat Potatoes (11 disciples and you?)	Water Walkers (Peter and you?)
Choose a safe and familiar environment	Choose an unfamiliar environment
Danger: stagnation and boredom	Advantage: growth and fulfillment

During the next five days, we will set out the *five steps* those who walk on the water follow. The next five days were inspired by the book *If You Want to Walk on Water, You've Got to Get Out of the Boat* by John Ortberg.

 Lord, help me to get out of my comfort zone. I want to live a fulfilled life.

To the degree we're not living our dreams, our comfort zone has more control of us than we have over ourselves.
—Peter McWilliams (1949–2000), *American writer, primarily of self-help books*

STEP 1 FOR WALKING ON THE WATER: RECOGNIZE YOUR CALLING!

Step 1 for those who want to step out of the boat and walk on the water is that *there is always a calling.* Learn to see it!

Matthew 14 (story)

[25]Early in the morning, Jesus went out to the disciples. He walked on the lake.

Tension: *The disciples get a fright*

[26]They saw him walking on the lake and were terrified. 'It's a ghost!' they said. And they cried out in fear.

Relief of tension: *Jesus comforts them*

[27]Right away Jesus called out to them, 'Be brave! It is I. Don't be afraid.'

Result: *Peter gets off the boat*

[28]'Lord, is it you?' Peter asked. 'If it is, tell me to come to you on the water.'
[29]'Come,' Jesus said.
So Peter got out of the boat. He walked on the water toward Jesus. [30]But when Peter saw the wind, he was afraid. He began to sink. He cried out, 'Lord! Save me!'
[31]Right away Jesus reached out his hand and caught him. 'Your faith is so small!' he said. 'Why did you doubt me?'
[32]When they climbed into the boat, the wind died down. [33]Then those in the boat worshiped Jesus. They said, 'You really are the Son of God!' (NIRV)

In the above passage, Peter is not an adrenaline junky but rather an obedient follower. He waits for Jesus' command before he gets off the boat: "'Come,' Jesus said" (v. 29). Those who walk on the water can distinguish between a calling and simply being careless. You have to be wise to distinguish your mission.

Wisdom tells you that *a calling is more than a career.* A career ends the day you retire, but a calling ends the day you die. Mother Teresa was a nun (her career), but her calling was to care for the poorest of the poor in Calcutta. Henry Ford was the managing director of a company (his career), but his calling was to make motor vehicles. Both individuals discovered this as time passed!

Wisdom also tells you that *you need others in order to see the blind spots (your limitations and potential).* Ask people who know you well what they think your calling in life is. In addition, *explore possibilities while you are in the boat.* Of course, you need to be responsible in doing this—do not resign from your job without thinking, to open a coffee shop. Finally, wisdom teaches that *a feeling of inadequacy is a good sign*—it makes you dependent on God.

Lord, help me to discover what my calling in life is.

Much of our activity these days is nothing more than a cheap anesthetic to
deaden the pain of an empty life.
—Author unknown

STEP 2 FOR WALKING ON THE WATER: OVERCOME YOUR FEAR!

Step 2 for those who want to step out of the boat and walk on the water is to recognize that *there will always be fear.* Overcome it!

Matthew 14 (story)

²⁵Early in the morning, Jesus went out to the disciples. He walked on the lake.

Tension: *The disciples get a fright*

²⁶They saw him walking on the lake and were terrified. 'It's a ghost!' they said. And they cried out in fear.

Relief of tension: *Jesus comforts them*

²⁷Right away Jesus called out to them, 'Be brave! It is I. Don't be afraid.'

Result: *Peter gets off the boat*

²⁸'Lord, is it you?' Peter asked. 'If it is, tell me to come to you on the water.'
²⁹'Come,' Jesus said.
So Peter got out of the boat. He walked on the water toward Jesus. ³⁰But when Peter saw the wind, he was afraid. He began to sink. He cried out, 'Lord! Save me!'
³¹Right away Jesus reached out his hand and caught him. 'Your faith is so small!' he said. 'Why did you doubt me?'
³²When they climbed into the boat, the wind died down. ³³Then those in the boat worshiped Jesus. They said, 'You really are the Son of God!' (NIRV)

"Don't be afraid" is the most common instruction in the Bible—it occurs 366 times. A possible reason for this is that fear prevents us from getting out of the boat (our comfort zone). We are afraid to swap the familiar for the unfamiliar. We have to choose between *fear* and *trust*. Fear tells us to *stay put* because we are comfortable where we are. Trust tells us to *move ahead* despite the risk involved. When failing becomes our greatest fear, we become paralyzed, procrastinate and see life as purposeless and boring.

How can you conquer your fear of failure? First, do not personalize failure. To sink does not turn you into a failure. Although Peter sank, Jesus called him a "rock" two chapters later (Matt. 16:18). Second, take action! You can't wait to be motivated—motivation is a byproduct of action. Action has a way of driving away fear. Finally, see failure as an opportunity to grow! Peter sank but found safety in the arms of Jesus.

 Lord, I confess that my fears prevent me from following my calling. Help me!

Fear defeats more people than any other one thing in the world.
—Ralph Waldo Emerson (1803–1882), *U.S. poet, essayist and lecturer*

STEP 3 FOR WALKING ON THE WATER: BE BOLD IN YOUR FAITH!

Step 3 for those who want to step out of the boat and walk on the water is to realize that *there is always assurance.* Be bold in your faith!

Matthew 14 (story)

²⁵Early in the morning, Jesus went out to the disciples. He walked on the lake.

Tension: The disciples get a fright

²⁶They saw him walking on the lake and were terrified. 'It's a ghost!' they said. And they cried out in fear.

Relief of tension: Jesus comforts them

²⁷Right away Jesus called out to them, 'Be brave! It is I. Don't be afraid.'

Result: Peter gets off the boat

²⁸'Lord, is it you?' Peter asked. 'If it is, tell me to come to you on the water.'
²⁹'Come,' Jesus said.
So Peter got out of the boat. He walked on the water toward Jesus. ³⁰But when Peter saw the wind, he was afraid. He began to sink. He cried out, 'Lord! Save me!'
³¹Right away Jesus reached out his hand and caught him. 'Your faith is so small!' he said. 'Why did you doubt me?'
³²When they climbed into the boat, the wind died down. ³³Then those in the boat worshiped Jesus. They said, 'You really are the Son of God!' (NIRV)

To walk on water (to explore new territories—for example, to pray in public for the first time) can be terrifying. Life's storms and winds can sink your lifeboat. Yet it is comforting to know that fearful incidents are met with the assurance that God is present in our storms: "Right away Jesus called out to them, 'Be brave! It is I. Don't be afraid'" (v. 27). It is also comforting to know God's ears are good and that His hands are safe: "Right away Jesus reached out his hand and caught him. 'Your faith is so small!' he said. 'Why did you doubt me?'" (v. 31).

The dark depths in which we sink are just the place where God works best! David hid in a dark cave when he fled from Saul (2 Sam. 22). It was in that dark cave that David discovered that God was his fortress and his deliverer (Ps. 18). Jesus, the Son of David, also ended up in a dark grave (cave) after His crucifixion. However, he did not stay there, because God does His best work where it is dark. Be bold in your faith!

 Thank You, Lord, that I may be bold where You are concerned. Help me to realize my calling.

Avoiding danger is no safer in the long run than outright exposure.
The fearful are caught as often as the bold.
—Helen Keller (1880–1968), American author and educator who was blind and deaf

STEP 4 FOR WALKING ON THE WATER: GET OUT OF THE BOAT!

Step 4 for those who want to step out of the boat and walk on the water is to realize that *there is always a choice*. Get out of the boat!

Matthew 14 (story)

²⁵Early in the morning, Jesus went out to the disciples. He walked on the lake.

Tension: The disciples get a fright

²⁶They saw him walking on the lake and were terrified. 'It's a ghost!' they said. And they cried out in fear.

Relief of tension: Jesus comforts them

²⁷Right away Jesus called out to them, 'Be brave! It is I. Don't be afraid.'

Result: Peter gets off the boat

²⁸'Lord, is it you?' Peter asked. 'If it is, tell me to come to you on the water.'
²⁹'Come,' Jesus said.
So Peter got out of the boat. He walked on the water toward Jesus. ³⁰But when Peter saw the wind, he was afraid. He began to sink. He cried out, 'Lord! Save me!'
³¹Right away Jesus reached out his hand and caught him. 'Your faith is so small!' he said. 'Why did you doubt me?'
³²When they climbed into the boat, the wind died down. ³³Then those in the boat worshiped Jesus. They said, 'You really are the Son of God!' (NIRV)

We have a choice. Not everybody is willing to take the risk (e.g., to visit a sick person for the first time); however, getting out of the boat (your comfort zone) will always be worth our while. To stay inside the boat can be a risk, because we will stagnate and get bored. Obstacles that can prevent us from leaving the boat:

- **Embarrassment**: Failure can be an embarrassment to us. In reality, success only comes after we have taken small steps.
- **Rationalization**: We might rationalize that taking the risk is not that important. The truth is that if we wait long enough, everything loses its importance.
- **Unrealistic expectations**: We say that we will get off the boat when the wind abates. Yet those who walk on water do not expect the wind to be favorable. Peter did not.
- **Fairness**: We believe that life should be fair. The truth is that life is often difficult and unfair.
- **Timing**: We say that we will wait for the right time to come. The truth is that there is not always a favorable time.

- **Inspiration**: We decide to wait for inspiration before we start. But sometimes this inspiration never comes. We have to consciously decide to take the first step.

Remember: you do not have to be great to start, but you have to start to be great!

 Lord, help me to leave my comfort zone and to reach out to those in need.

It is our choices that show what we truly are, far more than our abilities.
—Joanne Kathleen Rowling (b. 1965), *English writer; author of the Harry Potter series*

STEP 5 FOR WALKING ON THE WATER: REMEMBER THAT THERE IS ALWAYS HOPE!

Step 5 for those who want to step out of the boat and walk on the water is to recognize that *there is always hope for a changed life.* Praise the Lord!

Matthew 14 (story)

[25]Early in the morning, Jesus went out to the disciples. He walked on the lake.

Tension: The disciples get a fright

[26]They saw him walking on the lake and were terrified. 'It's a ghost!' they said. And they cried out in fear.

Relief of tension: Jesus comforts them

[27]Right away Jesus called out to them, 'Be brave! It is I. Don't be afraid.'

Result: Peter gets off the boat

[28]'Lord, is it you?' Peter asked. 'If it is, tell me to come to you on the water.'
[29]'Come,' Jesus said.
So Peter got out of the boat. He walked on the water toward Jesus. [30]But when Peter saw the wind, he was afraid. He began to sink. He cried out, 'Lord! Save me!'
[31]Right away Jesus reached out his hand and caught him. 'Your faith is so small!' he said. 'Why did you doubt me?'
[32]When they climbed into the boat, the wind died down. [33]Then those in the boat worshiped Jesus. They said, 'You really are the Son of God!' (NIRV)

The act of walking on water begins and ends with God. Jesus was the one who called Peter, and the disciples kneeled before Him in verse 33. To walk on water is a way to turn a boring life into one of fulfillment.

Walking on water can broaden our image of God. It is like looking through a telescope. If you look through the wrong end, everything looks small and distant. However, after an experience of walking on water, it is as if you are looking though the right end of the telescope—everything is large and close up. That is why the disciples say, "You really are the Son of God."

Walking on water can also help us to realize that we are dependent on God. As Blaise Pascal once said, "Lord, help me to do great things as though they were little, since I do them with your power; and little things as though they were great, since I do them in your name." *Praise God's greatness!* Handel composed his famous opera *Messiah* after he got off his boat of depression. If you want to walk on the water, you have to get off the boat!

 Lord, give me the courage to get out of my comfort zone. I praise You!

Life is change. Growth is optional. Choose wisely.
—Karen Kaiser Clark, *Educator and author of three books on growing through change*

DOES FORGIVENESS HAVE BOUNDARIES?

Can a person reach the point in which he or she has forgiven someone enough? Let us see.

Matthew 18 (parable)

[21]Then Peter came to him and asked, 'Lord, how often should I forgive someone who sins against me? Seven times?'
[22]'No, not seven times,' Jesus replied, 'but seventy times seven!
[23]'Therefore, the Kingdom of Heaven can be compared to a king who decided to bring his accounts up to date with servants who had borrowed money from him.

Tension: Too much debt

[24]In the process, one of his debtors was brought in who owed him millions of dollars. [25]He couldn't pay, so his master ordered that he be sold—along with his wife, his children, and everything he owned—to pay the debt.
[26]But the man fell down before his master and begged him, 'Please, be patient with me, and I will pay it all.'

Relief of tension: Free of debt

[27]Then his master was filled with pity for him, and he released him and forgave his debt.

Result: Ungratefulness

[28]'But when the man left the king, he went to a fellow servant who owed him a few thousand dollars. He grabbed him by the throat and demanded instant payment. [34]Then the angry king sent the man to prison to be tortured until he had paid his entire debt.
[35]'That's what my heavenly Father will do to you if you refuse to forgive your brothers and sisters from your heart.' (NLT)

According to Jewish Law, it was enough to forgive someone three times. Peter wanted to impress Jesus by moving the boundary to seven times. Jesus surprised him by moving it to 490 (70 times 7) times. But was that the new boundary?

In this parable, Jesus explained what he meant. Two extremes are in contrast: the king's (God's) inconceivable mercy in canceling the servant's debt that amounted to millions (vv. 24,27), and the inconceivable callousness of the acquitted person who refused to cancel the small amount owed to him by a fellow official (fellow believer). The point Jesus was making is that since God pardons our innumerable sins, we should show our gratitude by canceling other peoples' small debts.

To forgive 70 times 7 times does not literally mean to forgive 490 times but limitless times. Jesus told Peter that love cannot be calculated and that we should forgive one another from the heart. One does not count forgiveness! To forgive does not mean that you need to trust because forgiveness has to do with the past and trust with the future.

Lord, help me to use Your great mercy to forgive others with all my heart.

Forgiveness does not change the past, but it does enlarge the future.
—Paul Boese

TO BE DOUBTFUL IS NOT AS BAD AS WE THINK!

You might want to do more to expand God's kingdom on earth but feel totally incompetent to really make a difference. Perhaps you feel that you are not capable of praying well enough—that you cannot even pray out loud in front of others—or that you do not know your Bible that well or do not know how to talk to others about God. You might even have doubts about God Himself. But it will be good if today you can look beyond all your so-called incompetencies and focus on the last section of Matthew.

Matthew 28 (story)

Tension: Some of the disciples are doubtful

> [16]Then the 11 disciples went to Galilee. They went to the mountain where Jesus had told them to go. [17]When they saw him, they worshiped him. But some still had their doubts.

Relief of tension: Jesus approaches them

> [18]*Then Jesus came to them.* He said, 'All authority in heaven and on earth has been given to me.

Result: The Great Commission

> [19]So you must go and make disciples of all nations. Baptize them in the name of the Father and of the Son and of the Holy Spirit. [20]Teach them to obey everything I have commanded you. And you can be sure that I am always with you, to the very end.' (NIRV)

Matthew 28:19–20 are well-known verses because they have become known as the "Great Commission." Because of this, we can easily read the chapter without paying attention to verses 16 to 18. Let us have a quick look at what these verses say. The first part of Matthew 28 is about the resurrection, followed by Jesus' encounter with the disciples. Verse 17 tells us that the disciples worshiped Jesus when they saw Him. But then the last part of the verse says, "But some still had their doubts." What was Jesus' reaction to the doubting disciples who left Him in the lurch at the cross?

The first few words of verse 18 express it so well: "Then Jesus came to them . . ." This is unbelievable. Jesus did not turn His back on the disciples but went to them and gave them the greatest commission: to spread the gospel to the whole world. God does not expect us to be competent. He expects us to be obedient. It is our incompetence, our doubt, that creates the space in which God can and will achieve great things. In this way, all praise will go to Him!

You can find consolation for your incompetence in the last verse: "And you can be sure that I am always with you, to the very end." Incompetence alerts you to the fact that you can depend on God.

 Thank You, Lord, that You want to use me despite my doubt.

Faith lives in honest doubt.
—Alfred, Lord Tennyson (1809–1892), *English poet often regarded as the chief representative of the Victorian age in poetry*

HOW SHOULD WE UNDERSTAND MIRACLES?

Believers do not always agree on the subject of miracles—especially where healing the sick is concerned. Some feel that too much emphasis is placed on the "miracle worker" (or "faith healer"), while others may feel that "faith healing" is merely a show. The following passage in Mark will help us to understand miracles better.

Mark 2 (story)

Tension: The paralyzed man's desperate friends

³Four of those who came were carrying a man who could not walk. ⁴But they could not get him close to Jesus because of the crowd. So they made a hole in the roof above Jesus. Then they lowered the man through it on a mat.

Relief of tension: Healing and forgiveness

⁵Jesus saw their faith. So he said to the man, 'Son, your sins are forgiven.'
⁶Some teachers of the law were sitting there. They were thinking, ⁷'Why is this fellow talking like that? He's saying a very evil thing! Only God can forgive sins!'
¹¹'I tell you,' he said, 'get up. Take your mat and go home.'

Result: The amazed crowd praise Jesus!

¹²The man got up and took his mat. Then he walked away while everyone watched. All the people were amazed. They praised God and said, 'We have never seen anything like this!' (NIRV)

This section suggests that the miracles of Jesus should never be detached from His message. Miracles help to illustrate Jesus' message in a practical way. In this case, Jesus used a miracle to show the people—particularly the scribes—that He could pardon sins. According to the scribes, only God could forgive sins. By performing this miracle, Jesus confirmed that He was in fact God and that He could therefore forgive the paralyzed man's sins. Miracles should never focus on a person, but rather on Jesus' message. That is why the crowd was amazed and praised God (v. 12).

 Thank You, Lord, that Your miracles confirm that You are God and that You are able to forgive sins—even mine. I want to join the crowd in praise!

I am realistic; I expect miracles.
—Wayne Dyer (b. 1940), *American psychotherapist, author and lecturer*

IF WE LIE DOWN WITH THE DOGS WE WILL GET UP WITH FLEAS!

Is this true? Looking at Jesus' life, we find that He mingled with sinners and tax collectors ("dogs"), but that these people did not "infest" Him. Why not? This episode may help us to understand.

Mark 2 (story)

Tension: Jesus eats with the sinners

> [15]Later Jesus was having dinner at Levi's house. Many tax collectors and 'sinners' were eating with him and his disciples. They were part of the large crowd following Jesus.

Relief of tension: Jesus' actions are condemned

> [16]Some teachers of the law who were Pharisees were there. They saw Jesus eating with 'sinners' and tax collectors. So they asked his disciples, 'Why does he eat with tax collectors and 'sinners'?'

Result: The reason for Jesus' coming becomes clear

> [17]Jesus heard that. So he said to them, 'Those who are healthy don't need a doctor. Sick people do. I have not come to get those who think they are right with God to follow me. I have come to get sinners to follow me.' (NIRV)

In the above passage, Jesus ate in the house of Levi, a tax collector, along with many other "sinners" and tax collectors. The tax collectors were regarded as sinners because they were suspected of being dishonest. In those days, when you ate with someone, it meant that you showed your solidarity to those with whom you shared your meal. The "righteous" (Pharisees) did not like Jesus' actions at all, because they looked down on sinners. But these sinners did not influence Jesus negatively. Jesus did not become a dishonest tax collector or a sinner. Instead, He went to them to influence them positively.

Jesus compared these individuals to the sick and Himself to the doctor (v. 17). These people did not "infest" Him because they did not have a negative influence on Him. How ironic that it was the "righteous" who trampled on Jesus by letting Him die on the cross. It is very sad that many believers are guilty of looking down on others. May the Lord protect us from being prejudiced! We have to mix with the "dogs" of this world. How else will we be able to show them Christ's love?

 Thank You, Lord, for not distinguishing between people. Thank You that I can know You.

No prejudice has even been able to prove its case in the court of reason.
—Author unknown

WHAT DO WE MEAN WHEN WE SAY THAT JESUS IS THE "SON OF GOD"?

Mark wrote his Gospel in way that pointed out to his readers that Jesus was the Son of God. The Gospel begins with this (1:1) and also ends with it when the Roman officer says, "Surely this man was the Son of God" (15:39, NIV). It is also often mentioned in between the beginning and the end (e.g. 1:11; 5:7; 9:7; 14:61–62). But what does Mark mean when he writes that Jesus is the Son of God?

Mark 3 (story)

Tension: The crowds flock to Jesus

> [7]Jesus went off to the Sea of Galilee with his disciples. A large crowd from Galilee followed.

Relief of tension: Jesus heals the sick

> [10]Jesus had healed many people. So those who were sick were pushing forward to touch him. [11]When people with evil spirits saw him, they fell down in front of him. The spirits shouted, *'You are the Son of God!'*

Result: Jesus wants to hide His identity

> [12]But Jesus ordered them not to tell who he was. (NIRV)

The fact that Jesus is the "Son of God" should be understood in a spiritual sense. For example, Arabs are generally known as the "sons of the desert," yet nobody believes that the desert physically gave birth to them. No, the name "sons of the desert" should be understood in a spiritual sense. Arabs are given that name because they have such a thorough knowledge of the desert; they are one with it. In the same way, when Mark writes that Jesus is the "Son of God," he emphasizes the intimate bond between Jesus and the Father.

The early Christians did not consider the title "Son of God" unusual. The Israelites were given this name (Exod. 4:22–23), and it was common for Egyptians, Babylonians Canaanites and Romans to refer to their leader as a son of God. To them, "Son of God" indicated a special bond with God.

Yet there is something unique about calling Jesus the Son of God. Mark wrote that Jesus called God "Abba, Father" (14:36). "Abba" means "my father," and it was the name Jewish children used to address their fathers. By calling God "Abba," Jesus revealed the intimacy that existed between Him and His Father. John takes the name "Son of God" even further when Jesus refers to Himself as a "Son" who was sent by the father (John 3:16–17; 5:23; 6:40; 10:36). John uses this name to clearly indicate that Jesus, the Messiah, was indeed God (John 1:18).

Nobody has ever seen God. However, Jesus, as the Son of God, showed us what the Father is like (John 1:18). Therefore, if we want to know what God is like, we should look at Jesus. To confess that Jesus is the Son of God is to know, "Anyone who has seen me has seen the Father" (John 14:9, NIRV).

Lord, thank You that I know that You and the Father are one!

You should point to the whole man Jesus and say, "That is God."
—Martin Luther (1483–1546), *German priest and scholar whose questioning of certain Church practices led to the Protestant Reformation*

BLOOD IS THICKER THAN WATER, BUT . . .

People who work in orphanages have told me that children always have a desire to return home—no matter how bad things are at home. The tie between family members often overcomes and leads them to tolerate even the most adverse circumstances. This is why the saying that blood is thicker than water rings so true. Do other similar ties exist?

Mark 3 (story)

Tension: Jesus' family wanted to talk to Him

> [31]Then Jesus' mother and brothers arrived. Standing outside, they sent someone in to call him. [32]A crowd was sitting around him, and they told him, 'Your mother and brothers are outside looking for you.'

Relief of tension: Jesus responds by asking a counter question

> [33]'Who are my mother and my brothers?' he asked.

Result: Jesus' definition of family

> [34]Then he looked at those seated in a circle around him and said, 'Here are my mother and my brothers! [35]Whoever does God's will is my brother and sister and mother.' (TNIV)

At first glance, we might feel that Jesus acted rather rudely toward His family. But this is not the case. His family was very important to Him. His mother, Mary, and His brother, Jacob, joined the other believers in the upper room on Pentecost (Acts 1:14). Jesus did not reject His family, but showed us something comforting. In His comment in verse 35, He called those who were not His blood relatives His brothers and sisters.

Throughout the ages right up to this day, all believers can know that Jesus considers us part of His family. That is why all believers (those who do His will—v. 35) are brothers and sisters of each other and of Jesus. In this way, all of us, together with this Child, are children of the Father. Jesus taught His disciples to pray, "Our Father." His blood, which flowed for all of us, makes us His family. How comforting!

Jesus shows us that spiritual ties are just as strong and binding as family ties (v. 35). Jesus is busy preparing the way for a new community of believers—a new family. Jesus' family is no longer limited to His own blood relatives. Paul understood this when he wrote, "Consequently, you are no longer foreigners and aliens, but fellow citizens with God's people and members of God's household" (Eph. 2:19, NIV). Blood is thicker than water, but the ties of our spiritual family should not be underestimated.

 Thank You, Lord, that I can be part of Your family with God as our Father.

You don't choose your family. They are God's gift to you, as you are to them.
—Archbishop Desmond Tutu (b. 1931), *South African religious leader*
and winner of the Nobel Peace Prize in 1984

THE DAY WHEN A WOMAN'S FAITH MADE JESUS' NO CRUMBLE!

We all know the feeling of disappointment we have when an urgent request is turned down with a firm *no*. The following story tells us about a woman who would not accept no from Jesus. Perhaps she could teach us something.

Mark 7 (story)

Tension: An evil spirit lives in the woman's daughter.

[25]Soon a woman heard about him. An evil spirit controlled her little daughter. The woman came to Jesus and fell at his feet. [26]She was a Greek, born in Syrian Phoenicia. She begged Jesus to drive the demon out of her daughter.

Relief of tension: The woman impresses Jesus.

[27]'First let the children eat all they want,' he told her. 'It is not right to take the children's bread and throw it to their dogs.'
[28]'Yes, Lord,' she replied. 'But even the dogs under the table eat the children's crumbs.'
[29]Then he told her, 'That was a good reply. You may go. The demon has left your daughter.'

Result: Her daughter is freed from the evil spirit.

[30]So she went home and found her child lying on the bed. And the demon was gone. (NIRV)

Jesus went to the non-Jewish area to rest. His rest was disturbed when a Greek woman begged Him to deliver her daughter from a demon. Jesus politely told her that He could not help her. His words in verse 27 confirm this: "It is not right to take the children's [Jews] bread and throw it to their dogs [non-Jews]."

The Jews (the children) often insulted the heathen (non-Jews) by calling them dogs because they believed that God did not bless heathens. In today's terms, the word "dog" would be the equivalent of "bitch." However, in this story, the dog was not at a loss for words. She uses Jesus' own words to challenge His no: "Lord, but even the dogs under the table eat the children's crumbs."

By using these words, the woman admits that the Jews have the privilege to hear the gospel first but insists that the Lord should also think about her. Her faith turned Jesus' no into a yes. Let us take God's word for what it is worth—just like the woman did. He might also surprise us.

 Thank You, Lord, that we can come to You with supplications for our requests to be granted.

Faith is the art of holding on to things your reason has once accepted in spite of your changing moods.
—C.S. Lewis (1898–1963), *High-powered Oxford and Cambridge professor and perhaps the twentieth century's most famous convert to Christianity. Lewis was the creator of the Narnia series.*

338   PROSE   *Day 235*

DOES GOD ALSO HAVE SECRETS?

People often have secrets they are reluctant to share with others. Jesus also had a secret He did not want to reveal. Scholars call it the secret of the Messiah. This episode tells us more about this secret.

Mark 8 (story)

Tension: Jesus wants to know who the people think He is.

> [27]Jesus and his disciples went on to the villages around Caesarea Philippi. On the way he asked them, 'Who do people say I am?'

Relief of tension: The disciples' answer

> [28]They replied, 'Some say John the Baptist. Others say Elijah. Still others say one of the prophets.'
> [29]'But what about you?' he asked. 'Who do you say I am?'
> Peter answered, 'You are the Christ.'

Result: They have to remain silent.

> [30]Jesus warned them not to tell anyone about him. (NIRV)

I wonder how people would answer Jesus' question in verse 27: "Who do people say I am?" There are many answers to this question. Peter gives the best answer: "You are the Christ!" The word "Christ" is a Greek word that means "the anointed one" or "the one who was sent" ("Messiah" is the Hebrew word for the anointed one). In those days, a new king was sworn into office by pouring oil on his head. This is why the king was called the anointed one. Jesus was not anointed with oil, but with the Holy Spirit who descended on Him like a dove (John 1:32).

Jesus' secret was that He, as Christ (Messiah), was also the Son of God (Mark 3:11; see also day 232). He forbade His disciples to reveal this secret—and for good reason. Unlike us, the Jews did not expect that the Messiah would also be the Son of God, nor did they have the same expectations of the Messiah. In general, they expected a special person (someone like King David of old) who would usher in a new era for the Jews. They expected a political liberator who would free them from Roman rule.

Jesus realized that it was not the right time to tell the people that He was the long-awaited Messiah, as they would then have expected Him to topple the Roman rule. He first wanted to teach His disciples that His kingdom was not an earthly one and that He had come to serve and not to rule. When Jesus died, the Roman soldier said, "This man was surely the Son of God!" (Mark 15:39, NIRV). Jesus' secret was out! The world has to know this! Jesus was really the Son of God who suffered on our behalf.

 Thank You, Lord, that Your secret is the good news that brings hope!

A secret between two is God's secret, between three is all men's.
—Spanish proverb

IS THE LOTTO YOUR MOTTO?

What may a Christian do or not do? All Christians will not answer this question in the same way. What some believers might consider to be right may be unacceptable to others. This can be confusing. How do we know what is right and what is wrong?

Mark 12 (story)

Tension: What is the greatest commandment?

[28]One of the teachers of the law came and heard the Sadducees arguing. He noticed that Jesus had given the Sadducees a good answer. So he asked him, 'Which is the most important of all the commandments?'

Relief of tension: Jesus' answer.

[29]Jesus answered, 'Here is the most important one. Moses said, 'Israel, listen to me. The Lord is our God. The Lord is one. [30]Love the Lord your God with all your heart and with all your soul. Love him with all your mind and with all your strength.' [31]And here is the second one. 'Love your neighbor as you love yourself.' There is no commandment more important than these.'

Result: Fewer questions

[34]Jesus saw that the man had answered wisely. He said to him, 'You are not far from God's kingdom.'
From then on, no one dared to ask Jesus any more questions. (NIRV)

Many believers, especially children, often ask questions such as, "Is it wrong for a Christian to smoke, to visit night clubs, to have sex before marriage or to play the lotto?" Why do believers ask these questions? Perhaps they are afraid of God, or perhaps they want reassurance that the things they are doing are not really that bad. The Bible does not want us to function in this way.

In Jesus' time, the scribes were obsessed with what was wrong and what was right. This is why one of them asked Jesus to tell him what was the most important commandment. Jesus' answer showed him that there was something bigger than the commandments, namely love toward God and toward his neighbor. With this, Jesus wanted to show that religion was not about what should and what should not be done but about one's relationship with God and with one's neighbor. Love makes relationships meaningful. Therefore, we should rather learn to ask the right questions. We should ask, "What is edifying for my relationship with God and with my fellow human beings?"

A minister friend of mine used the following theme for one of his sermons: "Is the lotto your motto?" Members of the congregation had the opportunity to air their views during the service. An old lady came up to my friend after the sermon and remarked, "Pastor, I do not play the lotto because my relationship with God is too important." My friend answered, "My dear, you don't know what an important thing you have just said."

 Lord, help me to do what is edifying for my relationship with You and my neighbor.

You have a religion; I have a relationship.
—Anne Angelelli

SEVEN DAYS WITHOUT SUN: THE PALMS OF SUNDAY!

The Bible tells us in detail about two weeks in history when God made His presence felt. The first was the week of Creation, and the second was the week of Jesus' suffering—therefore, seven days without sun! The first day of Jesus' week of suffering was a Sunday. This week coincided with the Passover. Jerusalem was packed with people. God ordained that Jesus would be crucified during this festival. By doing this, He wanted to show the world that Jesus was the real paschal lamb.

Mark 11 (story)

[1]As they all approached Jerusalem, they came to Bethphage and Bethany at the Mount of Olives. Jesus sent out two of his disciples. [2]He said to them, 'Go to the village ahead of you. Just as you enter it, you will find a donkey's colt tied there. No one has ever ridden it. Untie it and bring it here. [3]Someone may ask you, 'Why are you doing this?' If so, say, 'The Lord needs it. But he will send it back here soon.' '

Tension: The question to the two disciples

[4]So they left. They found a colt out in the street. It was tied at a doorway. They untied it. [5]Some people standing there asked, 'What are you doing? Why are you untying that colt?'

Relief of tension: The disciples could leave

[6]They answered as Jesus had told them to. So the people let them go.
[7]They brought the colt to Jesus. They threw their coats over it. Then he sat on it.

Result: Triumphant entry!

[8] Many people spread their coats on the road. Others spread branches they had cut in the fields. [9] Those in front and those in back shouted,
'Hosanna!'
'Blessed is the one who comes in the name of the Lord!'
[10] 'Blessed is the coming kingdom of our father David!'
'Hosanna in the highest heaven!' (NIRV)

Jesus entered Jerusalem in royal fashion in the "limousine" of those times—on the back of a donkey. The crowd was excited and full of expectation that He would free them from Roman rule. Luke tells us that Jesus cried (19:41). He realized that they wanted to turn Him into a political liberator, while He wanted to free them from their sins. He wanted to become the king of their hearts and not the ruler of Israel. Jesus cried because in the cries of "praise Him" on Sunday, He could already hear the cries of "crucify Him" that would come on Friday. Even today, we should heed against using Jesus for our own gain.

 Thank You, Lord, for being the king of my life. I praise You for it!

Among politicians the esteem of religion is profitable; the principles of it are troublesome.
—Benjamin Whichcote (1609–1683), *British Establishment and Puritan divine, Provost of King's College, Cambridge, and leader of the Cambridge Platonists*

SEVEN DAYS WITHOUT SUN: THE WHIPPING ON MONDAY!

After His triumphant entry the previous day, Jesus went to the Temple and "looked around at everything" (Mark 11:11, *NIrV*). What he saw upset Him. He must have had a very disturbing night that Sunday after everything He saw in the Temple. When He returned to the Temple on Monday, He acted in a way that signed His own death warrant.

Mark 11 (story)

Tension: Jesus overturns the tables

> [15]When Jesus reached Jerusalem, he entered the temple area. He began chasing out those who were buying and selling there. He turned over the tables of the people who were exchanging money. He also turned over the benches of those who were selling doves. [16]He would not allow anyone to carry items for sale through the temple courtyards.
> [17]Then he taught them. He told them, 'It is written that the Lord said,
> ' 'My house will be called
> a house where people from all nations can pray.'
> But you have made it a 'den for robbers.''

Tension: Jesus' death is planned

> [18]The chief priests and the teachers of the law heard about this. They began looking for a way to kill Jesus. They were afraid of him, because the whole crowd was amazed at his teaching.

Relief of tension: Jesus leaves the city

> [19]When evening came, Jesus and his disciples left the city. (NIRV)

Who would have thought that Jesus would act in such a drastic way? John tells us that Jesus used a whip to drive out the people and the animals (2:15). Why did He act that drastically? The Temple was the heart of the Jewish religion. Jesus was shocked to see that instead of practicing their religion, the Jews were making money.

People who traveled from afar could buy sacrificial animals at the Temple. However, the prices they had to pay for these animals were exorbitant. Furthermore, one could not pay the Temple taxes in the Greek or Roman currency, because people were depicted on the coins. This was seen as a transgression of the second commandment, "Do not make statues of gods that look like anything . . ." (Exod. 20:4, NIRV). Travelers had to exchange their money for Temple money at great cost.

Because of these practices, Jesus had to act drastically. He wanted to save the Temple from being a den of robbers and turn it into a house of prayer again. However, Jesus sealed His own fate when he acted in this way. The one who tampers with the purse of another walks the path of death. Four days later, God's whip struck Him to ensure that we could live! The words of Psalm 69:9 came true: "My great love for your house destroys me. Those who make fun of you make fun of me also" (NIRV).

Lord, I shudder to think how much pain You had to endure—for me!

When it's a question of money, everybody is of the same religion.
—Voltaire (1694–1778), *French philosopher and writer—one of the greatest of all French authors*

SEVEN DAYS WITHOUT SUN: THE TRICKY QUESTION ON TUESDAY!

The Tuesday of that week must have been a very busy day for Jesus. He had to address people from early on that day. One of the delegations confronted Him with a tricky question, but Jesus dealt with it masterfully.

Mark 12 (story)

Tension: Tricky question

> [13]Later the religious leaders sent some of the Pharisees and Herodians to Jesus. They wanted to trap him with his own words.
> [14]They came to him and said, 'Teacher, we know you are a man of honor. You don't let others tell you what to do or say. You don't care how important they are. But you teach the way of God truthfully. Is it right to pay taxes to Caesar or not? [15]Should we pay or shouldn't we?'
> But Jesus knew what they were trying to do. So he asked, 'Why are you trying to trap me? Bring me a silver coin. Let me look at it.'
> [16]They brought the coin.
> He asked them, 'Whose picture is this? And whose words?'
> 'Caesar's,' they replied.

Relief of tension: Jesus' answer

> [17]Then Jesus said to them, 'Give to Caesar what belongs to Caesar. And give to God what belongs to God.'

Result: Surprise

> They were amazed at him. (NIRV)

The Pharisees and the Herodians disliked Jesus. The Pharisees disliked Jesus because He thought they were hypocrites—and told them so. The Herodians, who were in favor of Roman supremacy and believed that it brought stability in the world, disliked Jesus because they considered Him a threat to Roman authority.

Both these groups wanted to get rid of Jesus. They tried to achieve this by asking Him a tricky question. They did it very subtlety by first flattering Jesus (v. 14) in order to eliminate any suspicion He might have had about their motives and to force Him to answer them. The question about tax was exceptionally sly. If Jesus answered yes, the Jews would have turned against Him because they hated to pay taxes to the Romans. If He answered no, the Roman authority would have turned against Him.

Jesus answered their question by asking them a counter question: "Whose picture is this? And whose words? 'Caesar's' they replied." The coin bore the image of Caesar, and therefore it belonged to the emperor. In a very clever way, Jesus led them to realize that they also had to give to God that which bore His image. What could that be? Our lives—because we were created in His image. Therefore, we belong to Him!

Lord, my only comfort is that I know that I belong to You! Hallelujah!

Behavior is the mirror in which everyone shows their image.
—Johann Wolfgang Von Goethe (1749–1832), *German poet, novelist and dramatist*

SEVEN DAYS WITHOUT SUN: THE SUMS ON WEDNESDAY!

People often give things a monetary value. Is it possible to measure all things in terms of money? Let us have a look.

Mark 14 (story)

Tension: Expensive oil is 'wasted'.

³Jesus was in Bethany. He was at the table in the home of a man named Simon, who had a skin disease. A woman came with a special sealed jar of very expensive perfume. It was made out of pure nard. She broke the jar open and poured the perfume on Jesus' head.

Relief of tension: Jesus does not think that oil is being wasted.

⁴Some of the people there became angry. They said to one another, 'Why waste this perfume? ⁵It could have been sold for more than a year's pay. The money could have been given to poor people.' So they found fault with the woman.
⁶'Leave her alone,' Jesus said. 'Why are you bothering her? She has done a beautiful thing to me. ⁷You will always have poor people with you. You can help them any time you want to. But you will not always have me. ⁸She did what she could. She poured perfume on my body to prepare me to be buried.

Result: Everyone will hear of her deed.

⁹What I'm about to tell you is true. What she has done will be told anywhere the good news is preached all over the world. It will be told in memory of her.' (NIRV)

The woman (Mary, according to John 12:30) was harshly criticized because she used too much oil to anoint Jesus. Indirectly, those present were saying that Jesus was not worth it. They were more concerned about the poor than the Son of God who would suffer so much. The critics quickly did a few calculations and gave the woman's deed a monetary value (300 silver coins equaled a laborer's annual wages).

Jesus measured her deed in different terms. He was not blinded by the external, but saw the woman's heart. Her deed meant a lot to Him, and He also saw it as symbolically pointing toward His death. This same woman wanted to anoint Jesus' body at the tomb. However, she was too late, because He had already risen.

Jesus does not care about the value of the article but about the attitude of the heart. That was why Jesus could say the following about the widow who gave an offering of two coins: "This poor widow has put more into the treasury than all the others" (Mark 12:43, TNIV).

 Lord, help me not to measure everything in terms of money.

A healthy attitude is contagious but don't wait to catch it from others. Be a carrier.
—Author unknown

SEVEN DAYS WITHOUT SUN: THE BETRAYAL ON THURSDAY!

Thursday of that week was very busy, as the Jews were preparing to eat the Passover meal on that day. All forms of yeast—images of fermenting sins (1 Cor. 5:7)—had to be removed from their homes. For the next seven days, they would eat only unleavened bread. They also had to find and slaughter the paschal lamb before sunset.

The Passover reminded them of their liberation from Egypt. The bitter herbs reminded them of the bitter days they had spent in Egypt. Jesus wanted to spend this Passover alone with His disciples. Yet this Passover would turn out to be a devastating experience for Him.

Mark 14 (conversation)

[17]When evening came, Jesus arrived with the Twelve. [18]While they were at the table eating, Jesus said, 'What I'm about to tell you is true. One of you who is eating with me will hand me over to my enemies.'

[19]The disciples became sad. One by one they said to him, 'It's not I, is it?'

[20]'It is one of the Twelve,' Jesus replied. 'It is the one who dips bread into the bowl with me. [21]The Son of Man will go just as it is written about him. But how terrible it will be for the one who hands over the Son of Man! It would be better for him if he had not been born.' (NIRV)

It must have been an enormous shock to the disciples when Jesus told them about His fear: "One of you who is eating with me will hand me over to my enemies" (v. 17). Matthew states that the disciples became very sad when they heard this from Jesus. One after the other, they began to say to him, "It's not I, Lord, is it?" Jesus replied, "The one who has dipped his hand into the bowl with me will hand me over" (26:22–23, NIRV). Without realizing it, Judas revealed himself—even before he betrayed Jesus with a kiss later that evening. What happened here alludes to Psalm 41:9: "Even my close friend, whom I trusted, has deserted me. I even shared my bread with him" (NIRV).

Mark constantly emphasizes that everything that happened to Jesus was part of a divine plan. Therefore, Jesus was not left to His fate. That evening, Judas led the Roman soldiers to Jesus. It was not their handcuffs that bound Him but His obedience. Judas later declared his remorse to the Jewish leaders, but they were cold toward him. When he left them, he went and hanged himself (Matt. 27). His death and the insensitivity of the Jewish leaders toward Judas emphasized Jesus' innocence. He was the real paschal lamb!

 Lord, save me from betraying You by my conduct.

Judas heard all Christ's sermons.
—Thomas Goodwin (1600–1679), *A Puritan priest who served as chaplain to Oliver Cromwell*

SEVEN DAYS WITHOUT SUN:
THE AGONIZING CRY ON FRIDAY!

Jesus was crucified on Friday of that week. As He hung on the cross, darkness descended over the whole land. The darkness lasted for three hours—from 12 o' clock until 3 o'clock in the afternoon. The people had had it with Jesus. It was as if God had drawn a black curtain around Him so that people could not see anything, but only hear. And what was heard at the end of the three hours was an alarming cry in Armenian, Jesus' home language: "Eloï, Eloï, lemá sabagtani?"

Mark 15 (history)

[33]At noon, darkness covered the whole land. It lasted three hours. [34]At three o'clock Jesus cried out in a loud voice, *'Eloi, Eloi, lama sabachthani?'* This means 'My God, my God, why have you deserted me?'
[35]Some of those standing nearby heard Jesus cry out. They said, 'Listen! He's calling for Elijah.' [36]One of them ran and filled a sponge with wine vinegar. He put it on a stick. He offered it to Jesus to drink. 'Leave him alone,' he said. 'Let's see if Elijah comes to take him down.' [37] With a loud cry, Jesus took his last breath. (NIRV)

"My God, my God, why have you deserted me?" It is bad enough when people forsake us, but in Gethsemane not even Jesus' intimate friends were prepared to keep vigil with Him for one hour. His loneliness was aggravated when His disciples left Him. On that Friday afternoon, His loneliness reached a low point. He was nailed to the cross, separated from everything and everyone—even from God. Then He cried out the words of Psalm 22: "My God, my God, why have you deserted me?" (NIRV).

Yet this agonizing cry was already filled with triumph. It was uttered at the end of the three hours of darkness, when Jesus' work was done. Satan wanted Jesus to go one step further—He wanted Jesus to forsake the Father. During those three hours, the darkness must have tempted Him to repeatedly swear at God and die. Hell expected Jesus to swear, but instead it got the words from the Psalm!

Although God had left Him, Jesus did not turn His back on His Father. Because Jesus called out in bewilderment during that hour, "My God, my God, why have you deserted me?" we can now call out in wonder, "My God, my God why did You adopt me?" The Father left His own Son to ensure that you and I will never be forsaken. Therefore, we should feel free to say Psalm 23 in prayer.

The Lord is my shepherd. He gives me everything I need.
He lets me lie down in fields of green grass.
He leads me beside quiet waters.
He gives me new strength.
He guides me in the right paths
for the honor of his name

—(Ps. 23:1–3, NIRV)

Loneliness is the most terrible poverty.
—Mother Teresa of Calcutta (1910–1997), *Albanian born Indian missionary, founder of the Order of the Missionaries of Charity and winner of the Nobel Prize for Peace in 1979*

SEVEN DAYS WITHOUT SUN: THE IRONY OF SATURDAY!

Matthew is the only one of the Gospel writers who describes what happened on the Saturday of that week. On this Sabbath after the death of Jesus, the Jewish leaders still could not find peace. So they went to Pilate with a special request.

Matthew 27 (conversation)

[62]The next day was the day after Preparation Day. The chief priests and the Pharisees went to Pilate. [63]'Sir,' they said, 'we remember something that liar said while he was still alive. He claimed, 'After three days I will rise again.' [64]So give the order to make the tomb secure until the third day. If you don't, his disciples might come and steal the body. Then they will tell the people that Jesus has been raised from the dead. This last lie will be worse than the first.'
[65]'Take some guards with you,' Pilate answered. 'Go. Make the tomb as secure as you can.' [66]So they went and made the tomb secure. They put a seal on the stone and placed some guards on duty. (NIRV)

It is ironic that the spiritual leaders took Jesus' prediction that He would rise from the dead more seriously than the disciples did. The disciples forgot what Jesus had taught them about His resurrection (Matt. 20:17–19), but the spiritual leaders remembered. That is why they were just as afraid of Him after His death as they were when He was alive.

The religious leaders could not find peace on the Sabbath, so they went to Pilate to ensure that every possible precaution was taken to keep Jesus' body in the tomb. They were afraid that the disciples would steal it. (It is interesting to note that they addressed Pilate as "sir" and referred to Jesus as "that liar.") Pilate granted them their request, and the tomb was guarded and sealed.

All these precautions point to the fact that there could be only one reason for an empty tomb: Jesus had risen from the dead. The spiritual leaders wanted to prevent a "second deception." The first deception was to admit that Jesus was the Messiah, and the second was His resurrection.

Ironically, the spiritual leaders did not realize that they were not dealing with the disciples but with God Himself. The Jewish leaders harmed their own cause because the guard and the sealing of the tomb were under their own jurisdiction (vv. 65–66). If something had gone wrong, they would have been blamed for it. Jesus' resurrection turned their actions and precautions into the first argument in support of the resurrection. This was not deception, but the truth. This is why we can attend the service on Sundays and know that Jesus rose from the dead!

Thank You, Lord, that I can believe that You truly rose from the dead.

The greatest deception men suffer is from their own opinions.
—Leonardo da Vinci (1452–1519), *Italian draftsman, painter, sculptor, architect and engineer whose genius epitomized the Renaissance humanist ideal*

THE FIRST DAY OF THE FOLLOWING WEEK!

As we previously mentioned, the Bible tells us in great detail about the two weeks in history when God made His presence felt—the first week of God's creation and the last week of Jesus' suffering. Saturday was the last day of the Holy Week. The next day, a Sunday, was the first day of the following week. On this day, Jesus appeared to a woman first.

Mark 16 (history)

⁹Jesus rose from the dead early on the first day of the week. He appeared first to Mary Magdalene. He had driven seven demons out of her. ¹⁰She went and told those who had been with him. She found them crying. They were very sad. ¹¹They heard that Jesus was alive and that she had seen him. But they did not believe it.

¹²After that, Jesus appeared in a different form to two of them. This happened while they were walking out in the country. ¹³The two returned and told the others about it. But the others did not believe them either. (NIRV)

Mary Magdalene's life was dark before she met Jesus. Seven demons had taken possession of her life. When she met Jesus, He drove the evil spirits out of her, and light came into her life. After that, she became a devoted follower of Christ. At the cross, it became dark for her again because she had to witness her Master being nailed to the cross. Two days later, on a Sunday, Mary returned to Jesus' grave. There, she became the first person to see Jesus after His resurrection—an event that brought light back into her life. The Lord again opened up a future for her.

It is interesting to note that during these two weeks when God made His presence felt in history, something also closed. During the first week, the gate to the Garden of Eden was closed and guarded by angels. During the second week (Holy Week), Jesus' grave was closed and guarded by soldiers. On the first day after Holy Week, Jesus' grave was opened. The entrance to the Garden, which had been closed during the first week, was also opened on that Friday when Jesus told the thief who was crucified with Him, "Today you will be with me in paradise" (Luke 23:43 NIRV).

Jesus opens everything. When He died, the Holy of Holies was opened when the curtain was torn in two (Matt. 27:51). The graves opened (v. 52). The soldier's heart opened when he confessed that Jesus was indeed the Son of God (v. 54). The Holy Scripture opened when John wrote: "These things happened in order that Scripture would come true" (John 19:36, NIRV). During Jesus' ascension, the heavens were opened for us. Wow!

 Thank You, Lord, that everything is open. Thank You that we have a future!

To believe in something to yet proved and to underwrite it with our lives;
it is the only way we can leave the future open.
—Lillian Smith (1897–1966), *A writer and social critic of the American South who is best known for*
her best-selling novel Strange Fruit *(1944)*

NOBODY REALLY CARES!

It's interesting that people often use slogans on their T-shirts to convey messages. Just the other day, I read a message on the back of someone's T-shirt that said, "Guess what? Nobody cares!" This statement made quite an impression on me. I'm not sure whether the person experienced it firsthand, but I do know that in many respects, the fact that "nobody cares" has become characteristic of our society. Why is it like this?

Luke 3 (history)

[21]When all the people were being baptized, Jesus was baptized too. And as he was praying, heaven was opened. [22]The Holy Spirit came down on him in the form of a dove. A voice came from heaven. It said, 'You are my Son, and I love you. I am very pleased with you.' (NIRV)

In the time of Jesus, John the Baptist was baptizing people who repented of their sins. Baptism was therefore a sign of repentance. So, if this was the case, why did Jesus want to be baptized? After all, He was without sin. By being baptized, Jesus was identifying fully with us—especially with those who confess their sins. Further proof of His identification with human beings is that He was baptized with other people.

It is interesting that the place where Jesus was baptized and the person who baptized Him are not mentioned in this section in Luke. The reason for this is to emphasize that the heavens opened up. When the heavens opened, the Holy Spirit descended like a dove upon Jesus, while the Father called from heaven, "You are my Son, and I love you. I am very pleased with you." This gave Jesus divine authority. The involvement of the Holy Spirit and the Father is further proof that God identifies Himself with human beings. This is what makes God so laudable. He became part of our history—our world. He really cares!

Sadly, many people feel alone and actually believe that "nobody cares." Why would this be? Because people are just too busy with their own lives—and class distinctions still play a major role. Many people tend to think that they are better than others and are not keen to identify with just anybody. Fortunately, Christ was different. The point is that as believers, we have to reach out to others in order to tell those who are lonely that God—and us—really do care

 Thank You, Lord, that You care for me by truly identifying with me. Help me so that my life can proclaim that somebody cares!

I don't care how much you know until I know how much you care.
—Author unknown

EVANGELISM? NO THANKS!

I'm not sure what goes through your mind when you hear the word "evangelism." Perhaps you shrink back when you hear the word. It might sound too hypocritically pious. You might feel that you are not the kind of person who could go around knocking on people's doors. Leave that to the pastor—after all, he or she gets paid to do those kinds of things. However, perhaps we should learn to think differently about this matter. Let's first read what happens in the next episode in Luke.

Luke 5 (story)

Tension: Will they catch something?

> [4]When he finished speaking, he turned to Simon. He said, 'Go out into deep water. Let the nets down so you can catch some fish.'
> [5]Simon answered, 'Master, we've worked hard all night and haven't caught anything. But because you say so, I will let down the nets.'

Relief of tension: Nets that threatened to tear

> [6]When they had done so, they caught a large number of fish. There were so many that their nets began to break. [7]So they motioned to their partners in the other boat to come and help them. They came and filled both boats so full that they began to sink.

Result: Surprise and the command to catch people

> [8]When Simon Peter saw this, he fell at Jesus' knees. 'Go away from me, Lord!' he said. 'I am a sinful man!'
> [9]He and everyone with him were amazed at the number of fish they had caught. [10] So were James and John, the sons of Zebedee, who worked with Simon.
> Then Jesus said to Simon, 'Don't be afraid. From now on you will catch people.' (NIRV)

This episode concludes with a command: "From now on you will catch people." This command is nothing other than evangelism, a word that means "good news." The good news of God's love for us should be shared with others. But do we do this? And what is the best way to "do" evangelism? An opinion poll conducted by the American Bible Society found that people most often came to Christ due to the following influences:

1. **Family:** 32 percent of people said that a family member (or members) led them to Jesus.
2. **Friends:** Christian friends were the second most important influence.
3. **Atmosphere:** A third important factor was the atmosphere at the church itself in which the person received Christ.

All three factors involve relationships. Therefore, you need not approach strangers directly—just start with the people you know. You do not need to be a top chef in order to recommend a restaurant. All you have to do is tell people about the nice food. You also need not be a trained theologian to invite someone to a church service. Evangelism is everybody's task. So many people are just waiting for you to invite them! What are you waiting for?

 Lord, give me the confidence to share the good news with others.

Evangelism is just one beggar telling another beggar where to find bread.
—D.T. Niles, *Sri Lankan theologian*

WHAT IF THINGS BECOME TOO MUCH TO BEAR?

When computers entered our lives, we made plans about what we would do with all our free time, because computers would take over much of our work. Instead, the opposite happened: Computers often rob us of our time. Furthermore, life's demands are so great that we battle to stay afloat. Most of us lead very busy lives. Even retired people will tell you that their days are too short to do everything they want to do. However, in this next section in Luke, Jesus teaches us a very important lesson about this.

Luke 5 (story)

Tension: A leper comes to Jesus.

> ¹²While Jesus was in one of the towns, a man came along. He had a skin disease all over his body. When he saw Jesus, he fell with his face to the ground. He begged him, 'Lord, if you are willing to make me 'clean,' you can do it.'

Relief of Tension: Jesus cures him.

> ¹³Jesus reached out his hand and touched the man. 'I am willing to do it,' he said. 'Be 'clean'!' Right away the disease left him.
> ¹⁴Then Jesus ordered him, 'Don't tell anyone. Go and show yourself to the priest. Offer the sacrifices that Moses commanded. It will be a witness to the priest and the people that you are 'clean.' '

Result: Jesus gains in popularity.

> ¹⁵But the news about Jesus spread even more. So crowds of people came to hear him. They also came to be healed of their sicknesses. (NIRV)

Jesus changed many people's lives radically. In this passage, He gave a leper new hope by curing him. In those days, lepers were social outcasts. Nobody touched them. They were unable to work and had no income to support their families, and they could not attend religious assemblies. They were completely isolated from society and their friends. In our day, this could be compared to having AIDS.

Many people flocked to Jesus to listen to Him and to be cured by Him. His popularity increased and His days were busy. Jesus realized that He could not keep this schedule up. So He did what we often neglect to do—He went to a secluded spot to pray. Prayer and quiet time will help you to focus on God, and it is a source of strength. When things sometimes overwhelm you, the best thing to do is to isolate yourself and become quiet in prayer. If Jesus needed to do this, just imagine how much you need to do this from time to time.

 Thank you, Lord, that in Your presence I am able to experience quiet time in any place.

To be a Christian without prayer is no more possible than to be alive without breathing.
—Martin Luther King, Jr. (1929–1968), *American Baptist minister, Civil Rights leader and winner of the Nobel Prize in 1964*

THE WORST FORM OF DISABILITY . . .

Often, we find ourselves feeling uncomfortable when in the presence of disabled people. We would rather choose the easy option—namely, to ignore them or pretend not to see them. Jesus acted differently in this regard.

Luke 6 (story)

⁶On another Sabbath day, Jesus went into the synagogue and was teaching. A man whose *right hand was weak and twisted* was there.

Tension: Will Jesus cure someone on the Sabbath?

⁷The Pharisees and the teachers of the law were trying to find fault with Jesus. So they watched him closely. They wanted to see if he would heal on the Sabbath.

Relief of tension: Jesus cures someone on the Sabbath

⁸But Jesus knew what they were thinking. He spoke to the man who had the weak and twisted hand. 'Get up and stand in front of everyone,' he said. So the man got up and stood there.
⁹Then Jesus said to them, *'What does the Law say we should do on the Sabbath day? Should we do good? Or should we do evil? Should we save life? Or should we destroy it?'*
¹⁰He looked around at all of them. Then he said to the man, 'Stretch out your hand.' He did, and his hand was as good as new.

Result: Furious religious leaders

¹¹But the Pharisees and the teachers of the law were very angry. They began to talk to each other about what they might do to Jesus. (NIRV)

According to Jewish Law, healing was forbidden on the Sabbath. The religious leaders considered it more important to obey the Law than to relieve someone of his or her misery. However, Jesus considered a deed of mercy toward someone who was suffering the true fulfillment of the law of the Sabbath.

Jesus knew that the religious leaders objected to this, so He asked them, "What does the Law say we should do on the Sabbath day? Should we do good? Or should we do evil? Should we save life? Or should we destroy it?" (v. 9). His question assumed that if a person refused to do good, he or she was, in actual fact, doing wrong. This is the reason why Jesus' opponents did not have an answer. They were furious, because Jesus unmasked their traditional views as incorrect. The leaders used (abused) the Law to avoid disabled people.

Even today, it is easy (convenient) to ignore the disabled. However, if you are the kind of person who keeps others at a distance or does not want to get involved, Jesus considers you disabled, because you also keep Him at a distance. Even today, many people show by the way they live that they do not really need Jesus. They think that He is there for those who are weak—that they are the ones who need a crutch to lean on. This kind of attitude is the worst disability. We need each other—even those who are disabled.

 Lord, forgive me if I keep others—especially those who are physically disabled—at a distance.

The only disability in life is a bad attitude.
—Scott Scovell Hamilton (b. 1958), *An American figure skater and Olympic gold medalist known for his originality and engaging on-ice personalities*

THE GAME GOD WANTS TO PLAY WITH US

Jesus once compared a group of adults to children playing in the marketplace. This was because, just like today's children, the children in the marketplace imitated the grown-up world in playful fashion. The children imitated weddings and funerals in their games. Jesus wanted the adults to see something specific in the children's games. What could that be?

Luke 7 (conversation)

[31]'What can I compare today's people to?' Jesus asked. 'What are they like? [32] They are like children sitting in the market place and calling out to each other. They say,
"We played a flute for you.
But you didn't dance.
We sang a funeral song.
But you didn't cry.'
[33]'That is how it has been with John the Baptist. When he came to you, he didn't eat bread or drink wine. And you say, 'He has a demon.' [34]But when the Son of Man came, he ate and drank as you do. And you say, 'This fellow is always eating and drinking far too much. He's a friend of tax collectors and 'sinners.' ' [35]All who follow wisdom prove that wisdom is right.' (NIRV)

All children like to play. Yet we know that children's games can easily turn into fights because children tend not to stick to the rules. Then Mom and Dad have to listen to all the accusations: "I shot him, but he did not want to fall down" or, "I touched her, but she did not want to take her turn." This also happened in Jesus' comparison: When the one group played the flute, the others did not want to dance, and when the one group sang, the other group did not want to cry. They did not stick to the rules.

Jesus said that just like children, grown-ups do not always like to stick to the rules of life. Life is like a game. God plays a game of crying and laughing with us. He wanted us to lament the misery and chaos in the world, which is why God sent John the Baptist to sing a *lament*. He wanted the people to cry about their sins, but the people did not want to cry. In the same way, God wants us to laugh and dance about the good news of Jesus who offers us a life of hope. However, often people do not join in the game.

God uses children's games to show us that without Jesus in our homes, our relationships, our business ventures and our circle of friends, all of our games will degenerate into a game of death. Whenever you see children playing, ask yourself: *Am I keeping to the rules of the game?*

 Lord, help me to play the game of crying and laughing according to the rules of the game.

Life's a game, all you have to do, is know how to play it.
—Author unknown

PEOPLE ARE FREE TO RAISE THEIR EYEBROWS!

A young graphic arts student regularly attended our church services and Bible study groups. He often surprised us with the way he dressed. One morning, we got the surprise of our lives when he walked into the church with green hair. Needless to say, there was an audible silence, and many eyebrows were raised. In time, I got to know this young man, and I learned something from him that our society desperately needs.

Luke 8 (history)

> [1]After this, Jesus traveled around from one town and village to another. He announced the good news of God's kingdom. The Twelve were with him. [2]So were some women who had been healed of evil spirits and sicknesses. One was Mary Magdalene. Seven demons had come out of her. [3]Another was Joanna, the wife of Cuza. He was the manager of Herod's household. Susanna and many others were there also. These women were helping to support Jesus and the Twelve with their own money. (NIRV)

Jesus traveled constantly to spread the gospel and was accompanied on his journeys by the 12 disciples and some women. The Jews considered it shameful that women escorted Him and looked after Him. In their culture, it was unacceptable for women to follow a rabbi. These women, however, did not care that the public raised their eyebrows—they were grateful that Jesus had not only healed them physically but also liberated them spiritually and socially. Because of their gratefulness, they were prepared to follow Jesus.

Jesus did not mind that the women followed Him, and He allowed this apparent "shameful" conduct to continue. During His ministry, He penetrated many social structures without openly protesting against them. He merely did what was right—even though people raised their eyebrows when He did so. This was especially true when He mingled with sinners and tax collectors.

Like Jesus, the young student with the green hair acted in a stylish manner. He did not harm anyone, and the congregation eventually grew very fond of him and his girlfriend. His dress code was not a means of protest but merely the way he and his fellow students dressed. In his heart, he was grateful toward God that he had been saved and that he could be himself. The church is not a place for us to raise our eyebrows but a place for us to lovingly reach out to others and to give them the space to be themselves. Perhaps we should not place so much emphasis on the opinion of others and instead do what we believe is right. We can do this in style and without public protest.

 Thank You, Lord that I can always be myself.

People do not seem to realize that their opinion of the world is also a confession of character.
—Ralph Waldo Emerson (1803–1882), *American poet, lecturer and essayist*

STRANGE AND REVERSED!

People like to think that they are important and that they are first in line and blessed. The disciples once argued about which one of them was the most important in God's kingdom. Jesus was aware of their arguments and dealt with them by way of an illustration.

Luke 9 (conversation)

[46]The disciples began to argue about which one of them would be the most important person. [47]Jesus knew what they were thinking. So he took a little child and had the child stand beside him. [48]Then he spoke to them. 'Anyone who welcomes this little child in my name welcomes me,' he said. 'And anyone who welcomes me welcomes the One who sent me. The least important person among all of you is the most important.' (NIRV)

Jesus used a child to illustrate His point. A child cannot compete with adults and is therefore a symbol of someone who is the least among others. Jesus wanted to teach the disciples (and us) that the values of the kingdom of God are not what we expect them to be. Just consider the following:

So those who are last will be first. And those who are first will be last.

—Matt. 20:16, NIRV

Blessed are those who are spiritually needy. The kingdom of heaven belongs to them. Blessed are those who are sad. They will be comforted. Blessed are those who are free of pride. They will be given the earth. Blessed are those who are hungry and thirsty for what is right. They will be filled.

—Matt 5:3–6, NIRV

The least important person among all of you is the most important.

—Luke 9:48, NIRV

The values of the Kingdom are strange and different from what we are used to. We will have to learn to look at life differently, because this strange and reversed value system is not always apparent to the naked eye. The pity of it all is that the most important things in life are often right at the bottom of our list of priorities. Perhaps we should try to place the following three points right at the top of our list:

1. *Our relationship with God*: We often neglect this relationship because we feel that there is something more "important" to do. We need to decide to get more involved in this relationship.
2. *Our relationship with our family*. Our family often takes the back seat. However, no success at work can ever compensate for failure at home.
3. *Our relationship with ourselves*. We can only give others what we ourselves have. We also cannot lift others higher than we lift ourselves. We must invest in ourselves!

So the next time you feel that your priorities are out of place, just remember Jesus' words to the disciples: "The least important person among all of you is the most important" (v. 48).

 "I pray that your love will grow more and more. And let it be based on knowledge and understanding. Then you will be able to know what is best. You will be pure and without blame until the day Christ returns."

—Phil 1:9–10, NIRV

Success is only another form of failure if we forget what our priorities should be.
—Harry Lloyd

HOW DOES GOD JUDGE THE GOOD LIFE?

I once asked a friend of mine what he would like his life to look like in 10 years' time. His answer was short and sweet: "I want to be retired and on every golf course in the world." This next section in Luke also describes dreams of eating, drinking and living the good life. What is the Bible's view on this?

Luke 12 (parable)

¹⁵Then he said to them, 'Watch out! Be on your guard against wanting to have more and more things. *Life is not made up of how much a person has.*'

Tension: The rich man's harvest is too large for his barn.

¹⁶Then Jesus told them a story. He said, 'A certain rich man's land produced a good crop. ¹⁷He thought to himself, 'What should I do? I don't have any place to store my crops.'

Relief of Tension: He builds bigger barns.

¹⁸'Then he said, 'This is what I'll do. I will tear down my storerooms and build bigger ones. I will store all my grain and my other things in them. ¹⁹I'll say to myself, 'You have plenty of good things stored away for many years.
Take life easy. Eat, drink and have a good time.'

Result: God thinks he is a fool.

²⁰'But God said to him, 'You foolish man! This very night I will take your life away from you. Then who will get what you have prepared for yourself?'
²¹'That is how it will be for anyone who stores things away for himself but is not rich in God's eyes.' (NIRV)

This successful man in Jesus' parable enlarged his barns and pursued his dreams. This was very noble, yet God considered him a fool. Why? There are three distinct reasons why God called him a fool:

1. He was selfish, as he constantly referred to "my" and "I."
2. He thought he had control of his life, but when God demanded his life (v. 20), he discovered that he merely had control over his belongings.
3. He wanted to organize his own life—but without God. The words in verse 18 ("This is what I'll do") and those in verse 19 ("I'll say to myself") are proof of this.

It is not wrong to have ideals; God just wants us to have the right attitude and not be greedy. When we are greedy, it means that our life has become dependent on money and belongings. Jesus' parables generally had one main message. The point of this one was set out very clearly in verse 15:

"Life is not made up of how much a person has." Always remember Jesus' opening words in His first sermon: "Blessed are those who are spiritually needy" (Matt. 5:3, NIRV). This is wisdom!

 Lord, help me to have the correct attitude toward money and wealth.

Complete possession is proved only by giving. All you are unable to give possesses you.
—Andre Gide (1869–1951), French writer, humanist, moralist and winner of the
Nobel Prize for literature in 1947

EVERY HOUSE HAS ITS TRIALS!

There's no such thing as a perfect family, which is why we have the saying that "every house has its trials." In the following parable of the prodigal (lost) son told in Luke 15 (which is generally regarded as the best short story ever written), tension existed between the father and his two sons. This short story can be divided into four sections, so we will pause here over the next few days. Enjoy!

Luke 15 (parable—episode 1)

[11]Jesus continued, 'There was a man who had two sons.

Tension: Tension between father and son

[12]The younger son spoke to his father. He said, 'Father, give me my share of the family property.' So the father divided his property between his two sons.

Relief of Tension: Looking for 'greener' pastures

[13]'Not long after that, the younger son packed up all he had. Then he left for a country far away. *There he wasted his money on wild living.*

Result: Misfortune and disillusionment

[14]He spent everything he had.
'Then the whole country ran low on food. So the son didn't have what he needed. (NIRV)

The opening sentence of this wonderful short story is short and sweet: "There was a man who had two sons." The youngest of these sons yearned for excitement in his life. He wanted to have a bit of fun. He was a real party animal. However, to do this, he needed money, so he approached his dad with a strange and surprising request: "Father, give me my share of the family property" (v. 12). By making this request, the young man revealed that he wished his father were dead. The father's reaction was just as strange and surprising: "So the father divided his property between his two sons" (v. 12).

In other words, the father allowed his young son to go. He knew that there was only one way that he would learn his lesson—the hard way! Sadly enough, the younger son went looking for things that were already present in his father's house. He went looking for joy, security, love and his place in life. To put it bluntly, he went looking for a home away from home! Nor did he keep the backdoor open so that he could return.

Misfortune and disillusionment awaited the young man in the foreign places he visited. Two disasters hit him simultaneously: first he ran out of money (which, of course, was his own fault), and then famine hit the land (which was beyond his control but nevertheless aggravated his situation). This young man lacked wisdom. Wisdom will help us to not become totally disillusioned.

Lord, help me to live every day with wisdom and insight.

The function of wisdom is to discriminate between good and evil.
—Cicero (106 B.C.–43 B.C.), *Ancient Roman lawyer, writer, scholar, orator and statesman*

THE BIG QUESTION CONCERNING OUR PROBLEMS

Sooner or later, we all make mistakes. Unfortunately, our mistakes often have dire consequences. Some people's problems are just so much greater than others. However, the big question concerning our problems is not how we got into them in the first place but how we will get out of them. Let us see how this young man got out of his dilemma.

Luke 15 (parable—episode 2)

Tension: A Jew looks after pigs!

[15]He went to work for someone who lived in that country, who sent him to the fields to feed the pigs. [16]The son wanted to fill his stomach with the food the pigs were eating. But no one gave him anything.

Relief of Tension: The prodigal son sees the light!

[17]'Then he began to think clearly again. He said, 'How many of my father's hired workers have more than enough food! But here I am dying from hunger! [18]I will get up and go back to my father. I will say to him, 'Father, I have sinned against heaven. And I have sinned against you. [19]I am no longer fit to be called your son. Make me like one of your hired workers.''

Result: He returns to his father!

[20]So he got up and went to his father. (NIRV)

As we mentioned yesterday, the youngest son was hit hard in the foreign country. He lost all his money (because he squandered it,) all his values (because he practiced free sex) and all his dignity (because a Jew who looked after pigs was condemned by his fellow countrymen). His urge to eat the food of pigs was the lowest point to which a Jew could stoop. Furthermore, he also lost his right and claim to be acknowledged as a son.

The young man had bumped his head very hard. But there was one thing he could not lose—his father's love. This time, the young man did not long for what was in his father's hand but what was in his father's heart. The story's turning point is in verse 17, when he came to his senses. His need made him realize how stupid he had been, and his misery made him long for the abundance in his father's house. He decided to confess his sins to his father and to God.

The young man's sinful lifestyle and wrong attitude toward life landed him in big trouble. However, the most important thing to remember is not how he got into his situation but how he got out of it. Where does one start? Exactly where this young man started out. He realized that he had sinned. He did not make all kinds of excuses to justify himself or plead for leniency—just for mercy.

 Lord Jesus, help me to be honest in confessing my sins to You and to others.

The confession of evil works is the first beginning of good works.
—Saint Augustine (354–386), *Christian theologian, rhetor, North African bishop and doctor of the Roman Catholic Church*

THIS IS TOO GOOD TO BE TRUE!

We often use phrases such as "this is too good to be true" when we react to something wonderful that happens in our lives. In the following passage in Luke, we have an episode that is also too good to be true. Let's have a look!

Luke 15 (parable—episode 3)

Tension: A waiting father

> ²⁰'While the son was still a long way off, his father saw him. He was filled with tender love for his son. He ran to him. He threw his arms around him and kissed him.

Relief of Tension: The prodigal (lost) son shows remorse

> ²¹'The son said to him, 'Father, I have sinned against heaven and against you. I am no longer fit to be called your son.'

Result: His father forgives him

> ²²'But the father said to his servants, 'Quick! Bring the best robe and put it on him. Put a ring on his finger and sandals on his feet. ²³Bring the fattest calf and kill it. Let's have a big dinner and celebrate. ²⁴This son of mine was dead. And now he is alive again. He was lost. And now he is found.'
> 'So they began to celebrate. (NIRV)

The youngest son must have returned home with a fearful heart, wondering: *What will my father say?* Yet it is interesting to note that the father did five things before he even said *anything* to him. According to verse 20, these five reactions were:

1. He saw his son while he was still a long way off—which means that he had waited for him all the time!
2. He pitied him deeply—his eyes were not filled with anger but with tears.
3. He ran to meet him—he took the initiative.
4. He embraced him—the prodigal son experienced unconditional love.
5. He kissed him—this was considered undignified conduct for an Oriental father, but it did not bother him to act in this way because the news about his son's return was overwhelming.

In this manner, the father eased his son's final steps on his return. When his son expressed remorse (v. 21), the father did not answer directly but arranged a feast for him. The father's actions indicated that he had forgiven his son. In this parable, the prodigal son represents the sinners and tax collectors. The father is God. God is the father who always rejoices when someone who went astray returns home, shows remorse and confesses. The prodigal son's fear was unnecessary, because he was greeted with a feast instead of rejection. This seems too good to be true. But fortunately this is true, because God always shows mercy toward repentant sinners. Hallelujah!

Lord, I want to praise and glorify You for showing me so much mercy. Thank You that I can know that You always wait to receive me with open arms.

> *Every saint has a past and every sinner has a future.*
> —Oscar Wilde (1854–1900), *Irish poet and dramatist*

OBSTACLES TO JOY

The fourth and final episode of the parable of the prodigal son tells us about obstacles to joy. We should guard against this!

Luke 15 (parable—episode 4)

²⁵'The older son was in the field. When he came near the house, he heard music and dancing. ²⁶So he called one of the servants. He asked him what was going on.
²⁷"Your brother has come home,' the servant replied. 'Your father has killed the fattest calf. He has done this because your brother is back safe and sound.'

Tension: The eldest son is bitter.

²⁸'The older brother became angry. He refused to go in.

Relief of Tension: His father pleads with him!

So his father went out and begged him.
²⁹"But he answered his father, 'Look! All these years I've worked like a slave for you. I have always obeyed your orders. You never gave me even a young goat so I could celebrate with my friends. ³⁰But this son of yours wasted your money with some prostitutes. Now he comes home. And for him you kill the fattest calf!'
³¹"My son,' the father said, 'you are always with me. Everything I have is yours. ³²But we had to celebrate and be glad. This brother of yours was dead. And now he is alive again. He was lost. And now he is found." (NIRV)

Result: Open-ended!

The eldest son's bitter reaction stood in stark contrast to his father's joy. The eldest son felt that his younger brother did not deserve the festivities, because he had squandered all his money on prostitutes. He was bitter because he had been a loyal son all those years and yet did not receive festive recognition for it. The eldest son's reasoning was wrong. He thought in terms of reward, not in terms of his father's goodwill. In fact, he was the one who was lost. He was lost because he was Mr. Clean and Correct. He did not work for his dad out of love but in order to earn things, which is why he became bitter when his undeserving brother was welcomed in a festive manner.

Yet despite all this, the father showed great love to both his lost sons. He also tried to show his eldest son that his sense of duty and zeal had robbed him of his joy. He was the complacent eldest son who had stayed at home, but he still did not experience the joy of being home and feeling at home. We are not told whether the eldest son actually went inside and joined in the festivities. This open-ended parable is an invitation to each one of us to use our own lives to complete the story.

 Lord, I want to show by my way of living that I am part of the festivities.

Hurt leads to bitterness, bitterness to anger, travel too far that road and the way is lost.
—Terry Brooks (b. 1944), *Writer of fantasy fiction*

WHY IS PONTIUS PILATE'S NAME IN THE CREED?

On Sundays, believers all over the world profess the Creed of the Apostles. They use it to profess that Jesus suffered under Pontius Pilate. But why does the name of a heathen appear in our precious Creed?

Luke 23 (conversation)

[13]Pilate then called together the chief priests and the rulers and the people, [14]and said to them, 'You brought me this man as one who was misleading the people. And after examining him before you, behold, I did not find this man guilty of any of your charges against him. [15]Neither did Herod, for he sent him back to us. Look, nothing deserving death has been done by him. (ESV)

John 18 (conversation)

[37]Then Pilate said to him, 'So you are a king?' Jesus answered, 'You say that I am a king. For this purpose I was born and for this purpose I have come into the world—to bear witness to the truth. Everyone who is of the truth listens to my voice.' [38]Pilate said to him, 'What is truth?' After he had said this, he went back outside to the Jews and told them, 'I find no guilt in him. (ESV)

Pilate (full name Pontius Pilate) was the Roman governor of the provinces of Judea and Samaria from A.D. 26 to 36. According to non-biblical sources, he could be cruel and rigid. However, his behavior at Jesus' trial reveals a gentler side to his nature. If Pilate had wanted to be cruel, he could have crucified Jesus immediately, but he did not do so. Instead, he had a conversation with Jesus and the prosecutors.

Although Pilate was judicially competent, he seemed to waver at this point. He moved backward and forward between Jesus and the prosecutors. He dithered, because he realized that although Jesus was telling the truth, the Jews wanted him to be punished in any case. Pilate also realized that Jesus did not pose a threat to the Roman Empire, because He did not claim to be an earthly king. Pilate realized this when Jesus told him that if He were the king of an earthly kingdom, His followers would have already taken up the sword to free Him (John 18:36).

Pilate eventually reached a conclusion: "I find no guilt in him" (v. 38). This is repeated twice in the next chapter (19:4,6). The earthly judge confirmed Jesus' innocence. This is why we confess in the third article of the Creed of the Apostles that Jesus suffered under Pontius Pilate. He did not deserve to be crucified. His innocence intensified His suffering—the innocent for the guilty.

 Thank You, Lord, for carrying my guilt with You to the cross.

Innocence is lucky if it finds the same protection as guilt.
—François de la Rochefoucauld (1613–1680), *French classical author, leading exponent of the Maxime*

IF JESUS IS THE ANSWER, WHAT IS THE QUESTION?

The scientific formula for water is H_2O. However, the formula itself cannot quench your thirst—it is merely a symbol. Only water can quench your thirst. Unfortunately, many people want to turn Jesus into a formula. Just think of the graffiti and bumper stickers that say: "Jesus is the answer!" Someone once asked, "But what is the question?" Let us say that the question is: "What quenches my thirst?"

John 7 (conversation)

[37]On the last day of the feast, the great day, Jesus stood up and cried out, *'If anyone thirsts, let him come to me and drink.* [38]*Whoever believes in me, as the Scripture has said, 'Out of his heart will flow rivers of living water.'"* [39]Now this he said about the Spirit, whom those who believed in him were to receive, for as yet the Spirit had not been given, because Jesus was not yet glorified. (ESV)

A living relationship with Jesus is not enough to quench life's thirst. Now, before you object that this point of view is too risky, consider the example of Adam. Initially, he had a perfect relationship with God, but he still yearned for a companion. God noticed this yearning and gave him a wife.

Thirst is a concept that involves God and other people. If we want to quench our thirst only with God, we will lose out on people. Likewise, if we want to quench our thirst only with people, we will lose out on God. We all have different kinds of thirst. Our thirst might lie in unanswered questions such as: What is the meaning of life? Why did my relationship fail? Why am I still in the same job? Why do I have to endure so much pain? The answers to these questions do not lie in a formula but in a promise: "Out of his heart will flow rivers of living water" (v. 38).

Like the poet of Psalm 73, you might feel trapped in a cocoon of desperation. Yet it is important to remember that the Spirit did not break this psalmist's cocoon, because then his wings would not have been strong enough. Rather, the Spirit quenched his thirst by enabling him to feel secure. "But for me it is good to be near God" (Ps. 73:28, ESV). This sense of belonging proved sufficient for him. Although the psalmist's circumstances did not change, his perspective did.

Quenching thirst cannot be restricted to the individual. Think of Moses' thirst, which was caused by the fact that he could not enter the Promised Land. His descendents had this privilege, which teaches us that the tree we plant today might one day provide shade for our children. Quenching thirst is not a formula but an invitation with a promise: "If anyone thirsts, let him come to me and drink. Whoever believes in me, as the Scripture has said, 'Out of his heart will flow rivers of living water'" (vv. 37–38).

 Thank You, Spirit, that You quench thirst in different ways—and that You also quench my thirst!

Love shortens time, changes the hours. Love is invincible. Many waters cannot quench it nor the floods drown. The supreme happiness of life is the conviction that we are loved.
—Author unknown

DOES GOD HAVE A HANDLE?

I often hear how believers in difficulty comfort each other with these words: "Never mind, just hold on tightly to the Lord!" This often makes me wonder, *Does God have a handle?*

John 10 (conversation)

[22]At that time the Feast of Dedication took place at Jerusalem. It was winter, [23]and Jesus was walking in the temple, in the colonnade of Solomon. [24]So the Jews gathered around him and said to him, 'How long will you keep us in suspense? If you are the Christ, tell us plainly.' [25]Jesus answered them, 'I told you, and you do not believe. The works that I do in my Father's name bear witness about me, [26]but you do not believe because you are not part of my flock. [27]My sheep hear my voice, and I know them, and they follow me. [28]I give them eternal life, and they will never perish, and no one will snatch them out of my hand. [29]My Father, who has given them to me, is greater than all, *and no one is able to snatch them out of the Father's hand.* [30]I and the Father are one.' (ESV)

In this passage in John, Jesus attended the Feast of Dedication in Jerusalem. During this feast, the Jews called into remembrance the rededication of the Temple after the hated Syrian leader Antiochus IV Epiphanes had desecrated it in 186 B.C. During this feast, Jesus' identity became a burning issue. The Jews wanted to know if He was the Christ, the Messiah. They wanted to hold onto something solid—some kind of proof! They could no longer cope with the uncertainty (v. 24).

Jesus linked their unbelief to their own identity. Despite everything that they had seen of Jesus, they did not believe, because they were not part of His flock. His sheep, the believers, had a relationship with Him, which is why Jesus said that they knew Him. In two verses, Jesus showed the doubting Jews six certainties associated with His sheep: "My sheep [1] hear my voice, and [2] I know them, and [3] they follow me. I give them [4] eternal life, and they [5] will never perish, and [6] no one will snatch them out of my hand" (vv. 27–28,).

You cannot hold on to the Lord, because He does not have a handle. He holds you in His hand! In difficult times, you need not exhaust yourself even more in order to "hold on to" God. Rather, be assured that He holds you!

 Thank You, Lord, that You hold me tight. Thank You that I am safe in your arms!

We are all pencils in the hand of God.
—Mother Teresa of Calcutta (1910–1997), *Albanian born Indian missionary, founder of the Order of the Missionaries of Charity and winner of the Nobel Prize for Peace in 1979*

LIFE CAN SOMETIMES BE SO UNFAIR!

We have to accept the fact that life can sometimes be very unfair. This is often a bitter pill to swallow. Each of us undoubtedly has our own story to tell about how life treated us unfairly. Jesus also did not escape this. Let us see how He handled it.

John 18 (conversation)

[19]The high priest then questioned Jesus about his disciples and his teaching. [20]Jesus answered him, 'I have spoken openly to the world. I have always taught in synagogues and in the temple, where all Jews come together. I have said nothing in secret. [21]Why do you ask me? Ask those who have heard me what I said to them; they know what I said.' [22]When he had said these things, one of the officers standing by struck Jesus with his hand, saying, 'Is that how you answer the high priest?' [23]Jesus answered him, 'If what I said is wrong, bear witness about the wrong; but if what I said is right, why do you strike me?' [24]Annas then sent him bound to Caiaphas the high priest. (ESV)

Annas was no longer the high priest; his son-in-law, Caiaphas, had taken his place. Annas was the high priest from A.D. 6 to 15, while Caiaphas was high priest from A.D. 18 to 36/37. So why was Jesus first taken to Annas at His trial? This was done because Annas still had a lot of influence. Four of his sons had occupied the position of high priest. He was also a very rich man who sold sacrificial animals at exorbitant profits to pilgrims who came to Jerusalem for the Passover.

Jesus had become infuriated during the Passover when He saw that the Temple had been turned into a supermarket and the emphasis had been shifted from God to money. This is why Jesus cleansed the Temple by chasing away the traders and money-changers. Jesus was therefore a threat to Annas's business empire. Yet Jesus was not afraid of Annas, because He had no hidden agendas when He acted in public—unlike Annas, who was secretly involved in malpractices.

During the interrogation, Jesus pointed out to Annas that he was not acting in accordance with legal procedures. Annas was supposed to call in witnesses, which is the reason Jesus asked, "Why do you ask me?" It was then that the guard, who probably could not stand the fact that Jesus had rebuked the "godfather," struck Jesus. He wanted to put Jesus in His place. People usually start hitting and asking questions when they feel threatened.

When Annas realized that Jesus was blameless, he sent Him to his son-in-law, Caiaphas, the high priest. Despite the unjust treatment Jesus suffered, He acted in a dignified manner. The sad part is that Annas sent the Messenger away without listening to His message. Like Jesus, we should learn to act with style and dignity in all situations.

 Lord, help me to act with dignity if I am treated unjustly.

We only live once, but once is enough if we do it right. Live your life with class, dignity, and style so that an exclamation, rather than a question mark signifies it!
—Gary Ryan Blair, *Author, speaker, coach and consultant who focuses on people's goals*

WHAT CONSTITUTES A THREAT?

A threat forces us to act differently than the way we would actually want to act. This is exactly why we dislike threats so much. In the following conversation between Pilate and the Jews, we witness how a threat made Pilate act differently than the way he wanted to act. Let us have a look at how strong threats can be.

John 19 (conversation)

[10]So Pilate said to him, 'You will not speak to me? Do you not know that I have authority to release you and authority to crucify you?' [11]Jesus answered him, 'You would have no authority over me at all unless it had been given you from above. Therefore he who delivered me over to you has the greater sin.'

[12]From then on Pilate sought to release him, but the Jews cried out, 'If you release this man, you are not Caesar's friend. Everyone who makes himself a king opposes Caesar.' [13]So when Pilate heard these words, he brought Jesus out and sat down on the judgment seat at a place called The Stone Pavement, and in Aramaic Gabbatha. [14]Now it was the day of Preparation of the Passover. It was about the sixth hour. He said to the Jews, 'Behold your King!' [15]They cried out, 'Away with him, away with him, crucify him!' Pilate said to them, 'Shall I crucify your King?' The chief priests answered, 'We have no king but Caesar.' (ESV)

Pilate realized that Jesus was innocent and did everything in his power to set Jesus free. However, Pilate was confronted with a threat from the shouting Jews: "If you release this man, you are not Caesar's friend" (v. 12). The word "if" in the crowd's statement typifies a threat. Pilate had to choose: Either he was a *friend* of Caesar or he was an *enemy* of Caesar. If Pilate allowed Jesus to be crucified, he would be in the good books of Caesar and the Jews. However, if he let Jesus free, the Jews could report him to Caesar for freeing someone who had "slandered" Caesar. After all, Jesus did say that He was a king (John 18:37).

In order to retain his position, Pilate eventually gave in to the threat. He did not act according to the courage of his convictions, because the threat deterred him. The Sanhedrin's actions were also very unfortunate. Despite the Jews' hatred for the Romans, the Sanhedrin (a group of 70 men who were the religious political body for Israel) declared to Pilate that their only king was the Roman Caesar. In this way, they made it clear that they did not want to be associated with Jesus.

We should not allow a situation to arise in which we are threatened or one in which we pose a threat to others. We should learn to act according to our convictions. This is not always easy, however, because it requires much from us. But this is the honorable way we should act, for only by acting in this manner can we live in peace and with a clean conscience. Furthermore, it is proof of our character and integrity.

 Lord, help me to always act according to my convictions.

There is no pillow so soft as a clear conscience.
—French proverb

WHY WAS THE NOTICE ON JESUS' CROSS IN THREE LANGUAGES?

During the time of Jesus, the Roman Empire ruled Israel. Crucifixion was a Roman way of executing a death sentence. The custom was to write the nature of the crime the person was guilty of at the top of the cross. Pilate had the following written on Jesus' cross: "Jesus of Nazareth, the king of the Jews." This notice was written in three languages: Hebrew, Latin and Greek. Why did Pilate do this?

John 19 (history)

[16]So he delivered him over to them to be crucified. So they took Jesus, [17]and he went out, bearing his own cross, to the place called the place of a skull, which in Aramaic is called Golgotha. [18]There they crucified him, and with him two others, one on either side, and Jesus between them. [19]Pilate also wrote an inscription and put it on the cross. It read, 'JESUS OF NAZARETH, THE KING OF THE JEWS.' [20]Many of the Jews read this inscription, for the place where Jesus was crucified was near the city, and it was written in Aramaic, in Latin, and in Greek. [21]So the chief priests of the Jews said to Pilate, 'Do not write, 'The King of the Jews,' but rather, 'This man said, I am King of the Jews.'' [22]Pilate answered, 'What I have written I have written.' (ESV)

It was Passover in Jerusalem, and the streets were filled with people from all over the world. This feast lasted for seven days and was only celebrated in Jerusalem. It reminded the Jews of the events in Egypt when the angel of death saved Israel's firstborn sons. The blood on the doorposts of the Israelites was a sign that the angel should pass by their homes. The Jews crucified Jesus during this feast because He claimed to be the King of the Jews. They could not accept the fact that He was the promised Messiah because Jesus did not meet their expectations of a mighty political liberator.

However, Pilate did realize that Jesus was innocent, and in his heart of hearts he knew that Jesus was the King of the Jews (see Day 257). Pilate wanted everyone who attended the feast to know this, so he wrote the notice in three languages: Hebrew (Aramaic) for the Jews, Latin (the official language of the Roman Empire) for the Romans, and Greek (generally spoken throughout the Roman Empire) for the Jews and non-Jews who attended the feast.

Without realizing it, those who walked past Jesus that day were witnessing the true paschal lamb. Jesus' blood caused God's punishment to pass us by. This is mercy! Holy Communion and baptism reminds us of this!

 Thank You, Lord, that Your blood means that Your punishment passes me by.

Jesus, what made You so small? LOVE!
—Saint Bernard of Clairvaux (1090–1153), *French abbot and the primary builder of the reforming Cistercian monastic order*

WHY DOES LIFE SOMETIMES GET SO LONELY?

One of our basic human needs is to know that we belong and that people accept us. The sad fact, however, is that we are often lonely and alone. At Jesus' cross, something remarkable happened that can teach us something important.

John 19 (history)

²³After the soldiers had nailed Jesus to the cross, they divided up his clothes into four parts, one for each of them. But his outer garment was made from a single piece of cloth, and it did not have any seams. ²⁴The soldiers said to each other, 'Let's not rip it apart. We will gamble to see who gets it.' This happened so that the Scriptures would come true, which say,
'They divided up my clothes and gambled for my garments.'
The soldiers then did what they had decided.
²⁵Jesus' mother stood beside his cross with her sister and Mary the wife of Clopas. Mary Magdalene was standing there too. ²⁶When Jesus saw his mother and his favorite disciple with her, he said to his mother, 'This man is now your son.' ²⁷Then he said to the disciple, 'She is now your mother.' From then on, that disciple took her into his own home. (CEV)

On that Friday, Jesus was probably the loneliest person on earth. He experienced complete separation from God and helplessly watched as His last belongings, His clothes, were divided among four soldiers. In those days, it was the custom that the soldiers could take the clothes of those who were crucified as some kind of reward. In Jesus' case, the soldiers drew lots to determine who would get His undergarment. This was a fulfillment of the prophecy that had been foretold in Psalm 22:19.

Jesus' pain and loneliness intensified when He saw that only His mother, three other women and John attended the crucifixion. The other disciples had become filled with fear and had run away. The crucifixion was not only painful for Jesus but also humiliating, as those who were crucified hung between heaven and earth. Jesus was condemned, and therefore He belonged nowhere—not on earth or in heaven.

Although Jesus experienced enormous pain and loneliness, He was concerned about His family right up to the end. There on the cross, while experiencing pain and loneliness, He brought people together when He told John, "She is now your mother" (v. 27). It is remarkable that despite His own suffering, Jesus was able to bring people together so that they could care for each other and escape loneliness. Jesus also gave us the Holy Spirit to bind us to Him and to each other. The fruit of the Spirit (Gal 5:22) strengthen this bond: love, joy, peace, patience. . . . Jesus experienced separation from God so that we need never be without God and each other.

 Lord, help me to reach out to those who are lonely.

The eternal quest of the human being is to shatter his loneliness.
—Norman Cousins (1915–1990), *Prominent political journalist, author, professor and world peace advocate*

THE MOST FAMOUS DYING WORDS . . .

We should be grateful that so many famous people's dying words have been recorded, as their words reveal so much about their lives. Here are a few:

- Winston Churchill: "What a fool have I been."
- Karl Marx: "How pointless and empty life is!"
- Cecil John Rhodes: "So little done, so much to do."
- Alexander the Great: "There are no more other worlds to conquer!"
- Leonardo da Vinci: "I have offended God and mankind because my work did not reach the quality it should have."
- James Dean: "My fun days are over."

Fortunately, we also have a record of Jesus' last words before he died.

John 19 (history)

[28]Jesus knew that he had now finished his work. And in order to make the Scriptures come true, he said, *'I am thirsty!'* [29]A jar of cheap wine was there. Someone then soaked a sponge with the wine and held it up to Jesus' mouth on the stem of a hyssop plant.
[30]After Jesus drank the wine, he said, *'Everything is done!'* He bowed his head and died. (CEV)

Jesus' last words were, "Everything is done!" (In Greek, this only consists of one word: *tetelestai*!) What do these words reveal to you and me?

First, these words indicate the end of the complicated Jewish system of sacrificial offerings. The Jews had a very complicated system of sacrificial offerings, the purpose of which was to reestablish the right relationship between the people and God. Sin caused their relationship with God to suffer. The people's sins were forgiven when an animal was sacrificed in their place for their sins.

The frustration was that the people continually had to bring the offerings, because they continually committed sin. The good news is that Jesus' sacrificial death brought an end to the complicated system of offerings, because God considered the death of Jesus sufficient. By way of prayer, we now have direct access to God.

Jesus' words also indicate that there would now be peace between people and God. The words, "Everything is done!" means that Jesus paid the price for our sin in full because His death also made provision for all the generations to come. He completely removed the distance between us and God.

With these last words, Jesus confirmed that the task His father instructed Him to perform was finally completed. His last words therefore reveal that He is the Savior and the Prince of Peace of the entire human race. This is why these last words of Jesus are the most famous and meaningful dying words ever uttered.

Thank You, Jesus, that Your last words are my reassurance that You have paid the price for my sins.

God is dead.
—Friedrich Nietzsche (1844–1900), *German philosopher of the late nineteenth century who challenged the foundations of traditional morality and Christianity. Nietzsche died in spiritual darkness, a babbling madman. On a wall in Austria, someone wrote, "'God is dead,'—Nietzsche!" Beneath this, someone else wrote, "'Nietzsche is dead!' God."*

THE FIRST WITNESS TO JESUS' RESURRECTION

The first person to witness the resurrection of Jesus wasn't Herod, Pilate, the Sanhedrin or Caiaphas. She was a simple woman named Mary Magdalene. Jesus was first seen by a woman, even though women were not considered important in those days. Let us read about that special meeting.

John 20 (conversation)

¹¹Mary Magdalene stood crying outside the tomb. She was still weeping, when she stooped down ¹²and saw two angels inside. They were dressed in white and were sitting where Jesus' body had been. One was at the head and the other was at the foot.

¹³The angels asked Mary, 'Why are you crying?'

She answered, 'They have taken away my Lord's body! I don't know where they have put him.'

¹⁴As soon as Mary said this, she turned around and saw Jesus standing there. But she did not know who he was. ¹⁵Jesus asked her, 'Why are you crying? Who are you looking for?'

She thought he was the gardener and said, 'Sir, if you have taken his body away, please tell me, so I can go and get him.'

¹⁶Then Jesus said to her, 'Mary!'

She turned and said to him, 'Rabboni.' The Aramaic word 'Rabboni' means 'Teacher.'

¹⁷Jesus told her, 'Don't hold on to me! I have not yet gone to the Father. But tell my disciples that I am going to the one who is my Father and my God, as well as your Father and your God.' ¹⁸Mary Magdalene then went and told the disciples that she had seen the Lord. She also told them what he had said to her. (CEV)

On the Sunday after Jesus' death (v. 1) Mary Magdalene cried bitterly at the empty grave because she thought that somebody had removed Jesus' body. Why was she so passionate about Jesus? Jesus had previously exorcised seven demons from her (Luke 8:2). She was overjoyed at being set free and showed her gratitude by following Him everywhere. As we previously mentioned, this was against the social conventions of the time, but Jesus openly protested against any form of discrimination, especially women.

During the time of Jesus, women were regarded as inferior to men. However, Jesus treated women as equals, thereby going against the tradition of His time. At the cross, all the disciples (except John) ran away from the Roman soldiers. Yet Mary Magdalene and a few other women remained at the cross until the very end. Officially, she was not a member of Jesus' disciples, but her grateful conduct made her a true disciple. She also had the privilege to tell those who were so scared, "I saw the Lord!" We should follow her example!

 Lord, help me to follow You with grateful passion.

Discipleship means adherence to the person of Jesus, and therefore submission to the law of Christ which is the law of the cross.
—Dietrich Bonhoeffer (1906–1945), *Theologian, author of fiction and poetry and a central figure in the Protestant Church struggle against Nazism*

TO HAVE DOUBTS IS NOT AS BAD AS WE MIGHT THINK!

I was brought up knowing that I could be 100 percent sure about my faith in Jesus and, therefore, also of eternal life. I do not consider this to be wrong, but perhaps we did not leave enough room for the honest emotion of doubt. This next section in John shows us that doubt can be healthy and necessary for our faith.

John 20 (history)

²⁴Although Thomas the Twin was one of the twelve disciples, he wasn't with the others when Jesus appeared to them. ²⁵So they told him, 'We have seen the Lord!'
But Thomas said, 'First, I must see the nail scars in his hands and touch them with my finger. I must put my hand where the spear went into his side. I won't believe unless I do this!'
²⁶A week later the disciples were together again. This time, Thomas was with them. Jesus came in while the doors were still locked and stood in the middle of the group. He greeted his disciples
²⁷and said to Thomas, 'Put your finger here and look at my hands! Put your hand into my side. Stop doubting and have faith!'
²⁸Thomas replied, *'You are my Lord and my God!'*
²⁹Jesus said, 'Thomas, do you have faith because you have seen me? The people who have faith in me without seeing me are the ones who are really blessed!' (CEV)

Jesus never reprimanded Thomas for his doubt. His doubt led to a request: unless he could see the scars in Jesus' hands and side, he would not believe. Jesus dealt with his doubt by granting his request (v. 27). Doubt led Thomas to the confession that is also the climax of the Gospel: "You are my Lord and my God!"

The author of Psalm 73 also started doubting God's goodness (v. 1). He could not understand why things went well for unbelievers and not for him. However, his doubt and honest wrestling ended with him coming to a personal confession: "It is good for me to be near you" (v. 28, CEV).

In Matthew 28 is the well-known passage that contains the Great Commission for the Church: "Go to the people of all nations and make them my disciples. Baptize them in the name of the Father, the Son, and the Holy Spirit, and teach them to do everything I have told you. I will be with you always, even until the end of the world" (vv. 19–20, CEV). However, the previous verse reveals the emotions of some of the disciples Jesus sent out: "They saw him and worshiped him, but some of them doubted" (v. 17, CEV). Jesus sent a doubting group of people out into the wide world, but despite this doubt, the Church is visible nearly all over the world.

Doubt did not strip Thomas, the disciples or the author of Psalm 73 of their faith. Doubt can sometimes be the beginning of spiritual growth. Doubt may be a way of telling God, "Lord, I battle to believe, but I would like to continue believing." Mercifully, the Lord understands such honesty. If one is always sure and knows exactly how things work, it could lead to spiritual arrogance.

 Thank You, Lord, that doubt can help me to discover You.

Doubt is not the opposite of faith; it is one element of faith.
—Paul Tillich (1886–1965), *German born theologian and philosopher*

AFRAID TO WITNESS?

Luke wrote both the Gospel of Luke and the book of Acts. The Gospel of Luke is about Jesus' life on earth until the day of His Ascension. In Acts, Luke tells about the 30 years after the Ascension, during which time the Church was founded. The Church had to continue Christ's work, but how?

Acts 1

¹In the first book, O Theophilus, I have dealt with all that Jesus began to do and teach,
²until the day when he was taken up, after he had given commands through the Holy Spirit to the apostles whom he had chosen. ³To them he presented himself alive after his suffering by many proofs, appearing to them during forty days and speaking about the kingdom of God.
⁴And while staying with them he ordered them not to depart from Jerusalem, but to wait for the promise of the Father, which, he said, 'you heard from me; ⁵for John baptized with water, but you will be baptized with the Holy Spirit not many days from now.' *(history)*
⁶So when they had come together, they asked him, 'Lord, will you at this time restore the kingdom to Israel?' ⁷He said to them, 'It is not for you to know times or seasons that the Father has fixed by his own authority. ⁸But you will receive power when the Holy Spirit has come upon you, and you will be my witnesses in Jerusalem and in all Judea and Samaria, and to the end of the earth.' *(conversation)* ESV

Christians continue Christ's work by being witnesses. But in actual fact, many of us are afraid to bear witness. One of the main reasons is that we do not always know how the other person will react—we might be rejected. To overcome these fears, we need the power of the Holy Spirit. The power of the Holy Spirit is more than just the supernatural and the extraordinary workings of the Spirit. The power of the Spirit also means that one has the courage, fearlessness, insight and wisdom to testify with style.

We often worry about what we should say to people and how we will answer difficult questions that they may ask. However, to "bear witness" does not mean that we convince others or that we have answers to everything. Remember: Our lives speak louder than words. Our life is what people see. That is why the Spirit would rather use its power to change our lives than to give us answers to our arguments. It is interesting to note that in Greek, the same word is used for witness and martyr—*martus*. Thus, to bear witness also means to allow for animosity and misfortune. The Spirit will also help us in this regard.

 Lord, I realize anew what responsibility I have to live the right life.

The blood of the martyrs is the seed of the church.
—Tertullian (155–230), *Church leader and prolific author of early Christianity.*
He was born, lived and died in Carthage, in what is today Tunisia.

WHAT DO WE CELEBRATE WHEN WE CELEBRATE THE ASCENSION?

After the resurrection of Jesus, He spent 40 days teaching His disciples and then ascended to heaven to rule alongside His Father. Yet Christians are not always excited about the Ascension. Perhaps this is because the day falls on a weekday or because the world does not celebrate (exploit) this day commercially in the same way as it does Christmas.

Many of us have difficulty understanding how Christ could *ascend* into heaven—after all, the earth does not have a top part and a bottom part. However, we have to realize that during the time of Jesus, people still thought that the earth was flat and that the heavens were somewhere above them.

Yet there might be another reason why the Ascension does not fill us with excitement: perhaps we are not quite sure what to get excited about. It is interesting to note that Luke is the only Gospel writer who tells the story of the Ascension (Luke 24:50). Paul (in Ephesians) and the author of Hebrews do, however, enthusiastically refer to the Ascension. What do we really celebrate when we celebrate the Ascension?

Acts 1 (history)

⁹After Jesus had said this and while they were watching, he was taken up into a cloud. They could not see him, ¹⁰but as he went up, they kept looking up into the sky.
Suddenly two men dressed in white clothes were standing there beside them. ¹¹They said, 'Why are you men from Galilee standing here and looking up into the sky? Jesus has been taken to heaven. But he will come back in the same way that you have seen him go.' (CEV)

The Ascension does not mean that Jesus has left us but that He is with us in a different way. He is with us in a glorified way—in other words, in the Spirit. We do not have someone else with us in the Spirit. No, the Spirit is the new way, the glorified way, whereby Christ Himself is with us. This is why Matthew could use the following words of Jesus to conclude his Gospel: "I will be with you always, even until the end of the world" (CEV).

Jesus is not gone! We should get excited about this. There is also another reason why we should be excited: the Ascension declares that Jesus will return. But it will not be a return after a long absence—the second coming of Christ will be another way in which He will be with us. As a Church, we are not on our way to nowhere. History is not merely a series of unrelated facts. God is leading us to the second coming of Christ, and for this we have to be prepared. We cannot prepare for it by staring at the clouds all day long. No, we have to work hard to spread the gospel so that others can share in God's blessing.

 Thank You, Lord, that I can be excited about the Ascension.

As the Resurrection opened the grave, the Ascension opened heaven.
—Author unknown

THE REVENGE OF THE HOLY SPIRIT!

What do you do when you start noticing that your belief in Jesus and your conviction to do what is right counts against you at work or in your circle of friends? You pray for the "revenge" of the Holy Spirit! But what does that mean?

Acts 4 (story)

Tension: How will the fellow believers react?

²³As soon as Peter and John had been set free, they went back and told the others everything that the chief priests and the leaders had said to them.

Relief of tension: They pray

²⁴When the rest of the Lord's followers heard this, they prayed together and said:
Master, you created heaven and earth, the sea, and everything in them. ²⁵And by the Holy Spirit you spoke to our ancestor David. He was your servant, and you told him to say:
'Why are all the Gentiles so furious?
Why do people make foolish plans?
²⁶The kings of earth prepare for war,
and the rulers join together
against the Lord and his Messiah.'
²⁷Here in Jerusalem, Herod and Pontius Pilate got together with the Gentiles and the people of Israel. Then they turned against your holy Servant Jesus, your chosen Messiah. ²⁸They did what you in your power and wisdom had already decided would happen. ²⁹Lord, listen to their threats! We are your servants. *So make us brave enough to speak your message.* ³⁰Show your mighty power, as we heal people and work miracles and wonders in the name of your holy Servant Jesus.

Result: The 'revenge' of the Spirit

³¹After they had prayed, the meeting place shook. They were all filled with the Holy Spirit and bravely spoke God's message. (CEV)

The Sanhedrin forbade Peter and John to talk about Jesus and to teach others about Him. They probably threatened Peter and John by saying, "Remember what happened to Jesus? You will be next!" So how did the two disciples respond to this threat? They immediately went to their fellow believers and told them everything, and then they prayed! In their prayer, Peter and John confessed that God could do everything. They prayed that God would tackle this superior force because they were not able to. They prayed for the revenge of the Spirit.

How does the Spirit take revenge? The answer is in Peter and John's prayer: "So make us brave enough to speak your message" (v. 29). The revenge of the Spirit means that you will not be deterred by intimidation. The Spirit's "revenge" is a revenge of love. You bless others when they condemn you. When you are hit on the cheek, you turn the other one. May the Spirit also fill you!

Lord, I pray that I will boldly do what is right!

I don't deserve any credit for turning the other cheek as my tongue is always in it.
—Flannery O'Connor (1925–1964), *American writer*

A CONGREGATION'S BEST TESTIMONIAL

"There was not a needy person among them" (v. 34). The members of the first congregation in Jerusalem are described in this unbelievable way. This must be the best testimonial any congregation could have. But what was their secret? How did they achieve this? We will find the answer in this section!

Acts 4 (history)

[32]Now the full number of those who believed were of one heart and soul, and no one said that any of the things that belonged to him was his own, but they had everything in common. [33]And with great power the apostles were giving their testimony to the resurrection of the Lord Jesus, and great grace was upon them all. [34]*There was not a needy person among them*, for as many as were owners of lands or houses sold them and brought the proceeds of what was sold [35]and laid it at the apostles' feet, and it was distributed to each as any had need. [36]Thus Joseph, who was also called by the apostles Barnabas (which means son of encouragement), a Levite, a native of Cyprus, [37]sold a field that belonged to him and brought the money and laid it at the apostles' feet. (ESV)

Three factors contributed to the fact that nobody in this congregation was ever in need.

1. "*Now the full number of those who believed were of one heart and soul.*" People who were once strangers or even enemies all became believers. This made a difference to their lives! They no longer distrusted one another, opposed one another or ran one another down. Bosses and servants became brothers and sisters. This congregation had no dividing lines, and therefore no cliques. They were one in heart and soul.
2. "*And no one said that any of the things that belonged to him was his own, but they had everything in common.*" The Lord does not compel us to give away all our belongings—that would make us bankrupt in no time. No, He prefers that our hearts have ample space for the needs of others. This will help us to rid ourselves of the grip of selfishness and the sickly rush to gain more possessions.
3. "*And with great power the apostles were giving their testimony to the resurrection of the Lord Jesus, and great grace was upon them all.*" With the Ascension, Jesus conquered our biggest enemy, death. The first congregation realized that the Ascension of Jesus made eternal life a reality. This made them to realize that everything on earth, including their possessions, were temporary.

These three factors enabled this congregation to share the things we so easily cling to with others! They were free! Barnabas is an example to all of us. What about you?

 Lord, I want to help to turn my congregation into a caring community.

Without a sense of caring, there can be no sense of community.
—Anthony J. D'Angelo, *Founder of The Collegiate EmPowerment Company and creator of the Inspiration book series*

WHAT "GOOD" PEOPLE ALSO NEED!

Life is not only filled with bad people. There are also many good people—people who care about other people and who are hardworking, loyal, exemplary, conscientious and honest. This next episode in Acts tells us about what all people need—including the good ones.

Acts 9 (story)

Tension: Saul persecutes the church

[1]Saul kept on threatening to kill the Lord's followers. He even went to the high priest [2]and asked for letters to the Jewish leaders in Damascus. He did this because he wanted to arrest and take to Jerusalem any man or woman who had accepted the Lord's Way.

Relief of tension: The Damascus experience

[3]When Saul had almost reached Damascus, a bright light from heaven suddenly flashed around him. [4]He fell to the ground and heard a voice that said, 'Saul! Saul! Why are you so cruel to me?' [5]'Who are you?' Saul asked.

'I am Jesus,' the Lord answered. 'I am the one you are so cruel to. [6]Now get up and go into the city, where you will be told what to do.'

[9]and for three days he was blind and did not eat or drink.

Result: Persecutor becomes follower!

[18]Suddenly something like fish scales fell from Saul's eyes, and he could see. He got up and was baptized. [19]Then he ate and felt much better. For several days Saul stayed with the Lord's followers in Damascus. [20]Soon he went to the Jewish meeting places and started telling people that Jesus is the Son of God. (CEV)

We all know this story. It is a story of conversion—perhaps the best known one of all. It is the story of an archenemy of the Church who became a brother—Saul, who became Paul! Even today, many Christians use Paul's conversion as the model for their own story—stories such as, "I was wild, bad and sinful. Then I had a Damascus experience—the Lord intervened and I was made new! I was addicted, but now I am free. I only want to live for the Lord!"

These stories are gripping. But we should realize that Paul was not a wild or bad person. He was a "good" person. Yet after his Damascus experience, he makes the following remark about his good virtues: "But Christ has shown me that what I once thought was valuable is worthless. Nothing is as wonderful as knowing Christ Jesus my Lord. I have given up everything else and count it all as garbage. All I want is Christ" (Phil. 3:7–8, CEV). Being a good person does not mean that you know Jesus. For this reason, good people also need to be converted.

 Lord, I want to be more than a good person. I want to know and serve You!

Conversion for me was not a Damascus Road experience. I slowly moved into an intellectual
acceptance of what my intuition had always known.
—Madeleine L'Engle (b. 1918), *American writer best known for her children's books*

SOMETHING GOD NEVER DOES
BUT WE DO SO OFTEN!

Acts 10 tells the story of one of the most important turning points in the history of the Church. The chapter starts with Cornelius, a Roman officer who was converted. The Lord wanted to send Peter to welcome him to the Church, but before this could happen, He first had to teach Peter a very important lesson. This lesson showed Peter something that God never does but that we do so often.

Acts 10 (conversation)

[9]The next day about noon these men were coming near Joppa. Peter went up on the roof of the house to pray [10]and became very hungry. While the food was being prepared, he fell sound asleep and had a vision. [11]He saw heaven open, and something came down like a huge sheet held up by its four corners. [12]In it were all kinds of animals, snakes, and birds. [13]A voice said to him, 'Peter, get up! Kill these and eat them.' [14]But Peter said, 'Lord, I can't do that! I've never eaten anything that is unclean and not fit to eat.' [15]The voice spoke to him again, 'When God says that something can be used for food, don't say it isn't fit to eat.'
[16]This happened three times before the sheet was suddenly taken back to heaven.
[17]Peter was still wondering what all of this meant, when the men sent by Cornelius came and stood at the gate. They had found their way to Simon's house [18]and were asking if Simon Peter was staying there. (CEV)

During his prayer, Peter went into a trance. This means that the Holy Spirit worked in him to such an extent that he had a vision. While the others were preparing the meal, in the vision the Lord presented Peter with an unusual menu—one from which Peter was unwilling to eat. The problem was that the Lord's menu contained foods that were forbidden according to Jewish law (Lev. 11:29–30). These strict rules regarding food were the reason why Jews did not easily share their dinner table with non-Jews. They even went so far as to consider non-Jews "unclean."

The lesson Peter had to learn from this vision was that non-Jews, like Cornelius, were not to be regarded as inferior. Before this vision, Peter would have thought it impossible for a non-Jew to want to become a Christian. After the vision, Peter realized that he had to join the messengers when they went to Cornelius. There, in the Roman officer's house, Peter spoke these words: "Now I am certain that God treats all people alike" (Acts 10:34, CEV). We easily discriminate between rich and poor, white and black, skinny and fat, pretty and ugly, heterosexual and homosexual. Let us stop doing this!

 Thank You, Lord, that You do not discriminate against people.

I want to be the white man's brother, not his brother-in-law.
—Martin Luther King, Jr. (1929–1968), *American Baptist minister, Civil Rights leader and winner of the Nobel Prize in 1964*

WHAT EUROPE'S FIRST CONVERT CAN TEACH US!

The book of Acts is divided based on the ministries of the two people who were the main characters in the formation and development of the early Church, namely Peter (1–12) and Paul (13–28). This next section in Acts describes Paul and his friends' first missionary journey to Europe. They went to the city of Philippi, a very important town in Macedonia (today in the northern part of Greece). Paul always visited the synagogue when he visited a new city. However, Philippi did not have a synagogue, because few Jews lived there (at least 10 men were needed to establish a synagogue). So Paul and his friends went to the river on the Sabbath, because they thought that they could find a place of worship there. While there at the river, something wonderful happened.

Acts 16 (history)

[11]We sailed straight from Troas to Samothrace, and the next day we arrived in Neapolis. [12]From there we went to Philippi, which is a Roman colony in the first district of Macedonia. We spent several days in Philippi. [13]Then on the Sabbath we went outside the city gate to a place by the river, where we thought there would be a Jewish meeting place for prayer. We sat down and talked with the women who came. [14]One of them was Lydia, who was from the city of Thyatira and sold expensive purple cloth. She was a worshiper of the Lord God, and he made her willing to accept what Paul was saying. [15]Then after she and her family were baptized, she kept on begging us, 'If you think I really do have faith in the Lord, come stay in my home.' Finally, we accepted her invitation. (CEV)

At the river, Paul shared the gospel with a few women, and the Lord made Lydia's heart receptive to the gospel (v. 14). We can assume that Lydia was wealthy, because she traded in expensive purple woolen cloth. After her conversion, she immediately showed hospitality towards Paul and his friends by inviting them to stay over at her house. Later on when Paul describes the Christian character, he mentions that believers should be hospitable (Rom. 12:13).

Paul experienced hospitality in Philippi. Hospitality lets the guest feel special and at ease. Peter, the other main character in Acts, added his voice to this: "Show hospitality to one another without grumbling" (1 Pet. 4:9, ESV). Hebrews 13:2 expands on this thought: "Be sure to welcome strangers into your home. By doing this, some people have welcomed angels as guests, without even knowing it" (CEV).

 Lord, I want to use my hospitality to let others feel like angels.

He who practices hospitality entertains God himself.
—Author unknown

PRAISE DOES NOT ALWAYS REQUIRE AN ORGAN OR A GUITAR . . .

Although innocent, Paul and Silas sat in prison in Philippi with sore and bleeding bodies (Acts 16:24–34). Then something happened!

Acts 16 (story)

[25]About midnight Paul and Silas were praying and singing praises to God, while the other prisoners listened.

Tension: Earthquake and suicide attempt

[26]Suddenly a strong earthquake shook the jail to its foundations. The doors opened, and the chains fell from all the prisoners.
[27]When the jailer woke up and saw that the doors were open, he thought that the prisoners had escaped. He pulled out his sword and was about to kill himself.

Relief of tension: Paul shouts

[28]But Paul shouted, 'Don't harm yourself! No one has escaped.'
[29]The jailer asked for a torch and went into the jail. He was shaking all over as he knelt down in front of Paul and Silas.

Result: A prison guard repents

[30]After he had led them out of the jail, he asked, 'What must I do to be saved?'
[31]They replied, 'Have faith in the Lord Jesus and you will be saved! This is also true for everyone who lives in your home.'
[32]Then Paul and Silas told him and everyone else in his house about the Lord. [33] While it was still night, the jailer took them to a place where he could wash their cuts and bruises. Then he and everyone in his home were baptized. [34] They were very glad that they had put their faith in God. After this, the jailer took Paul and Silas to his home and gave them something to eat. (CEV)

How is it possible that one can praise the Lord in such a painful situation? Paul and Silas understood the meaning of praise. Praise is more than happily singing along to organ or guitar music. Unfortunately, we have reduced it to music, when it actually involves one's whole life. In Romans 12:1 Paul says. "Dear friends, God is good. So I beg you to offer your bodies to him as a living sacrifice, pure and pleasing. That's the most sensible way to serve God" (CEV).

Worship therefore concerns God, and we can summarize it in one word: *offering!* Praise is not there for our pleasure but for God's pleasure. It must have pleased God when Paul saved the life of his torturer by shouting, "Don't harm yourself! No one has escaped." Paul and Silas's praise led to the conversion and baptism of a whole family. We should not let our praise depend on music and the ideal circumstances.

Lord, I realize that praise consists of more than music. I want to praise You with all my life!

I never knew how to worship until I knew how to love.
—Henry Ward Beecher (1813–1887), *American politician*

MEET THE SPIRIT OF GOD ANEW . . . BUT NOT AS A STEPCHILD OF FAITH

The Holy Spirit is often treated as the stepchild of faith. Perhaps this is because the word "Spirit" conjures up something spooky, or perhaps it is because a lot of people see the Spirit as a vague and impersonal force. Consequently, we are not always concerned about the Holy Spirit. The Spirit of God, however, wants us to be concerned about Him. The following six daily readings will help you to meet the Spirit anew . . . but not as stepchild of your faith.

John 14 (conversation)

[16]Then I will ask the Father to send you the Holy Spirit who will help you and always be with you. [17]The Spirit will show you what is true. The people of this world cannot accept the Spirit, because they don't see or know him. But you know the Spirit, who is with you and will keep on living in you. [18]I won't leave you like orphans. I will come back to you. (CEV)

John 15 (conversation)

[26]I will send you the Spirit who comes from the Father and shows what is true. The Spirit will help you and will tell you about me. [27]Then you will also tell others about me, because you have been with me from the beginning. (CEV)

John 16 (conversation)

[7]But I tell you that I am going to do what is best for you. That is why I am going away. The Holy Spirit cannot come to help you until I leave. But after I am gone, I will send the Spirit to you. [13]The Spirit shows what is true and will come and guide you into the full truth. The Spirit doesn't speak on his own. He will tell you only what he has heard from me, and he will let you know what is going to happen. [14]The Spirit will bring glory to me by taking my message and telling it to you. (CEV)

These passages in John make it clear that the Holy Spirit is not a vague and impersonal force. The Holy Spirit is a personal being that is equal to God the Father and God the Son. According to the Bible, the Holy Spirit has an intellect (1 Cor 2:11), emotions (Rom 15:30) and a will (1 Cor 12:11).

He is regarded as the third person of the Holy Trinity. As Jesus told His disciples, "I have been given all authority in heaven and on earth! Go to the people of all nations and make them my disciples. Baptize them in the name of the Father, the Son, and the Holy Spirit, and teach them to do everything I have told you. I will be with you always, even until the end of the world" (Matt. 28:18–20, CEV). God revealed Himself as the Father, the Son and the Holy Spirit. All the godly attributes of the Father and the Son also apply to the Holy Spirit.

A special bond exists between the Holy Spirit and Jesus. The Spirit first sent Jesus into the world through the pregnancy of Mary, Jesus' mother (Matt. 1:18). At Jesus' baptism, He saw the heavens open and the Spirit descend on Him like a dove (Mark 1:10). The Holy Spirit supported everything that Jesus did (Luke 10:21).

Jesus then sent the Spirit into the world. Jesus' ascension to heaven took place 40 days after His resurrection. Ten days later, Jesus sent the Spirit (John 15:26). It is for this reason that we refer to the outpouring of the Holy Spirit as Pentecost, because Pentecost means "50" (40 + 10). Jesus said that it was to our advantage that He had to leave (John 16:7). Why would He say this? His life, His death and His resurrection made many things possible for us. For instance, Jesus made it possible for us to know the Father; to forgive; to experience love, joy and peace; to be patient, friendly, kind-hearted, faithful and humble; and to apply self-constraint. He sent His Spirit to live within us and *to turn all these possibilities into realities.*

In Romans 8:9–10, Paul wrote, "You are no longer ruled by your desires, but by God's Spirit, who lives in you. People who don't have the Spirit of Christ in them don't belong to him. But Christ lives in you. So you are alive because God has accepted you, even though your bodies must die because of your sins" (CEV). When the Spirit turns the possibility Jesus created into reality in our lives, John 16:14 is fulfilled: "The Spirit will bring glory to me by taking my message and telling it to you" (CEV).

We therefore cannot treat the Holy Spirit as a stepchild of our faith. The question is: How does this become a reality? The answer is fulfillment. The theme of the following section is fulfillment.

 Thank You, Lord, for sending the Spirit to make everything that You made possible a reality for me.

The Holy Spirit wants to turn that which Jesus made a possibility into a reality in your life!

MEET THE SPIRIT OF GOD ANEW . . . THROUGH A SPIRIT-FILLED LIFE

In the previous reading, we saw that the Holy Spirit turns that which Jesus made a possibility into reality. The question is: How does it become a reality for us? As we mentioned, this occurs through fulfillment! This immediately brings us to the next question: What does it mean to be filled with the Holy Spirit?

Ephesians 5 (instruction)

[18]Don't destroy yourself by getting drunk, but let the Spirit fill your life. [19]When you meet together, sing psalms, hymns, and spiritual songs, as you praise the Lord with all your heart. [20]Always use the name of our Lord Jesus Christ to thank God the Father for everything. [21]Honor Christ and put others first. (CEV)

Colossians 3 (instruction)

[16]Let the message about Christ completely fill your lives, while you use all your wisdom to teach and instruct each other. With thankful hearts, sing psalms, hymns, and spiritual songs to God.
[17]Whatever you say or do should be done in the name of the Lord Jesus, as you give thanks to God the Father because of him. (CEV)

What does it mean to be filled with the Holy Spirit? To be filled with the Holy Spirit is not a mystical, secretive or supernatural matter but rather a process of choices, attitudes and actions. The word for "be filled" in the original text (*plerousthe*) proves this. *Plerousthe* is a warning and a command: "let the Spirit fill you." This means that we have to make a conscious choice to be filled with the Spirit. It is also a present-tense verb, which indicates that being filled with the Spirit is a process that occurs daily. It is also in the passive form: "*be* fulfilled," which shows that fulfillment is not something that we can do. We have to expose ourselves and allow ourselves to be filled with the Spirit. It is therefore all about attitude. Finally, *plerousthe* is in the plural. It is therefore aimed at every believer.

To be filled with the Spirit is thus not limited to just the "super Christians." If we believe in Christ, *we* have the Holy Spirit. In Romans 8:9, Paul confirms this: "People who don't have the Spirit of Christ in them don't belong to him" (CEV). To be filled with the Spirit also means that we are free of selfishness. As 1 Peter 5:5 states, "All of you young people should obey your elders. In fact, everyone should be humble toward everyone else. The Scriptures say, 'God opposes proud people, but he helps everyone who is humble'" (CEV). Humility allows the Spirit to turn that which Christ made possible into a reality that we can experience in our lives.

So, how are we filled with the Spirit? Or, formulated differently, how can we meet the Spirit of God anew? First, we have to have the desire to be filled. "God blesses those people who want to obey him more than to eat or drink. They will be given what they want!" (Matt. 5:6, CEV). Second, we must confess our sins. "Don't make God's Spirit sad. The Spirit makes you sure that someday you will be free from your sins" (Eph. 4:30, CEV). Third, we must make ourselves available. "Don't turn away God's Spirit" (1 Thess. 5:19, CEV).

What happens when we are filled with the Spirit of God? Or, to put it another way, what happens when we meet the Spirit of God anew? Is the experience marked by signs and wonders? This could be the case, but it is more likely that we will experience the fruit of the Spirit. "But the fruit of the Spirit is love, joy, peace, patience, kindness, goodness, faithfulness, gentleness, self-control" (Gal. 5:22–23, ESV).

Finally, what does a Spirit-filled life look like? According to Ephesians 5, a fulfilled person sings with joy, is grateful and has respect for others. Colossians 3 says exactly the same, but states that the cause of this fulfillment is the study of the Word. In short, the result of a life filled by the Spirit (Ephesians) and filled by the Word (Colossians) are always the same. This confirms that the Holy Spirit always acts in accordance with the Word of God. After all, the Spirit wants to lead us in truth, which is why it is so important for us to study the Bible. "The Spirit shows what is true and will come and guide you into the full truth" (John 16:13, CEV).

Peter is a good illustration of what it means to be filled with the Spirit. He confessed in the presence of Jesus, "You are the Messiah, the Son of the living God" (Matt. 16:16, CEV). In the presence of Jesus, Peter could walk on water. But in the absence of Jesus, he renounced Him three times and was afraid (Matt. 26:69–75). Given this pattern of behavior, when Jesus completely disappeared after He ascended to heaven, one would have thought that Peter would have freaked out. However, he instead gave a powerful sermon (Acts 2:14) and no longer feared the Sanhedrin (Acts 4).

What was the secret of Peter's transformation? Peter was filled with the Holy Spirit after Jesus' ascension (Acts 2). Jesus therefore did not disappear after His ascension, but was with him in a new way. In the same way, the Spirit connects us to Jesus and turns that which Jesus made possible into reality. To be filled with the Holy Spirit is a daily process whereby we commit ourselves anew to Christ and His Word. This is possible because the Spirit allows Jesus to be present!

 Thank You, Lord, that the Spirit allows You to be present in my life. Please fill me!

The Spirit enables Jesus to be present in our lives!

MEET THE SPIRIT OF GOD ANEW . . . IN THE SHADOWS OF LIFE

You can meet the Spirit anew in your daily life. The secret is to learn to look at your situation differently. But how? The book of Esther can help in this regard. Apart from the Book of Ruth, Esther is the only book in the Bible that is named after a woman. The events take place in the Persian Empire during the reign of king Xerxes, who reigned from 486 to 465 B.C., and deals with the Jews in exile. The story of Esther is a remarkable one, but there is no reference to God in the original text. Does this mean that the events in this story are merely accidental?

Esther 1

King Xerxes summoned queen Vasthi to appear before him, but she did not obey his order and was consequently dismissed as queen.

Esther 2

Esther, the Jewess became King Xerxes's new wife after a beauty pageant had been held in the kingdom.

Esther 3 (story)

Tension 1: Mordecai refuses to kneel before Haman.

[1]Later, King Xerxes promoted Haman the son of Hammedatha to the highest position in his kingdom. Haman was a descendant of Agag, [2]and the king had given orders for his officials at the royal gate to honor Haman by kneeling down to him. All of them obeyed except Mordecai.

Relief of tension: Mordecai is reported to Haman.

[3]When the other officials asked Mordecai why he disobeyed the king's command, [4]he said, 'Because I am a Jew.' They spoke to him for several days about kneeling down, but he still refused to obey. Finally, they reported this to Haman, to find out if he would let Mordecai get away with it.

Result: Haman is furious and makes plans against the Jews.

[5]Haman was furious to learn that Mordecai refused to kneel down and honor him. [6]And when he found out that Mordecai was a Jew, he knew that killing only Mordecai was not enough. Every Jew in the whole kingdom had to be killed. (CEV)

When Mordecai, Esther's uncle, refused to kneel before Haman, the king's right-hand man, the situation became very intense. The power-crazy Haman then decided not only to destroy Mordecai but also all the Jews who were in exile in the Persian Empire. Haman persuaded the king to sign a dangerous proclamation, which ordered that on a certain day all the Jews would be destroyed. The exiled Jews cried, fasted and lamented when they heard about this. In the meantime, Mordecai informed Esther, who had become queen, about these events and told her that her people needed her. So she put her own life in danger to save the nation. Esther's courage brought about a *drastic turn* in the situation.

Esther invited the king and Haman to dinner. At first, she did not discuss the matter regarding the Jews but simply invited them again for dinner the next day. That night, the king was unable to sleep and read his palace documents. When he did so, he discovered that Mordecai had saved his life some time ago. Mordecai had heard about a plot to murder the king and had told the king about it. However, he had never been rewarded for this deed. The next day, the king asked Haman for advice on how to reward someone. Haman was under the impression that the king wanted to reward him and immediately made a suggestion about how it should be done. To his shock and dismay, Haman was told that the king wanted to reward Mordecai—and Haman was forced to honor him. During the dinner, Esther told the king about Haman's plot to kill her and the Jews. The king commanded that Haman be hanged on the gallows that had originally been built for Mordecai.

The king then made a second proclamation in favor of the exiles that enabled them to defend themselves on the day that Haman had initially planned to kill them. The Jews did this very successfully, and the day of their destruction became a day of victory. Up to this day, the Jews celebrate this day as the Purim festival. All these things happened without any reference to God in the original text. However, this did not mean that God was absent but rather that He was working behind the scenes to ensure that:

- an orphan (a Jewess) became queen
- Mordecai heard about the plot to murder the king
- the king could not fall asleep one night
- the king read in the palace documents that Mordecai had saved his life
- the plot of Haman was uncovered and he was executed

We could so easily ascribe this to chance. Yet those things we so easily attribute to chance, intuition, premonition and fate could very well be the Spirit of God wanting to meet us again. The working of the Spirit is often not a spectacle but a graceful work in the shadows of our lives!

 Thank You, Lord, that You are involved in the shadows of my life.

The working of the Spirit is often not a spectacle but graceful work in the shadows of our lives!

MEET THE SPIRIT OF GOD ANEW . . . IN WRESTLING WITH GRIEF

Grief is part of our lives. The question is whether we can also meet the Spirit when we experience grief. The book of Ruth will help us with this.

Ruth 1 (story)

Tension: Famine

¹In the days when the judges ruled there was a famine in the land,

Relief of tension: Naomi and her family move away

and a man of Bethlehem in Judah went to sojourn in the country of Moab, he and his wife and his two sons. ²The name of the man was Elimelech and the name of his wife Naomi, and the names of his two sons were Mahlon and Chilion. They were Ephrathites from Bethlehem in Judah. They went into the country of Moab and remained there.

Result: Naomi's husband and her two sons die

³But Elimelech, the husband of Naomi, died, and she was left with her two sons. ⁴These took Moabite wives; the name of the one was Orpah and the name of the other Ruth. They lived there about ten years, ⁵and both Mahlon and Chilion died, so that the woman was left without her two sons and her husband. (ESV)

During times of sorrow, we often ask, "Why? Why me?" The truth of the matter is that we are not always able to explain everything. We might as well admit this. We are like fragile clay pots. However, although we cannot explain everything, we can be comforted by the thought that the Spirit is involved in our sorrow.

The Spirit groans with us and intercedes on our behalf when our prayers only seem to be reaching as far as the ceiling. "The Spirit helps us in our weakness. For we do not know what to pray for as we ought, but the Spirit himself intercedes for us with groanings too deep for words" (Rom. 8:26, ESV). The Spirit provides peace and joy. "For the kingdom of God is not a matter of eating and drinking but of righteousness and peace and joy in the Holy Spirit" (Rom. 14:17, ESV). The Spirit also provides wisdom and insight. For instance, after an intense struggle, the author of Psalm 73 came to the conclusion that the end result of the wicked was something terrible, that he had been unfair toward God, and that God had always been with him.

It is like the man who was marooned on an island and waited for a ship to rescue him. One day as he walked along the beach, he saw a crate that had been washed up on the shore. When he opened it, he found that it contained a small gas stove and all kinds of useful things. The man then thanked God for not forgetting him.

One day, the man made some nice food on the stove. While the food was cooking on the stove, he went to the beach to pray. When he looked up, he saw that his hut and wooden plate were on fire. The wind had blown over the small gas stove. In anger, he returned to the beach to wrestle with God in prayer, crying, "Why? Why?"

Then the man looked out over the ocean and saw a ship heading straight toward the island. It was a ship that had come to rescue him. When he was safely on board, the man asked the captain of the ship, "How did you know that I was there?" The captain answered, "We saw the fire that you made."

The Spirit creates new possibilities for our lives. The book of Ruth is a good example of this. When Naomi and her family move to Moab because of a drought, she loses her husband and, later, her two sons. Naomi's future is dark—she is in a dead-end street! But then she gets out of her comfort zone and returns to Judah with her daughter-in-law, Ruth. Naomi soon arranges for Ruth to marry Boaz, an unmarried relative of Naomi. Obed is born from this marriage. Naomi's life changed from that of a helpless widow to that of a joyful grandmother. The Spirit led her through her pain—and not just from it! This happened because she was prepared to step out of her comfort zone and get on with life.

So, where does the story end? Although Naomi did not realize it at the time, her descendents would one day unlock a part of world history, as her family would eventually become part of Jesus' genealogy (Matt. 1).

 Oh Spirit, thank You for being involved in the struggles of my heartache.

The Spirit does not lead us from heartache but rather through it!

MEET THE SPIRIT OF GOD ANEW . . . IN EMOTIONS

Emotions are part of our humanness. But is it possible to also meet the Holy Spirit there? In other words, can the Spirit also meet us there? This is an important question, because many believers consider the combination of emotion and faith to be a thorny issue. Many believers think that emotions are not important in religion. Just think about some of the following well-known warnings:

- Be careful not to get too emotional.
- You cannot trust your feelings.
- Beware not to build your faith on feelings.

Consequently, emotions have received second-class status in the lives of many believers. Therefore, emotions are either ignored or suppressed (e.g., such as at funerals). This could be the reason why we often refer to "cold" and "dead" churches. The Bible, however, teaches us to think differently about emotions. God made us total people. We have a mind (cognitive), a will (conative) and emotions (affective). Thus, the Spirit cannot be restricted to certain segments of humanness. Indeed, the Bible is loaded with emotions.

Some examples of emotions in Scripture include:

- **Love:** Love is a crucial emotion. According to the Bible, love is the greatest attainment. "For now there are faith, hope and love. But of these three, the greatest is love" (1 Cor. 13:13, CEV). "God loved the people of this world so much that he gave his only Son, so that everyone who has faith in him will have eternal life and never really die" (John 3:16, CEV). Jesus commanded His followers to love God with all their heart (Matt. 22:37). Furthermore, Paul lists love as the first fruit of the Spirit (Gal. 5:22).
- **Praise:** Psalm 149:1–2 states, "Shout praises to the LORD! Sing him a new song of praise when his loyal people meet. *People of Israel, rejoice* because of your Creator. *People of Zion, celebrate* because of your King" (CEV).
- **Happiness and Joy:** Second Corinthians 9:7 states, "God loves a cheerful giver" (ESV). Instructions for a Christian life are full of emotions (Rom. 12:9–18).
- **Peace:** Jesus left us a legacy of peace. "Each one of you is part of the body of Christ, and you were chosen to live together in peace. So let the peace that comes from Christ control your thoughts. And be grateful" (Col. 3:15, CEV). When Paul was in jail, the peace of Christ carried him through. "Always be glad because of the Lord! I will say it again: Be glad. Always be gentle with others. The Lord will soon be here. Don't worry about anything, but pray about everything. With thankful hearts offer up your prayers and requests to God. Then, because you belong to Christ Jesus, God will bless you with peace that no one can completely understand. And this peace will control the way you think and feel" (Phil. 4:4–7, CEV).

As far as the Church is concerned, I believe that we have attenuated our emotions of raising our hands, using music and even giving hugs. The emotions mentioned in the Bible do not exclude these acts, but it also definitely includes more than this. When you express your feelings, you show that you are honest and sincere toward yourself and others. These are the two ingredients for any successful relationship.

To conclude, God gave us a *mind*—use it to get to know Him better. He gave us a *will*—use it to obey Him. And He gave us *emotions*—we need to show them.

 Thank You, Spirit of God, that I can experience You working in my life.

The essence is that the Holy Spirit expects sincerity deep in one's heart!

MEET THE SPIRIT OF GOD ANEW . . . IN CHURCH

It sounds strange that one should meet the Spirit anew in church. However, it would be a good idea to gain some clarity on the Spirit's workings in church, because this has caused so much discord. The working of the Spirit in church can be divided into three main sections: tongues, the fruit of the Spirit, and the gifts of the Spirit.

1. The *Tongues* of the Holy Spirit: Acts 2 (story):

Tension: The disciples speak in other languages

[7]They were excited and amazed, and said:
Don't all these who are speaking come from Galilee? [8]Then why do we hear them speaking our very own languages? [9]Some of us are from Parthia, Media, and Elam. Others are from Mesopotamia, Judea, Cappadocia, Pontus, Asia, [10]Phrygia, Pamphylia, Egypt, parts of Libya near Cyrene, Rome, [11]Crete, and Arabia. Some of us were born Jews, and others of us have chosen to be Jews.

Relief of tension: Everyone could listen to the gospel in his or her own language!

[11]Yet we all hear them using our own languages to tell the wonderful things God has done.

Result: Amazement and mockery

[12]Everyone was excited and confused. Some of them even kept asking each other, 'What does all this mean?'
[13]Others made fun of the Lord's followers and said, 'They are drunk.' (CEV)

The coming of the Spirit goes hand in hand with speaking in other languages. Which languages? All the languages of the known world at that time. At Pentecost, all of the Jews were present in Jerusalem. These Jews spoke different languages, but during the outpouring of the Holy Spirit, all the disciples, to the amazement of everyone present, spoke all the languages of the visiting Jews. What caused this? It was the Holy Spirit.

The meaning of speaking in different languages was therefore the bonding of all those who believed. The Bible also talks about a different form of speaking—*glossolalia,* or the gift of tongues—which describes the ability or phenomenon to utter words or sounds of a language unknown to the speaker, especially as an expression of religious ecstasy. Paul suggests that when such speaking occurs, it should be explained (1 Cor. 14:5). His reason for this is so that it can be for the edification and unity of the congregation.

2. The *Fruit* of the Spirit: Galatians 5 (explanation)

[19]The acts of the sinful nature are obvious: sexual immorality, impurity and debauchery; [20]idolatry and witchcraft; hatred, discord, jealousy, fits of rage, selfish ambition, dissensions, factions [21]and envy; drunkenness, orgies, and the like. I warn you, as I did before, that those who live like this will not inherit the kingdom of God.

²²But the fruit of the Spirit is love, joy, peace, patience, kindness, goodness, faithfulness, ²³gentleness and self-control. Against such things there is no law. (TNIV)

Sin might seem very enticing at first, but it eventually leads to division and destroys people and communities. The fruit of the Spirit stands in direct contrast to sinful practices such as hatred, discord and jealousy. The meaning of the fruit of the Spirit is to bind people together. Love, joy and peace are precisely those things that prevent relationships from disintegrating.

3. The *Gifts* of the Spirit: 1 Corinthians 12 (explanation)

¹Now concerning spiritual gifts, brothers, I do not want you to be uninformed. ⁴Now there are varieties of gifts, but the same Spirit;
⁵and there are varieties of service, but the same Lord; ⁶and there are varieties of activities, but it is the same God who empowers them all in everyone. ⁷To each is given the manifestation of the Spirit for the common good. (ESV)

A variety of gifts were distributed among the believers: the gift of teaching (Rom. 12:7), the gift of serving (v. 7), the gift of encouraging (v. 8), the gift of generosity (v. 8), the gift of being a leader (v. 8), the gift of showing mercy (v. 8), the gift of wisdom and knowledge, and many others. Each believer received a gift. The fact is that we should not regard someone's gift as superior to that of another, as this will cause discord. After all, the gifts of the Spirit should be to everyone's advantage. The meaning of the gifts is to unite all the believers in one body.

The languages, fruit and gifts of the Spirit were given to unite believers. The reason for this is spelled out in John 13:35: "If you love each other, everyone will know that you are my disciples" (CEV). The essence is thus that *the Spirit binds all God's children together!*

 Spirit of God, I want to speak the language of love. I want to give expression to Your fruit and use my gifts to the advantage of everyone.

We do not need to wait for the Holy Spirit to come: he came on the day of Pentecost.
He has never left the church.
—John R. W. Stott (b. 1921), *English pastor and evangelist*

ARE WE GOOD ENOUGH FOR HEAVEN?

When we look at our lives and notice all the defects we have, we sometimes wonder whether we are really worthy of going to heaven. The truth is nobody is good enough to go to heaven; therefore, this question need no longer worry us. All people are equal in this regard. Fortunately, the gates of heaven are open. But for whom?

Romans 4 (explanation)

[13]God promised Abraham and his descendants that he would give them the world. This promise wasn't made because Abraham had obeyed a law, but because his faith in God made him acceptable. [14]If Abraham and his descendants were given this promise because they had obeyed a *law*, then faith would mean nothing, and the promise would be worthless. [15]God becomes angry when his *Law* is broken. But where there isn't a *law*, it cannot be broken. (CEV)

No one, not even the Pharisees, could meet the standards required by the Law, for if you transgressed one law, you were guilty. This is why Paul wrote in Romans 3:23 that everyone has sinned and is far from God. The only way to have the right relationship with God is through faith.

The Jews thought that Abraham came to be in God's good book because he lived a good live. The Jews were of the opinion that a person could have this right relationship with God by adhering to the Law of Moses. Of course, Abraham could not do this, as he lived about 400 years before Moses and his Law. It must have come as a surprise to the recipients of the letter to hear that Abraham received the promise and, through faith, had the right relationship with God. He trusted God when God called him to leave everything behind and move to a foreign land. He trusted God that he would have a child despite his old age. He trusted God when he had to sacrifice Isaac.

Faith in God means to trust Him. Faith enables us to focus on Christ and not on ourselves. Nobody is good enough for heaven. We do not build our religious assurance on our good works—which is just as well, as nobody would have made it. Fortunately, the gates of heaven are wide open to those who trust in Christ. The anchor of a ship is not cast on the first deck but over the side of the ship. Similarly, our religious anchor does not rest in ourselves but outside ourselves—in Jesus Christ. That is where our security rests. This is why believers—those who trust in God—go to heaven. Do you believe this?

 Thank You, Lord, that my religious anchor rests outside myself—in You!

If you read history you will find that the Christians who did most for the present world were precisely those who thought most of the next. It is since Christians have largely ceased to think of the other world that they have become so ineffective in this.
—C.S. Lewis (1898–1963), *High-powered Oxford and Cambridge professor and perhaps the twentieth century's most famous convert to Christianity. Lewis was the creator of the Narnia series.*

WHAT MAKES FAITH SO SPECIAL?

The word "faith" is very important to Christians and is used again and again in the Bible. But what makes it so special to have faith? In this next section in Romans, Paul gives us two clear reasons why faith is so special.

Romans 4 (explanation)

[16]That is why it depends on faith, in order that the promise may rest on grace and be guaranteed to all his *offspring*—not only to the adherent of the law but also to the one who shares the faith of Abraham, who is the father of *us all*, [17]as it is written, 'I have made you the father of *many nations*'—in the presence of the God in whom he believed, who gives life to the dead and calls into existence the things that do not exist. (ESV)

First, according to verse 16, we believe by grace. In yesterday's reading, we saw that God's favor cannot be acquired by doing good deeds and by obeying rules. We are like beggars when it comes to God's promises. We have nothing to offer God and are merely the recipients of his grace. God never asked us what we would offer Him in return for the wonderful promises in the Bible. There was nothing in it for Him, except risk. And the worst that could possibly happen happened: His only Son was crucified. People disappointed God so much at that time, and we continue to do so today. Even Abraham could not offer God anything. Instead, God was the one who reached out to him. This is grace—undeserved favor. This is why faith is so special!

Second, faith is not only something individualistic but also something that concerns relationships. This is why Paul uses the following words when he speaks about faith: "offspring," "us all" and "many nations." Faith does not only bind us to Jesus but also to our fellow believers. Faith is not something we do on our own; it makes us part of other believers. Faith prevents us from becoming lonely and ensures that we can enjoy intimacy within relationships. This is why faith is so special!

 Lord Jesus, today I give thanks that I can be a beggar for Your grace. Thank You that faith unites me with You and with others!

Faith is to believe what we do not see; and the reward of this faith is to see what we believe.
—Saint Augustine (354–386), *Christian theologian, rhetor, North African bishop and doctor of the Roman Catholic Church*

WE DOUBT SO EASILY . . .

It is easy to have faith when things go well, but so easy to doubt as soon as things begin to go wrong. In this section, Paul uses Abraham as an example of someone who kept on believing despite a bad situation in which he found himself.

Romans 4 (explanation)

[18]God promised Abraham a lot of descendants. And when it all seemed hopeless, Abraham still had faith in God and became the ancestor of many nations. [19]Abraham's faith never became weak, not even when he was nearly a hundred years old. He knew that he was almost dead and that his wife Sarah could not have children. [20]But Abraham never doubted or questioned God's promise. His faith made him strong, and he gave all the credit to God. [21]Abraham was certain that God could do what he had promised. (CEV)

God asked Abraham to move from Ur in order to become the father of many nations. At that stage, Abraham and his wife had no children. Abraham moved, and when he reached the age of 100, he was still childless. By this time, he and Sarah were too old to have children. It seemed that no hope remained for them. But Abraham continued to trust in God and believe that God would fulfill His promises.

Someone once said that God can be very slow but is never late. Our timing and God's timing are not always the same. Things might happen in your life that seem to indicate that God wants to send you in a certain direction. Later on, you might discover that this is not the case. This means that you do not understand God. On the other hand, wonderful things that you did not ask for might happen to you.

Someone else once said that if God had answered all his prayers, he would not have been married to his wife and would not have been as successful as he was. God closed doors that he wanted open. Looking back, he was grateful because God blessed him abundantly. Abraham focused on God and trusted that He would not disappoint him. May the Lord help you when you doubt and help you to gain confidence in Him merely because He is God. Abraham set an example for us in this regard.

 Lord, help me to carry on believing, despite my circumstances.

Doubt is the beginning not the end of wisdom.
—Author unknown

HAVE WE BEEN ACCEPTED BY GOD?

Paul often used the word "accepted" in his letter to the Romans. We should therefore know what this word means and whether we have been accepted (acquitted).

Romans 4 (explanation)

[22]That's why 'God *accepted* Abraham because he believed. So his faith made him right with God.'
[23]The words 'God *accepted* Abraham's faith' were written not only for Abraham. [24]They were written also for us. We believe in the God who raised Jesus our Lord from the dead. So God will *accept* our faith and *make us right* with himself.
[25]Jesus was handed over to die for our sins. He was raised to life in order to *make us right* with God.
(NIRV)

At the beginning of the previous century, the idea that "accepted" should be understood from a legal perspective was very prevalent in the Church. God was depicted as the judge, Jesus the advocate, Satan the accuser and the Holy Spirit the witness, while each of us were in the dock. We are found guilty and sentenced to death. Jesus, as our advocate, pleads for our acquittal because He died on our behalf. The Holy Spirit is called on as a witness to confirm this. Then the verdict is read that we have been *acquitted* on the basis of what Jesus did and because of the Holy Spirit's testimony (Rom 8:16). This means that we are free of all guilt.

This sounds fine, but I think we should think differently about the matter. The Greek word *dikaiosune* (righteousness), which is translated as "accepted" or "make right with God" (v. 25) should be understood differently. Why? Because the Bible does not teach that we have a legal relationship with God (judge and accused) but that we have a father-child relationship with Him instead. When Jesus taught His disciples to pray, He started with "Our Father in heaven," not "our Judge in heaven." The father-child relationship projects love and warmth, but the judge-accused relationship projects distance and fear. If we believe and confess that Jesus' blood has redeemed us, then we are acquitted and accepted because only faith in Jesus can ensure that we have the correct relationship with God.

 I want to honor and praise You so that by faith I can enjoy the right relationship with You once more.

There is no justification without sanctification, no forgiveness without renewal of life, no real faith from which the fruits of new obedience do not grow.
—Martin Luther (1483–1546), *German priest and scholar whose questioning of certain Church practices led to the Protestant Reformation*

ARE YOU SUPER-RELIGIOUS?

A young lady once knocked on my door, hoping that I would subscribe to one of the series of books she was promoting. She wanted to know what work I did. When I answered her that I was a church minister, she responded by saying, "So you are super-religious!" I surprised her by saying that in actual fact I was not very religious. She frowned and asked me how I could be a minister and not be religious. The following section formed the basis of what I answered her.

Romans 12 (explanation and instruction)

[1]And so, dear brothers and sisters,
I plead with you to give your bodies to God *(instruction)*
because of all he has done for you. (explanation)
Let them be a living and holy sacrifice—
the kind he will find acceptable. *(instruction)*
This is truly the way to worship him. *(explanation)* NLT

My answer to the young lady was that in essence, religion focuses on what we can do for God, while being a Christian focuses on what God can do for us. This is very different! Before Paul asked the believers to do anything, he used the words "because of all he has done for you" to justify his warnings. We should focus on God's mercy and His grace—that which God in Christ did for you and me! Our response to His great mercy should be to dedicate ourselves fully to Him. Paul calls this "truly the way to worship him," meaning that to live for Christ, is the most *logical reaction* to God's grace.

Blaise Pascal, the seventeenth-century French philosopher, said: "There are only two classes of persons who can be called reasonable: those who serve God with all of their hearts because they know Him and those who seek God with all of their hearts because they do not know Him."

 Lord, Help me to serve You with much more enthusiasm and dedication.

Religion is like holding on to a rock in the middle of a raging river; faith is learning how to swim.
—Author unknown

SOMETHING A GOVERNMENT CANNOT CONQUER BUT WE CAN!

The citizens of a country are not always positive about their government. There are many reasons for this, such as corruption, bad administration and the wanton waste of taxpayers' hard-earned money. When these things occur, the government is blamed for the inability to set things in order. Paul, however, writes very positively about government. He tells us that we should submit ourselves to our governing authorities. Before we set about criticizing Paul, we should briefly consider why Paul made this request.

Romans 13 (explanation and instruction)

[1]Obey the rulers who have authority over you. (*instruction*)
Only God can give authority to anyone,
and he puts these rulers in their places of power.
[2]People who oppose the authorities are opposing what God has done, and they will be punished. (*explanation*) CEV

Although Jesus died and rose again and there is now a Church on earth, sin still prevails. For this reason, God established authorities (v. 1) to prevent things from getting out of hand. Paul realized that if the government of his day (namely, the Roman government) were not respected, there would be chaos. The laws of government that instill fear in people prevent society from deteriorating into chaos. Governments can never conquer the evil in people, but they can prevent it from erupting into violence and chaos.

The Church cannot fulfill this function, because it has not been called to keep people in check through authority and violence. Instead, the Church has been called to conquer evil through good. This means that a believer's behavior is motivated from the inside by means of love and not from the outside by means of punishment and fear for authority. Love says "I want to," while fear says "I have to." As believers representing the Church of Christ, we are called to use the good—from the inside—to conquer evil. We should keep on praying for the authorities to perform their duties and responsibilities to the benefit of us all.

 Lord, I pray that the Holy Spirit will enable me to conquer evil with good.

The church must be reminded that it is not the master or the servant of the state, but rather the conscience of the state. It must be the guide and the critic of the state, and never its tool.
—Martin Luther King, Jr. (1929–1968), *American Baptist minister, Civil Rights leader and winner of the Nobel Prize in 1964*

THE ONE ACCOUNT WE WILL NEVER BE ABLE TO SETTLE!

It is so much easier to incur debt than to repay it. It is possible to settle all our debt, but there is one account we can never settle.

Romans 13 (explanation and instruction)

[8]Let love be your only debt! (instruction) If you love others, you have done all that the Law demands. [9]In the Law there are many commands, such as, 'Be faithful in marriage. Do not murder. Do not steal. Do not want what belongs to others.' But all of these are summed up in the command that says, 'Love others as much as you love yourself.' [10]No one who loves others will harm them. So love is all that the Law demands. (explanation) (CEV)

Love is what we owe to each other. We can never settle the debt of love, because each of us needs it every day. In this passage, Paul mentions twice that love is the complete fulfillment of the Law. By this, he means that love makes the Law perfect. The Pharisees tried to obey the Law, but without love. This is why Jesus reprimanded them and healed people on the Sabbath—to their great dismay. The Pharisees did not understand that love makes the Law perfect.

If we love God, we will not want to commit adultery, murder or steal. We need to focus on our love for God and not, like the Pharisees, on the Law. A golf player focuses on the ball and not on the hole. If he or she hits the ball well, it will hopefully bear good results. In the same way, we should focus on God's love—and then love for our neighbor will come naturally. If we know that Jesus forgives us, we will be able to forgive our neighbor. If we love God, we will never go bankrupt because of the love account you have to pay! Let us pay our debts of love!

 Lord, help me to start immediately to pay my accounts of love.

There is no remedy for love but to love more.
—Henry David Thoreau (1817–1862), *American naturalist, poet and philosopher*

WHAT IF CHRISTIANS DIFFER AMONG THEMSELVES?

It is sad when Christians fight among themselves—usually about trivial matters! However, should Christians always agree about everything?

Romans 14 (explanation and instruction)

[1]Accept those whose faith is *weak*. Don't judge them where you have differences of opinion. (*instruction*)

[2]The faith of some people allows them to eat anything. But others eat only vegetables because their faith is weak. (*explanation*)

[3]People who eat everything must not look down on those who do not. And people who don't eat everything must not judge those who do. *God has accepted them.* (*instruction*) (NIRV)

In Paul's day, the believers differed among themselves on what food was pure and what food was impure. Some believers only ate vegetables, because they considered all other food impure. According to these believers, the other Christians were committing sin by eating the so-called impure food. Paul referred to these believers as weak, because they did not realize that they were free and could eat any food they wished. They desperately clung to their beliefs and considered certain things impure and sinful that clearly were not so.

Although Paul spoke to both groups, he agreed with the strong ones. He asked them to accept the weak ones and not to despise them. The strong ones could win the argument that all food was pure but could lose the person. It was therefore good not to get involved in such unnecessary arguments. Paul also instructed the weak believers, who considered all kinds of things sinful, not to judge the believers who differed from them in their beliefs.

A wonderful explanation then follows: "God has accepted them." Even today, believers have different opinions on moral issues (such as drinking, visiting night clubs and homosexuality) and dogmatic issues (such as baptism). Instead, we should all agree to disagree. Let's learn to accept one another and not condemn each other . . . because God has accepted us!

 Lord, forgive me for judging others so easily. Help me to accept them, even though I might not always agree with them on certain things.

In essentials, unity; in differences, liberty; in all things, charity.
—Philipp Melanchthon (1497–1560), *German professor and theologian, key leader of the Reformation and a friend and associate of Martin Luther*

GODLY NONSENSE?

Just the other day, someone told me nonchalantly that he was not a churchgoer. Speaking to him made me realize that more and more Christianity doesn't appeal to people. In fact, it often pushes people away! Paul understood only too well why people consider Christianity nonsense. Let us call it godly nonsense!

1 Corinthians 1 (explanation)

[22]Jews ask for miracles, and Greeks want something that sounds wise.
[23]But we preach that Christ was nailed to a cross. Most Jews have problems with this, and most Gentiles think it is foolish.
[24]Our message is God's power and wisdom for the Jews and the Greeks that he has chosen.
[25]Even when God is foolish, he is wiser than everyone else, and even when God is weak, he is stronger than everyone else. (CEV)

The Jews and the Greeks regarded the message of the cross as nonsense. The Jews expected a Messiah who would act with power and authority. They therefore considered it repulsive that someone whose life ended shamefully on a cross could be the Son of God. The Greeks believed that it was an insult to God to get involved in human matters. They believed that God was *apathetic* and devoid of emotion. If God were to show any emotion, it would mean that the behavior of human beings could influence Him. Therefore, the message of the cross, which demonstrated God's passion for people, made no sense to them.

Throughout the New Testament we discover this godly nonsense. For instance, do you know of any other God who came to earth as a baby? Do you know of any other God who was born in a stable? (Buckingham Palace would have made more sense!) Do you know of any other God who was brought up in poverty or who died as a criminal and was buried in a borrowed grave? Do you know of any other God whose teachings were regarded as total nonsense? After all, who could really take Jesus' teachings seriously when He taught, "Love your enemies, and be good to everyone who hates you" (Luke 6:17, CEV)? Or, "If someone slaps you on one cheek, don't stop that person from slapping you on the other cheek" (Luke 6:29, CEV)? This just doesn't make sense.

However, the incredible part is that this godly nonsense contains more wisdom than the wisdom of human beings. It shows that God's supposed weakness (His death on the cross) was greater than the power of human beings (1 Cor. 1:25). God showed this by using His tender love to turn a cross—a symbol of hate—into a symbol of hope. With time, human beings discovered that this godly nonsense was the only way to real happiness.

 Thank You, Lord that the so-called godly nonsense is in fact wisdom and strength!

*God heals the sicknesses and the griefs by making the sicknesses and the griefs his suffering
and his grief. In the image of the crucified God the sick and dying can see themselves,
because in them the crucified God recognizes himself.*
—Jürgen Moltmann (b. 1926), *German theologian*

THERE IS MORE ON THE MENU THAN JUST MILKSHAKES!

Many believers have a longing to grow in their faith. They are tired of being spiritual babies who live on milk alone. They realize that there is more on the menu than just milkshakes. Let us call this the "steaks," or "solid food," of the Bible.

1 Corinthians 3 (explanation)

[1]My friends, you are acting like the *people of this world*. That's why I could not speak to you as spiritual people. You are like babies as far as your faith in Christ is concerned.
[2]So I had to treat you like babies and feed you milk. You could not take solid food, and you still cannot, [3]because you are not yet spiritual. You are jealous and argue with each other. This proves that you are not spiritual and that you are acting like the people of this world.
[4]Some of you say that you follow me, and others claim to follow Apollos. Isn't that how ordinary people behave? (CEV)

Paul had promised to speak to the Corinthians on more profound matters. However, he could not do this, because they would not have been able to understand it. They were still like babies in their faith (v. 1) and had not grown spiritually since the previous time when Paul had brought them the gospel. How did Paul know this? The believers in Corinth were fighting and were jealous of each other (v. 3). This had led to the formation of different groups in the congregation: on the one side those who supported Paul; on the other side those who supported Apollos.

Such conduct belonged to worldly people, which is why Paul compared them to worldly people. It does not befit a spiritually mature person to form groups and to be jealous! Such behavior harms relationships and leads to the formation of cliques. A spiritually mature person focuses on good relationships and unity. A spiritually mature person does not study the Children's Bible (milk) but obtains his or her solid food in the books of the Bible (v. 2). Milk can easily be drunk straight from a glass while a person is standing at the fridge, but to eat solid food you have to sit at a table. So let's partake of the books of the Bible and allow this solid food to give us strength of faith to grow away from jealousy and the formation of cliques!

 Lord, I want to feed my faith with the solid food of Your word!

It ain't those parts of the Bible that I can't understand that bother me,
it is the parts that I do understand.
—Mark Twain (1835–1910), *American humorist, writer and lecturer*

EFFECTIVE PEOPLE LIVE ACCORDING TO THIS PRINCIPLE!

To be effective in the race of life, it is important to live according to the principle Paul describes in the next section. In this passage in 1 Corinthians, Paul refers to the Istmic games. This was a big sports event that was held in Corinth every other year.

1 Corinthians 9 (explanation and instruction)

[24]You know that many runners enter a race,
and only one of them wins the prize. (*explanation*)
So run to win! (*instruction*)
[25]Athletes work hard to win a crown that cannot last,
but we do it for a crown that will last forever. (*explanation*) CEV

Paul noticed that the athletes at the Istmic games in Corinth followed the principle of "begin with the end in mind!" To live according to this principle meant that you worked backward from where you wanted to end up and made choices that would lead you there. The athletes were disciplined and motivated because they had set their minds on the crown of victory, which Paul understood was exactly what would help believers to be effective.

In his book *Seven Habits of Highly Effective Families*, Stephen Covey tells about a three-year old boy who waited for his dad to return home from work. He greeted his dad with these words: "Daddy, I'm a hard-working boy." What the father didn't know was that half an hour before, the kitchen floor had been under water. The boy had wanted to help his mother (who was busy elsewhere in the house) wash the dishes, but had not been able to reach the sink. So he had decided to take water from the fridge instead. Unfortunately, he dropped the bottle of water on the floor.

When his mother saw the mess in the kitchen, she asked him very calmly, "Son, what's going on here?" After the boy had explained what had happened, she helped him to mop up the floor. She then asked her son to tell her the next time he wished to wash the dishes, because then she could pull up a chair for him and help him. This little boy experienced appreciation and love. If the mother had scolded him, he would have felt guilty and embarrassed. Then he would have been his father's bad boy.

This mother realized that the education of her child was more important than a clean floor. In the race of faith, we should also realize that the everlasting crown of eternal life surpasses all other ultimate destinations. May this motivate us not to despair but to run the race of life with faith, hope and love.

 Lord, thank You that I can start the race of faith every day with the end in sight.

We may be very busy, we may be very efficient, but we will also be truly effective
only when we begin with the end in mind.
—Stephen R. Covey (b. 1932), *Author of the international best-selling book* The Seven Habits of
Highly Effective People, *first published in 1989*

SETTING A GOOD EXAMPLE

As the saying goes, "example is better than precept." In this next section, Paul explains how we can set a good example. He encourages us to surround ourselves with something specific, because this will inspire us to set a good example.

1 Corinthians 10 (explanation and instruction)

[31]When you eat or drink or do anything else,
always do it to honor God.
[32]Don't cause problems for Jews or Greeks or anyone else who belongs to God's church.
-*(instruction)*
[33]I always try to please others instead of myself,
in the hope that many of them will be saved. *(explanation)*
11 [1]You must follow my example,
as I follow the example of Christ. *(instruction)* CEV

It is not always easy to set a good example. What one person might consider to be right might be totally unacceptable to the next person—for instance, things such as smoking, visiting night clubs, playing the lotto and drinking alcohol. In this passage, however, Paul gives us three clear instructions to help us set a good example.

First, we should do everything for God's glory (v. 31). God should be part of our lives to such an extent that we will do everything to glorify His name. For instance, how we talk to people, our attitude while waiting in long lines and how we handle criticism should always reflect a lifestyle that will honor God.

Second, Paul instructs us not to offend anyone. How do we do this? Paul gives us the answer in verse 33: We should consider God's interests and those of other human beings above our own. This means that we should sometimes refrain from doing things that are not really wrong in the true sense of the word but which could offend other people.

Third, Paul says that we should follow his example. He was a good role model because he strived to follow Jesus' example. If we imitate good role models, we will be a good example to others. So let's surround ourselves with good role models, for this will inspire us!

 Lord, help me to be a good role model. Please give me the wisdom to act in a way that does not dishonor You.

Example is not the main thing in influencing others. It is the only thing.
—Albert Schweitzer (1875–1965), *German theologian, philosopher and physician*

IS THERE LIFE AFTER DEATH?

We have so many questions about God and the Bible, but we do not always have the answers. Do we have an answer to the question whether there is life after death? Let us have a look.

1 Corinthians 15 (explanation and instruction)

> [56]Sin is what gives death its sting,
> and the Law is the power behind sin.
> [57]But thank God for letting our Lord Jesus Christ
> give us the victory! *(explanation)*
> [58]My dear friends, stand firm and don't be shaken.
> Always keep busy working for the Lord. *(instruction)*
> You know that everything you do for him
> is worthwhile. *(explanation)* CEV

The entire chapter of 1 Corinthians 15 deals with the question of whether there is life after death. In this chapter, Paul compares death to a bee with a dangerous sting—the sting of sin. God allowed the "bee of death" to pierce Jesus (and not us) on the cross with its sting of *sin*, thereby causing His death. However, when Jesus was resurrected from the grave, the bee of death was conquered and lost its poisonous sting of sin (v. 57). Our relationship of faith with Jesus enables us to share in this victory. We should thank God for this (v. 57).

Although we might at times feel that being a Christian is all in vain (v. 58), the fact that there is life after death makes it worth our while to persevere. We should, however, not content ourselves with the question whether there is life after death. The following graffiti was once seen on a wall: "Is there life after death?" Someone then came and wrote the following beneath it: "Is there life before death?" Considering all the hurt and sorrow of life, this is a very significant question. Sometimes we worry so much about life after death that we battle to lead a meaningful life on this side of the grave (v. 58). Paul therefore warns us to stand firm, to let nothing move us and to give ourselves fully to God's work (v. 58). We therefore have the responsibility to convince humankind that we can live completely before death.

 Lord, thank You that You made life after death possible. Help me to live a full life before death.

> *If I think more about death than some other people, it is probably*
> *because I love life more than they do.*
> —Angelina Jolie (b. 1975), American actress

WHAT DO WE ALL NEED FROM TIME TO TIME?

Life, with all its sharp edges, has a way of getting us down. From time to time, despondency bowls us over. During such times, we need something specific to help us carry on with life. Paul writes about this in the following section.

2 Corinthians 1 (explanation)

> ³Praise God, the Father of our Lord Jesus Christ! The Father is a *merciful* God, who always gives us *comfort*. ⁴He *comforts* us when we are in trouble, so that we can share that same *comfort* with others in trouble. ⁵We share in the terrible sufferings of Christ, but also in the wonderful *comfort* he gives. (CEV)

Paul experienced great difficulties as a missionary, but he did not seek sympathy in his letter to the Corinthians. Instead, He thanked God. Paul looked back and realized that God had compassion on him and saved him from every difficult situation (v. 3). He compared the comfort he enjoyed to a relay stick that had to be passed on to those who, like him, experienced difficulties (v. 4).

Difficult times are just a part of life, and during such times the saddened heart seeks comfort. Paul felt so strongly about this that he used the word "comfort" four times in the above three verses. The question is how we can pass on the relay stick of comfort. We can do this by simply showing sincere interest in someone who is in need and by listening to that person before giving answers or making comments prematurely. The person should know and feel that we truly care. A person in need does not expect us to provide the answers, but simply to be sincere in caring. Paul called this "comfort" (v. 3). Let us pass that which we receive from God and others on to each other: the relay stick of comfort!

 Lord, help me to pass on the comfort I receive to others.

God didn't promise days without pain, laughter without sorrow, sun without rain, but He did promise strength for the day, comfort for the tears, and light for the way.
—Author unknown

IS THE GOSPEL STILL RELEVANT?

The gospel is the good news of God who loved the world so much that He gave His only Son so that those who believe in Him would not be lost but enjoy eternal life (John 3:16). Does the gospel still appeal to people today? Let us read.

2 Corinthians 2 (explanation)

[14]I am grateful that God always makes it possible for Christ to lead us to victory. God also helps us spread the knowledge about Christ everywhere, and this knowledge is like the *smell of perfume.* [15-16]In fact, God thinks of us as a *perfume* that brings Christ to everyone. For people who are being saved, this *perfume* has a *sweet smell* and leads them to a better life. But for people who are lost, it has a *bad smell* and leads them to a horrible death. No one really has what it takes to do this work. (CEV)

Today, people do not always see the messenger of the gospel, the Church, in a positive light. But the gospel itself, the good news, will always be relevant because it deals with love. Love transcends time and boundaries. We all look for love, security and acceptance. Through the death and resurrection of Jesus, God proved that He loves us.

However, the gospel also passes judgment. One cannot be neutral toward it. To those who accept it, Paul states, it is like incense, the aroma of victory—a thought that comes from the triumphal procession (v. 14) of a Roman officer after battle. The triumphant officer would show off his captives and his loot in a street parade. Incense was burnt during such an event. The aroma was sweet to the victors but carried the smell of death (v. 16) to those who were conquered.

The gospel is *good news to* those who accept it but *repulsive* to those who reject it. The Church, as the messenger of the gospel, has a major task to do this responsibly and with style—to spread the aroma in a polluted world. May our lives be an example of style and love!

 Almighty God, together with Paul, I thank You that I can be part of Your triumphal procession.

The real truth is that while He came to preach the gospel, His chief object in coming was that there might be a gospel to preach.
—R. W. Dale (1829–1895), *Theologian, pastor and preacher of the civic gospel*

WHAT NOBODY CAN DETECT

We like it when other people meet our expectations. The problem is that we don't always say this to them. For example, spouses expect certain things from each other without communicating it to each other. They assume that their partner simply knows what they want. This is not fair, as nobody can simply detect another person's expectations. Expectations should be shared. Fortunately, God spelled out His expectations to us.

2 Corinthians 5 (explanation and instruction)

[19]That is, in Christ God was *reconciling* the world to himself, not counting their trespasses against them, and entrusting to us the message of reconciliation.
[20]Therefore, we are ambassadors for Christ, God making his appeal through us. We implore you on behalf of Christ, *(explanation)*
be *reconciled* to God. *(instruction)*
[21]For our sake he made him to be sin who knew no sin, so that in him we might become the righteousness of God. *(explanation)* ESV

Paul is very clear on our task as believers, namely to promote reconciliation (v 19). What does "reconciliation" mean? Reconciliation happens when a broken relationship is restored and there is peace. This is exactly what God came to do. Reconciliation was necessary, because sin disrupted all relationships. So God took the initiative by using an exchange to restore peace between Himself and us. He exchanged our sins for His goodness and our disobedience for His Son's obedience.

Jesus became what He was not, being treated as a sinner in order for us to attain what we do not deserve—namely, an acquittal of all guilt (v. 21). Reconciliation is the work of God, and He asks us to be agents of reconciliation (v. 20). We do this by thanking God every day for the restored relationship and by asking Him for the strength to help us live in peace with others. After all, the main commandment is to love God and our fellow human beings. This is the essence of the gospel!

 Lord, help me to fulfill my role as an agent of peace.

True reconciliation is never cheap, for it is based on forgiveness which is costly. Forgiveness in turn depends on repentance, which has to be based on an acknowledgment of what was done wrong, and therefore on disclosure of the truth. You cannot forgive what you do not know.
—Archbishop Desmond Tutu (b. 1931), *South African religious leader and winner of the Nobel Peace Prize in 1984*

HOW MUCH MONEY SHOULD WE GIVE TO THE CHURCH?

Christians differ on giving tithes. Should it be a full tenth? Those who say yes differ on whether it should be a tenth of gross income or net income. Some argue that the tithe is a law of the Old Testament and no longer applies to Christians. This section will shed some light on this important issue.

2 Corinthians 9 (explanation and instruction)

[6]The point is this: whoever sows sparingly will also reap sparingly, and whoever sows bountifully will also reap bountifully. (*explanation*)
[7]Each one must give as he has made up his mind,
not reluctantly or under compulsion, (*instruction*)
for God loves a *cheerful giver.*
[8]And God is able to make all grace abound to you, so that having all sufficiency in all things at all times, you may abound in every good work. [9]As it is written,
'He has distributed freely, he has given to the poor;
his righteousness endures forever.' (*explanation*) ESV

Paul does not ask money for the church's building project or to balance the books. (In those days, "church" referred to a movement rather than to expensive structures.) Instead, he asks for money for the believers in Judea. He does not prescribe how much they should give, but gives a general *guideline* (v. 6). He uses an example from nature of sowing seed. The more seed you sow, the more you will reap. Of course, this might not be in material things but in treasures of the heart—you will become richer in love, friends, helpfulness and peace in God. You never lose your harvest when you sow in the fields of people's needs.

Paul also states that it is important to have the right *attitude* when you give. God loves a cheerful giver (v. 7). Nobody can prescribe how much you should give; the amount should stem from your heart. In addition, Paul notes that *God* is the One who gives us the resources and the attitude in which we should give (v. 8). God knows that generosity works miracles. It does something for the needy: their distress is relieved and their trust in their fellow human beings (and quite often in God) is restored. It does something for the giver: he or she gains friends and has peace in God. And it also does something for God: He is honored and worshiped by grateful hearts.

 Thank You, Lord, for the privilege to give and to receive.

Never measure your generosity by what you give, but rather by what you have left.
—Bishop Fulton J. Sheen (1895–1979), *Roman Catholic bishop*

BEWARE OF THE PLUS FACTOR!

There are people who distort the gospel in subtle ways and then present their distorted gospel as absolute truth. This often leads to spiritual confusion among people, which makes them feel unsure and deprives them of the joy and peace of salvation. This section will help us to keep our cool and beware of the plus factor!

Galatians 1 (explanation)

[6]I am shocked that you have so quickly turned from God, who chose you because of his wonderful kindness. You have believed another message, [7]when there is really only one true message. But some people are causing you trouble and want to make you turn away from the good news about Christ. (CEV)

The first few verses of Paul's letters usually start with a salutation that is followed by thanksgiving: "I thank my God . . ." However, his letter to the believers in Galatia does not contain thanksgiving. Instead of "I thank my God," Paul starts with "I am shocked." Why did he choose to start his letter this way? Because he was very upset that the Galatians had accepted another gospel to the one he had preached to them. He was upset, because the other gospel was a distortion of the true gospel. It had a plus factor—the death of Jesus on the cross plus the Jewish laws and customs were necessary in order to be saved.

This gospel maintained that the death of Jesus was not enough: individuals had to contribute something in addition to the crucifixion of Jesus. Paul saw this as a rejection of Jesus' mercy—something believers receive at no cost. Even today, we should beware of the plus factor. People can tell us very subtly that we have not been (fully) saved if we have not fasted, spoken in tongues or been baptized. But we do not need all these plusses to be saved. Following such a doctrine confuses us and imprisons us. It affects the essence of the gospel, which states that Jesus paid the price for all our sins. His death on the cross was a complete offering. We only have to accept it in faith.

If ever we hear about plusses, it means that another gospel is being exposed. Christians may differ, but we should agree on the essence of the truth in the Bible. It is liberating to go to sleep at night, knowing that our salvation does not depend on what we do but on what Jesus has already done. Our response to the gospel should be a grateful life of dedication to our only Savior, Jesus Christ. We need not be confused! Rest in His mercy!

 Thank You, Jesus, that You paid the full price for me on the cross.

The greatest enemy to human souls is the self-righteous spirit which makes men look to themselves for salvation.
—Charles Spurgeon (1834–1892), *British Baptist preacher who remains highly influential amongst Reformed Christians of different denominations, among whom he is still known as the "prince of preachers"*

WHY DO YOU BELIEVE?

Take a moment to think how you would complete the following sentence: "I believe in Jesus because . . ." This next section in Galatians will help you to complete this sentence. However, realize that there is more than one answer!

Galatians 2 (explanation)

[15]We ourselves are Jews by birth and not Gentile sinners; [16]yet we know that a person is not *justified* by works of the law but through faith in Jesus Christ, so we also have believed in Christ Jesus, in order to be *justified* by faith in Christ and not by works of the law, because by works of the law no one will be *justified*. (ESV)

Paul repeats the word "justified" three times in verse 16. Paul often used this word in his letters. "Justified" means to have the right relationship with God. It is God's desire that we should have the right relationship with Him. But how do we do this?

The Jews believed that if you obeyed the Law of Moses, you would have the right relationship with God. They believed that if you obeyed the Law, you were no longer a sinner. However, Paul, who himself had adhered to the Law, realized after his conversion that the Law cannot ensure that you are in the right relationship with God. He realized that only faith in Jesus could help you to establish the right relationship with God. By believing in Jesus, you confess that you are not in a position to offer God anything for your salvation. You cannot do anything to be in God's good books; it was Jesus' crucifixion alone that restored the right relationship between God and human beings.

Therefore, we are all like beggars who have nothing to offer God in return for our salvation—we can only receive. By believing in Jesus, all of our sins are forgiven. This ensures that we have the right relationship with God. However, this does not render the Law of Moses unimportant. The Jews saw the Law as a *prerequisite* for salvation, but to us, as beggars of God's mercy, it is the *guideline* for our lives. "I believe in Jesus because . . ." it places us in the right relationship with God.

 Lord, thank You that faith helps me to have the right relationship with You.

I believe in Christianity as I believe that the sun has risen: not only because I see it,
but because by it I see everything else.
—C.S. Lewis (1898–1963), *High-powered Oxford and Cambridge professor and perhaps the twentieth*
century's most famous convert to Christianity. Lewis was the creator of the Narnia series.

WHAT HAPPENS WHEN GOD FORGIVES US?

The essence of the gospel is that Christ died in our place and paid the price for our sins. When we accept this in faith, something wonderful happens. Let us read about this!

Galatians 2 (explanation)

¹⁸Suppose I build again what I had destroyed. Then I prove that I break the Law.
¹⁹Because of the law, *I died as far as the law is concerned.* I died so that *I might live for God.*
²⁰*I have been crucified with Christ.* I don't live any longer. *Christ lives in me.* My faith in the Son of God helps me to live my life in my body. He loved me. He gave himself for me. (NIRV)

Paul was very excited about the gospel because he realized that Jesus Christ had done for him what he could not do for himself. His focus shifted from the Law to the cross. The death of Jesus on the cross gave him access to something the Law could not do—forgiveness of sins. This is why his focus shifted from the Law to the cross. With these insights, he realized that wonderful changes occur in people when they realize that their sins are forgiven. What are these changes?

Paul writes, "I died as far as the law is concerned" (v. 19). We no longer need to desperately try and earn salvation by good works. "I might live for God" (v. 19). We already enjoy eternal life because we believe in Jesus and He makes us children of God the Father. "I have been crucified with Christ" (v. 20). The death and resurrection of Jesus means victory over death and forgiveness of sins. The word "with" signifies that we share in the benefits of Jesus' death and resurrection. Finally, "Christ lives in me" (v. 20). The essence of our personality is taken over by the Holy Spirit, and through this we become new.

 Lord Jesus, thank You for doing for me what I could never do for myself. Thank You for forgiving me, not because I am so smart but because You are so merciful. Thank You for all the wonderful changes that become part of me through forgiveness.

Socrates taught for 40 years, Plato for 50, Aristotle for 40, and Jesus for only three. Yet the influence of Christ's three-year ministry infinitely transcends the impact left by the combined 130 years of teaching from these men who were among the greatest philosophers of all antiquity.
—Author unknown

WHY ABRAHAM IS STILL A HERO!

Abraham lived around ±2000 B.C. and is one of the biggest heroes in Jewish history. Today, there are still many reasons why we should be excited about Abraham. Let us read why Paul got so excited about him.

Galatians 3 (explanation)

⁶The Scriptures say that God accepted Abraham because Abraham had *faith*.

⁷And so, you should understand that everyone who has *faith* is a child of Abraham.

⁸Long ago the Scriptures said that God would accept the Gentiles because of their *faith*. That's why God told Abraham the good news that all nations would be blessed because of him.

⁹This means that everyone who has *faith* will share in the blessings that were given to Abraham because of his *faith*. (CEV)

Abraham was the ancestor of the Israelites with whom God made an everlasting covenant. Circumcision was the sign of the covenant. After the coming of Jesus, the gospel was also spread among non-Jews. Unfortunately, those who spread heresy led these non-Jewish Christians astray by encouraging them to continue obeying Jewish customs (e.g. circumcision) and the Law. They implied that this would help them to become descendents of Abraham and to share in the blessing of the covenant of forgiveness.

This heresy upset Paul tremendously. He tried to expose the misconception by drawing the Galatians' attention to Abraham, the great hero of the Israelites. Paul pointed them to the Old Testament and reminded them of the words in Genesis 15:6, which states that Abraham was acquitted because he believed in God. Paul showed how Abraham could not have been acquitted because he obeyed the Law, as he had lived 400 years before the Law of Moses. It was never necessary for the Israelites to be acquitted because they obeyed the Law.

The Old Testament and the New Testament demand faith. Hebrews 11 refers to the figures in the Old Testament as "heroes of faith," not "heroes of the Law." Abraham's name is also listed here! He was prepared to leave everything behind to travel to a foreign land. It is wonderful to read in the very first verse of the New Testament that Jesus was a descendent of Abraham. In this way, God blessed Abraham. Faith in Jesus makes us all children of Abraham. Abraham is an example of someone who had unyielding faith in God.

 Lord, thank You that faith enables me to share in Abraham's blessing.

The legacy of heroes is the memory of a great name and the inheritance of a great example.
—Benjamin Disraeli (1804–1881), *British politician and author*

JESUS HAD TO SUBMIT TO THE LAW, BUT WE DO NOT!

Paul's whole purpose for the book of Galatians was to convince the believers that they were not saved because they obeyed the Law but because they had faith. Yet despite this, Jesus had to submit Himself to the Law. Why did Jesus have to do this, but we do not?

Galatians 4 (explanation)

[1]Children who are under age are no better off than slaves, even though everything their parents own will someday be theirs.

[2]This is because children are placed in the care of guardians and teachers until the time their parents have set.

[3]That is how it was with us. We were like children ruled by the powers of this world.

[4]But when the time was right, God sent his Son, and a woman gave birth to him. His Son obeyed the Law,

[5]so he could set us free from the Law, and we could become God's children. (CEV)

Paul uses the example of a minor to explain spiritual immaturity. A minor could only inherit from his father on the day that his father determined he would be mature. Up until that day, the minor's position was equal to that of a slave—even though the whole inheritance belonged to him. Like a slave, his whole life was ruled by others and his belongings were under their control (vv. 1–2). The age of the minor stood in his way.

Similarly, the Law stands in the way preventing human beings from inheriting eternal life. The Law keeps us spiritually immature because we constantly stumble over the demands (obedience) of the Law. Stumbling (disobedience) means that the punishment of the Law, eternal death, awaits us—which means we inherit nothing.

However, when Jesus became human and submitted to the Law, He did not falter. As a perfect human being, He could meet the demands of the Law. He conquered the consequence of our stumbling—namely, eternal death—on the cross. Believing in Him enables us to share in this triumph and inherit eternal life. The Law has now become a guideline instead of a precondition.

 Thank You, Lord, for enabling me to have eternal life.

If God would have wanted us to live in a permissive society He would have given us
Ten Suggestions and not Ten Commandments.
—Zig Ziglar, *American motivational speaker and author*

WHAT WORD WOULD SUMMARIZE THE GOSPEL?

Do you think it is possible to capture the gospel in one word? If this were possible, what word do you think it would be? Let's see if this section can help!

Galatians 5 (explanation and instruction)

[1]Christ has set us *free!* This means we are really *free. (explanation)*
Now hold on to your *freedom* and don't ever become slaves of the Law again. *(instruction)*
[2]I, Paul, promise you that Christ won't do you any good if you get circumcised. [3]If you do, you must obey the whole Law. [4]And if you try to please God by obeying the Law, you have cut yourself off from Christ and his wonderful kindness. *(explanation)* CEV

Paul used a series of arguments to convince the Galatians to give up the heresies they believed in. The arguments in his letter culminate in these verses, and he concludes with a word that embraces the essence of Christianity: *Freedom!* Of course, "freedom" is easily misinterpreted. It does not mean that we are free to do as we like. We cannot drive a car and ignore all the road signs. Reckless behavior (so-called freedom) has the potential to destroy people's lives. Our freedom does not rest on obeying a set of rules but on lovingly following Jesus Christ. By focusing on the Law, we give more value to human achievement than to God's grace.

Paul used strong reprimanding language to warn the Galatians not to fall back on a religion that appeared Christian on the surface but was in fact enslavement, for this type of religion would never set them free. Today, there are also modern misconceptions that lead people to think that if they do certain things, it will help them in some way or another to be saved. However, even if we think that our good behavior makes us better than other people, it only serves to show that we do not understand the gospel.

A good way to discriminate between a true and a false gospel is to ask: "What role does God's grace play in the gospel that is offered to me?" Let us live every day with the freedom for which Jesus paid so dearly as our point of departure.

 Thank You, Lord, that I can be truly free!

Freedom is a package deal—with it comes responsibilities and consequences.
—Author unknown

WHAT DOES FAITH LOOK LIKE?

Children are able to draw a tree, a house or a person of some sort because they know what those objects look like. But would it be possible to ask a child to draw a picture of faith? He or she might ask you what faith looks like. How would you answer this question?

Galatians 5 (explanation)

> [5]But we expect to be made completely holy because of our *faith* in Christ. Through the Holy Spirit we wait in *hope*. [6]Circumcision and uncircumcision aren't worth anything to those who believe in Christ Jesus. The only thing that really counts is faith that shows itself through *love*. (NIRV)

To Paul, there were three words that described a Christian's life: faith, hope and love. He begins in Galatians 5 by talking about hope and expectation and then uses this to illustrate that Christians are geared toward the future. Hope is normally a reaction to uncertainty. When someone says he "hopes" his team wins, he is not sure that it will indeed happen. But in the Bible the word "hope" is used completely differently. It expresses absolute certainty. Paul was absolutely certain that a believer did not have to fear the day of judgment, because he or she has already been acquitted on the ground of his or her faith. The word "wait" is used in the same verse as "hope." Therefore, hope means to look forward to the second coming of Jesus, because it is based on certainty and not on something that "might" happen.

In verse 6 Paul uses the words "faith" and "love" to emphasize that we as Christians are not only geared toward the future but are also people of action. Surely, we can't sit around idly waiting for Jesus to come. We have to keep ourselves busy in a meaningful way, and the only way to keep busy meaningfully is to live a life of faith. We can do this by performing good deeds. These deeds are not performed in a clinical and cold-hearted way, but with a heart filled with love. Faith never operates in isolation. True faith always becomes actions through love. It is therefore wrong to regard faith and deeds as separate entities. Paul saw them as a unity of believing and doing. Doing is not less important than believing.

What does faith look like? Faith is deeds that are demonstrated through love! Let us live each day in such a way that small children (and the world) will know how to depict faith. This, and not legalistic religious rules, is what is important to Jesus. It is what we all need.

 Lord, help me to show others what faith looks like by the way I live.

Faith is the strength by which a shattered world shall emerge into the light.
—Helen Keller (1880–1968), *American author and educator who was blind and deaf*

THE CIVIL WAR WITHIN US!

It is sad to see how often we give in to temptation. Many times we know that we do not want to do certain things, but we end up doing them anyway. Why does this happen? This next section in Galatians looks at this problem.

Galatians 5 (explanation and instruction)

[16]So I say, let the Holy Spirit guide your lives. (*instruction*)
Then you won't be doing what your sinful nature *craves*.
[17]The sinful nature *wants* to do evil, which is just the opposite of what the Spirit *wants*. And the Spirit gives us desires that are the opposite of what the sinful nature desires. These two forces are constantly fighting each other, so you are not free to carry out your good intentions. (*explanation*) NLT

Paul's arguments in this letter clearly show that only faith in Christ places us in the right relationship with God. The question is: How does someone who has been acquitted of sin live? Paul's answer is short and sweet: "Let *the Holy Spirit guide your lives*" (v. 16).

But this is where the struggle within us starts. We still harbor a sinful nature—our natural instinct to do bad rather than good—that does not disappear when we are filled with the Holy Spirit. The Spirit, who wants us to do what is good, is then in direct conflict with our sinful nature, which wants you to do what is bad. Our choice lies between what the Spirit wants and what our sinful nature desires. This often becomes such a struggle to choose that we end up being at war with ourselves. We are torn between the wishes of the Spirit and our desires.

It is not easy to act against our natural instincts. To live by the Spirit means that we consciously choose the side of the Holy Spirit. Fortunately, the Lord does not turn His back on us when we make the wrong choices. May we taste the sweetness of victory when we make the right choices!

 Lord, today I want to choose the Holy Spirit anew. I want to allow You to fill me anew.

The greatest conflicts are not between two people but between one person and himself.
—Garth Brooks (b. 1956), *American Country singer who was the first to win six Academy of Country Music Awards (1991)*

WHAT DOES LOVE LOOK LIKE?

Love is the one theme that people like to sing about—usually about lost love. We all search for love, but in this process so many of us fall along the way and get hurt. Perhaps we do not know what the love we are looking for looks like. This section in Galatians shows us two of the many sides of love.

Galatians 6 (instruction)

¹Brothers and sisters, if someone is caught in a sin, you who live by the Spirit should restore that person gently. But watch yourselves, or you also may be tempted. ²Carry each other's burdens, and in this way you will fulfill the law of Christ. (TNIV)

In this section, Paul's warnings highlight two of the many sides of love. First, love means that we should help (direct) each other with a *Spirit of gentleness*. Those who commit sin should see from our attitude that we do not regard ourselves as superior to them and that we are not insensitive. They should see us act humbly because we know that we can be led into temptation. It is unfortunate that so many believers often come across as moralizing and self-righteous.

Second, love means that we should carry each other's burdens. What are these burdens? They are anything that makes life difficult for fellow believers. Many of us were raised to be independent and not to rely on anyone else. We often feel embarrassed when we have to depend on others for help. We react to those who want to help us by saying, "I do not want to be a burden to you." But it should be regarded as a privilege to help one another. We need other people, and other people need us.

By showing these two sides, it becomes evident that the principle Paul wants to stress is that believers should sympathize with each other in love. This is where the strength of the Church lies. Jesus said: "If you love each other, everyone will know that you are my disciples" (John 13:35, CEV). Churches will grow if there is a loving sympathy among its members.

I want to be bold here and state that many congregations tend to focus on the wrong things in their efforts to increase church attendance. A professor once summed it up very accurately when he said, "We have to decide whether we want to entertain the goats or let the sheep graze!" To amuse people in church is entertaining at that moment, but people need loving sympathy. It makes them feel cherished and creates a feeling within them that they belong. We need to restore love and carry each other's burdens, because that is what love looks like.

 Lord, help me to build loving relationships with others.

Love is like heaven, but it can hurt like hell.
—Author unknown

IS IT "BECAUSE" OR "IN SPITE OF"?

People will generally like us because they see something good in us. It could be our pleasant personality, our loyalty or simply because we are kind to people. Is this how our relationship with God works? Does God like us because He sees something good in us? Let us read what Paul says.

Ephesians 1 (explanation and instruction)

[3]Give praise to the God
and Father of our Lord Jesus Christ. *(instruction)*
He has blessed us with every spiritual blessing. Those blessings come from the heavenly world. They belong to us because we belong to Christ.
[4]God chose us to belong to Christ before the world was created. He chose us to be holy and without blame in his eyes. He loved us. [5]So he decided long ago to adopt us as his children. He did it because of what Jesus Christ has done. It pleased God to do it. [6]All those things bring praise to his glorious grace. God freely gave us his grace because of the One he loves. [7]We have been set free because of what Christ has done. Through his blood our sins have been forgiven. We have been set free because God's grace is so rich. [8]He poured his grace on us by giving us great wisdom and understanding.
[12]We were the first to put our hope in Christ. We were chosen to bring praise to his glory. *(explanation)* NIRV

Paul's tone in this text is one of awe, adoration, worship, gratefulness and joy. The reason for Paul's praise is because God loves us not because we are good but rather in spite of all our shortcomings. Despite who we are, God has chosen *us*. We do not deserve it; it is a gift of grace (v. 6). God takes the initiative and makes us His children (v. 5), forgives us our sins (v. 7) and gives us grace (v. 8). He did all this even before the world was made (v. 4), even before we deserved anything.

Our only reaction to this can be to praise God! God's love for us is amazing. Are you still astounded by this? Nietzsche, the French philosopher, commented on Christians as follows: "You will have to look much more saved if you want me to believe in your Savior." Let us take up this challenge to "look" more saved!

 Lord, it surprises me that You love me in spite of who I am. I praise You for this!

I like your Christ, I do not like your Christians. Your Christians are so unlike your Christ.
    —Mahatma Gandhi (1869–1948), *Preeminent leader of Indian nationalism*

A THREE-LETTER WORD THAT ALWAYS GIVES THINGS A NEW TURN!

In any conversation, it is advisable to always take note of one particular three-letter word. Although the word itself is not very significant, it does indicate that we should listen carefully to what is said. Paul liked to use this word. It is the word "but." The short word "but" normally steers a conversation in a totally different direction. Someone could tell us a lot of things, but if the word "but" is used, it means that the person's true intentions will follow. Let us see how it works in the following verses.

Ephesians 2 (explanation)

[1]In the past you were dead because you sinned and fought against God. [2]You followed the ways of this world and obeyed the devil. He rules the world, and his spirit has power over everyone who doesn't obey God. [3] Once we were also ruled by the selfish desires of our bodies and minds. We had made God angry, and we were going to be punished like everyone else.
[4-5]But God was merciful! We were dead because of our sins, but God loved us so much that he made us alive with Christ, and God's wonderful kindness is what saves you. (CEV)
[10]For we are God's workmanship, created in Christ Jesus to do good works, which God prepared in advance for us to do. (NIV)

In this section in Ephesians, Paul begins by painting a gloomy picture in verses 1 to 3: *What a mess!* We are lost sinners! But then in verse 4, his argument takes a wonderful turn when he uses the word "but." This word leads us to what Paul actually wants to say: *What a God!* He saves us through grace! We do not deserve this. Then in verse 10, Paul points out: *What a difference!* Paul states that we should show our gratitude by performing good deeds. Our good deeds should not be performed in order for us to be saved but because we are grateful that God has saved us through Jesus. Many centuries ago, a Sunday school manual (the Heidelberg Catechism) was compiled according to these three points: sin, salvation and gratitude. These are the three things any believer should know: We are sinners (vv. 1–3) who have been saved by grace (vv. 4–9) and therefore now want to live a life of gratitude (v. 10)!

 Thank You, Lord, for Your abundant grace and for loving me dearly. I thank You wholeheartedly!

Our favorite attitude should be gratitude.
—Author unknown

HOW CAN WE MAKE THE HOLY TRINITY PART OF OUR PRAYERS?

Prayer should never be complicated, because it is communication with God. We know that God reveals Himself to us in three Persons, namely the Father, the Son and the Holy Spirit. Sometimes, people find it difficult to include all three Persons in their prayers. Let us see how Paul did this.

Ephesians 3 (explanation)

[14]I kneel in prayer to the Father. [15]All beings in heaven and on earth receive their life from him. [16]God is wonderful and glorious. I pray that his Spirit will make you become strong followers [17]and that Christ will live in your hearts because of your faith. Stand firm and be deeply rooted in his love. [18]I pray that you and all of God's people will understand what is called wide or long or high or deep. [19]I want you to know all about Christ's love, although it is too wonderful to be measured. Then your lives will be filled with all that God is. (CEV)

Paul starts his prayer with the *Father* to remind us that we should be very grateful to God. We owe our salvation to the Father who, on His own initiative, sent His Son to die on the cross on our behalf, and in our prayers we could thank Him for so many things. Paul then directs his prayer to the *Spirit,* who gives us what we need every day, namely inner strength. We can pray that the Spirit (Gal. 5:22) will reveal His fruit in our life. The fruit of the Spirit are signs of inner strength because love, joy, peace, patience, friendliness and happiness begin deep in our hearts. Finally, Paul directs his prayer to *Jesus,* who lives within us through our faith. His prayer to Jesus deals specifically with love. He reminds us that the love of Jesus is so all-embracing that we are never beyond its reach. We are now free to involve all three Persons in our prayers.

 Father, I am grateful that through the power of Your Spirit, You enable me to experience and share the love of Jesus.

When you pray, rather let your heart be without words than your words without heart.
— John Bunyan (1628-1688) *English minister and author*

HOW CAN WE CONVINCE THE WORLD THAT IT IS MEANINGFUL TO BE A CHRISTIAN?

It sometimes feels as if the Church has lost its impact on society. In some congregations, fewer people attend church, and some churches even have had to shut down. Complaints about moral decay are heard everywhere. What can we as believers do to bring about change in society?

Ephesians 4 (instruction)

[1]As a prisoner of the Lord, I *beg* you to live in a way that is worthy of the people God has chosen to be his own. [2]Always be humble and gentle. Patiently *put up with* each other and love each other. [3]Try your best to let God's Spirit *keep* your hearts united. Do this by living at peace. (CEV)

One of my lecturers once told our class, "If we want to have any impact at all in this world, we will have to learn to be better people." I think he was right. If the gospel does not bring about change in our lives, we might as well forget about convincing the world that it is meaningful to be a Christian. This is exactly the point Paul wants to make here.

Paul's words, "I beg you to live in a way that is worthy of the people God has chosen to be his own" are, in a sense, a summary of everything he will say up to Ephesians 6:20. The way we live will make the difference—not arguments and doctrines. Many people do not read the Bible, but they do notice the way we live. Paul names five virtues that will have an impact on those around us: humility, gentleness, patience, tolerance and peace.

These five virtues give value to the people around us and make them feel safe in our presence. They help us to establish sound relationships that will enable us to find what we are all looking for: intimacy. They require us to set aside our own interests. If we live according to these virtues, the world will regard the Church as meaningful, because these virtues will enable people to have what society so often lacks: happy and sound relationships.

You might ask, "How do I manage to live according to these virtues?" Words such as "beg," "put up with" and "keep" in Paul's letter to the Ephesians indicate very clearly that it is a choice.

 Spirit of God, help me to live out these virtues.

All virtue is summed up in dealing justly.
—Aristotle (384–322 B.C.), *Greek philosopher*

SHH! NOBODY SHOULD HEAR ABOUT THIS!

Many people shut up their heartache and secrets with a lock that says: "Nobody is allowed to hear about this." These locks should be unlocked. Why?

Ephesians 5 (explanation en instruction)

⁹The light produces what is completely good,
right and true. *(explanation)*
¹⁰Find out what pleases the Lord.
¹¹Have nothing to do with the acts of darkness. *(instruction)*
They don't produce anything good. *(explanation)*
Show what they are really like. *(instruction)*
¹²It is shameful even to talk about what people who don't obey do in secret.
¹³But everything the light shines on can be seen.
¹⁴Light makes everything clear. That is why it is said,
'Wake up, sleeper.
Rise from the dead.
Then Christ will shine on you.' *(explanation)* NIRV

If we were to lock a dead animal away in one of the rooms in our house, the stench would gradually spread to the rest of the house and overpower us. In the same way, the shame and hurt we lock away will eventually have a visible effect on our lives. We do not solve our problems by locking them away. On the contrary, they only get worse.

Paul called the key to unlock the locks of our inner rooms "light." This key of light produces the *good fruit* of that which is good, right and true (v. 9), *exposes hurt and pain* (vv. 10–13) and *heals*, because Christ makes our lives visible (v. 14) by healing our wounds. To open up our heart in prayer or to someone we trust gives us an opportunity to have remorse and to be forgiven.

Things that keep on happening in the dark will spread insidiously. This is why women nowadays are urged to unlock the locks of molestation, rape and abuse and expose these deeds in order to hopefully bring an end to them. So many people have told about the liberating feeling they experienced after they unlocked the hurt within them. So don't wait any longer to unlock your heartache. Dare to trust someone else to help you open the locks. This will be worth the trouble and pain!

 Lord, help me to unlock the locks of my pain.

There is a crack in everything. That's how the light gets in.
—Leonard Cohen (b. 1934), *Canadian folk singer, songwriter, poet and novelist*

AN E-MAIL TO FATHER AND CHILD

In this next section, Paul gives some practical advice to a father and his children. Mothers could find this equally useful.

Ephesians 6 (explanation and instruction)

[1]Children, you belong to the Lord, and you do the right thing when you obey your parents. The first commandment with a promise says, [2]'Obey your father and your mother, [3]and you will have a long and happy life.' *(explanation)*
Parents, don't be hard on your children. Raise them properly. Teach them and instruct them about the Lord. *(instruction)* CEV

The following words of wisdom, which link up with those of Paul, were once e-mailed to me:
Children have the right to

- be taken seriously, but the responsibility to listen to others
- medical treatment, but the responsibility to take care of themselves
- a good education, but the responsibility to do their work well and to behave in class
- be loved and protected, but the responsibility to care for and to love others
- special attention for special problems, but the responsibility to be the best persons they can possibly be
- be proud of their heritage and faith, but the responsibility to respect its origin and those who believe differently
- grow up in a safe and comfortable home, but the responsibility to keep the house tidy and clean
- make mistakes, but the responsibility to learn from their mistakes
- good nutrition, but the responsibility to appreciate their food and not waste it

Fathers [parents] could spare their children a lot of injustice if they would realize that their children

- grow up in different times than the ones they grew up in
- want to be trusted—err by trusting too much than by restricting too much
- need encouragement more than criticism—constant criticism crushes their self-image

My mother gave my daughter a Bible on her seventh birthday. This Bible had a very special bookmark that read: "Our children are our most important guests. They stay with us in our house for a while, require attention and care . . . and then travel along their own path." This made me think!

 Lord, give me the wisdom to be a good family member.

There are only two lasting bequests we can give our children. One is roots;
the other, wings.
—Author unknown

HOW DO WE KNOW
IF SOMEONE IS A LEADER?

What exactly makes someone a leader? Is it someone with a title or someone who occupies a high position? Should a leader be well spoken and knowledgeable? Books on leadership will tell you that these things do not make you a leader. For example, Moses was slow of speech but was a great leader despite this handicap. So what makes a true leader? This section might help to answer this question.

Philippians 1 (explanation)

²⁰I honestly expect and hope that I will never do anything to be ashamed of. Whether I live or die, I always want to be as brave as I am now and bring honor to Christ.
²¹If I live, it will be for Christ, and if I die, I will gain even more. (CEV)

Paul, who was writing this letter from the prison in Rome, states that he eagerly desires to live in such a way that he will never have to be ashamed of anything. His reason is simple: He wants to glorify Christ. Paul realizes that a leader is measured in terms of his or her followers. A Christian's conduct often determines what other Christians think about him or her. Our conduct is to Christ's honor or shame.

Someone once said that "life is the theatre where God's honor, God's greatness, is enacted." Paul wanted his life to be a testimony to the fact that Christ was the greatest influence in His life. For this reason, he confessed that "If I live, it will be for Christ, and if I die, I will gain even more" (v. 21)—gain because death would free him of his sins and he would enjoy glory in the presence of Christ.

Leadership is therefore not measured according to someone's position or knowledge but according to the person's influence on others. Mother Teresa was a leader because she influenced people all over the world. Princess Diana was a leader (although people seldom spoke about her in this way) because she had millions of followers all over the world. During His life on earth, Jesus had followers everywhere He went. As a leader, His command is still, "Anyone who intends to come with me has to let me lead. You're not in the driver's seat; I am" (Matt. 16:24, MSG). By doing this, Jesus confirmed that a leader is measured according to his or her followers. He therefore asked for total commitment! May your life also be a theatre where the honor of God is enacted.

 Lord, I pray that my life will be a theatre where the honor of God is enacted.

Leadership is influence.
—John C. Maxwell, *American entrepreneur, author and motivational speaker*

HOW CAN WE SOLVE DISCORD?

The book of Philippians is a letter of joy in which Paul wrote about joy no less than 16 times. But then he realized that one thing could rob us of all joy: discord. What is the solution to this? Here is some good advice!

Philippians 2 (explanation and instruction)

[1]Are you cheerful because you belong to Christ? Does his love comfort you? Is the Holy Spirit your companion? Has Christ been gentle and loving toward you? *(explanation)*
[2]Then make my joy complete by agreeing with each other. Have the same love. Be one in spirit and purpose.
[3]Don't do anything only to get ahead. Don't do it because you are proud. Instead, be free of pride. Think of others as better than yourselves.
[4]None of you should look out just for your own good. You should also look out for the good of others. *(instruction)* NIRV

In verse 1, Paul gives us four reasons why we should try to avoid discord at all cost. These reasons are like four cables that join believers to Jesus:

1. "Are you cheerful because you belong to Christ?" Our comfort lies in the fact that Jesus' blood places us in the right relationship with Him. However, nobody can live in unity with Jesus while being in discord with others.
2. "Does his love comfort you?" Christian love does not impose conditions but is marked by forgiveness. This alone is enough to avoid discord.
3. "Is the Holy Spirit your companion?" The Spirit ties us to God and to each other. The fruit of the Spirit (i.e., love, patience, humility) is particularly aimed at building sound relations and is there to ensure that the Church functions as a unit. Discord hampers the fruit and gifts of the Spirit.
4. "Has Christ been gentle and loving toward you?" We all need lovingness and gentleness at some time or another. Discord prevents this from happening.

The abovementioned four cables link us to Jesus and motivate us to be joined to one another by other cables. These other cables are practical guidelines to prevent discord. For instance, when we *agree* with each other (v. 2), we create a recipe for success in working together. When we think of others *as better than ourselves* (v. 3), we are kept humble and work toward unity. When we have *humility* (v. 3) and are free of pride, we obtain the right attitude for working on a sound relationship. And finally, when we *look out for the good of others* (v. 4), we take the focus off our own needs, which so often leads to competition among people and creates adversarial relationships.

To summarize: Selfishness is the seed of discord. Humility is the root of unity.

Lord Jesus, help me to avoid discord at all cost.

Three Rules of Work: Out of clutter find simplicity; from discord find harmony;
in the middle of difficulty lies opportunity.
—Albert Einstein(1879–1955), *German-Swiss-American scientist*

THE WHAT SHOULD CHANGE TO WHO!

What saves us? The "teachers" in Philippi had a simple answer: Trust in exterior things such as circumcision. Paul, who had originally founded the congregation, later wrote from prison (probably in Rome) that he differed totally from these teachers. He called them "dogs" (Phil. 3:2, NIRV). Why would Paul react so strongly?

Philippians 3 (explanation)

[4]I have many reasons to trust in my human nature. Others may think they have reasons to trust in theirs. But I have even more. [5]I was circumcised on the eighth day. I am part of the people of Israel. I am from the tribe of Benjamin. I am a pure Hebrew. As far as the law is concerned, I am a Pharisee. [6]As far as being committed is concerned, I opposed and attacked the church. As far as keeping the Law is concerned, I kept it perfectly. [7]I thought things like that were for my benefit. But now I consider them to be nothing because of Christ. (NIRV)

The "dogs" to whom Paul refers wanted the newly converted to be circumcised before they could become Christians. In other words, they wanted to first make them Jews before they could become Christians (3:2). However, in these verses Paul says that if there was one person who could silence these dogs, it was he. The reason was because Paul had perfected the *what* that the heretics expected. He could trust in exterior things to be saved if he wanted to, because:

- "circumcised on the eight day"—he had been part of Judaism since his birth
- "of the people of Israel"—he emphasized his true descent
- "from the tribe of Benjamin"—like King Saul, he was part of this elite tribe
- "a pure Hebrew"—many Jews in other parts of the world had lost the ability to speak Hebrew, but Paul still could speak this language
- "I am a Pharisee"—he was part of the spiritual elite
- "I opposed and attacked the church"—he had been fanatical about Judaism
- "I kept [the Law] perfectly"—He had followed the law conscientiously

After meeting Jesus, Paul realized that external matters could not save us. The peace Jesus brings is not found in external things. External things merely quiet our conscience. For example, I was in church this morning and I gave my thanksgiving offering. That is why the question should rather be *Who* saves me? This is how the *What* changes to *Who*! (Jesus).

 Lord, I realize that exterior things cannot save me. Thank You for my salvation!

Grace is given to heal the spiritually sick, not to decorate spiritual heroes.
—Martin Luther (1483–1546), *German priest and scholar whose questioning of certain Church practices led to the Protestant Reformation*

WHAT DOES A CHRISTIAN LOOK LIKE?

It would be interesting to walk around and ask people, "What does a Christian look like?" I am sure that some of the answers would be embarrassing to us as Christians. Perhaps we should change the question somewhat. Let's rather ask, "What *should* a Christian look like?"

Philippians 4 (explanation and instruction)

[4]Rejoice in the Lord always.
I will say it again: Rejoice!
[5]Let our gentleness be evident to all. *(instruction)*
The Lord is near. *(explanation)* (TNIV)

In this passage, Paul tells us very clearly what a Christian should look like: joyful and gentle! Both of these characteristics are based on choice. We therefore have no excuse not to have these two qualities. Both of them are also focused: Joy focuses on the Lord and gentleness focuses on all people.

Why does joy not focus on circumstances instead? Perhaps because then we would believe the lie that we could only be happy under favorable circumstances. Paul found himself in unsuitable circumstances—a prison—but urged the people to rejoice in the Lord. The lesson Paul teaches us is that joy should not be dependent on circumstances. Paul was happy and joyous because he knew that Jesus Christ was with him in all circumstances. Therefore, his joy was in the Lord. This joy should flow over to all people in the form of gentleness, which means that we will act kindly toward all people.

The following example will explain this. Two students were writing an exam. One of them received a score of 80 percent, while the other received a score of 50 percent. However, the student who had received a 50 percent score had experienced a death in his family the prior week before the exams. Now, a rigid lecturer would regard the student who received the 80 percent score as excellent and the one who received the 50 percent score as mediocre. But an accommodating lecturer would, in the light of the events, congratulate the student who got 50 percent. A rigid person is cold and clinical, while a gentle and accommodating person is warm and reasonable.

Paul tried to motivate us to choose joy and gentleness by writing, "The Lord is near" (v. 5). In this way, Paul stated that life is short and that the end is a reality. This end does not mean nothingness but rather Jesus, who stands with outstretched arms to embrace His bride, the Church. Let us therefore choose today to look like a Christian (bride). By doing this, we will captivate the world. Life is too precious not to do this.

 Lord, I confess that I do not always live with joy and gentleness. I now choose to live my life this way.

If you would fall into any extreme, let it be on the side of gentleness. The human mind is so constructed that it resists rigor, and yields to softness.
—Saint Francis de Sales (1567–1622), *French Roman Catholic bishop of Geneva*

WHAT DO FAITH, HOPE AND LOVE HAVE IN COMMON?

Three words describe the Christian life: faith, love and hope. Paul liked to write about these three important issues and always related them to each other. Let us see what they have in common.

Colossians 1 (explanation)

[3]Each time we pray for you, we thank God, the Father of our Lord Jesus Christ. [4]We have heard of your faith in Christ and of your love for all of God's people, [5]because what you hope for is kept safe for you in heaven. You first heard about this hope when you believed the true message, which is the good news. (CEV)

This congregation made Paul grateful because they reflected the essence of the Christian religion, namely faith and love. The substance of the Christian faith does not involve a set of rules and laws, but a Person. For this reason we believe in *Jesus*. Faith implies that we know and trust Him. Yet it is not enough for a Christian to believe only with the mind. Faith requires us to act, and this action involves love toward our *neighbor*. The love that streams from our heart is God's way to show the world what He is like.

Love is God's invitation to the world to believe in Him, the origin of life. Christians thus have a dual commitment: they are committed to Jesus Christ and to their neighbors. Christian faith is not merely a religious conviction but also an act of love. Faith and love are therefore two sides of the same coin. These two pillars of the Christian life are built on the foundation of hope. In colloquial language, "hope" means "maybe"—you hope it will rain next week, but you are not sure. Biblical hope, however, means "definitely." Hope directs faith and love to our future in heaven—something that is fixed and certain (v. 5).

Hope implies that we should not only be concerned about the here and now but also about the future. Hope is like a pair of binoculars that brings that which is far away (eternal life) closer. This helps us to gain perspective on the here and now. Hope is the knowledge that our future is safe with God. Hope fuels faith and love. It drives faith and inspires love.

To sum up: *faith* gives *love* and *hope* substance—Jesus Christ.
Love gives *faith* and *hope* a heart—the love of Jesus Christ.
Hope gives *faith* and *love* a future—eternal life.

 Thank You, Lord, that I can live in faith, hope and love!

Nothing worth doing is completed in our lifetime; therefore we must be saved by hope.
Nothing true or beautiful makes complete sense in any immediate context of history;
therefore we must be saved by faith. Nothing we do, however virtuous, can be
accomplished alone; therefore, we are saved by love.
—Reinhold Niebuhr (1892–1971), *American theologian*

WE ARE CHRISTIANS BECAUSE . . .

The Colossian church was a young congregation without a spiritual leader, and it was led astray. According to the heresy that led them astray, a person was a Christian because he or she believed in Christ *and* adhered to all kinds of additional demands (rules and doctrines) (2:8,23). Paul reacted fiercely to this and wrote that one is a Christian because . . .

Colossians 2 (explanation)

[13]And you, who were dead in your trespasses and the uncircumcision of your flesh, God made alive together with him, having forgiven us all our trespasses, [14]by canceling the record of debt that stood against us with its legal demands. This he set aside, nailing it to the cross. [15]He disarmed the rulers and authorities and put them to open shame, by triumphing over them in him. (ESV)

Paul brilliantly described what makes a person a Christian. He used three images to explain this. First, he used the image of *death*. This image refers to someone who does not yet have a living relationship with Jesus. To give life to such a relationship, the obstacle had to be eradicated, namely sin. Only one Person could do this: Christ. We are Christians because Christ gives us life! Believe this!

Second, Paul used the image of *debt*. Debt should be settled. It can also be written off as bad debt. God does not write off our sin as bad debt, but settles it by His Son's death. We do not have any IOUs. A legalistic rule is a way to tell God that we owe Him something, but this is heresy. We need not have any feelings of guilt towards God, merely gratefulness.

The third image Paul used is a *triumph*. A general's triumph after a battle was celebrated with a procession in the streets so that all the people knew that he had won. The conquered king and his soldiers had to walk naked behind the triumphant king. This is exactly what Jesus did to the evil spirits. He disarmed them (stripped them of their clothes). Jesus Christ is Lord! Paul used these three images to say that we are Christians because faith in Christ makes us Christians.

 Thank You, Lord, that my faith enables me to be a Christian!

Faith . . . is the art of holding on to things your reason once accepted, despite your changing moods.
—C.S. Lewis (1898–1963), *High-powered Oxford and Cambridge professor and perhaps the twentieth century's most famous convert to Christianity. Lewis was the creator of the Narnia series.*

HOW SERIOUSLY SHOULD ONE APPROACH LIFE?

When reading this next section in Colossians, one gets the feeling that Paul suggests that we should not take life seriously. In a way, his two instructions create the impression that we should strive for heavenly things and direct our thoughts toward heavenly things. Did Paul really mean this?

Colossians 3 (explanation and instruction)

¹You have been raised to life *with Christ. (explanation)*
Now set your heart on what is in heaven,
where Christ rules at God's right side.
²Think about what is up there,
not about what is here on earth. *(instruction)*
³You died, which means that your life is hidden *with Christ,*
who sits beside God.
⁴Christ gives meaning to your life, and when he appears,
you will also appear *with him* in glory. *(explanation)* CEV

If our life centers on sport, that is where our thoughts will be. A Christian's thoughts should be centered on Christ (v. 4). The word "with Christ" is used three times in this section and should give us enough reason to make Christ everything. Paul states that Christ gave us three things: *life* (v. 1), *safety* (v. 3) *and a secure future* (v. 4). Jesus is sitting at the right hand of God. This position is an image of power and strength in the Bible. When Jesus ascended to heaven, He took on a position of power. Because Christ is our life and He is with God above, it should therefore be logical that our thoughts and aspirations should be on the things above.

But does this mean that we should no longer regard ordinary earth life as worthy? No! These four verses are merely a transition, an introduction, to the rest of chapters 3 and 4. In this passage, Paul, in a very practical and concrete way, speaks about all the relationships we could possibly have on this earth: family, work, political, everything. Paul means that we should consider the heavenly matters in order to deal with ordinary matters in a new and different way.

By focusing on what is above, you bring elements of heaven to the earth. If you want to balance a broom in your hand, you look up and not down at your hand. In the same way, you should look up when you want to bring about change on earth.

 Lord, help me to fulfill my obligations here on earth.

My soul can find no staircase to heaven unless it be through earth's loveliness.
—Michelangelo (1475–1564), *Italian sculptor, painter, architect and poet, considered to be the creator of the Renaissance*

SHOULD WE HONESTLY BELIEVE THAT PEOPLE CAN CHANGE?

A journalist once interviewed Dorothee Sölle, a German minister. During the interview, Sölle spoke enthusiastically about the changes that took place in people's lives when Christ became their master. The journalist interrupted her by asking the following question: "Do you honestly believe that people can change?" This section can help us to answer this important question.

Colossians 3 (explanation and instruction)

[5]Don't be controlled by your body. *Kill* every desire for the wrong kind of sex. Don't be immoral or indecent or have evil thoughts. Don't be greedy, which is the same as worshipping idols. (*instruction*)
[6]God is angry with people who disobey him by doing these things.
[7]And that is exactly what you did, when you lived among people who behaved in this way. (*explanation*)
[8]But now you must *stop doing* such things. You must quit being angry, hateful, and evil. You must no longer say insulting or cruel things about others.
[9]And stop lying to each other. (*instruction*)
You have given up your old way of life with its habits.
[10]Each of you is now a *new person*. You are becoming more and more like your Creator, and you will understand him better. (*explanation*) CEV

In this passage, Paul makes it clear that people *can* change. A few strong words emphasize this: "kill" (v. 5), "stop doing" (v. 8) and "new person" (v. 10). These words lead to a change of character and eradicate sin in our lives. We can divide sin into the following categories:

- **Sexual sins:** "Kill every desire for the wrong kind of sex. Don't be immoral or indecent or have evil thoughts" (v. 5).
- **Greed:** "Don't be greedy, which is the same as worshipping idols" (v. 5).
- **Sins in relationships:** anger (being cross), hate (having hostility), evil (harboring feelings of hate), insult and lying (vv. 8–9.)

Let's be honest. The journalist asked Sölle a valid question—our own experiences have taught us that it is very difficult to break away from the above-mentioned sins. Sölle's answer to the journalist's question was as clear as daylight. She told the journalist that this was the most atheistic question to ask, because to doubt that one could change was to doubt the living God Himself. Whoever doubts this doubts the power of the Spirit who lives and works within us. Renewal and change are possible. This is the good news! Hallelujah!

 Thank You, Lord, that I can change through the power of the Spirit that lives within me.

You must be the change you wish to see in the world.
—Mahatma Gandhi (1869–1948), *Preeminent leader of Indian nationalism*

WHAT IF WE ARE NOT CHOSEN BY GOD?

Have you ever wondered, *Have I been chosen by God?* Perhaps you are too afraid to give a thought to this. What if you are not chosen? Relax and read the next section in 1 Thessalonians, because being chosen should be a comfort to you and not a threat.

1 Thessalonians 1 (explanation)

²We thank God for you and always mention you in our prayers. Each time we pray,
³we tell God our Father about your faith and loving work and about your firm hope in our Lord Jesus Christ.
⁴My *dear friends,* God loves you, and we know he has chosen you to be his people. (CEV)

Paul thanked God for this young congregation because he knew that they were chosen. He knew this because the three pillars of the Christian life (namely faith, hope and love) were present in their lives. How comforting it must have been for this young congregation to hear Paul say, "You are chosen!" But what about you? Perhaps you still view this idea of being chosen by God as a threat. Perhaps it could be ascribed to the following *two misunderstandings:*

1. **Being chosen only concerns individuals.** In the Old Testament, God did not choose individuals but Israel as a nation. The Church is the continuation of Israel. It is therefore not strange that Paul mentions in this passage that those in the *congregation* ("dear friends") were the chosen ones.
2. **If God had chosen some, the implication is that he had rejected others.** Israel was to serve a purpose on this earth: to be a blessing to the nations. "Everyone on earth will be blessed because of you" (Gen, 12:3, CEV). Congregations do this by following the words Jesus gave us in the Great Commission: "Go to the people of all nations and make them my disciples" (Matt. 28:19, CEV). Therefore, being chosen concerns a *task* and not a *place* (hell or heaven).

Perhaps you could ask, "What about Matthew 22:14, which says: 'Many are invited, but only a few are chosen'? (CEV)." It is important to remember that this verse is the culmination of three parables (Matt. 21:28–22:13). The essence of the three parables is that God calls people but they fail to react. The fact that they are not chosen means that they did not want to come. Thus, people who are rejected have no one to blame but themselves, because they do not want to believe the gospel. If you believe in Jesus, you can be certain that you have been chosen—chosen to make the *task* of faith, hope and love visible in this world.

 Thank You, Lord, that I can know that You have chosen me to be subservient.

When you put faith, hope and love together, you can raise positive kids in a negative world.
—Zig Ziglar, *American motivational speaker and author*

ONE OF THE GREATEST MISTAKES IN OUR PRAYER LIFE

Long ago, three young gentlemen completed a yacht race on the west coast of Scotland. After the successful expedition, one of the men commented, "When I am at home, I do not listen to the weather forecast. But when I was on the yacht, I listened to it every day." It is possible to do without the weather forecast when we are safely home in our comfort zone, but when our life depends on the weather, it becomes very important. We often act like the yachtsman where prayer is concerned and only use it when there is uncertainty in our lives. Paul teaches us an important lesson about this in the next section.

1 Thessalonians 3 (explanation)

[10]Day and night we sincerely pray that we will see you again and help you to have an even stronger faith.
[11]We pray that God our Father and our Lord Jesus will let us visit you. [12]May the Lord make your love for each other and for everyone else grow by leaps and bounds. That's how our love for you has grown. [13]And when our Lord comes with all of his people, I pray that he will make your hearts pure and innocent in the sight of God the Father. (CEV)

Prayer is our way of telling God, "I depend on You." In verse 10, Paul says, "I need You at all times—not only when I find myself in troubled waters." Paul prayed night and day. Of course, this does not mean that he was constantly on his knees, just that he was constantly aware that he depended on God. In this prayer, we see how he depended on God for everything:

- "We pray that God our Father and our Lord Jesus will let us visit you" (v. 11)
- "May the Lord make your love for each other and for everyone else grow by leaps and bounds" (v. 12)
- "I pray that he will make your hearts pure and innocent" (v. 13)

If God, our Father, knows how many hairs we have on our heads, should we not pray for the small things in our lives? God does not want us to only know Him during the storms of our lives but also when we are on calm waters. He wants to be the Father who travels with us and not merely the spare wheel in the trunk that we pull out when we have a flat tire.

 Lord, in my prayers I want to tell You that I am dependent on You for everything.

Prayer does not change God, but it changes him who prays.
—Søren Kierkegaard (1813–1855), *Danish philosopher and theologian who is generally recognized as the first existentialist philosopher*

THE SERMON THAT WILL REACH PEOPLE OUTSIDE THE CONGREGATION!

The majority of people never go to church to listen to a sermon. Despite this, there is a sermon that reaches them every week. How is this possible? Paul tells us about this.

1 Thessalonians 4 (explanation and instruction)

⁹We don't have to write you about the need to love each other. God has taught you to do this, ¹⁰and you already have shown your love for all of his people in Macedonia. *(explanation)*
But, my dear friends, we ask you to do even more. ¹¹Try your best to live quietly, to mind your own business, and to work hard, just as we taught you to do. *(instruction)*
¹²Then you will be respected by people who are not followers of the Lord, and you won't have to depend on anyone. *(explanation)* CEV

The congregation in Thessalonica resigned from their work because they expected the second coming of Jesus to happen during their lifetime. Many of them used this as an excuse not to work. Consequently, the people who were not part of the congregation did not have much respect for their way of living (v. 12). In the same way, while the people outside our congregations do not hear the sermons, they see how we live. Our life is a visible sermon to those on the outside.

Paul was aware of this. He wrote very diplomatically in order not to quell the congregation's enthusiasm and gave them some practical advice on how to await Jesus' second coming. First, he encouraged them to dedicate themselves even more to mutual love. Love always commands respect because it is unselfish, unconditional and forgiving. Love gives to us and others what is needed: worth!

Second, Paul encouraged them to have the right attitude to work. They had to carry on with their daily tasks to ensure that they did not unnecessarily become dependent on other people. They also had to concern themselves with their own matters and not poke their noses in other people's business.

The following story can help illustrate these points. One Sunday, a young girl attended church alone. When she returned home, her father asked her, "Why are you back so early?" She answered, "Half of the sermon has been delivered. I must now live the other half." May this also be our attitude.

 Lord, help me to live in such a way that my life will be a good sermon to all.

A good example is the best sermon.
—Benjamin Franklin (1706–1790), *American statesman, scientist, philosopher, printer, writer and inventor*

HOW CAN WE PREPARE OURSELVES FOR THE SECOND COMING?

A friend of mine once painted a very encouraging picture of our position as Christians. He said that behind us are God's outstretched arms, with which He freed us on the cross, and in front of us are God's welcoming arms, with which He will welcome us at His second coming. The question is, how can we prepare ourselves for the second coming?

1 Thessalonians 5 (explanation and instruction)

²You surely know that the Lord's return will be as a thief coming at night.
⁵You belong to the light and live in the day. We don't live in the night or belong to the dark. *(explanation)*
⁶Others may sleep, but we should stay awake and be alert. *(instruction)*
⁷People sleep during the night, and some even get drunk. ⁸But we belong to the day. *(exposition)*
So we must stay sober and let our faith and love be like a suit of armor. Our firm hope that we will be saved is our helmet. *(exhortation)* CEV

Although there is much speculation about the second coming, the Bible is very clear about one thing: the second coming will catch us unaware (v. 2). Nobody can predict it. The Bible warns us repeatedly about this: "So, my disciples, always be ready! You don't know the day or the time when all this will happen" (Matt. 25:13, CEV). Therefore, we should be ready for Christ's return at all times. But how do we do this? Paul tells us to be level headed and alert. How does a person look who is alert? Three famous words in verse 8 describe the life of a person who is alert: faith, love and hope.

Christians who are alert in *faith* have a living relationship with the Lord. To them Christ is everything, and therefore they will not be caught unaware when He returns. They live in the light. Christians who are alert through *love* get involved in people's needs. They are the ones who are willing to give others their time and money and who take on a subservient position. They are the ones who realize that we, as people, owe each other only one thing in these final days: to love each other. These Christians will be ready. Finally, Christians who are alert live with *hope*. This does not mean that they merely "hope for the best." No, they realize that hope means God promised us more than this life.

Our future is safe with God. Hope helps us to live knowing that Jesus is on His way. Therefore, faith and love cannot exist without hope. It urges faith on and inspires love so that we can be level headed and alert.

 Lord, help me to be ready for Your coming through faith, hope and love.

All human wisdom is summed up in two words—wait and hope.
—Alexandre Dumas (1802–1870), *One of the most famous French writers of the nineteenth century*

WHEN WILL JESUS COME?

The Bible is filled with moving events such as the creation, the crucifixion, the resurrection and the ascension. The one big event we should look forward to with great expectation is the second coming of Jesus. But when will this happen?

2 Thessalonians 2 (explanation)

[3]Don't let anyone trick you in any way. That day will not come until people rise up against God. It will not come until *the man of sin* appears. He is a marked man. He is sentenced to be destroyed. [6]Now you know what is holding the man of sin back. He is held back so that he can make his appearance at the right time. [7]The secret power of sin is already at work. But the one who now holds that power back will keep doing it until he is taken out of the way.
[8]Then the man of sin will appear. The Lord Jesus will overthrow him with the breath of his mouth. The glorious brightness of Jesus' coming will destroy the man of sin. (NIRV)

The young congregation in Thessalonica was confused about the return of Jesus. As we mentioned previously, many of them had stopped working because they expected Jesus to come at any time. Paul wrote this second letter to explain to them that certain things had to happen before Jesus' return: "The man of sin" first had to be revealed before the day of the Lord would come (v. 3). Paul said that after he appeared, the coming of Jesus would be close.

In the letters of John, this lawless man is called the "antichrist." According to 1 John 2:18, the man of lawlessness had already appeared and the coming of Jesus was close: "Children, it is the last hour, and as you have heard that antichrist is coming, so now many antichrists have come. Therefore we know it is the last hour" (ESV).

This seems to be a contradiction: Paul told the congregation in Thessalonica that the antichrist still had to come, while John had already pointed him out. How do we explain this? Paul was already dead when the letters of John were written. Many scholars believe that the book of 2 Thessalonians was written at about A.D. 50, while the letters of John were written around A.D. 90. This means that the one who was holding back "the man of sin" (v. 6) had been removed before the letters of John were written.

In Paul's time, the man of lawlessness had not yet appeared because he was held back. We do not know exactly who or what held him back, but it was most likely the Roman government, which was well disposed toward Paul (there are also other explanations). However, between A.D. 63 and 90, the Roman government turned against the Christians. This gave Caesar Nero, as antichrist, the opportunity to persecute the Christians. No one knows when Jesus will return, but His return is certain. The comfort is that Jesus will destroy and eradicate the man of sin (the antichrist) when He comes (v. 8).

 Lord, it is comforting to know that the antichrist will not be able to resist Your splendor.

Jesus Christ: The meeting place of eternity and time, the blending of deity and humanity, the junction of heaven and earth.
—Source unknown

WHERE DOES THE CHRISTIAN LIFE BEGIN?

The believers in Thessalonica (like many of us) battled to persevere as Christians. In the following section, Paul encouraged them by reminding them of their early days as Christians.

2 Thessalonians 2 (explanation and instruction)

[13]My friends, *the Lord loves you,* and it is only natural for us to thank God for you. *God chose* you to be the first ones to be *saved.* His Spirit made you holy, and you put your faith in the truth. [14]God used our preaching as his way of *inviting you* to share in the glory of our Lord Jesus Christ. *(explanation)*
[15]My friends, that's why you must remain faithful and follow closely what we taught you in person and by our letters. *(instruction)*
[16]God our Father loves us. He is kind and has given us eternal comfort and a wonderful hope. We pray that our Lord Jesus Christ and God our Father [17]will encourage you and help you always to do and say the right thing. *(explanation)* CEV

The Christian life always begins with God, who took the initiative to approach human beings. Unfortunately, human beings were not always approachable and often preferred to hide from God and carry on with their own lives. Think about Adam and Eve, who hid from Him in the garden. God was the One who went to them and asked, "Where are you?" (Gen. 3:9, CEV). We find God because He found us first.

In this section, Paul uses charged words to confirm this: "the Lord loves you," "chose you," "saved" and "inviting you." The result of God's initiative is that we can share in His glory (v. 14). But God is not only the beginning of everything; He is also the end. The last line confirms this: God showed us His love and gave us *eternal encouragement* and *good hope.* Everything begins and ends with God. Therefore, we are called to remain faithful, follow His Word closely and live according to it (vv. 15–16). In this way, our lives become an invitation to others to let them be found by God!

 Thank You, Lord, that You came looking for me and showered me with Your love!

Some people talk about finding God—as if He could get lost.
—Author unknown

A LIBERATING REQUEST OF ONLY THREE WORDS!

Life is not easy, and many people find life's challenges just too much to handle. Often times, people would rather just throw in the towel than persevere. Divorce, nervous breakdowns and suicides—to mention but a few—point to this fact. Paul, despite being a spiritual giant, also went through difficult times (2 Cor. 11:16–33). I must admit that after reading what Paul had to go through, I would have thrown in the towel a long time ago if I were in his shoes. But despite all of his hardships, Paul persevered. He could do so because he was prepared to make a very important request—one that we often neglect to make.

2 Thessalonians 3 (explanation and instruction)

¹Finally, our friends, please pray for us. (*instruction*)
This will help the message about the Lord to spread quickly, and others will respect it, just as you do. (*explanation*)
²Pray that we may be kept safe from
worthless and evil people. (*instruction*)
After all, not everyone has faith.
³But the Lord can be trusted to make you strong and protect you from harm. ⁴He has made us sure that you are obeying what we taught you and that you will keep on obeying. ⁵I pray that the Lord will guide you to be as loving as God and as patient as Christ. (*explanation*) CEV

This spiritual giant was willing to ask the young congregation: "Pray for us" (v. 1). He made the same request in his other letters (1 Thess. 5:25; Philem. 22; Rom. 15:30). Paul realized that the gospel was not a one-man show. He was a realistic believer. He realized that not all people were believers and that there would be hostility (v. 2). Furthermore, he was aware of the workings of evil and realized that intercession helps to focus on another more comforting reality: the God who is faithful and who strengthens and protects us (v. 3).

Intercession helps you to focus on God's love. God's love ensures that you will not heartlessly criticize those for whom you pray. Therefore, if you find it difficult to forgive someone, you should start praying for that person. If you do so, verse 3 will eventually become reality in your life. It is very liberating to pray for others and to ask others to pray for you. Imagine how your child would feel if he or she opened his or her lunchbox just before an exam and found a note with these words: "Mommy and Daddy love you and are praying for you!" Imagine a girl asking her friend to pray for her when she goes on her first date. It is liberating and will help you uphold your moral values in the heat of the moment. In this way, intercession leads to perseverance!

 Thank You, Lord, for the privilege to pray for one another. I want to treat this seriously!

Prayer may not change things for you, but it for sure changes you for things.
—Samuel M. Shoemaker, *Pastor at Calvary Episcopal Church in New York, where he headed the Oxford Group. He was also a great friend of the early Alcoholics Anonymous (AA).*

IT IS GOOD TO REMEMBER OUR SINS!

When Paul was in Macedonia (in modern day Greece), he wrote encouraging words to Timothy, a young preacher in Ephesus. This letter clearly shows that Paul remembered his sins. He mentions how inhumanly cruel he was and that he sees himself as the greatest sinner. What comfort could this hold for Timothy?

1 Timothy 1 (explanation)

[12]I thank Christ Jesus our Lord. He has given me the strength for my work because he knew that he could trust me. [13]I used to say terrible and insulting things about him, and I was cruel. But he had mercy on me because I didn't know what I was doing, and I had not yet put my faith in him. [14]Christ Jesus our Lord was very kind to me. He has greatly blessed my life with faith and love just like his own. [15]'Christ Jesus came into the world to save sinners.' This saying is true, and it can be trusted. I was the worst sinner of all! [16]But since I was worse than anyone else, God had mercy on me and let me be an example of the endless patience of Christ Jesus. He did this so that others would put their faith in Christ and have eternal life. [17]I pray that honor and glory will always be given to the only God, who lives forever and is the invisible and eternal King! Amen. (CEV)

According to Paul, it is advantageous to remember your sins for several reasons. First, it keeps your gratefulness and love to God alive. When you remember how your sins broke the hearts of God and other people and how they forgave you, you cannot help but be grateful (v. 12). Second, it prevents you from becoming spiritually arrogant. You come to realize that you owe everything to God's abundant grace (v. 14). Third, it reminds you of the essence of the gospel: "Christ Jesus came into the world to save sinners" (v. 15). Fourth, remembering your sins urges you on to greater dedication to God. It allows you to realize anew that Jesus died in your place on the cross and that you therefore have to live with greater dedication (v. 16).

Paul's sinful past encouraged Timothy and also serves to encourage us. Before he was converted, Paul persecuted the Christians in an inhumane way, and therefore he viewed himself as the biggest sinner. It is comforting to know that nobody is beyond the reach of God's grace. God's grace is always greater than our sins (v. 16)! Honor and glory to God (v. 17)!

 Thank You, Lord, that my sinful past enables me to focus on Your grace!

Nothing emboldens sin so much as mercy.
—William Shakespeare (1564–1616), *British poet and playwright*

HOW CAN WE SILENCE OUR CRITICS?

As a young minister, Timothy had to prepare himself to handle criticism and opposition. The experienced Paul understood this and gave Timothy (and us) excellent advice on how to handle criticism.

1 Timothy 4 (instruction)

[12]Don't let anyone make fun of you, just because you are young. Set an *example* for other followers by what you say and do, as well as by your love, faith, and purity.
[13]Until I arrive, be sure to keep on reading the Scriptures in worship, and don't stop preaching and teaching. [14]Use the gift you were given when the prophets spoke and the group of church leaders blessed you by placing their hands on you. [15]Remember these things and think about them, so everyone can see how well you are doing. [16]Be careful about the way you live and about what you teach. Keep on doing this, and you will save not only yourself, but the people who hear you. (CEV)

According to Paul, there were two primary ways that Timothy should handle criticism. First, Timothy had to concentrate on setting a *good example*. Good arguments and polemics do not necessarily silence your critics. You might win the argument but lose the person in the process. You will only have an impact on the world when your conduct surpasses the world's standards. Someone once remarked that Christian standards have dropped to such an extent that everyone qualifies to be a Christian. The impact of your example is greater than the impact of your arguments. Example is better than precept.

A second way that Paul told Timothy to handle criticism was to stay focused on his mission: "Be sure to keep on reading the Scriptures in worship, and don't stop preaching and teaching" (v. 13). Criticism is usually aimed at the person and not the calling, so a good way to handle criticism is to divert the attention it brings away from yourself and remain fixed on your purpose. Paul knew that there was nothing as enriching as focusing on your mission and nothing as taxing as meddling in peripheral matters.

It is so easy to get involved in less important matters while neglecting the important ones. This is why Paul asked Timothy not to neglect his gift (v. 14). We have no control over what others say about us, but we do have control over the example we set and the calling on which we focus!

 Thank You, Lord, that I need not fear criticism. Thank You for Paul's advice! I realize anew that my example and my calling are extremely important.

There is nothing so annoying as a good example.
—Mark Twain (1835–1910), *American humorist, writer and lecturer*

WHAT DO A SOLDIER, AN ATHLETE AND A FARMER HAVE IN COMMON?

The experienced Paul was very honest when he wrote to Timothy, the young spiritual leader of Ephesus. Paul knew that life was not always sunshine and roses for a Christian—especially for a leader. He knew that it often involved disappointment and was an uphill battle. So in this next section, Paul encouraged Timothy by means of three different images: the soldier, the athlete and the farmer. Although one finds a soldier on the battlefield, an athlete on the track and a farmer in the fields, they all have something in common. What was it that they shared in common?

2 Timothy 2 (explanation and instruction)

³As a good soldier of Christ Jesus you must endure your share of suffering. *(instruction)*
⁴Soldiers on duty don't work at outside jobs. They try only to please their commanding officer. ⁵No one wins an athletic contest without obeying the rules. ⁶And farmers who work hard are the first to eat what grows in their field.
⁷If you keep in mind what I have told you, the Lord will help you understand completely. *(explanation)* CEV

Paul asks us to look to the soldier, the athlete and the farmer when our spirits are low and we feel that being a Christian no longer makes any sense. A soldier, an athlete and a farmer will tell us about the days when they also felt like throwing in the towel. But there was always something that motivated them and encouraged them not to lose hope but carry on. They all share a common motivation! In all three cases, this motivation concerns the future:

- A soldier is motivated by the *thought* of victory.
- An athlete is encouraged by the *dream* of a crown of victory.
- A farmer is motivated by the *hope* of a harvest.

As believers, we should realize that our life is not a road that leads to nowhere but that there is something wonderful waiting for us in the future: heavenly glory! In the meantime, we should, like the soldier, remain focused on our calling and not be fazed by the ordinary things of life. We should stick to the rules like the athlete. Many athletes have had to endure the pain of being banned from their sport because they tested positive for certain substances. We need to stick to God's rules: It is good to love God and our neighbor! Like a farmer who has to wait for the results of his labor, we too have to learn to persevere—especially as spiritual leaders!

 Thank You, Lord, that Paul was so honest. I sometimes also feel disheartened. But like the soldier, the athlete and the farmer, I will learn to preserve!

Be like a postage stamp. Stick to one thing until you get there.
—Josh Billings (1818–1885), *The pen name of humorist Henry Wheeler Shaw, who was perhaps the second most famous humor writer and lecturer in the United States during the second half of the nineteenth century after Mark Twain*

EVER DOUBT THE VALUE OF THE BIBLE?

After all these centuries, the Bible remains the bestseller of all times. Despite this, many people doubt the value of the Bible. Is it possible that a book, written so many years ago, still has application to people's lives today? Timothy most likely also had doubts about the Bible's value. He was one of the first second-generation Christians. This means that his conversion was not the result of the ministry of a traveling apostle—he grew up in a Christian home (2 Tim. 1:5). This, however, does not free one of doubt. In the following section, Paul used encouraging words to address Timothy's possible doubt about the validity of Scripture.

2 Timothy 3 (explanation and instruction)

[14]But as for you, continue in what you have learned and have firmly believed, (*instruction*) knowing from whom you learned it [15]and how from childhood you have been acquainted with the sacred writings, which are able to make you wise for salvation through faith in Christ Jesus. [16]All Scripture is breathed out by God and profitable for teaching, for reproof, for correction, and for training in righteousness, [17]that the man of God may be competent, equipped for every good work. (*explanation*) ESV

Paul was a brilliant theologian, but in his attempt to convince Timothy about the value of the gospel, he did not use theological arguments. Instead, he referred to people—people whom Timothy knew very well. Paul referred to Timothy's grandmother, Loïs, and his mother, Eunice, who taught him about the Holy Scriptures from an early age (v. 15; see also 1 Tim. 2:5). More importantly, they lived according to the truth revealed in Scripture. The lives of his grandmother and mother confirmed that Scripture had made a difference in their lives. Timothy's mentor, Paul, was further proof that Scripture does bring about change in people's lives. Changed lives speak stronger than theological arguments.

Paul continued by stating, "All Scripture is breathed out by God" (16). This is exactly what the Bible does: It gives life! This means that God made provision for everything that is recorded in the Bible. He used people to do this—the Bible did not fall down from heaven. To summarize what Paul says: the Bible should direct our teaching and our lives. What we teach and the way we lead our lives should be in harmony. After all, as the saying goes, "practice what you preach and preach what you practice."

 Lord, I realize anew that I have a great responsibility to lead a righteous life.

The only objection against the Bible is a bad life.
—John Wilmot (1647–1680), *English poet and the second Earl of Rochester*

WE DO NOT LIKE TO TALK ABOUT DEATH!

People do not like to talk about death, yet it casts a shadow over our lives on a daily basis. Nobody can escape it. However, thinking about death should not make us feel negative—especially after reading this section.

2 Timothy 4 (explanation)

[6]For I am already being poured out as a *drink offering,* and the time of *my departure* has come. [7]I have fought the good fight, I have *finished the race,* I have kept the faith.
[8]Henceforth there is laid up for me the crown of righteousness, which the Lord, the righteous judge, will *award* to me on that Day, and not only to me but also to all who have loved his appearing. (ESV)

Paul did not deny or ignore his impending death, nor was he afraid to talk about it. In this passage, he uses four images to discuss his death: the *drink offering* (v. 6a), the *departure* (v. 6b), *finishing the race* (v. 7) and the *reward* (v. 8).

The *drink offering* was the very last part of the Israelites' process of offerings (Num. 15) in which wine was poured on the altar. Paul used this image to ensure that the last part of his life, like the rest of his life, would be an offering to God. In describing the *departure* from this world, Paul used a word (*analusis*) that in those days was also used to describe a ship that was about to depart. It literally meant "the time of loosing." Death should let us live daily with the realization that we should not cling to this world.

Paul saw his impending death as the *finish to a race.* We know that Paul's life involved a lot of hardship; however, he persevered because he knew that he would eventually be victorious at the end of the race, at which point he would receive the *reward.* Paul expanded this image by comparing his death to a prize-giving ceremony. In those days, winners received a crown of bay leaves at athletic meetings. This gave the winner many advantages, such as tributes, free meals and invitations to visit the homes of famous people. For Paul, the advantage of death was that he would be with God. These positive images help us to speak more freely about death.

 Thank You, Lord, that death is a finishing line with a reward.

Do not seek death. Death will find you. But seek the road which makes death a fulfillment.
—Dag Hammarskjöld (1905–1961), *Swedish diplomat and the second Secretary-General of the United Nations. He served from April 1953 until his death in a plane crash in September 1961.*

WHERE DO WE BEGIN TO HEAL A SICK SOCIETY?

In A.D. 60, Titus was the spiritual leader in Crete, an island located in the Mediterranean Sea. This island did not have a good name back then. Evidence from non-Biblical sources indicates that in those days the name *Cretan* was synonymous with pirates, thieves, guzzlers, liars, sluggards and beasts (Titus 1:12). Paul's command to Titus to bring order to such a sick society was indeed a tremendous task (v. 5). Where would he begin?

Titus 1 (instruction)

⁵I left you in Crete to do what had been left undone and to appoint leaders for the churches in each town. As I told you, ⁶they must have a good reputation and be faithful in marriage. Their children must be followers of the Lord and not have a reputation for being wild and disobedient. ⁸Instead, they must be friendly to strangers and enjoy doing good things. They must also be sensible, fair, pure, and self-controlled. ⁹They must stick to the true message they were taught, so that their good teaching can help others and correct everyone who opposes it. (CEV)

The healing of a sick society starts with leadership. This is the reason why Paul told Timothy to appoint elders who conformed to strict requirements. These elders had to be irreproachable role models who were aware of their responsibility toward God. The way they lived had to show the Cretans that Christianity could add value to society.

Families are the building blocks of a healthy society because they provide a safe haven in which children can grow up. In a sick society, these family structures seem to disintegrate completely and become a place of much violence. If we as Christian leaders, fathers, mothers, ministers or pastors want to contribute to building a healthy society, it would be wise for us to give first priority to our family life. No success at work can make up for failure at home. Let's put our families first!

 Lord, I would like to be a role model to others in the way I live—in Your honor!

I start with the premise that the function of leadership is to produce more leaders, not more followers.
—Ralph Nader (b. 1934), *American attorney and political activist who ran for President of the United States three times (1996, 2000 and 2004)*

IS THE BIBLE STILL CREDIBLE?

There are many different answers to this question. Arguments, no matter how good, will not easily convince opponents of the Word about its credibility. But there is something else which will embarrass the critics of God's Word.

Titus 2 (explanation and instruction)

[1]Titus, you must teach only what is correct. [2]Tell the older men to have self-control and to be serious and sensible. Their faith, love, and patience must never fail. [3]Tell the older women to behave as those who love the Lord should. They must not gossip about others or be slaves of wine. They must teach what is proper, (*instruction*)
[4]so the younger women will be loving wives and mothers. (*explanation*)
[5]Each of the younger women must be sensible and kind, as well as a good homemaker, who puts her own husband first. (*instruction*)
Then no one can say insulting things
about God's message. (*explanation*)
[6]Tell the young men to have self-control in everything.
[7]Always set a good example for others. Be sincere and serious when you teach.
[8]Use clean language that no one can criticize. Do this, and your enemies will be too ashamed to say anything against you. (*instruction*) CEV

Paul states that our exemplary conduct will make opponents of the Bible think twice before criticizing us (v. 8). This is why Paul asks Titus to spread sound doctrine, because the fruit it bears is a healthy lifestyle. An irreproachable life will confirm the virtuous, good and sound doctrines of the Bible. However, we should live out what we learn, for if we listen to the doctrines of God's grace and forgiveness but do not live accordingly, we discredit the Word of God (v. 4).

This kind of conduct provides the opponents of the Church with ammunition. This is why Paul advised the groups in the congregation in Crete to live according to sound doctrine. Believers of all ages should live in such a way that they will be assets to society. They should excel in those things non-Christians also regard as virtuous—things such as honesty, fidelity, sincerity, punctuality and trustworthiness, to mention just a few.

Saint Francis of Assisi once said, "Preach the gospel at all times, and if necessary, use words." Test yourself: If you were accused of being a Christian, would there be enough witnesses to prove that you are guilty? Martin Luther said that you should live in such a way that even your dog would know that you are a Christian.

 Lord, I want to commit myself anew to live according to Your will.

Faith makes a Christian. Life proves a Christian. Trial confirms a Christian.
Death crowns a Christian.
—Author unknown

WALLS THAT DON'T BELONG IN CHURCHES!

The short letter of Philemon, which consists of 25 verses that Paul wrote from prison to his friend Philemon in Colosse around A.D. 60, contains a very important message for us. It requires us to break down the walls in our churches—not the concrete walls, but the barriers of race, sexism, social status, gender and personality differences that so often exist. The two characters in the letter, namely Philemon and Onesimus, are striking examples of such barriers.

Philemon was the master, and Onesimus the slave. The separation between them grew when Onesimus ran away. However, this runaway slave's path crossed with that of Paul, and their meeting led to Onesimus's conversion. Paul sent Onesimus, the slave, back to Philemon with a letter addressed to his master. In those days, slavery was a common practice, and it is clear from Paul's letter that Christians also participated in the practice. Paul never openly criticized slavery, but in this letter he dealt the barrier a devastating blow. How did he do this?

Philemon (explanation and instruction)

¹From Paul, who is in jail for serving Christ Jesus, and from Timothy, who is like a brother because of our faith. Philemon, you work with us and are very dear to us. This letter is to you
⁸Christ gives me the courage to tell you what to do.
⁹But I would rather ask you to do it simply because of love. Yes, as someone in jail for Christ, *(explanation)*
¹⁰I beg you to help Onesimus! *(instruction)*
He is like a son to me because I led him to Christ here in jail.
¹¹Before this, he was useless to you, but now he is useful both to you and to me.
¹²Sending Onesimus back to you makes me very sad.
¹⁵Perhaps Onesimus was taken from you for a little while so that you could have him back for good. *(explanation)* CEV

Paul did not oppose slavery as a social structure, but dealt it a blow when he asked Philemon to take back his slave, Onesimus, as a brother in Christ. He told Philemon that their relationship had changed from that of a master and slave to one between fellow believers. In Christ, all of us belong to one big family. No barriers should bring discord between believers.

Christ came to break down all the barriers. It was for this reason Paul could write, "It doesn't matter if you are a Greek or a Jew, or if you are circumcised or not. You may even be a barbarian or a Scythian, and you may be a slave or a free person. Yet Christ is all that matters, and he lives in all of us" (Col. 3:11, CEV). Let us break down the barriers with our chisels of love and forgiveness.

 Lord, I want to break down the barriers that exist in my life!

The people to fear are not those who disagree with you, but those who disagree with
you and are too cowardly to let you know.
—Napoleon Bonaparte (1769–1821), *French Emperor*

HOW DO WE PUT THE SPARKLE BACK INTO OUR RELIGIOUS LIFE?

Life's burdens can deplete the sparkle, joy, newness and freshness of our faith. This was the exact position in which the recipients of the letter of Hebrews found themselves. In brilliant language (perhaps the best Greek in the New Testament), the author tried to encourage them by means of a pastoral sermon. How did he do this?

Hebrew 1 (explanation and poetry)

[1]Going through a long line of prophets, God has been addressing our ancestors in different ways for centuries. [2]Recently he spoke to us directly through his Son. By his Son, God created the world in the beginning, and it will all belong to the Son at the end. [3]*This Son perfectly mirrors God, and is stamped with God's nature.* He holds everything together by what he says—powerful words!
After he finished the sacrifice for sins, the Son took his honored place high in the heavens right alongside God,
[4]far higher than any angel in rank and rule. [5]Did God ever say to an angel, 'You're my Son; today I celebrate you'? Or, 'I'm his Father, he's my Son'? [6]When he presents his honored Son to the world, he says, 'All angels must worship him.' (*explanation*)
[7]Regarding angels he says,
The messengers are winds,
the servants are tongues of fire.
[8]But he says to *the Son*,
You're God, and on the throne for good;
your rule makes everything right. (*poetry*)

Hebrews 2 (explanation)

[1]It's crucial that we keep a firm grip on what we've heard so that we don't drift off. (MSG)

Fortunately, the author of Hebrews did not bombard his readers with a foolproof recipe or a list of do's and don'ts. Instead, he shifted the focus away from their gloomy situation to Someone who emanates the glory of God—who is the very image of God. This person was no less than Jesus! In order to put the sparkle back in their faith, they first and foremost had to realize who Jesus was and what He had done for them.

The reason the author needed to point this out was because the recipients thought that other practices (such as honoring the angels) would return the sparkle to their faith. The author wanted to eradicate this heresy by stressing that Jesus is far superior to the angels—He is *God!* Few verses state this clearer than verse 8: "But he says to the Son, You're God, and on the throne for good; your rule makes everything right."

Only after talking so splendidly about the divinity of Jesus did the author then turn to his list in chapter 2, where he asks them to cling to God's Word! This is why he asks in Hebrews 12:2–3 that we keep our eyes on Jesus, because Jesus is the Beginning and the End of our faith.

Thank You, Lord, that I can know who You are. Thank You that Your grace is sufficient for me.

I am trying here to prevent anyone saying the really foolish thing that people often say about Him: "I'm ready to accept Jesus as a great moral teacher, but I don't accept His claim to be God." That is the one thing we must not say. A man who was merely a man and said the sort of things Jesus said would not be a great moral teacher. He would either be a lunatic—on the level with the man who says he is a poached egg—or else he would be the Devil of Hell. You must make your choice. Either this man was, and is, the Son of God: or else a madman or something worse. You can shut Him up for a fool, you can spit at Him and kill Him as a demon; or you can fall at His feet and call Him Lord and God. But let us not come with any patronizing nonsense about His being a great human teacher. He has not left that open to us. He did not intend to.

—C.S. Lewis (1898–1963), High-powered Oxford and Cambridge professor and perhaps the twentieth century's most famous convert to Christianity. Lewis was the creator of the Narnia series.

WHY DIDN'T AN ANGEL COME TO DIE FOR US INSTEAD?

As a child, I often wondered why God did not use an angel to die for our sins. Why did He let His only Son? Why did Jesus and not an angel choose to become a human being? Or are God's promises not perhaps intended for angels (v. 5)? This section will eliminate all the doubt.

Hebrews 2 (explanation)

[5] God didn't put angels in charge of this business of salvation that we're dealing with here.
[14] Since the children are made of flesh and blood, it's logical that the Savior took on flesh and blood in order to rescue them by his death. By embracing death, taking it into himself, he destroyed the Devil's hold on death
[15] and freed all who cower through life, scared to death of death.
[16] It's obvious, of course, that he didn't go to all this trouble for angels. It was for people like us, children of Abraham.
[17] That's why he had to enter into every detail of human life. Then, when he came before God as high priest to get rid of the people's sins,
[18] he would have already experienced it all himself-all the pain, all the testing—and would be able to help where help was needed. (MSG)

In this passage, the author of Hebrews makes it very clear that Jesus did not become an angel but a *human being* and that by becoming fully human He fully identified Himself with human beings. The author gives three reasons why Jesus became a human being.

The first reason was to *destroy* the devil and *free* human beings from death (vv. 14–15). Before Jesus' death and resurrection, death instilled fear in people because the devil had dominion over death. However, with the death and resurrection of Jesus, the one who had dominion over death was conquered. Because a human being conquered death, death no longer had power over human beings.

The second reason Jesus became human was to save people from their sins (v. 17). Reconciliation means that broken relationships are restored. Sin had caused a rift between God and human beings. God wanted to bring peace between Himself (not angels) and human beings. This is why God, in the form of Jesus, became a human being. When a husband quarrels with his wife, he can't send his friend so that he can be reconciled with her. Therefore, God is concerned with human beings, not angels (v. 16).

The third reason Jesus became human was to *help those who needed help* (v. 18). It is almost impossible to understand other people's hurt and temptations if we do not experience them ourselves. The fact that Jesus Himself was tested and suffered (v. 18) enables Him to help us to handle the temptation and suffering in our own lives. Therefore, this invitation is extended to us: "So let's walk right up to him and get what he is so ready to give. Take the mercy, accept the help" (4:16). He understands!

Thank You, Lord, for understanding my pain and my temptations.

In Jesus, God wills to be true God not only in the height but also in the depth—in the depth of human creatureliness, sinfulness and mortality.
—Karl Barth (1886–1968), *Swiss theologian, among the most influential of the twentieth century*

HOLDING ON TO FAITH CAN BE A BATTLE!

It is very easy for us to hold on to our faith when things are going well. However, the reality is that things do not always go well, and it is exactly then that it becomes not so easy to hold onto our faith. During such times, we easily become rebellious and stubborn. The author of Hebrews does not sidestep this reality but talks about it quite openly.

Hebrews 3 (explanation and poetry)

[7]That's why the Holy Spirit says,
Today, please listen;
[8]don't turn a deaf ear as in 'the bitter uprising,'
that time of wilderness testing!
[9]Even though they watched me at work for forty years,
your ancestors refused to let me do it my way;
over and over they tried my patience.
[10]And I was provoked, oh, so provoked!
I said, 'They'll never keep their minds on God;
they refuse to walk down my road.'
[11]Exasperated, I vowed,
'They'll never get where they're going,
never be able to sit down and rest.' *(poetry)*
[12]So watch your step, friends. Make sure there's no evil unbelief lying around that will trip you up and throw you off course, diverting you from the living God. [13] For as long as it's still God's *Today*, keep each other on your toes (instruction) so sin doesn't slow down your reflexes. *(explanation)* MSG

The poetry the author of Hebrews uses in this passage (vv. 7–11) is from Psalm 95:7–11, which refers to the difficult times the Israelites had to endure in the desert. The author used the Israelites' wandering in the desert as an example to encourage those for whom he wrote his sermon. Like the Israelites, they had also become stubborn and lost their faith. The author made it very clear that such an attitude would eventually lead to their self-destruction.

For the stubborn Israelites, the loss of their faith had meant that they could not experience God's peace. The first generation of Israelites who came out of Egypt could not enter the Promised Land. Their stubbornness was so unnecessary. They should have noticed all of the things that God had done for them in the desert: the water from the rock, the quails and the manna, the cloud during the day and the pillar of fire at night. God helped them not to get lost but unfortunately, they did not notice these things.

It is when we think God has forsaken us that He is there with us to help us. If we choose not to notice this but remain rebellious and stubborn, it will lead to our destruction. The good news is that we still have time left to change. We still have today (v. 13) in which to learn to look differently at our situation—to see God!

Lord, I confess my rebelliousness. Today is the day I want to control it!

Yesterday, we can't do anything; tomorrow, we don't know. Today.
—Celine Dion (b. 1968), *French-Canadian music artist and the best-selling female artist of all time*

A DUEL WE CAN NEVER WIN

The Bible challenges us to a duel. When we open its pages and seriously engage with what it teaches, we become involved in a duel that we cannot win. Why is this?

Hebrews 4 (explanation and instruction)

[12]God means what he says. What he says goes.
His powerful Word is sharp as a surgeon's scalpel, cutting through everything, whether doubt or defense, laying us open to listen and obey.
[13]Nothing and no one is impervious to God's Word.
We can't get away from it-no matter what.
[14]Now that we know what we have-
Jesus, this great High Priest with ready access to God-*(explanation)*
 let's not let it slip through our fingers. *(instruction)*
[15]We don't have a priest who is out of touch with our reality.
He's been through weakness and testing, experienced it all-
all but the sin. *(explanation)*
[16]So let's walk right up to him and get what he is so ready to give.
Take the mercy, accept the help. *(instruction)* MSG

When we read the Word of God, we are not dealing with dead letters on paper. When we read the Word of God, it comes to life and is powerful. When God's Word starts working in us, it cuts through our spirit and soul with its two sharp edges.

In Greek, soul (*psuche*) refers to the physical, earthly life. According to the Greeks, both human beings and animals have *psuche*. In Greek, the spirit (*pneuma*) refers to the spiritual aspect that is only present in human beings. The gospel therefore tests both our physical and our spiritual life. The Word cuts through our joints and marrow—in other words, it does not only judge what our muscles do but also reveals the driving force (the marrow) behind it.

The sharp blades of the gospel reveal our hidden positive and negative intentions and the thoughts of our hearts. At the end of this duel with the gospel, we lie completely exposed before our own eyes. It is at this point that we see ourselves the way God has always seen us and realize that in the final moment of *reckoning* we are like a sacrificial animal on the altar waiting for the final blow of the sharp sword.

But verse 13 then leads us to the good news of the next verses of this chapter: the High Priest (Jesus) sacrificed Himself on our behalf. This is mercy! We need not fear the sword of God's Word. Our weaknesses (v. 15) that are revealed by the Word give us the opportunity to freely approach Jesus and thank Him for sacrificing Himself on our behalf. This is why prayer is an essential means of showing our gratitude.

 Thank You, Lord, for not judging me but acquitting me through Your grace.

Jesus is the God whom we can approach without pride and before whom we can humble
ourselves without despair.
—Blaise Pascal (1623–1662), *French mathematician, physicist and philosopher*

WHERE WAS GOD ON SEPTEMBER 11, 2001?

The world, especially America, will never be the same again after September 11, 2001. When people think about the tragic events that occurred on that day, they often ask each other, "Where were you when it happened?" But there is a much more difficult question that is also often asked, namely: "Where was God when it happened?"

Hebrews 4 (explanation and instruction)

14Now that we know what we have-
Jesus, this great High Priest with ready access to God-*(explanation)*
let's not let it slip through our fingers. *(instruction)*
15We don't have a priest who is out of touch with our reality.
He's been through weakness and testing, experienced it all-
all but the sin. *(explanation)*
16So let's walk right up to him and get what he is so ready to give.
Take the mercy, accept the help. *(instruction)* MSG

The following story illustrates something we cannot accuse God of doing. During the 1930s, a father found his daughter crying next to the radio in her room. When he asked her why she was so sad, she told him that she had heard a news report over the radio that said Japanese tanks had invaded Canton that day. This had very little significance for most of the people who listened to the news that day. So why was the girl in tears? It was because she was born in Canton. To her, Canton meant a loving home, school and friends. She could say, "I was there!"

For each human experience, God can also say, "I was there!" Through Jesus, God became a human being so that He could experience every possible human experience (v. 15). Because of this, we should feel free to approach the Lord with all of our pain and joy, because He has been there! This is why He finds it easy to forgive us. God understands our problems because, through Jesus, He overcame them. Nobody can accuse God of being harsh, cold and distant. The life and crucifixion of Jesus proclaim loud and clear: *God was there!*

God was even there on September 11, 2001. I believe He was disgusted that human beings abused their freedom and responsibility in the way they did. Although the Twin Towers fell, the following stands firm: "Though he was God's Son, he learned trusting-obedience by what he suffered, just as we do. Then, he became the source of eternal salvation to all who believingly obey him" (Heb. 5:8–10).

 Thank You, Lord, that I know that You are not distant and cold. I praise You!

The flood that devastates a town is not an "act of God," even if the insurance companies find it useful to call it that. But the efforts people make to save lives, risking their own lives for a person who might be a total stranger to them, and the determination to rebuild their community after the flood waters have receded, do qualify as acts of God.
—Harold Kushner, *Prominent American rabbi who wrote the immensely popular book* When Bad Things Happen to Good People

THE ONLY WAY TO HAVE PEACE

We all have a deep yearning for peace, but it often eludes us. Perhaps this is because we look for peace in all the wrong places. Many of us look for peace in *escapism,* but the problem with this is that at some stage we have to return to reality. Another way we search for peace is to deny and suppress our problems, but this also does not work because a problem is like an illness—the longer we ignore it, the worse it becomes. Another popular way we look for peace is in compromise, but the problem with compromise is that it does not always satisfy all parties. In fact, compromise often goes hand in hand with underlying tension, which is precisely what hampers peace. This next section in Hebrews shows us the correct way to find peace.

Hebrews 7 (explanation)

[1]Melchizedek was king of Salem and priest of the Highest God. He met Abraham, who was returning from 'the royal massacre,' and gave him his blessing.
[2]Abraham in turn gave him a tenth of the spoils. 'Melchizedek' means 'King of Righteousness.' 'Salem' means 'Peace.' So, he is also 'King of Peace.'
[3]Melchizedek towers out of the past—without record of family ties, no account of beginning or end. In this way he is like the Son of God, one huge priestly presence dominating the landscape always.
[15]But the Melchizedek story provides a perfect analogy: Jesus, a priest like Melchizedek,[16] not by genealogical descent but by the sheer force of resurrection life-he lives![17]priest forever in the royal order of Melchizedek.' (MSG)

The prerequisite for peace is contained in the name "Melchizedek." His name means "king of righteousness." Only then does his title follow: "king of *Salem,*" which means "king of *peace.*" It is clear from Melchizedek's name and title that righteousness always precedes peace. It is also clear that Melchizedek pointed towards Jesus, whose ministry was characterized by righteousness and peace.

We are not exactly sure who Melchizedek was, because he suddenly appeared on the scene and disappeared just as quickly (Gen. 14:17–20). However, the author of Hebrews saw Melchizedek as a *mysterious figure* from the past and he used him to explain that Jesus' priesthood replaced and surpassed the Levitical priesthood. The Levitical priesthood was based on genealogical descent, while Jesus, like Melchizedek, was not appointed as a priest on the grounds of heritage but is a priest for eternity.

Jesus came from the lineage of Judah. When He was born, the angels sang, "Glory to God in the heavenly heights" (Luke 2:14, MSG), and just before His ascension, He said the following to His disciples: "Peace be with you" (Luke 24:36, MSG). Jesus could say this because between the time of His birth and His ascension, He shared in our sins when He was on the cross. Righteousness triumphed when He paid for our sins.

Mercifully, Jesus endured this on our behalf. Although His crucifixion did not rid the earth of all injustice, it did guarantee that there will eventually be a future in which righteousness and peace will embrace each other. Until that time, we should be peacemakers by ensuring that righteousness prevails.

Lord, I no longer want to turn a blind eye to all the injustice of life.

If I must choose between peace and righteousness, I choose righteousness.
—Theodore Roosevelt (1858–1919), *Twenty-sixth President of the United States (1901–1909)*

WHY IS THE CHRISTIAN "RELIGION" SO UNIQUE?

There are many religions, and all of them believe that they are right. Why does religion exist? The reason religion exists is because human beings have an inherent need for a deity. Religion provides access to such a deity. We believe that the Christian "religion" differs from all the other religions. But what makes it so unique?

Hebrews 7 (explanation)

[1]Melchizedek was king of Salem and priest of the Highest God.
[24]But Jesus' priesthood is permanent. He's there from now to eternity
[25]to save everyone who comes to God through him, always on the job to speak up for them.
[26]So now we have a high priest who perfectly fits our needs: completely holy, uncompromised by sin, with authority extending as high as God's presence in heaven itself.
[27]Unlike the other high priests, he doesn't have to offer sacrifices for his own sins every day before he can get around to us and our sins. He's done it, once and for all: offered up himself as the sacrifice.
[28]The law appoints as high priests men who are never able to get the job done right. But this intervening command of God, which came later, appoints the Son, who is absolutely, eternally perfect. (MSG)

The Jewish religion was designed to bring human beings closer to God. This would be achieved in two ways: First, by establishing obedience to the Law, which brought a person closer to God; and second, through the introduction of the sacrificial system, which was necessary because it was impossible to achieve this kind of obedience to the Law. The priests' function was to open a way to God by means of this system. However, the system as a whole was ineffective because it failed to establish true peace between God and human beings. The offerings could not pay the price for sin, and the priests themselves had weaknesses (v. 28). The answer to this problem rested in another high priest and another offering.

In order to open a way to God, a high priest had to be fully in touch with human beings and with God. He had to know human beings and God perfectly. Only one person on earth could satisfy these requirements: Jesus. This is why the author of Hebrews makes it very clear in chapter 1 that Jesus was truly human and truly God. Although this is not always easy to understand, it makes sense: as a *human being*, Jesus represented us before God, but as *God,* He represented God before us. Jesus was therefore the perfect High Priest. Furthermore, Jesus was the perfect sacrifice who died on our behalf.

It is not religion with all its customs and rituals that opens the way to God, but the person of Jesus Christ. He is the way, the truth and life (John 14:6). In the heading to today's reading, the word "religion" is placed in quotes because the Christian faith is not really a religion but a relationship with the living God. Faith in Jesus, not religion, makes us children of the heavenly Father. This is what makes the Christian faith so unique.

 Thank You, Lord, that Your sacrificial death opened the way to God for me.

Jesus does not give recipes that show the way to God as other teachers of religion do. He is himself the way.
—Karl Barth (1886–1968), *Swiss theologian, among the most influential of the twentieth century*

WHAT SHOULD WE DO
WHEN WE ARE SPIRITUALLY TIRED?

Because we are vulnerable, we often have to deal with life's sharp edges. During these times, it becomes very difficult to hold on to our faith. Constantly having to search for meaning in our hurt can drain us spiritually. This next section gives us hope!

Hebrews 11 (explanation)

¹The fundamental fact of existence is that this trust in God, this faith, is the firm foundation under everything that makes life worth living. It's our handle on what we can't *see.* ²The act of faith is what distinguished our ancestors, set them above the crowd. ³By faith, we *see* the world called into existence by God's word, what we *see* created by what we don't *see.* ⁷By faith, Noah built a ship in the middle of dry land. He was warned about something he couldn't *see,* and acted on what he was told. The result? His family was saved. His act of faith drew a sharp line between the evil of the unbelieving world and the rightness of the believing world. As a result, Noah became intimate with God. ¹³Each one of these people of faith died not yet having in hand what was promised, but still believing. How did they do it? They *saw* it way off in the distance, waved their greeting, and accepted the fact that they were transients in this world. ²⁴By faith, Moses, when grown, refused the privileges of the Egyptian royal house. ²⁶He valued suffering in the Messiah's camp far greater than Egyptian wealth because he was *looking* ahead, anticipating the payoff. ²⁷By an act of faith, he turned his heel on Egypt, indifferent to the king's blind rage. He had his *eye* on the One no *eye* can *see,* and kept right on going. (MSG)

Hebrews 12 (explanation and instruction)

¹Do you see what this means—all these pioneers who blazed the way, all these veterans cheering us on? . . . ²Keep your *eyes* on Jesus, who both began and finished this race we're in. Study how he did it. (*instruction*)
Because he never lost *sight* of where he was headed—that exhilarating finish in and with God—he could put up with anything along the way: cross, shame, whatever. And now he's there, in the place of honor, right alongside God. (*explanation*)
³When you find yourselves flagging in your faith, go over that story again, item by item, that long litany of hostility he plowed through. (*instruction*)
That will shoot adrenaline into your souls! (*explanation*) MSG

The people the author mentions in chapter 11 all experienced difficult and tiring times. Despite this, they did not give up spiritually, and they eventually rejoiced. Verse 13 gives an impressive summary of their lives: "Each one of these people of faith died not yet having in hand what was promised, but still believing. How did they do it? They saw it way off in the distance, waved their greeting, and accepted the fact that they were transients in this world." Faith helped them to look beyond the horizons of their lives—to see the future of God.

Faith helped Noah to see what others were unable to see with their ordinary eyes—namely, what would still happen, the flood—and he adjusted his life accordingly. Moses also chose suffering instead of the treasures of Egypt because he looked forward to the heavenly reward. *Faith enables us to see better—to see Jesus.* This is why we are commanded to keep our eyes on Jesus (vv. 2–3). The eyes of faith enable us to look beyond our hurt and suffering. Faith helps us to endure.

Thank You, Lord, that faith enables me to see better.

Fear can keep us up all night long, but faith makes one fine pillow.
—Author unknown

BITTER OR BETTER?

From time to time, we all find ourselves in a situation (often because of our own doing) from which we would like to escape. No one is immune to affliction and suffering, and it can make us extremely bitter. But the author of James asks us to change our attitude toward suffering. It is interesting to note that it is generally accepted that the author of this letter, who is identified as James, was Jesus' brother. He wrote to the believers who fled from Jerusalem after Stephan's martyrdom. The believers who fled experienced a lot of suffering. His opening words in verse 2 may surprise you. Be prepared!

James 1 (explanation and instruction)

¹I, James, am a slave of God and the Master Jesus, writing to the twelve tribes scattered to Kingdom Come: Hello!
²Consider it a sheer gift, friends, when tests and challenges come at you from all sides. (*instruction*)
³You know that under pressure, your faith-life is forced into the open and shows its true colors. ⁴So don't try to get out of anything prematurely. Let it do its work so you become mature and well-developed, not deficient in any way. (*explanation*) (MSG)

The tone of James' opening words to the believers who fled is not gloomy. On the contrary, he asks them to be happy. One is tempted to tell James that he is out of his mind to ask them to be happy when bitterness would be the logical emotion. However, James then explains in striking terms why they should rather be happy: suffering is a religious exercise.

Faith is precious, and in order for us to be strengthened against dejection and bitterness, we should exercise our faith. The purpose of suffering is not to lead us to a fall but for us to conquer it by overcoming. It does not exist to make us weaker and bitter but to make us stronger and better. We are put to the test because God is more interested in our character than in our comfort. Just think about Paul, who had to endure so much suffering and discomfort. Despite all his suffering, he was able to write, "There's more to come: We continue to shout our praise even when we're hemmed in with troubles, because we know how troubles can develop passionate patience in us, and how that patience in turn forges the tempered steel of virtue, keeping us alert for whatever God will do next" (Rom. 5:3–4, MSG).

God considers faith to be more precious than comfort. On August 3, 2004, I tuned in to Larry King Live to see an interview he was conducting with the famous Joni Eareckson Tada. Joni had become a quadriplegic in 1967 after a diving accident. While in a wheelchair, she wrote bestsellers and received many tributes and awards. When asked about her life in a wheelchair, she answered with a smile, "Larry, this wheelchair is my freedom. This wheelchair was instrumental in bringing me to Christ." She wasn't bitter but better—a symbol of hope!

 Thank You, Lord, that suffering helps me to be a better person!

What seems to us as bitter trials are often blessings in disguise.
—Oscar Wilde (1854–1900), *Irish poet, novelist, dramatist and critic*

WHAT IS MORE IMPORTANT THAN APPEARANCE?

These days, appearance is of the utmost importance. It is unbelievable how much money people spend on their external appearance. Of course, many see this as their ticket to acceptance. However, the author of James uses an instruction and a parable to tell us that there are more important things in life than appearance.

James 2 (parable and instruction)

[1]My dear friends, don't let public opinion influence
how you live out our glorious, Christ-originated faith. (*instruction*)
[2]*If* a man enters your church wearing an expensive suit, and a street person wearing rags comes in
right after him, [3]and you say to the man in the suit, 'Sit here, sir; this is the best seat in the house!' and
either ignore the street person or say, 'Better sit here in the back row,' [4]haven't you segregated God's
children and proved that you are judges who can't be trusted? (*parable*) MSG

This section in James gives us two reasons why we as believers should not judge others on their appearance. The first reason is because we should not bestow the honor that belongs to God on people (v. 1). Differences of "magnificence" may exist between people, but in the magnificence of God's glory, these differences disappear, just as the stars—even those that shine brightly—disappear when the sun rises. All people are equal before God!

The second reason why we should not judge others is given in the form of a parable. Perhaps one could call this the "parable of snobbishness." In this parable, people make a fuss of a smartly dressed person in the congregation, while the members look down on the person who is not dressed as well. The smartly dressed person receives a place of honor, while the other one has to be content with a bench at the back. It is wrong to judge people on their appearance, because believers should be measured in terms of faith and love, not wealth and poverty.

There is a story told of a former slave who at the end of the Civil War attended the communion service of a very "smart" church. When the time came to serve the communion, the slave walked down the aisle and knelt before the altar. The congregation was noticeably shocked and angered. But then one of the members stood up, walked to the front and knelt down beside the man. This moved the other members of the congregation to such an extent that they all stood up, walked forward and knelt at the altar. The congregation member who knelt beside the slave showed that love and faith surpass outward appearance.

Likewise, these four verses in James clearly show that the glory of God and character is more important than appearance.

Lord, forgive me when I judge people on their appearance.

Let us be grateful to the mirror for revealing to us our appearance only.
—Samuel Butler (1835–1902), *British writer best known for his satire* Erewhon *and his posthumous novel* The Way of All Flesh

CAN FAITH WITHOUT GOOD DEEDS SAVE US?

The Bible is very clear that we are saved through faith alone. So where do good deeds fit in? Can faith without good deeds save us? This is a very important question that James answered clearly.

James 2 (explanation)

[14]Dear friends, do you think you'll get anywhere in this if you learn all the right words but never do anything? Does merely talking about faith indicate that a person really has it? [15]For instance, you come upon an old friend dressed in rags and half-starved [16]and say, 'Good morning, friend! Be clothed in Christ! Be filled with the Holy Spirit!' and walk off without providing so much as a coat or a cup of soup—where does that get you? [17]Isn't it obvious that God-talk without God-acts is outrageous nonsense? [26]The very moment you separate body and spirit, you end up with a corpse. Separate faith and works and you get the same thing: a corpse. (MSG)

James' answer was very clear: faith without deeds cannot save us. To understand James' words, we first need to distinguish between two kinds of faith. With intellectual faith, you believe that the earth is round but that it does not really have an influence on your life. On the other hand, because you believe that 2 plus 2 adds up to 4, you will not pay more than $4.00 for 2 chocolates that cost $2.00 each. You accept the fact that 2 plus 2 makes 4, and this determines your actions. This faith leads to action.

Intellectual faith merely accepts the facts, but it does not influence your behavior. This is like believing that Jesus died on the cross for you but not being affected when you encounter people who do not have clothes to wear and who are hungry. Such faith does not mean a thing. Faith is therefore more than intellectual knowledge; it should result in active deeds. Faith is like a carpenter's square. The one arm points upward to God while the other one points straight to your fellow human beings. If you only have one arm, the structure will be incomplete and deformed.

The dual truth is that we are not saved *by* good deeds but *for* good deeds. Paul placed much emphasis on the first part (faith), while James emphasized the second part (deeds). Paul and James do not contradict one another but rather complement each other. In the last verse, James compares faith and deeds to a body and breath. Faith is like a body that has to use deeds to breathe or else it dies. Faith without good deeds cannot save us.

 Lord, I pray that my faith will make a difference.

The smallest good deed is better than the grandest intention.
—Author unknown

WHAT DO OUR TONGUES AND A TUBE OF TOOTHPASTE HAVE IN COMMON?

The tongue and a tube of toothpaste have one thing in common: once their contents are out, it cannot be put back. There are times when we reproach ourselves for saying the wrong thing or we think we should have kept quiet instead. Yet as James states in the following section, it is possible to control our tongue. How?

James 3 (explanation and instruction)

¹Don't be in any rush to become a teacher, my friends. *(instruction)*
Teaching is highly responsible work.
Teachers are held to the strictest standards.
²And none of us is perfectly qualified.
We get it wrong nearly every time we open our mouths.
If you could find someone whose speech was perfectly true, you'd have a perfect person, in perfect control of life.
³A bit in the mouth of a horse controls the whole horse.
⁴A small rudder on a huge ship in the hands of a skilled captain sets a course in the face of the strongest winds.
⁵A word out of your mouth may seem of no account, but it can accomplish nearly anything—or destroy it! *(explanation)* MSG

The tongue performs the same work as the bit of a bridle or the rudder of a ship. In the same way the bit and the rudder control something large, the tongue has the ability to control major things in our lives. In reality, we often stumble. The question is, How can we keep our tongues in check? Perhaps the first two words of the Lord's prayer can help us here: our Father! These are words of faith that have the ability to change our speech because it can teach us three important things.

First, it can teach us *modesty*. Notice in the Lord's Prayer that Jesus used the words "our Father," not "my Father." This means that we should learn to listen to the opinion of others. We should learn to regard others in a serious light, because together we pray, "Our Father."

Second, the words of the Lord's Prayer teach us *solidarity*. We are not the only ones who believe—many other people share our faith and have the same Father. This is the reason why the needs of others should touch us. We cannot keep quiet if we witness injustice being done toward others because together we pray, "Our Father."

Third, it teaches us *inclusivity*. We cannot exclude others. The world does not, for example, only consist of males. We may not look down on others, because together we pray, "Our Father." The Lord's Prayer teaches us to think differently, which in turn will help us to speak differently. Remember: the way we speak is the way we live and think.

 Thank You, Lord, that Your prayer can help me to think differently so that I can speak differently.

Speaking without thinking is shooting without taking aim.
—Author unknown

HOW WILL WE BE ABLE TO PERSEVERE IN TROUBLED TIMES?

In about A.D. 65, Peter wrote his first letter to the devastated believers in Asia Minor who were suffering greatly because society had rejected them. Peter wanted to give them hope to carry on with their lives. He did this by showing them how they had to see themselves in the world.

1 Peter 1 (explanation)

> ¹I, Peter, am an apostle on assignment by Jesus, the Messiah,
> writing to *exiles* scattered to the four winds.
> Not one is missing, not one forgotten. (MSG)

1 Peter 2 (explanation and instruction)

> ¹¹Friends, this world is not your home, *(explanation)*
> so don't make yourselves cozy in it.
> Don't indulge your ego at the expense of your soul. *(instruction)* MSG

Peter showed the believers—and us—that they should regard themselves as strangers in this world. He felt very strongly about this, which is why the two main sections of the book start with this thought. Before telling them anything else, Peter wanted them to understand that they were strangers in this world. But why would Peter want believers to regard themselves as strangers?

First, by regarding ourselves as strangers, many things become clear to us. The criticism, insults and suffering we experience as a Christian are precisely because our values and approach to life make us different from the rest of the world. We are different because we represent the values of Christ, which is often contrary to how the world sees things. In this way, we become Christ's conscience to the world.

Second, it emphasizes the difference between the Church and the world. Three things are important in the world: money, sex and power. The Church (hopefully) revolves around faith, hope and love. These differences will obviously alienate us in a world that places so much emphasis on money, sex and power!

Third, knowing that we are strangers in this world is comforting! Hebrews 11 tells us about the "heroes of faith" of the Old Testament and summarizes their lives very succinctly in verse 13: "Each one of these people of faith died not yet having in hand what was promised, but still believing. How did they do it? They saw it way off in the distance, waved their greeting, and accepted the fact that they were transients in this world" (MSG). To us as believers, this brings everlasting comfort because faith enables us to look beyond our alienation. Faith enables us to see the Promised Land—eternal life with God. May this help us to persevere!

 Thank You, Lord, that my alienation from the world enables me to see everything in perspective.

In faith there is enough light for those who want to believe and enough shadows to blind those who don't.
—Blaise Pascal *(1623–1662), French mathematician, physicist, and religious philosopher*

SOMETHING A CHRISTIAN SHOULD NEVER BE SURPRISED ABOUT

As believers, we are often disillusioned because certain things happen to us. Peter is very clear about what should never surprise us.

1 Peter 4 (explanation and instruction)

[12-13]Friends, when life gets really difficult, don't jump to the conclusion that God isn't on the job. Instead, be glad that you are in the very thick of what Christ experienced. *(instruction)*
This is a spiritual refining process, with glory just around the corner. *(explanation)*
[14-16]If you're abused because of Christ, count yourself fortunate. *(instruction)*
It's the Spirit of God and his glory in you that brought you to the notice of others. If they're on you because you broke the law or disturbed the peace, that's a different matter. *(explanation)*
But if it's because you're a Christian, don't give it a second thought. Be proud of the distinguished status reflected in that name! *(instruction)* MSG

1 Peter 3 (explanation)

[13-14]If with heart and soul you're doing good, do you think you can be stopped? Even if you suffer for it, you're still better off. MSG

Peter makes it clear that we should never be surprised to find that being a Christian is no easy task. We should expect this because we will, in fact, experience opposition. This is because we begin to expect the world to have Jesus' standards, and we become the world's conscience. Of course, those in the world will not always like this—especially if we are the conscience of, for example, honesty or conjugal fidelity, and if we uphold what is right and truthful.

Peter did not get depressed about the matter. He wanted believers to approach suffering from the right perspective. First, he saw this as a crucial test of people's faith (v. 12). The test for them was whether they would continue loving Christ even though they did not see Him, just as the test for us is whether we will continue loving Him even though we do not see Him now (vv. 8–9). Faith should be tested, because we are tempted to consider the reality we can see in a more serious light than God whom we cannot see.

Second, Peter says that suffering makes us part of Christ (v. 13). This means that we can participate in the sufferings of Christ. Furthermore, Peter says that suffering helps us to share in the glory of God (v. 13). Paul said exactly the same thing: "We go through exactly what Christ goes through. If we go through the hard times with him, then we're certainly going to go through the good times with him!" (Rom. 8:17, MSG). The cross, the suffering, is the way to glory. It is for this reason that we are, according to Peter, privileged and blessed.

 Thank You, Lord, that I need not be ashamed to be Your child.

We were promised sufferings. They were part of the program. We were even told, "Blessed are they that mourn.'
—*C.S. Lewis (1898–1963), Oxford and Cambridge professor and perhaps the twentieth century's most famous convert to Christianity. Lewis was the creator of the Narnia series.*

GRACE IN SUFFERING

Suffering on its own does not make much sense. It can make us bitter and strip us of all hope. This is what happened to the believers in Asia Minor. They experienced opposition and discrimination because they were Christians and because they did certain things. Peter wrote this letter to them to encourage them during their times of suffering.

1 Peter 5 (explanation and instruction)

[9]Resist him, standing firm in the faith, (*instruction*)
because you know that your fellow believers throughout the world are undergoing the same kind of sufferings.
[10]And the God of all grace, who called you to his eternal glory in Christ, after you have suffered a little while, will himself restore you and make you strong, firm and steadfast.
[11]To him be the power for ever and ever. Amen.
[12]With the help of Silas, whom I regard as a faithful brother, I have written to you briefly, encouraging you and testifying that this is the true grace of God. (*explanation*)
Stand fast in it. (*instruction*) TNIV

Peter did not give believers a 10-point plan on how to handle or avoid suffering. In reality, a Christian will always accept suffering, because he or she applies Christ's standards to the world. But in this letter, Peter wanted to convince his readers that there was hope despite the suffering. Peter encapsulated the purpose of the letter by saying, "I have written to you briefly, encouraging you and testifying that this is the true grace of God." (v. 12). What a thing to say—namely, that suffering is God's true grace—to a people who were being prosecuted.

In 1 Peter 2:19–20, Peter repeats what he often says in the letter: "For this is a *gracious thing*, when, mindful of God, one endures sorrows while suffering unjustly. For what credit is it if, when you sin and are beaten for it, you endure? But if when you do good and suffer for it you endure, this is a *gracious thing* in the sight of God" (*ESV*). How can he say this?

According to Peter, suffering basically does two things for believers. First, suffering allows Christians to share in the suffering of Christ because of their different lifestyle and unites them with Him. This also means that we will share in His glory (1 Pet. 4:13). What a tremendous thought! The second reason appears in 1 Peter 4:14: "If you are insulted because of the name of Christ, you are *blessed*, for the Spirit of glory and of God rests on you" (*TNIV*). To know this is the greatest blessing, and it is our hope. Uphold this!

 Lord, thank You that suffering carries hope!

Although the world is full of suffering, it is also full of the overcoming of it.
—Helen Keller (1880–1968), American author and educator who was blind and deaf

I OFTEN STUMBLE! WHAT DO I DO?

To believe in Christ does not necessarily safeguard us against temptation. Every day, so many fall prey to temptation. Yet we shouldn't feel alone in this. Think about David, who committed adultery, and even Peter, who betrayed Jesus on three occasions. For Peter, betraying Christ was the low point of his life. But fortunately, God did not turn his back on him. In his later years, the cowardly and impulsive Peter preached the gospel with great commitment. Peter wanted to prevent us from making the same mistakes. He therefore gives us excellent advice that will help us to keep from stumbling.

2 Peter 1 (explanation and instruction)

3-4Everything that goes into a life of pleasing God has been miraculously given to us by getting to know, personally and intimately, the One who invited us to God. The best invitation we ever received! We were also given absolutely terrific promises to pass on to you—your tickets to participation in the life of God after you turned your back on a world corrupted by lust. *(explanation)*
5-7So don't lose a minute in building on what you've been given, complementing your basic faith with good character, spiritual understanding, alert discipline, passionate patience, reverent wonder, warm friendliness, and generous love, each dimension fitting into and developing the others. *(instruction)*
10. . . Do this, and you'll have your life on a firm footing. *(explanation)* MSG

Christian life starts with faith, but does not end there. It must develop to reach maturity. Peter calls this growth "goodness." Faith is enriched by being virtuous. To be virtuous means that we have the ability to give practical meaning to our faith. This is followed by knowledge that helps us to act effectively. In order to always act effectively, we need to apply self-control, and then it will become obvious that this self-control should be enhanced by perseverance.

We are only able to persevere because God stands by us. We will come to realize that it is imperative for us to live our life close to God. This living in the presence of God is called "godliness." Godliness is then enriched with the love we have for each other and, eventually, for all people.

Christian life starts with faith and turns to love through enrichment. One could say that the enrichment of our faith ends with God, because God is love. Peter is therefore convinced that the enrichment of our faith will help us not to falter. He is so convinced that he pleads with us to make every effort to achieve this.

 Lord, I want to do everything possible to add goodness to my faith.

When you want it the most, there's no easy way out. When you're ready to go, and your heart's left in doubt. Don't give up on your faith, love *comes to those who believe it . . . and that's the way it is.*
—Celine Dion (b. 1968), *French-Canadian music artist and the best-selling female artist of all time*

GUARD AGAINST THEM!

Peter warned the disillusioned second generation of Christians against false prophets and religious teachers. That generation was disillusioned because they were convinced that Jesus would come during their lifetime. When the first Christians started to die before Jesus' promise was fulfilled, some of the believers started to doubt and gave up hope that Jesus would ever return. False prophets and religious teachers exploited this situation. Peter warned the believers against these false teachers by pointing out the characteristics these individuals would possess. Consider these characteristics and judge for yourself whether false prophets and religious teachers still exist today.

2 Peter 2 (explanation)

¹But there were also lying prophets among the people then, just as there will be lying religious teachers among you. They'll smuggle in destructive divisions, pitting you against each other—biting the hand of the One who gave them a chance to have their lives back! They've put themselves on a fast downhill slide to destruction,
²but not before they recruit a crowd of mixed-up followers who can't tell right from wrong. They give the way of truth a bad name.
³They're only out for themselves. They'll say anything, anything that sounds good to exploit you. They won't, of course, get by with it. They'll come to a bad end, for God has never just stood by and let that kind of thing go on. (MSG)

The Old Testament tells us about false prophets, and it is interesting that their characteristics also appear in the New Testament. False prophets and religious teachers basically have the following four characteristics:

1. *They are more concerned about their own popularity than the gospel.* They therefore tell people what they would like to hear instead of what they ought to hear. Peter calls this tactic "smuggling." They sneak their lies in among the truth.
2. *They often lead an immoral life.* Jeremiah described false prophets as follows: "And the Jerusalem prophets are even worse—horrible!—sex-driven, living a lie, subsidizing a culture of wickedness, and never giving it a second thought. They're as bad as those wretches in old Sodom, the degenerates of old Gomorrah" (Jer. 23:14, MSG). These false teachers follow this lifestyle because they abuse the Lord's grace as justification for their sins.
3. *They are interested in personal gain.* They are driven by greed and "think that godliness is a means to financial gain" (1 Tim. 6:5, MSG).
4. *They lead people away from the Lord.* Above all, a false prophet leads people away from the Lord instead of closer to Him. The reason for this is because they do not know the Way of truth.

Sadly, many of these characteristics are still present in the Church, and this sheds a bad light on Christianity. The false prophet's path will eventually lead to destruction. Guard against them!

Thank You, Lord, that I can be warned against false prophets and religious teachers.

Watch out for false prophets.
They come to you in sheep's clothing, but inwardly they are ferocious wolves.
—Jesus (Matthew 7:15, NIV)

WHY DOES GOD WAIT SO LONG?

One of the most frustrating things is to wait. After waiting for almost 40 years for Jesus to return, the second generation of Christians to whom Peter wrote his second letter were very tired of waiting. We have been waiting 2,000 years for Jesus to return, and many of us might be wondering whether He has forgotten about us. Will Jesus really still come?

2 Peter 3 (explanation and instruction)

⁸Don't overlook the obvious here, friends. (*instruction*) With God, one day is as good as a thousand years, a thousand years as a day.

⁹God isn't late with his promise as some measure lateness. He is restraining himself on account of you, holding back the End because he doesn't want anyone lost. He's giving everyone space and time to change.

¹⁰But when the Day of God's Judgment does come, it will be unannounced, like a thief. The sky will collapse with a thunderous bang, everything disintegrating in a huge conflagration, earth and all its works exposed to the scrutiny of Judgment. (*explanation*)

¹⁵Interpret our Master's patient restraint for what it is: salvation. (*instruction*) MSG

God has not forgotten us. Peter gives two reasons why God is still waiting to send Jesus back to earth. First, Peter reminds us that time is not the same for us as it is for God. God lives in eternity. Eternity is not the sum total of time plus time plus time eternal but most likely the total absence of time. This is why one day is like 1,000 years and 1,000 years like one day to God. The author of Psalm 90 stated it in the following way: "Patience! You've got all the time in the world—whether a thousand years or a day, it's all the same to you" (v. 4, MSG). For this reason, human beings cannot calculate when the second coming will occur.

Second, Peter calls this time of waiting a time of grace. What we consider waiting is actually an expression of God's patience with us. God wants to give people the opportunity to be saved. He does not want anyone to be lost (1 Tim. 2:3–4). As the prophet Ezekiel wrote, "Do you think I take any pleasure in the death of wicked men and women? Isn't it my pleasure that they turn around, no longer living wrong but living right—really living?" (18:23, MSG).

This truth is echoed throughout the Bible. Nowhere are we prohibited from believing that God, who loves the world, will somehow bring the whole world to Him. Every new day echoes this truth! For those of us who have been saved, each day is a grateful opportunity to show by the way we live that we are ready for the coming of Jesus.

 Thank You, Lord, for Your grace and Your great patience with me!

Teach us, O Lord, the disciplines of patience, for to wait is often harder than to work.
—Peter Marshall (b. 1927), American TV game show host

THE ESSENCE OF THE CHRISTIAN FAITH

Around A.D. 90, a few non-Jewish congregations in Asia Minor were experiencing problems due to some false teachings. In response, the author of 1 John (most likely John the apostle and author of the fourth Gospel) wrote to the Christians to encourage them and warn them against false teachings. Some of these false teachers were preaching that sin should not be regarded too seriously. John used five "ifs" to encourage the believers to refute this heresy.

1 John 1 (explanation)

⁵This is the message we have heard from him and declare to you:
God is light; in him there is no darkness at all.
⁶If we claim to have fellowship with him yet walk in the darkness,
we lie and do not live by the truth.
⁷But if we walk in the light, as he is in the light,
we have fellowship with one another, and the blood of Jesus,
his Son, purifies us from all sin.
⁸If we claim to be without sin, we deceive ourselves and the truth is not in us.
⁹If we confess our sins, he is faithful and just and will forgive us our sins
and purify us from all unrighteousness.
¹⁰If we claim we have not sinned, we make him out to be a liar
and his word has no place in our lives. (MSG)

John's five "ifs" center on the essence of the Christian faith. It can be summarized under three headings: *What a mess! What a God!* and *What a difference!*

What a mess! First, John states that believers should realize that they are sinners. We do not like to think about ourselves in this way. We would rather like to believe that each of us is inherently good. However, if we believe this, we are only deceiving ourselves (v. 8) and make God out to be a liar (v. 10). As Paul states, "We've compiled this long and sorry record as sinners (both us and them) and proved that we are utterly incapable of living the glorious lives God wills for us" (Rom. 3:23, MSG). This brings us to the second point of the essence of our faith:

What a God! The good news is that we can share in God's glory despite our sins. How? "If we confess our sins, he is faithful and just and will forgive us our sins; and purify us from all unrighteousness" (v. 9). This knowledge brings us to the third point:

What a difference! As Christians, we consider the truth to be something we discover and, after discovering it, we have no choice but to live it out. We discover that God is light and that grace alone enables us to be part of God. This fills us with such gratitude that we want to live in the light (v. 6). It does not mean that we are perfect. A musician need not be good in order to love music passionately, and in the same vein, we need not be perfect in order to love Christ.

 Thank You, Lord, that I can share in Your glory despite my shortcomings.

In the New Testament, religion is grace and ethics is gratitude.
—Thomas Erskine (1788–1870), *Scottish theologian*

WE EASILY STUMBLE OVER
THIS FOUR-LETTER WORD . . .

First John 4:7–21 contains a superb section on love. In this section, John mentions love 27 times. Even today, love is an overwhelming theme. The Beatles sang about it in the 1960s. Their message to a broken world was, "Love is all you need." According to Amazon.com (2007), there are at least 470,950 printed books and more than 38,500 albums/CDs with the word "love" in their titles. In 2007 I did a Google-search and discovered that there are at least 936,000,000 websites with "love" as their main word. There is no doubt that love is still very important. Yet it is sad that we often get hurt while looking for love. Why do we so easily stumble over this four-letter word?

1 John 4 (explanation and instruction)

[7]My beloved friends, let us continue to *love* each other *(instruction)*
since *love* comes from God.
Everyone who *loves* is born of God
and experiences a relationship with God.
[8]The person who refuses to *love* doesn't know the first thing about God, because God is *love*-so you can't know him if you don't *love*.
[9]This is how God showed his *love* for us:
God sent his only Son into the world so we might live through him.
[10]This is the kind of love we are talking about –
not that we once upon a time *loved* God,
but that he *loved* us and sent his Son as a sacrifice
to clear away our sins
and the damage they've done to our relationship with God.
[21]The command we have from Christ is blunt:
Loving God includes *loving* people. *(explanation)*
You've got to *love* both. *(instruction)* MSG

We often stumble in our search for love. Perhaps this is because we often talk about love without realizing what love really is. The Greek word for love that is used in this passage is *agape*. In fact, the Greeks used four words for love: *eros* (romantic love), *philia* (love of friendship), *storge* (love for family) and *agape* (charity). The authors of the Bible used the word *agape* to describe God's love for human beings. This love was manifested in Jesus' life. It is *unselfish, unconditional, willing to make sacrifices* and *forgiving*. We do not deserve this love. *Agape* is therefore, grace in action. It is a love that starts with God, which is why the author of this section declares that God is love. We often understand this incorrectly and assume that love is God. However, love cannot define God; God defines love. We will stumble less in our search for love if we realize that love is grace in action.

 Thank You, Lord, that Jesus was our example of grace in action.

We come to love not by finding a perfect person, but by learning to see an imperfect person perfectly.
—Author unknown

WHAT IS ETERNITY?

How would you define eternity? A mother who has to wait 40 seconds for a bottle to heat up while her baby is crying in the background might feel that these seconds are an eternity. For some, the last minutes of a match can feel like an eternity. During the fifth century, Augustine, the great church father, said that time only exists within creation. God exists outside time. He does not have a past or a future, only an eternal now. Eternal life is therefore nothing else but God's life. The good news is that we can be part of this eternal life and that we can be certain about it. But how?

1 John 5 (explanation)

[10]Whoever *believes* in the Son of God inwardly
confirms God's testimony.
Whoever refuses to *believe* in effect calls God a liar,
refusing to *believe* God's own testimony regarding his Son.
[11]This is the testimony in essence:
God gave us eternal life; the life is in his Son.
[12]So, whoever has the Son, has life;
whoever rejects the Son, rejects life.
[13]My purpose in writing is simply this:
that you who *believe* in God's Son
will know beyond the shadow of a doubt
that you have eternal life, the reality and not the illusion. (MSG)

In this section, John repeatedly refers to the "Son" when he talks about eternal life. John was convinced that eternal life could only become a reality for us through Jesus Christ. Why is this so? If eternal life is the life of God, it means that we can only share in it if we know God and have access to Him. This became a reality for us in Jesus. Jesus knows the Father fully and gives us access to Him.

The following analogy may help to clarify this idea. If we want to meet someone who moves outside our circle of friends, the best course of action would be for us to find someone who knows the person and who is willing to introduce us to him or her. This is what Jesus achieved for us with regard to God. Previously, John wrote, "No one has ever seen God, not so much as a glimpse. This one-of-a-kind God-Expression, who exists at the very heart of the Father, has made him plain as day" (John 1:18, MSG). Now, John says repeatedly that if we believe in Jesus, we have the testimony. The testimony is stated very clearly: those who believe in Jesus have eternal life. John states that this is the reason why he wrote this letter (v. 13).

What a wonderful comfort it is to know that in the midst of all the uncertainties of life, we have *eternal* life—because God says so! To be certain of our faith does not mean that we are sure of our religion but rather that we are sure about the God in whom we believe.

 "Lord, I don't know whether I believe. But I do know in Whom I believe." (Paul Althaus, 1888–1966, prominent German theologian).

Life: a front door to eternity.
—Author unknown

THAT WHICH WE ALL SEEK, BUT WHICH IS SO HARD TO FIND . . .

In the letter of 2 John, which consists of only 245 words, John delivers a short but powerful message. He wrote the letter around A.D. 95, possibly from a mother church (the recipients of 1 John) to a sister church (the recipients of 2 John) to point out the two fundamental principles of the Christian faith to them. These principles would protect them against the false doctrines of heretics. Even today, we are all still looking for these two principles, but unfortunately they are so difficult to find.

2 John (explanation and instruction)

¹My dear congregation,
I, your pastor, *love* you in very truth.
And I'm not alone-everyone who knows the Truth
²that has taken up permanent residence in us loves you.
³Let grace, mercy, and peace be with us in truth and *love*
from God the Father and from Jesus Christ, Son of the Father!
⁴I can't tell you how happy I am to learn
that many members of your congregation
are diligent in living out the Truth,
exactly as commanded by the Father.
⁵. . . that we *love* each other.
⁶*Love* means following his commandments,
and his unifying commandment is *(explanation)*
that you conduct your lives in *love. (instruction)*
This is the first thing you heard, and nothing has changed. *(explanation)* MSG

John refers to the two principles of truth and love. These two principles give meaning to life. Unfortunately, they are very hard to find. Think about it: one cannot build healthy relationships without truth. How many scars have been left because of lies? Without truth, there can be no integrity or credibility. Even today, people in a court of law have to take an oath to ensure that they speak the truth.

Truth and love are inseparably linked in all John's letters. The Beatles were right in 1967 when they sang "All You Need Is Love." However, as mentioned previously, we often stumble in our search for love because we do not understand love correctly—especially the *agape* form of love that John talked about. *Agape* is the form of love spoken about in the New Testament that each of us should have because it is not self-seeking and requires us to love even our enemies. If we adhere to this type of love we live according to the truth. Be strong!

 Lord, today I want to start anew to show *agape* love toward others.

The whole being of any Christian is faith and love. Faith brings the man to God; love brings him to men.
—Martin Luther (1483–1546), *German priest and scholar whose questioning of certain Church practices led to the Protestant Reformation*

THIS CAUSES NO ONE ANY HARM . . .

John, the apostle and author of the fourth Gospel, most likely also wrote the pastoral letter of 3 John sometime between A.D. 90 and 95. This short letter consisting of only a few words, differs from the first two letters because it is addressed to a person and not a congregation. In this letter, John asks his friend Gaius to show something specific toward the traveling preachers. What John required of Gaius causes no one any harm; in fact, it makes people feel very special. What was this?

3 John (explanation)

[1]The Pastor, to my good friend Gaius:
How truly I love you!
[2]We're the best of friends,
and I pray for good fortune in everything you do,
and for your good health—that your everyday affairs prosper,
as well as your soul!
[3]I was most happy when some friends arrived
and brought the news that you persist in following the way of Truth.
[4]Nothing could make me happier than getting reports
that my children continue diligently in the way of Truth!
[5]Dear friend, when you extend hospitality to Christian brothers and sisters, even when they are strangers, you make the faith visible.
[6]They've made a full report back to the church here,
a message about your love.
It's good work you're doing, helping these travellers on their way,
hospitality worthy of God himself!
[7]They set out under the banner of the Name, and get no help from unbelievers.
[8]So they deserve any support we can give them.
In providing meals and a bed, we become their companions in spreading the Truth. (MSG)

John's request to Gaius can be expressed in one word: hospitality! Hospitality means to open our homes and our hearts (and maybe even our wallets) to other people—especially those who are involved in spreading the gospel. In the early years of the Church, there were many traveling preachers. These preachers were completely dependent on the hospitality of believers. Gaius was an example to others. He showed hospitality to all the preachers, even when they were strangers to him (v. 5). Someone once said that he could not understand how Christians could bestow love on each other without knowing each other. Hospitality harms no one. It allows people to feel comfortable and at home because hospitality is God's love in action. Hospitality enables people to experience God's love.

 Thank You, Lord, that I can use hospitality to make Your love visible.

When hospitality becomes an art it loses its very soul.
—Sir Max Beerbohm (1872–1956), *English parodist and caricaturist*

SOMETHING WITH WHICH
WE SHOULD NEVER GAMBLE . . .

The author of the letter/sermon of Jude was most likely the brother of James and Jesus. The letter was probably written sometime between A.D. 60 and 70. It is not clear to whom the letter was written, but it would appear as if the author knew the believers to whom it was directed. It is clear that the tone of his letter is personal, serious and urgent. The urgency of the letter was fueled by a dangerous gamble in the congregation.

Jude (explanation)

> ³Dear friends, I've dropped everything to write you
> about this life of salvation that we have in common.
> I have to write insisting—begging!—
> that you fight with everything you have in you
> for this faith entrusted to us as a gift to guard and cherish.
> ⁴What has happened is that some people have infiltrated our ranks
> (our Scriptures warned us this would happen),
> who beneath their pious skin are shameless scoundrels.
> *Their design is to replace the sheer grace of our God with sheer license—*
> which means doing away with Jesus Christ, our one and only Master.
> ⁵I'm laying this out as clearly as I can, even though you once knew all this well enough
> and shouldn't need reminding. Here it is in brief:
> The Master saved a people out of the land of Egypt.
> Later he destroyed those who defected. (MSG)

At first, Jude wanted to write about salvation. But when he saw how some people in the congregation were gambling with God's grace, he changed the theme of his letter. He wanted to urgently warn the congregation against individuals who had secretly infiltrated the congregation and were leading them to gamble with God's grace. These individuals believed that God's grace provided them with a free ticket to immorality, as they were under the impression that God's grace was encompassing enough to compensate for their immoral life.

These individuals' view was that people should sin bravely because they know that the grace of God is great. They abused God's grace to justify their immoral lifestyle. They committed sin without a conscience because they believed that grace would take care of it! They saw God's grace as an invitation to be sinful. Yet no one should gamble with God's grace.

However, the real issue Jude wanted raised was why the rest of the congregation meekly accepted this teaching (v. 5)! This conduct should not be allowed, because people who act in this way discredit the gospel. People outside the Church could see the immoral life of these churchgoers and conclude that there was very little difference between their lives and those of the "believers." If you are in the grasp of God's grace, you will not want to commit sin.

 Lord, forgive me if I have gambled with Your grace.

Laughter is the closest thing to the grace of God.
—Karl Barth (1886–1968), *Swiss theologian, among the most influential of the twentieth century*

EVIL TRIUMPHS—OR SO IT SEEMS!

The recipients of the book of Revelation were Christians who were persecuted terribly. In such trying times, one may feel like throwing in the towel because it seems as if evil triumphs. Today, it still seems as if the Church has lost its impact on society. Yet in such times, the book of Revelation brings us hope.

Revelation 5 (apocalypse)

¹I saw a *scroll* in the right hand of the One Seated on the Throne. It was written on both sides, fastened with *seven seals.*
²I also saw a powerful Angel, calling out in a voice like thunder, 'Is there anyone who can open the scroll, who can break its seals?'
³There was no one—no one in Heaven, no one on earth, no one from the underworld—able to break open the scroll and read it.
⁴I wept and wept and wept that no one was found able to open the scroll, able to read it. ⁵One of the Elders said, *'Don't weep. Look—the Lion from Tribe Judah, the Root of David's Tree, has conquered. He can open the scroll, can rip through the seven seals.'*
⁶So I looked, and there, surrounded by Throne, Animals, and Elders, was a Lamb, slaughtered but standing tall. Seven horns he had, and seven eyes, the Seven Spirits of God sent into all the earth. (MSG)

John had a poignant vision of God. God sat on His throne, holding a scroll with seven seals in His right hand. The scroll represented God's final plan for the world, while the seven seals indicated that the content of the book was a secret. John cried because nobody was worthy to open the scroll, which meant that no one could open it and execute it. Consequently, God's decree could not be carried out. But then John heard an elder say that there was someone who was worthy enough to open the scroll: Jesus Christ. He is the Lion from the tribe of Judah (Gen. 49:9), a descendent of David (Isa. 11:1,10; Rom. 15:12). He is worthy to open the scroll because He conquered death and is truly God and human.

After John had heard this, he saw a Lamb but not a Lion. Who was this Lamb? The Lamb was Jesus Christ, who died as the paschal lamb on Golgotha (John 1:29, 36). So the Lion is also the Lamb. How is this possible? One is a hunter, while the other is the prey. God allowed Jesus to become the prey of our sins. In this way, He conquered death and became worthy to open the scroll. God did not conquer the earth with the power of a lion but with the love of the Lamb's blood.

On October 30, 1974, Mohammad Ali and George Foreman fought against each other in Zaire (now the Democratic Republic of the Congo). Ali held his hands in front of his face, leaned against the ropes and allowed Foreman, the overwhelming favorite, to have a go at him for eight rounds. When the right moment came, Ali bounced off the ropes and knocked out Foremen, sending him into retirement. Ali called his technique "rope-a-dope." Even though it looked as if he was losing the fight—and losing badly—he was in control the whole time. He took all those punches because he knew that he would deliver the final blow. In the same way, God is in control—even if this does not always seem to be the case.

Thank You, Lord, that I can find peace in knowing that You are the victor.

I have been asked on hundreds of times in my life why God allows tragedy and suffering.
I have to confess that I really do not know the answer totally, even to my own satisfaction.
I have to accept, by faith, that God is sovereign, and He is a God of love and mercy
and compassion in the midst of suffering.
—Billy Graham (b. 1918), *American evangelist*

WHAT DOES THE FUTURE HOLD FOR US?

An unknown future often leaves us without hope. This is why we would like to know what will happen in the future. For this, we need not visit a fortune-teller or read the stars. There is something that enables us to see the future better and clearer: the telescope of Revelation. Let's have a look!

Revelation 7 (apocalypse)

9–12I looked again. I saw a huge crowd, too huge to count. Everyone was there—all nations and tribes, all races and languages. And they were standing, dressed in white robes and waving palm branches, standing before the Throne and the Lamb and heartily singing:
Salvation to our God on his Throne!
Salvation to the Lamb!
All who were standing around the Throne—Angels, Elders, Anmals—fell on their faces before the Throne and worshiped God, singing:
Oh, Yes!
The blessing and glory and wisdom and thanksgiving,
The honor and power and strength,
To our God forever and ever and ever!
Oh, Yes!
13–14Just then one of the Elders addressed me: 'Who are these dressed in white robes, and where did they come from?' Taken aback, I said, 'O Sir, I have no idea—but you must know.'
14–17Then he told me, 'These are those who come from the great tribulation, and they've washed their robes, scrubbed them clean in the blood of the Lamb. That's why they're standing before God's Throne. They serve him day and night in his Temple. The One on the Throne will pitch his tent there for them: no more hunger, no more thirst, no more scorching heat. The Lamb on the Throne will shepherd them, will lead them to spring waters of Life. And God will wipe every last tear from their eyes.' (MSG)

John's vision is like a telescope that allows us to see the future. Everything John saw in his vision is big and overwhelming, which is why he could only describe it by way of imagery. First, John sees a huge crowd standing in front of the throne (v. 9). This crowd is the struggling Church on earth that John describes in verses 1–8 that has become the triumphant church in heaven. Through the telescope of Revelation, we see that we are wearing white clothes that have been washed clean with the blood of the lamb (vv. 9,14). We carry palm branches that represent triumph. However, on earth our calls of distress still reveal our struggle. Just think about Paul, who said, "I've tried everything and nothing helps. I'm at the end of my rope. Is there no one who can do anything for me? Isn't that the real question?" (Rom. 7:24, MSG).

But then, John hears a loud cry that surpasses all previous ones. It is the Church shouting, "Salvation to our God on his Throne! Salvation to the Lamb!" (v. 10). John sees the angels, the elders (an image of the Church) and the four living beings (an image of creation) all standing before the throne. They then kneel before the throne and worship God. One of the elders explains to John that those who wore white clothes had come from the great tribulation.

There has been much speculation about what this means. Perhaps the best way to understand it is to see it as the sum total of all the suffering and persecution the Church has had to endure on earth. The good news is that the struggling Church will make it through the great tribulation and will share in God's triumph. Revelation tells us that history is not a road that leads to nowhere, but one that leads to a place in front of God's throne—in His arms! May this give you hope!

 Lord, open my eyes so that I can look beyond the horizon of my daily struggle and see You.

Some see a hopeless end, while others see an endless hope.
—Author unknown

THE ONSLAUGHT OF THE EVIL TRIO: THE DRAGON

The book of Revelation can help us to understand life better. It was not only intended to comfort the Christians who suffered under the persecution of the Roman Empire in Asia Minor during the end of the first century but also intended to incorporate the Church during all times. After all, the symbolic world depicted in Revelation deals with the happenings of the end. The readings that will follow during the next few days will help us to better understand the times in which we live. We will see how the satanic trio will stand up against the Holy Trinity. This evil trio consists of the dragon, the beast from the sea and the beast from the earth. This first section is about the fiery dragon!

Revelation 12 (apocalypse)

[1-2]A great Sign appeared in Heaven: a Woman dressed all in sunlight, standing on the moon, and crowned with Twelve Stars. She was giving birth to a Child and cried out in the pain of childbirth. [3-4]And then another Sign alongside the first: a huge and fiery Dragon! It had seven heads and ten horns, a crown on each of the seven heads. With one flick of its tail it knocked a third of the Stars from the sky and dumped them on earth.

Tension: The dragon waits to devour the child!

The Dragon crouched before the Woman in childbirth, poised to eat up the Child when it came.

Relief of tension: The child is born and is safe!

[5-6]The Woman gave birth to a Son who will shepherd all nations with an iron rod. Her Son was seized and placed safely before God on his Throne.

Result: God looks after the woman in the desert!

The Woman herself escaped to the desert to a place of safety prepared by God, all comforts provided her for 1,260 days. (MSG)

This vision is symbolic. The woman is the Church (Rev. 19:7; 21:9). The fact that she is *dressed all in sunlight* emphasizes her radiant and elevated, unchallengeable position. The fact that she *stands on the moon* depicts her position of authority. The *crown of twelve stars* that she wears is symbolic of her power and alludes to the 12 tribes of Israel.

The woman (the Church) is on the verge of giving birth to a child: Jesus. Then a dragon appears— the personification of Satan. In the Bible, evil is often depicted as a dragon. The dragon's fiery red color indicates a bloodthirsty nature, his 7 heads indicate his supposed perfect ability to lay plans, his 10 horns his power and might (Dan. 7:7), and his 7 *crowns of glory* indicate his presumptuous authority. The dragon uses his tail to knock a third of the stars down to the earth (v. 4), which hints at Daniel 8:10 and probably refers to the fallen angels (Dan. 9:1). In short: he is dangerous!

The dragon then stands in front of the woman to prevent the birth and ministry of Jesus. Think back to Herod, who wanted to kill all the babies at the time of Jesus' birth; Satan, who tempted Jesus in the desert; and Judas, who betrayed Him. Yet Satan, the dragon, fails because the child is born and *taken to God on His throne*. This refers to the suffering, death, resurrection and ascension of Jesus. The woman (the Church) then flees to the desert, where she will suffer for 1,260 days. This period of time probably refers to the ±3½ years (1,260 days) during which Antiochus IV Epiphanes cruelly persecuted the Jews (Dan 7:25; 12:7). According to Daniel 7:25 and 12:7, Antiochus IV Epiphanes would reign only for "a time [12 months] and times [24 months] and half a time [6 months]." This gives us 3½ years, which consists of 1,260 days.

The desert that John refers to should be seen against the background of the Israelites' travels through the desert on their way to the Promised Land. The desert is the symbolic home of believers—a place where God looks after them because no help is available for them in the desert. In short, Satan failed to prevent the birth and ministry of Jesus. For this we should praise and honor God! Satan then turned his fury against the Church. In the following devotions, this onslaught against the Church will become even clearer.

 Thank You, Lord, that You conquered the dragon and still look after Your church!

We must remember that Satan has his miracles, too.
—John Calvin (1509–1564), *French Christian theologian during the Protestant Reformation and the originator of the system of Christian theology known as Calvinism*

THE ONSLAUGHT OF THE EVIL TRIO: THE ANTICHRIST!

Revelation is a pastoral book in symbolic form that encourages Christians throughout the ages. Christians need encouragement, because the evil trio are still busy with their evil deeds. As we saw in the previous reading (Rev. 12:1–6), the dragon (Satan) could not prevent the birth and ministry of the child (Jesus), so he then focused his attack on the woman (the Church). According to Revelation, the dragon uses his ground staff to execute this onslaught. This brings us to the other two members of the evil trio, namely the beast out of the sea (Rev. 13:1–10) followed by a beast out of the earth (Rev. 13:11–18). In this section, we will see how the beast from the sea, the antichrist, is still at work today.

Revelation 13 (apocalypse)

[1-2] And the Dragon stood on the shore of the sea. I saw a Beast rising from the sea. It had *ten horns and seven heads*—on each horn a crown, and each head inscribed with a *blasphemous name*. The Beast I saw looked like a *leopard* with *bear paws* and a *lion's mouth*.

Tension: The dragon hands his power to the beast

The Dragon turned over its power to it, its throne and great authority.
[3-4] One of the Beast's heads looked as if it had been struck a deathblow, and then healed. The whole earth was agog, gaping at the Beast. They worshiped the Dragon who gave the Beast authority, and they worshiped the Beast, exclaiming, 'There's never been anything like the Beast! No one would dare go to war with the Beast!'
[5-8] The Beast had a loud mouth, boastful and blasphemous. It could do anything it wanted for forty-two months. It yelled blasphemies against God, blasphemed his Name, blasphemed his Church, especially those already dwelling with God in Heaven. It was permitted to make war on God's holy people and conquer them. It held absolute sway over all tribes and peoples, tongues and races. Everyone on earth whose name was not written from the world's foundation in the slaughtered Lamb's Book of Life will worship the Beast.

Relief of tension: Punishment to the beast's followers

[9-10] Are you listening to this? They've made their bed; now they must lie in it. Anyone marked for prison goes straight to prison; anyone pulling a sword goes down by the sword.

Result: Believers should be spiritually vigilant!

Meanwhile, God's holy people passionately and faithfully stand their ground. (MSG)

In his vision, John saw a beast emerging from the sea. The sea was the symbolic dwelling place of evil. This was a strange animal with 10 horns and 7 heads. The book of Daniel can help us to understand these symbols. Daniel saw 4 animals: a lion, a bear, a leopard and a monster. The fourth animal, the monster, had 10 horns (Dan 7:19). The animal that John saw is a combination of the four animals Daniel saw in his visions (Dan. 7). In the book of Daniel, the four animals were symbolic of four cruel world powers. The animal John saw personified the Roman Empire, which during John's time was persecuting the Church cruelly. This animal is therefore the antichrist.

Perhaps it is necessary to say something more about the antichrist at this stage. (You are welcome to disagree!) After a thorough study of the sections in the Bible that deal with the antichrist, I believe that we can draw several conclusions about this entity. First, the antichrist takes on different forms in different prophecies. According to Paul, the antichrist is an individual who had not yet arrived in his day and would only come when the obstructer was removed (2 Thess. 2). It is interesting to note that the letters of John already pointed out the antichrist. How does one explain this difference?

Paul had already died when the letters of John were written. As we mentioned previously, 2 Thessalonians was written around A.D. 50, while John's letters were written around A.D. 90. This means that the obstructer had already been removed by the time the letters of John were written—which leads us to conclude that this obstructer was most likely the Roman government who was well disposed toward Christians before A.D. 63. According to John's letters, the antichrist is a group of people who advocate a dangerous heresy and originates in the Church. John saw the antichrist as a reality in his time, not as something in the distant future. (It is wise to read what John had to say on this in 1 John 2:18–23, 1 John 4:1–3 and 2 John 7.) According to Revelation 13, the antichrist was a government (the Roman authority) that persecuted the Church forcefully from A.D. 63. Thus, we can say that the antichrist is mainly opposed to Christ and His ministry and that he should therefore be regarded as the false messiah of Satan.

Second, the antichrist imitates Jesus. The 10 crowns symbolize the false messiah's supposed royal authority. The blasphemous names on his heads allude to the claims the false messiahs/Roman Caesars made to enable them to use godly titles. In the same way that the Lamb of God was slaughtered, the animal has scars on his head (v. 3). However, his deadly wound had healed. This might refer to one of the Caesars, who persecuted the church and then lost his power. The wound had healed when another Caesar continued to persecute the Church. People follow the antichrist and worship him because they are deeply impressed by his power and his wondrous scars (vv. 3–4). He rules the world and deceives people.

The Antichrist is therefore a false messiah. In Revelation, the antichrist appears in the form of anti-Christian governments. Even today, Satan uses anti-Christian authorities to oppress the Church. However, the encouraging news is that this onslaught will only last for a short period of time! Revelation speaks about 42 months—a period representing the time between the first and second coming of Jesus—that is mentioned a few times in Revelation (11:2, 3; 12:6; 12:14; 13:5). Therefore, we can know for sure that Jesus will come again!

 Lord, today I remember the believers in anti-Christian countries.

Where God has his church, the Devil will have his chapel.
—Spanish proverb

THE ONSLAUGHT OF THE EVIL TRIO:
THE FALSE PROPHET!

The dragon does not only use anti-Christian governments to persecute the Church. In this section in Revelation, we see how the next animal, the beast out of the earth, is used against the Church. The beast out of the earth completes the evil trio that opposes the Holy Trinity. The Father stands in opposition to the dragon, Christ stands in opposition to the beast out of the sea, and the Holy Spirit and His testimony stand in opposition to the beast out of the earth. Later on, the beast out of the earth is identified as the false prophet (16:13; 19:20). Let us look at how he operates.

Revelation 13 (apocalypse)

[11]I saw another Beast rising out of the ground. It had two horns like a lamb but sounded like a dragon when it spoke.
[12]It was a puppet of the first Beast, made earth and everyone in it worship the first Beast, which had been healed of its deathblow.
[13]This second Beast worked magical signs, dazzling people by making fire come down from Heaven.
[14]It used the magic it got from the Beast to dupe earth dwellers, getting them to make an image of the Beast that received the deathblow and lived.
[15]It was able to animate the image of the Beast so that it talked, and then arrange that anyone not worshipping the Beast would be killed.
[16]It forced all people, small and great, rich and poor, free and slave, to have a mark on the right hand or forehead.
[17]Without the mark of the name of the Beast or the number of its name, it was impossible to buy or sell anything.
[18]Solve a riddle: Put your heads together and figure out the meaning of the number of the Beast. It's a human number: six hundred sixty-six. (MSG)

The fact that the beast from the earth has two horns like that of a lamb and a voice like that of a dragon reveals his true character. On the surface he seems gentle and harmless like a lamb, but he uses evil utterances to seduce people. One could say that the false prophet is the religious arm that propagates the political power of the antichrist. Just like the Holy Spirit inspires believers to serve Christ, the beast persuades the godless to worship the antichrist.

In the process, the false prophet uses signs and wonders, such as sending fire down from heaven to the earth. This reminds us of the prophet Elijah, who used fire to emphasize his message to the prophets of Baal (1 Kings 18:38). The false prophet also erects an image of the beast, which is most likely a reference to the statue of a Roman Caesar who had to be honored during John's time. Those who worshiped the beast had to carry a mark on their right hand or forehead. This means that all people can therefore be identified: the servants of God are marked by a seal on their foreheads (7:2–3), and those who worship the beast also carry a mark (13:16).

The mark of the beast is the opposite of the mark believers received to indicate that they belonged to God (7:2–3). This mark should therefore be understood in a symbolic sense. The mark on people's right hands symbolizes that their ability to work has been affected, while the mark on their foreheads indicates that their ability to think has been affected. The mark is the name of the beast, or the number of his name (13:17), which is 666 (13:18).

Unfortunately, throughout the ages so much time and effort has been spent trying to establish who 666 is that the essence of what he does has been overlooked. The real meaning is that the false prophet takes a firm stand against God and seduces the Church. We do not know for sure who 666 is—some people argue that it is the number of a person, while others believe it to be the number of the evil trio. In addition, if 7 is the number of perfection, and 777 is ultimate perfection, it would mean that 666 is symbolic of ultimate deficiency.

In ancient times, numerical values were assigned to the letters of the alphabet. Someone's name could therefore be expressed in numerical form. It is interesting to note that the numerical value of Nero's name in Aramaic (John's mother tongue) was 666. The early Christians therefore associated Caesar Nero with 666, because he persecuted the Church terribly. During the Second World War, people associated 666 with Hitler. It is interesting to note that if you give the first letter of the alphabet (*a*) a numerical value of 100 and add one number for each consecutive letter (b=101, c=102, d=103, and so forth), the numerical value for Hitler would be 666 (H = 107, I =108, T = 119, L = 111, E = 104, R = 117 = 666).

There is much to speculate about. Whichever way we want to apply the number, it remains a symbol of the supposed supremacy of evil in the world that seeks to destroy Christ's work. The false prophet does this by means of his propaganda, which includes false ideologies and philosophies. If we consider the background of the Roman Empire during the time of John, we realize how false religions and anti-Christian governments worked together to persecute the Christians.

During the time of the Early Church, Roman power was closely linked to the Roman religions. Before an important military decision could be taken, the priest first had to consult the gods. At times, the Caesars were honored and worshiped as gods. This led to clashes between the Christians, who refused to join the Roman religions, and the Roman government. The Roman government persecuted Christians with great cruelty.

Throughout history, governments have used religion and ideologies to promote their ideals. In the twentieth century, communist countries were known for their propaganda that promoted the communist ideology. Today, governments continue to use religion and ideologies to promote their ideals. This can be very dangerous. The Church should never be an instrument in the hands of the state. For this reason, many people feel that the Church and the state should not be associated too closely.

Revelation 13 reminds us that Satan uses the religions and ideologies of anti-Christian governments to oppress and persecute the Church. Mercifully, this will change with the coming of Jesus. For as Paul states in Romans 14:11, "'As I live and breathe,' God says, 'every knee will bow before me; Every tongue will tell the honest truth that I and only I am God'" (MSG).

 Thank You, Lord, that I can already confess today that You are God!

The church must be reminded that it is not the master or the servant of the state, but rather the conscience of the state. It must be the guide and the critic of the state, and never its tool.
—Martin Luther King, Jr. (1929–1968), *American Baptist minister, Civil Rights leader and winner of the Nobel Prize in 1964*

ANOTHER STRATEGY OF THE EVIL TRIO!

In this next section in Revelation, we witness a strategy that evil has used so successfully. To this day, it is one of its most successful strategies.

Revelation 17 (apocalypse)

[1]One of the seven angels who had the seven bowls came and said to me, 'Come, I will show you the punishment of *the great prostitute, who sits on many waters.* [2]With her the *kings* of the earth committed adultery and the *inhabitants* of the earth were intoxicated with the wine of her adulteries.'
[3]Then the angel carried me away in the Spirit into a desert. There I saw a *woman* sitting on a *scarlet beast* that was covered with *blasphemous names* and had *seven heads and ten horns.* [4]The woman was dressed in *purple and scarlet,* and was glittering with *gold, precious stones and pearls.* She held a *golden cup* in her hand, *filled with abominable things and the filth of her adulteries.* [5] This title was written on her *forehead*:
MYSTERY
BABYLON THE GREAT
THE MOTHER OF PROSTITUTES
AND OF THE ABOMINATIONS OF THE EARTH.
[6]I saw that the woman *was drunk with the blood of the saints,* the blood of those who bore testimony to Jesus. When I saw her, I was greatly astonished. (MSG)

In John's time, one could sum up Roman culture in three words: money, sex and power! In this section, the immoral and materialistic lifestyle of Roman culture is presented as a prostitute. The prostitute is presented as Babylon (v. 5), a symbolic name for Rome because Rome, like Babylon of old, threatened the existence of God's new people, the Christians. Rome is also called Babylon because, like that nation, Rome destroyed the Temple in Jerusalem.

John's vision implies that in the same way that Babylon fell during the sixth century B.C., so Rome will come to a fall. The seven bowls are the symbols of God's wrath and the punishment that He will mete out. Knowing that Rome would fall must have been a great encouragement to the Christians who had to submit to the yoke of the Romans. The *many waters* where this prostitute lives refer to the Euphrates River that flowed past Babylon. The prostitute was very popular among the *kings* and *inhabitants* of the earth (v. 2), which is proof that the immoral and materialistic culture of Rome exerted an influence on the rich and the poor.

John was carried away in a vision to look at the woman in the desert. This was in the same spot where the Church was (Rev. 12:6), which shows that the Church was not immune to the influence of this infamous woman. The woman sits on a *scarlet beast* that is covered with blasphemous names and has seven heads and 10 horns. All this confirms that it is the beast from the sea: the antichrist (13:1). It shows that materialism and immorality are part of Satan's strategy to seduce Christians.

It is sad to see how many Christians have stumbled before the temptations of money, sex and power. After all, the prostitute is an attractive woman. She dresses impressively. Her *purple and scarlet clothes are* a testimony of great wealth, because these articles were very rare and expensive. The *gold, precious stones and pearls* are proof of her wealth, and her *golden cup filled with abominable things* refers to her ability to deceive nations. Following the custom of the time in which prostitutes wrote their names on their foreheads, her forehead bears the name, "Great Babylon," which reminds us of the signs on the forehead of the Lamb's followers and the signs on the foreheads and hands of the beast's followers (Rev. 7:3; 9:4; 13:16; 14:1, 9; 20:4; 22:4). The woman is also called the *"mother of the prostitutes and of the abominations of the earth."* She is the fountain and nutritive source of all immorality.

In his vision, John saw that the woman was intoxicated with the blood of the believers. This indicates that the bloodthirsty persecution of Christians intoxicated her. Caesar Nero accused the Christians of starting the fire that devastated Rome (A.D. 64) and then severely persecuted them for it. The fact that the Christians' leader (Jesus) had been executed by the Roman power contributed to the tension between the Christians and Rome. The immoral woman is also depicted in sharp contrast to the bride of Christ, the Church. The bride of Christ is pure and righteous (19:6–9)—the exact opposite of this immoral woman. The evil city of Babylon is therefore the opposite of the New Jerusalem, the heavenly city (21:10–22:5).

This section in Revelation makes it clear that the culture in which we live can exert an enormous influence over our lives. As Christians, we must be aware of the temptations of money, sex and power. We must be honest and admit that it is not always easy to resist them! Materialism and immorality lead to an addiction to gambling, illicit sex and pornography and eventually causes our downfall. If you are caught up in this evil grip, it would be wise to talk about it with someone whom you trust. It will not disappear spontaneously—the best way to free yourself from the clutches of immorality and materialism is to admit to it.

Evil wants to convince you that you are *okay*. Start working on it today. Thank God if you are not in the clutches of these forces, and show mercy toward those who struggle and stumble!

 Lord, please protect me from the dangers of money, sex and power.

The best things in life aren't things.
—Arthur "Art" Buchwald (b. 1925), *American humorist best known for his long-running column in the* Washington Post *newspaper that concentrated on political satire and commentary*

FROM PARADISE TO PARADISE

I've heard of people who first read the last page of a book before they decided to read the whole book. I am convinced that the last page of the Bible will motivate us not only to read the Bible but also to study and live it!

Revelation 22 (conversation)

[16]'I, Jesus, sent my Angel to testify to these things for the churches. I'm the Root and Branch of David, the Bright Morning Star.'
[17]'Come!' say the Spirit and the Bride.
Whoever hears, echo, 'Come!'
Is anyone thirsty? Come!
All who will, come and drink,
Drink freely of the Water of Life!
[18–19]I give fair warning to all who hear the words of the prophecy of this book: If you add to the words of this prophecy, God will add to your life the disasters written in this book; if you subtract from the words of the book of this prophecy, God will subtract your part from the Tree of Life and the Holy City that are written in this book.
[20]He who testifies to all these things says it again: 'I'm on my way! I'll be there soon!'
Yes! Come, Master Jesus!
[21]The grace of the Master Jesus be with all of you. Oh, Yes! (MSG)

If Genesis describes the beginning of God's history with human beings, the book of Revelation describes its conclusion. The very first verse in the Bible begins with God: "First this: God created the Heavens and Earth" (Gen 1:1, MSG). The very last verse of the Bible also ends with God: "The grace of the Master Jesus be with all of you. Oh, Yes!" (Rev. 22:21). One could put this differently: the Bible starts with paradise and ends with paradise. But there is one big difference—in Revelation, evil is destroyed forever.

Genesis tells us about a garden of paradise with an evil snake, while the book of Revelation sketches a picture of a perfect city without evil. Sin destroyed the Garden of Eden for us, but the spiritual paradise is created anew in the New Jerusalem (Rev. 21). Our journey on the roads of the Bible takes place between these two paradises. We became aware of human failures that occurred during the early stages of our journey when human beings listened to the serpent instead of to God. The first murder took place as early as the fourth chapter of Genesis, when Cain killed Abel. But despite our failures, suffering and hardships, our history ends with us being in paradise once again.

How did this happen? The answer lies in the fact that God did not turn His back on us. The anticipation of a Savior is evident throughout the Old Testament, such as in Isaiah where the prophet wrote, "A green Shoot will sprout from Jesse's stump, from his roots a budding Branch" (11:1, MSG). Jesus called Himself the Root, the descendent of David, and thereby applied Isaiah 11:1–10 to Himself. He made the expectations in the Old Testament real.

Jesus also calls Himself the Bright Morning Star (Rev. 22:16). According to Numbers 24:17, Balaam the prophet said that a star would come out of Jacob. In that case it was applied to David;

now it had bearing on the "second" David. The second coming of Jesus, the appearance of the Bright Morning Star, will signify the dawning of a new day for all of us—a new day after a long night of pain and oppression. When that day comes, there will no longer be any pain and suffering. We (the bride) are called upon to pray that the Lord should come (v. 17). In the meantime, God carries on inviting people to come to Him.

This invitation is portrayed in Revelation as an image of water that quenches thirst. This image was also used in John 4:10–15, in which Jesus told the Samaritan woman at the well that He would give her living water that would quench her thirst forever. Jesus meant that He was the living water that would quench her spiritual thirst. The water was free, because He already paid the full price when He was crucified. However, we also find a warning (vv. 18,19) that is aimed at those who want to distort the message of Revelation. (It was the custom in those days for an author to include a curse at the end of his work to serve as a warning to people not to falsify, steal or distort the document.)

In the last verse of Revelation, Jesus confirms once more that He will come soon. John confirmed this in his prayer: "Yes! Come, Master Jesus!" Two thousand years have passed since this prayer was uttered, but still the Lord has not come. However, we should interpret the words "I'm on my way! I'll be there soon!" as, *"Expect me at any time!"*

Revelation lifts the veil on the end of time. We could act like a naughty child and ask, "So what? What does this mean to me today while I'm struggling with all my pain, trying to keep my head above water amidst all the chaos in the world?" Revelation wants to encourage us in the midst of our suffering and pain by saying that:

- The world is not heading towards an aimless end, but to God as the final destination. Jesus Himself said, "I'm A to Z, the First and the Final, Beginning and Conclusion" (Rev. 22:13, MSG).
- We can expect Jesus at any moment and should believe He will come again.
- We do not travel alone. Apart from our fellow believers, God is our travel companion! This is echoed in Matthew's last verse when Jesus says: "And surely I am with you always, to the very end of the age" (Matt. 28:20, MSG).

It is because of God's grace that He is prepared to accompany us on our journey through life. Therefore, it is fitting that the last verse in the Bible ends with these wonderful words of comfort: "The grace of the Master Jesus be with all of you."

 Thank You, Lord, that You embrace me with Your grace!

I haven't a clue as to how my story will end. But that's all right. When you set out on a journey and night covers the road, you don't conclude the road has vanished. And how else could we discover the stars?
—Author unknown

INDEX

PERIOD	DAY	BIBLE BOOK	PAGE
Pre-history	1–5	Genesis	27–34
The Patriarchs	6–10	Genesis	37–46
(±2000 B.C.)			
Exodus and Conquest	11–17	Exodus	47–59
(±1250 – 1220 B.C.)	18–24	Leviticus	60–66
	25–31	Numbers	67–73
	32–38	Deuteronomy	74–80
	39–45	Joshua	81–88
Judges	46–54	Judges	91–101
(±1200 – 1020 B.C.)	55–60	Ruth	102–109
United Kingdom	61–68	1 – 2 Samuel	113–120
(±1020 – 925 B.C.)	69–70	1 Kings 1–11	121–122
	71–77	1 Chronicles – 2 Chronicles 9	123–131
	78–84	Job	132–138
	85–92	Psalms	139–146
	93–99	Proverbs	147–153
	100–107	Ecclesiastes	154–161
	108–114	Song of Solomon	162–168
Divided Kingdom	115–119	1 Kings 12 – 2 Kings 25	171–175
(925 – 586 B.C.)	120	2 Chronicles 10–36	176
	121–124	Jonah	177–183

PERIOD	DAY	BIBLE BOOK	PAGE
	125–128	Amos	184–188
	129–133	Hosea	189–197
	134–136	Isaiah 1–39	198–201
	137–141	Micah	202–207
	142–144	Nahum	208–210
	145–147	Zephaniah	211–214
	148–155	Jeremiah	215–225
	156–159	Lamentations	226–229
	160–162	Habakkuk	230–233
	163–164	Obadiah	234–237
	165–169	Isaiah 40–66	238–242
Exile	170–177	Ezekiel	245–254
(597 – 538 B.C.)	178–184	Daniel	255–266
Return from Exile	185–186	Haggai	269–270
(538 – 420 B.C.)	187–191	Zechariah	271–276
	192–193	Joel	277–278
	194–201	Esther	279–289
	202–205	Ezra	290–293
	206–209	Nehemiah	294–298
	210–213	Malachi	299–302
400 Silent Years			
(420 – 6 B.C.)			
-6 B.C. ± A.D. 100	214–229	Matthew	309–331
	230–244	Mark	332–350
	245–257	Luke	351–370
	258–266	John	371–380
	267–274	Acts	381–390
	275–280	*Pentecost**	391–402
	281–288	Romans	403–410
	289–297	1 – 2 Corinthians	411–419
	298–306	Galatians	420–428
	307–312	Ephesians	429–434
	313–316	Philippians	435–439
	317–320	Colossians	440–443

PERIOD	DAY	BIBLE BOOK	PAGE
	321–327	1 – 2 Thessalonians	444–450
	328–332	1 – 2 Timothy	451–455
	333–334	Titus	456–457
	335	Philemon	458
	336–343	Hebrews	459–471
	344–347	James	472–475
	348–353	1 – 2 Peter	476–482
	354–358	1 – 3 John	483–487
	359	Jude	488
	360–366	Revelation	489–502

*   *Pentecost:* The six daily readings are summaries of Pentecost meetings I held at the Port Natal Congregation in 2002.